The International Politics of the Asia-Pacific

This fully revised third edition of Michael Yahuda's extremely successful textbook brings the region fully up-to-date, introducing students to the international politics of the Asia-Pacific region since 1945. As well as assessing the post-Cold War uncertainties that challenged balance and power with the region, Yahuda also examines the first decade of the new millennium, which includes no let up on the 'war on terror', new political administrations in all the key player-states and increased cooperative security between some nations, polarized by volatile relationships between others. Anyalsing politics in terms of global, regional and local trends, this new edition features:

- in-depth discussion of the Bush administration legacy and where the Obama administration's vision takes their policy
- analysis of post-Koizumi/post-Abe Japan
- examination of the continued rise of China in terms of politics, security and economic dominance
- ongoing debates concerning the 'war on terror' and how this shifts, forms and reforms relationships
- Asia-Pacific security issues

This new third edition will continue to be a core text for students of Asian politics, international relations and Cold War history.

Michael Yahuda is Professor Emeritus of International Relations at the London School of Economics, UK and visiting scholar at the Sigur Center for Asian Studies, the Elliott School, George Washington University.

D0711374

Politics in Asia series
Formerly edited by Michael Leifer
London School of Economics

**ASEAN and the Security of
South-East Asia**
Michael Leifer

**China's Policy Towards
Territorial Disputes**
The case of the South China
Sea islands
Chi-kin Lo

India and Southeast Asia
Indian perceptions and policies
Mohammed Ayoob

**Gorbachev and
Southeast Asia**
Leszek Buszynski

**Indonesian Politics Under
Suharto**
Order, development and pressure
for change
Michael R.J. Vatikiotis

**The State and Ethnic Politics
in Southeast Asia**
David Brown

**The Politics of Nation
Building and Citizenship
in Singapore**
Michael Hill and Lian Kwen Fee

Politics in Indonesia
Democracy, Islam and the ideology
of tolerance
Douglas E. Ramage

**Communitarian Ideology
and Democracy in Singapore**
Beng-Huat Chua

**The Challenge of Democracy
in Nepal**
Louise Brown

Japan's Asia Policy
Wolf Mendl

**The International Politics of
the Asia-Pacific, 1945–95**
Michael Yahuda

**Political Change in
Southeast Asia**
Trimming the banyan tree
Michael R.J. Vatikiotis

Hong Kong
China's challenge
Michael Yahuda

Korea versus Korea
A case of contested legitimacy
B.K. Gills

China's Rise, Taiwan's Dilemma's and International Peace
Edited by Edward Friedman

Japan and China in the World Political Economy
Edited by Saadia M. Pekkanen and Kellee S. Tsai

Order and Security in Southeast Asia
Essays in memory of Michael Leifer
Edited by Joseph Chinyong Liow and Ralf Emmers

State Making in Asia
Edited by Richard Boyd and Tak-Wing Ngo

US–China Relations in the 21st Century
Power transition and peace
Zhiqun Zhu

Empire and Neoliberalism in Asia
Edited by Vedi R. Hadiz

South Korean Engagement Policies and North Korea
Identities, norms and the sunshine policy
Son Key-young

Chinese Nationalism in the Global Era
Christopher R. Hughes

Indonesia's War over Aceh
Last stand on Mecca's porch
Matthew N. Davies

Advancing East Asian Regionalism
Edited by Melissa G. Curley and Nicholas Thomas

Political Cultures in Asia and Europe
Citizens, states and societal values
Jean Blondel and Takashi Inoguchi

Rethinking Injustice and Reconciliation in Northeast Asia
The Korean experience
Edited by Gi-Wook Shin, Soon-Won Park and Daqing Yang

Foreign Policy Making in Taiwan
From principle to pragmatism
Dennis Van Vranken Hickey

The Balance of Power in Asia-Pacific Security
US–China policies on regional order
Liselotte Odgaard

Taiwan in the 21st Century
Aspects and limitations of a development model
Edited by Robert Ash and J. Megan Green

Elections as Popular Culture in Asia
Edited by Chua Beng Huat

Security and Migration in Asia
The dynamics of securitisation
Edited by Melissa G. Curley and Wong Siu-lun

Political Transitions in Dominant Party Systems
Learning to lose
Edited by Edward Friedman and Joseph Wong

Torture, Truth and Justice
The case of Timor-Leste
Elizabeth Stanley

A Rising China and Security in East Asia
Identity construction and security discourse
Rex Li

Rise of China
Beijing's strategies and implications for the Asia-Pacific
Edited by Hsin-Huang Michael Hsiao and Cheng-yi Lin

Governance and Regionalism in Asia
Edited by Nicholas Thomas

Constructing a Security Community in Southeast Asia
ASEAN and the problem of regional order
Second edition
Amitav Acharya

East Asia's New Democracies
Deepening, reversal, non-liberal alternatives
Yin-Wah Chu and Siu-lun Wong

China's Multilateral Co-operation in Asia and the Pacific
Institutionalizing Beijing's 'Good Neighbour Policy'
Chien-peng Chung

The International Politics of the Asia-Pacific
Third edition
Michael Yahuda

The International Politics of the Asia-Pacific

Third and revised edition

Michael Yahuda

Routledge
Taylor & Francis Group

LONDON AND NEW YORK

First published 1996 by RoutledgeCurzon
Reprinted 1997, 1998, 2000, 2003,

Second edition published
2004 by Routledge
2 Park Square, Milton Park, Abingdon, Oxon OX14 4RN

Simultaneously published in the USA and Canada
by Routledge
711 ThirdAvenue, New York, NY10017
Reprinted 2006 (three times) 2007, 2009

Third edition published
2011 by Routledge
2 Park Square, Milton Park, Abingdon, Oxon OX14 4RN

Simultaneously published in the USA and Canada
by Routledge
270 Madison Avenue, New York, NY10016
Routledge is an imprint of the Taylor & Francis Group, an Informa business

© 2011 Michael Yahuda

Typeset in Baskerville by Glyph International Ltd.

British Library Cataloguing in Publication Data
A catalogue record for this book is available from the British Library

Library of Congress Cataloging in Publication Data
Yahuda, Michael B.
The international politics of the Asia-Pacific / Michael Yahuda. – 3rd and
rev. ed.
    p. cm. – (Politics in Asia series)
Includes bibliographical references and index.
1. World politics–1945-1989. 2. World politics–1989-. 3. East Asia–Politics and
government. 4. Southeast Asia–Politics and government–1945-. 5. East Asia–
Foreign relations. 6. Southeast Asia–Foreign relations. I. Title.
DS518.1.Y35 2011
320.95–dc22   2010033757

ISBN 13: 978-0-415-47479-5 (hbk)
ISBN 13: 978-0-415-47480-1 (pbk)
ISBN 13: 978-0-203-83098-7 (ebk)

Contents

Acknowledgements

As before, an enduring debt of gratitude is owed to the students, scholars and practitioners who contributed over the years to the annual seminars on the Asia-Pacific at the London School of Economics and Political Science, from which I learned a great deal in my thirty years at the LSE, before retiring in 2003. In particular I would like to register my indebtedness to my late colleague and a truly great scholar of the region, Michael Leifer, without whose constant encouragement this book would not have been written and whose advice greatly improved the first edition.

A book of this breadth of subject matter that deals with developments of an enormous region over a period of some sixty-five years owes a great deal to the insights, observations and analyses of many people – too numerous to be acknowledged individually. But a special mention must be made of my colleague David Shambaugh, whose scholarship, organizing abilities and advice have been a constant source of encouragement over many years. Thanks are also due to the Sigur Center for Asian Studies of the Elliott School for International Affairs at the George Washington University and its director Dr Shawn McHale, for providing all the facilities one could wish for as a visiting scholar intent on writing.

The editors at Routledge (now part of Taylor & Francis), notably Stephanie Rogers, deserve special thanks for their patience and gentle encouragement as they waited for this third (revised) edition.

I must thank my wife Ellen, for her invaluable contribution as a note-taker of the numerous interviews I conducted with officials and scholars in many countries of Asia over the years. These interviews have been invaluable in shaping my understanding of the politics of the region. I have not cited them in the text as the book is primarily aimed at students, who may wish to pursue further the references I have cited. Another debt of gratitude is owed to her for enduring long periods of my withdrawal from normal life as I prepared the new chapters.

Of course I alone am responsible for any shortcomings the book may have.

Introduction to the third edition

This edition follows on from the first, published in 1996, and the second, published in 2004. It includes four wholly new major chapters on the period since the end of the Cold War. It is therefore more than an update of the previous edition. As before, the approach is eclectic in the sense that it uses insights drawn from the main theories of International Relations including Realism, Liberalism and Constructivism. None of them by itself has provided the necessary methodological tools to encapsulate the main developments in the region, yet each has much to offer, especially in the post-Cold War period, where, for example, considerations of power relations, the significance of institutions and the importance of how states conceive of their identities must be taken into account.[1]

The two decades since the end of the Cold War in the Asia-Pacific, as elsewhere, have been marked by rapid change and uncertainty. Globalization has spread without obstacles and interdependencies have increased, but at the same time the significance of statehood has also grown. The last ten years in particular have witnessed the extraordinarily rapid rise of China, whose economic and political reach extends to every region of the world. India has also risen and Russia has re-emerged as a major player. Japan, however, has declined, literally in terms of population and relatively as an economic power. The United States meanwhile has been bogged down by two long wars in Iraq and Afghanistan and has suffered economically from the 'great recession' of 2008. While it remains the world's only superpower, capable of providing leadership on global issues and indeed the provider of public goods in the Asia-Pacific, there is no denying that its relative power and influence have declined as a result of these setbacks.

These developments, which were not easily foreseeable when the second edition was written in late 2003 and early 2004, required a rewriting of the whole post-Cold War period. As before, the analysis attempts to show the interaction between politics at international, regional and domestic levels. The character of relations between the great powers and changes in the nature of power as non-traditional security acquired great salience, meaning that the entire section on the last twenty years had to be rewritten. Only thus would it be possible to try and distinguish the enduring trends from those of passing or temporary significance. Arguably the geography of the Asia-Pacific has changed to include both India and Central Asia. But it was decided not to devote separate chapters to them, important though they are. Apart from considerations of space, which would have made the book too long and unwieldy, neither India, nor Central Asia could be addressed satisfactorily by focusing only on those aspects of their relationships that involved other Asia-Pacific countries, yet to go beyond that would have taken the focus of the book beyond its core regional concerns. A similar decision was made with regard to Russia, which clearly exercises some influence in the region, and its Far East is part of the region. But that part of Russia is not central to its broad state interests and, unlike during the Cold War period, Moscow's impact on the Asia-Pacific is marginal. Thus consideration of India, Central Asia and Russia have been incorporated into the four new chapters as appropriate.

It was decided not to alter the section on the Cold War period. Since the publication of the first edition in 1996 new materials have become available on many aspects of the Cold War and several fine books have been published to enhance our understanding of particular events and developments. But in my judgement the core arguments in that section of the book still hold and the call for alteration is less pressing. The Cold War provided a framework of bipolarity in which international politics was shaped very much by the incipient conflict between the two superpowers who not only headed two opposing alliance systems, but who also led two competing ideologies and economic and political systems. That international axis of conflict affected the world as a whole and determined very much when and how the United States and the Soviet Union intervened in Third World countries. The bipolar system was complicated in the Asia-Pacific region by the defection of China from the Soviet camp and its formation of an alignment with the United States in 1971. Nevertheless the main lines of conflict in the region were determined by the Cold War, even though many had local roots.

The end of the Cold War was abrupt and not anticipated by either academics or diplomats. It gave rise to a new situation of great complexity and uncertainty, so that more than twenty years after the fall of the Berlin Wall in 1989 it is still customary to describe the current period as 'post-Cold War' – which of course tells us little about the contemporary characteristics of the new period and indeed may even be misleading, as it implies that the period is still shaped by the legacy of the Cold War.

The dissolution of the Soviet Union in 1991 left the United States as the sole superpower. Such was the scale of American predominance that it seemed as if the forty-year period of bipolarity had been replaced by the unipolarity of the United States. The United States was the major economic power (as Japan's challenge burst with the collapse of its economic bubble in 1992) and the leader of the new surge of globalization that no longer faced the barriers of the Soviet-led communist camp. America was by far the world's greatest military power and its lead in the so-called revolution in military affairs enabled it to sweep away Saddam Hussein's Iraqi armed forces, despite the latter being armed with the latest Soviet weapons. So great was American power that it virtually ruled out warfare between the remaining major powers. However, that had the effect of giving greater salience to conflicts within states and of persuading Western governments of the merits of humanitarian intervention. One authoritative view of the new role of the United States was that it should actively promote the spread of democracy and free markets. The problems, however, were in determining the priorities for intervention. Bereft of the disciplines of the Cold War's bipolar order, the strategic priorities for the United States were not immediately apparent. For example, after much hesitation the Clinton administration intervened successfully in the former Yugoslavia, and intervened in Somalia only to withdraw under humiliating circumstances, never to return. It decided not to intervene to prevent genocide in Rwanda, only for President Clinton to regret not having done so ever since.

Globalization led to the deepening of interdependencies, but as these took root so did the growth of regionalization. The different regions were no longer linked by Cold War contingencies and they took different forms in different areas. If the European Union was based on legal obligations and formal rules for advancing integration, multilateral organizations in the Asia-Pacific focused on informal arrangements, consensus, non-interference and the enhancement of sovereignty.

Major security threats came to be seen as deriving less from conflicts between established states than from 'rogue states', non-state terrorist groups and the proliferation of weapons of mass destruction (WMD). Moreover, the concept of security was enlarged to encompass threats to civil order as posed by transnational crime involving narcotics, trafficking in people and money laundering. Similarly, threats of disease spread by the ease of communications, notably HIV/AIDS, were increasingly seen as security issues. Environmental degradation too increasingly began to be seen in security terms. These new perceptions of threat required new policies and methods of coordination between agencies and bureaucracies previously considered to be confined in scope to their domestic spheres. After the terrible attacks of 11 September 2001 on the symbols of American economic and political power in New York and Washington, American attention focused exclusively on the so-called war on terror, which led to the wars against Afghanistan and Iraq. In one sense, this intensified the significance of international cooperation to meet the new kinds of security threat, but in another, it widened the gap between the concerns of the United States and those of its partners, new and old.

The consequence of these trends for the Asia-Pacific region has been to narrow the range of the junctions between the global interests of America and those of the region. The principal concerns of the countries of the Asia-Pacific region have been to develop their economies and to consolidate the political order of their respective states in the face of greater exposure to exigencies of the international economy and rapid social change at home. To these ends there has been a trend towards enhancing cooperative security through an array of multitiered and overlapping economic and security associations. That has been accompanied by a strengthening of America's alliances with several countries in the region.

However, the key changes in the region's international politics have been the rise of China, followed by the rise of India and the relative decline of Japan. In particular the rise of China has been welcomed as the new locomotive driving the economies of the other regional states. China's embrace of multilateralism has been welcomed by many of its smaller neighbours who see this as signifying China's acceptance of the regional norms of conflict avoidance. But as against that there is concern about Chinese nationalism and the modernization of the Chinese military and in particular of its naval forces, which have begun to be more active in the Pacific and Indian Oceans in a context in which China is beginning to claim its EEZs and adjacent seas, including the Yellow and South China Seas, as areas of core Chinese national interests. At issue is the extent to which the United States may be relied upon to continue its naval activities in these maritime areas as before. Up until the present, China's maritime neighbours have relied upon the United States as a hedge against Chinese assertiveness, but more recently doubts have emerged as to how steadfast the United States will be against what is seen as a Chinese tendency to extend the areas, which it claims as its exclusive domain. In other words the immediate future of the region will depend on the character of Sino-American relations, specifically as to whether the United States can be relied upon to resist China's encroachments into areas deemed beyond its existing domain.

Note

1 For an argument to this effect, see Amitav Acharya, 'Theoretical Perspectives on International Relations in Asia', in David Shambaugh and Michael Yahuda (eds), *International Relations of Asia* (Lanham, MD: Rowman & Littlefield 2008).

Section I

The Cold War, 1945–89

Part I

The international politics of the Asia-Pacific

Introduction

The Atlantic Era is now at the height of its development and must soon exhaust the resources at its command. The Pacific Era, destined to be the greatest of all, is just at its dawn.

Theodore Roosevelt, 1903[1]

It still remains to be seen whether the 'Pacific Era' has at last begun to unfold, a hundred years after President Roosevelt proclaimed its dawn. But one important difference between his time and the beginning of the twenty-first century is that the Asian countries had long since ceased to be pawns of the major external powers and had increasingly become masters of their own destinies. Accordingly, it is more appropriate to describe the region as the Asia-Pacific.

The emergence of the Asia-Pacific as a region in international politics is a modern phenomenon. Indeed, it might best be conceived as a region that is still in the process of evolution and whose identity has yet to be clearly defined. It is a product of several developments associated with the modernization and globalization of economic, political and social life that has involved the spread of what might be called industrialism and statehood throughout the world. Derived from Europe and still bearing the marks of their origin, these great forces have shaped and continue to shape what we understand to be the contemporary Asia-Pacific. At the same time, their implantation in this part of the world has involved accommodation and adaptation to prior non-European traditions and institutions. Thus, although the states of the Asia-Pacific may be defined in common legal terms (involving concepts of sovereignty, territoriality and citizenship) that would be recognizable to Europeans of the nineteenth century, the governance of the states of, say, contemporary China, Japan or, indeed, Indonesia cannot be fully understood without reference to their respective different historical antecedents.

The regional identity of the Asia-Pacific may be said to derive from geopolitical and geo-economic considerations rather than from any indigenous sense of homogeneity or commonality of purpose. Unlike Europe, the Asia-Pacific cannot call upon shared cultural origins or proclaim attachment to common political values as a basis for regional identity. But the Asia-Pacific can claim to have been located at an important geographical junction of post-Second World War politics, where the competing Cold War interests of the two superpowers intersected with each other, with those of the two major regional powers and with those of the smaller resident states. The way in which these different sets of competing and cooperative interests have interacted has given this region its distinctive if evolving identity, which has acquired recent significance through geo-economic factors. The development of what the World Bank once called 'the East Asian economic miracle' has transformed East Asia from a region of poverty and insurgency into one of the most important centres of the international economy. The pattern of consistent high rates of economic growth and an increasing share of the world's GNP and trade that began with Japan and became true of the four little dragons (South Korea, Taiwan, Hong Kong and Singapore) has become true of southern China and most of the countries of the Association of Southeast Asian Nations (ASEAN – Brunei, Indonesia, Malaysia, the Philippines, Singapore and Thailand). Vietnam too is on the threshold of participating in the 'miracle'.[2] The continuing economic dynamism of the region and the confidence that resident governments have drawn from their economic achievements have enhanced a new sense of national pride and assertiveness that is in the process of acquiring regional expression.

It was only once the great powers began to treat the diverse countries of the area as a distinct arena of international politics and economics that it became possible to identify the area with some sense of coherence. It was first treated as a separate geographical region at the Washington Conference of 1921–22 when the great powers of the day formally agreed to fix the ratio of the warships they would deploy in the Pacific. That was designed to limit the geographical and military scope of the challenge of Japan – the first state in the Asia-Pacific to adapt to the modernizing imperatives. By the 1930s the Japanese had not only repudiated the agreement that had restricted their naval deployments, but they sought to exclude the Western powers altogether from the region as proposed in the scheme formally declared in 1938 as the East Asia Co-Prosperity Sphere. It had appeared in different guises earlier in the decade as in the concept of a 'new order in East Asia'.[3] Japan's initial victories over the Western powers and its attempts to encourage anti-Western sentiments around the slogan 'Asia for Asians' stimulated local nationalism.[4] However, the brutality and domineering behaviour of the Japanese conquerors undermined their image as liberators and engendered fears and animosities among local peoples that have yet to be expiated more than sixty years later. However, the Japanese sphere of military operations also defined the sphere of the allied response in the Pacific War. The several agreements among the wartime allies, beginning in 1941, followed by the Quebec Conference of 1943 which set up the South East Asian Command, continuing with the 1943 Cairo Declaration and culminating in the Yalta and Potsdam agreements of 1945, helped to give parts of the region greater geopolitical coherence. But they also marked the last time in which the region would be defined by the great powers in accordance with their interests without even informing the local states, let alone consulting them.

It was not until after the Pacific War (fought partly to deny Japan an exclusive sphere) that the local countries of the region acquired independence and began (or in some cases resumed) asserting their own identities and developing patterns of conflict and cooperation among themselves, and the region began to be shaped by its variety of indigenous forces. But the region was still largely defined in terms of the international struggle for the balance of power, with the Soviet Union and communist China replacing Japan as the object of Western (primarily American) containment.

The evolution of the region may therefore be seen as beginning with great power arrangements to accommodate the distribution of power within the Asia-Pacific to the global balance of power. Or put another way, it began with the recognition by the Western powers of the rise of Japan as a major power within a geographically circumscribed part of the world. Following the defeat of Japan, a new balance of power emerged as, under the impact of the Cold War, the United States sought to contain the challenge of the two major communist powers. That was seen to be linked to the struggles for independence from colonial rule and the subsequent attempts to consolidate independence and build new nations. In some states the nationalist challenge was led by communist forces and in others they constituted a threat, sometimes by armed insurgencies to incumbent governments. Local elites tended to seek external support and patronage. Thus linkages were formed between external balance of power considerations and regional and local conflicts that were defined primarily in terms of the Cold War.

The next major stage in the development of the region was its transformation from being merely an object of geopolitical interest to the great powers of global significance to one in which its constituent members as independent states sought to articulate an independent approach to international politics in the guise of what was later called non-alignment. The first notable expression of this was the Asian–African conference in Bandung, Indonesia, in 1955. Although this helped to identify what was later called the Third World as a new dimension in international politics and, indeed, contributed to developing the agenda that emphasized anticolonialism and the need for economic development, it was unable to overcome the differences of interests and competing security concerns of the resident Asian states. Indeed the enormous diversities of the region have militated against the development of the kind of integrative regionalism associated with Western Europe since the end of the Second World War. Interestingly, the one relatively successful regional organization, the Association of Southeast Asian Nations (ASEAN) which was formed in 1967, as its name implies, is restricted to Southeast Asia and was designed in practice to enhance the effective independence of its members. Far from seeking to integrate the region by merging sovereignty and unifying the operations of their economies, the national leaders sought to strengthen their hard won and vulnerable separate systems of government. They sought to reduce the challenges to their domestic rule by containing intraregional disputes through the recognition of the junction between the stability of the region and that of the domestic order of member states.[5]

The Asia-Pacific became a region of global significance, counting as it does as its resident members both the global powers, the United States and the Soviet Union (although its successor state, Russia, is less than global in its scope), and the major regional powers of international significance, China and Japan. The two major wars of the Cold War were fought in the region, and developments within the region have contributed to changing global alignments of great import. Thus the transformation of China from an ally of the Soviet Union to a position of revolutionary isolationism and then to alignment with the United States helped to undermine the congruence between ideological and strategic affinities that typified the early stages of the Cold War. The Chinese 'defection' from the alliance with the Soviet Union introduced a third factor into the global strategic equation, which was increasingly regarded as tripolar. But the main ramifications of this change were felt within the region, where the Soviet–American axis of conflict was joined by a parallel Soviet–Chinese one whose outcome was a Sino-American alignment and the end of the Vietnam War (or Second Indo-China War), followed by the outbreak of the Cambodian War (or Third Indo-China War). Similarly, developments within the region played a part in the ending of the Cold War for the world as a whole, but its impact upon the communist regimes in Asia has been altogether different from that experienced by their European former counterparts.

The end of the Cold War and the disintegration of the Soviet Union was not accompanied by the collapse of the key communist regimes in the Asia-Pacific of China, Vietnam and North Korea. And, as a result, an element of the Cold War has survived in the region, as they fear the political agenda of the United States, the sole surviving superpower. The end of bipolarity has brought to an end the central strategic balance that had hitherto dominated international politics and as a result it has detached regional and sub-regional conflicts from the larger global axis of conflict to which they had previously been joined. The ending of the international and then the regional dimensions of the Cambodian conflict facilitated a settlement brokered by the United Nations, and has reduced the ensuing domestic struggles within the country to primarily local significance. The Korean conflict has also been transformed, but its resolution is more complex as it involves two separate states in an area of geopolitical significance to four of the world's greatest powers. In so far as it involves global dimensions, these centre on the acquisition by the North of nuclear weapons, the challenge to the Nuclear Non-Proliferation Treaty regime and the proliferation of Weapons of Mass Destruction (WMD).

The new strategic situation in the region is regarded as uncertain. A predominant America is more focused on the global war on terror, while the region is adjusting to the rise of China. New patterns of multilateralism and greater fluidity in relations between the major powers have emerged in the region. Immediate concerns about the management of the rising power of China prompted the establishment in 1993 of the ASEAN Regional Forum (ARF) as an embryonic regional security organization. It may be seen as paralleling the Asia-Pacific Economic Cooperation forum (APEC) that was established in 1989, which (although also essentially consultative in character) has been boosted by American-led attempts since 1993 to enlarge its scope to promote an Asian-Pacific community dedicated to free trade. The global economic significance of the region has already been noted, but the political and strategic significance of the region's economic dynamism should also be appreciated. These economic changes are beginning to challenge the character and the distribution of global power. They have already transformed thinking about the character of security and political stability of so-called Third World states.

Accordingly, this book is concerned with the interplay between the interests of the great, the regional and the local powers in this part of the world. These may conveniently be depicted as operating simultaneously at three levels – the global, the regional and the local. During the period of the Cold War, the first may be said to have involved the dynamics of the central balance between the United States and the Soviet Union, the manner in which that impacted upon the other two levels and the way in which these also fed back into the first. The second involved the conflicts and accommodations affecting the major regional powers in their relations with the other two levels. The third involved the problems of identity and security as played out by the elites of the new or newly established states.

At the local level, security tended to be defined, especially in the first two or three decades after the Second World War, less in terms of conventional military threats than in terms of the survival of the ruling elites and the socio-economic systems that sustained them. In the period immediately following that war, the states of contemporary East and Southeast Asia either re-established themselves anew after civil war and alien military occupation or they acquired independence from colonial rule. The experience contributed to shaping their territorial bounds (and territorial claims) as well as the character of their social and economic development. Their domestic political cultures and their views of the outside world were also shaped by historical experiences that in most cases long predated the advent of the Europeans and the modern era. Nevertheless the majority of what might be called these new states were not secure initially in their social and political orders – and indeed some are still insecure or have acquired new sources of instability.

These domestic insecurities have had regional and international dimensions, first because competing elites have sought support from beyond their own states and external powers have in turn competed for regional influence by supporting them, and second because the outcomes were sometimes perceived as potentially significant for the management of the central or global balance of power by the two superpowers, the United States and the Soviet Union.

Therefore, this book will examine the interactions between three factors which have shaped the evolution of the political and security developments in the region since 1945. These may be characterized as: first, the impact of the dynamics of the central balance; second, the conflicts and accommodations involving the regional great powers; and third, the problems of identity and national security of the new or newly established states. The junctions and disjunctions of security and political interests between these three levels may be seen as having occasioned such patterns of order or disorder that have emerged from time to time within the region. The book will conclude with an assessment of the impact of the end of the Cold War upon the region and of the new significance of the region in international politics.

The region: an overview 信仰 统一 多为仿

The region may be defined in a broad fashion so as to include the littoral states of the Pacific of North, Central and South America; the island states of the South Pacific; Australasia; and Northeast, Southeast and South Asia. A more common definition includes the states of North America, Australasia and Northeast and Southeast Asia. But in order to keep this study manageable, we have defined the Asia-Pacific somewhat narrowly to include the two superpowers, the United States and the Soviet Union (and its more circumscribed successor, Russia); the two regional great powers, China and Japan; and the local countries of Northeast and Southeast Asia. Other parts of what may legitimately be regarded as the Asia-Pacific, namely South Asia, Australasia, the South Pacific, Canada and parts of Latin America, will be included only when necessary to explain the international politics of the others.

Even as defined in this relatively restricted way, the scope of the region is immense and hugely diverse. That in itself is detrimental to the emergence of an indigenous sense of a common regional identity. Leaving aside the United States and those former members of the Soviet Union that have claims to being Asian-Pacific countries in their own right, the region embraces eighteen countries and territories that vary from, at one extreme, China, with a territory of more than 9,561,000 square kilometres and a population in 2003 of 1,300 million people, to Singapore, at the other, with a territory of only 625 square kilometres and a population of 3.2 million people. The two countries also serve to point up further disparities as the per capita GNP in Singapore in 2003 was US$24,000 compared to US$1,084 in China (although it should be noted that in terms of purchasing power parity the Chinese figure was US$5,000; that was still only 13.1 per cent of that of America as compared to 63.4 per cent for Singapore).[6] As can be seen from these figures, China essentially still belongs to the Third World whereas Singapore is classified as a newly industrialized country or economy (NIC or NIE). The economic disparities of the region would loom even larger if Japan were to be compared with Vietnam or Burma.

In addition to these geographical and economic factors, attention is usually drawn to the wide divergences in religion, culture, historical associations, social traditions, language, ethnicity and political systems that further divide the region. Many of these divisions cut across state borders and not only make for tensions between regional states, but also exacerbate the problems of nation building and consolidating state power from within. This is particularly true of the states of Southeast Asia where the colonial experience promoted links with the metropolitan power. Thus the Indo-Chinese states were tied to France; Burma, through

India, was orientated to Britain, as were Malaya and Singapore; Indonesia, however, was attached to Holland (with the island of Borneo divided between the Dutch and the British). And the Philippines was under Spanish rule until 1898, when it was taken over by the United States and remade in its image. Indeed some of the states were actually the creations of the colonial powers. Indonesia and Malaysia, for example, in their present forms do not have precise historical antecedents, although their nationalistic elites draw on pre-colonial traditions. At the same time, the borders which all the Southeast Asian states inherited from the colonial period have left them with territorial disputes with neighbours, and the colonial legacy has also given rise to highly complex domestic communal problems, highlighted, for example, by the ethnic Chinese.

The region is also marked by considerable diversity in its security arrangements. The situation in the Asia-Pacific for most of this period and certainly for the duration of the Cold War was more fluid than in Europe, where two tightly coordinated military alliance systems confronted each other across clearly defined lines in seemingly implacable hostility. And although it was in the Asia-Pacific that the two major wars of the Cold War were fought, in Korea and in Vietnam, the fact that they were 'limited' and that they did not become general wars is indicative of the greater flexibility that applied in the region. It was possible to insulate conflicts and prevent them from engulfing the entire region. The different countries of the region did not on the whole join multiple or regional alliance systems. The alliance systems that have predominated in the region have tended to be of the bilateral kind – typically between a superpower and a regional partner. Such arrangements have allowed for significant variation within the region with regard to how the links or junctions between the global, regional and local levels could apply at any given time. China's evolution from a close ally of the Soviet Union in the 1950s to being aligned with the United States in the 1970s perhaps illustrates the point most clearly.

The diversity within the region and the fluidity of the security arrangements are indicative of the absence of what might be called a regional order. There is as yet no basis for the establishment of a regional order, if that is taken to mean the existence of stable relationships based on accepted rules of conduct between states, of shared views about the legitimacy of government within states and of common assumptions about the interrelationships among regional and external states.[7]

Until the establishment of the ASEAN Regional Forum in 1993, there were no intra-regional political institutions that linked together the various parts of the region, and even the ARF is best considered as an embryonic rather than a fully fledged security organization. Unlike in Europe, there are no effective institutional arrangements that would facilitate collective consideration by the states of the Asia-Pacific of the security problems of, say, Northeast Asia such as the disputed territories between Japan and the Soviet Union or the division of Korea. Similarly, the complexities involving the questions of Taiwan and Hong Kong are left to the parties directly involved. Even the one inter-state organization in the region that is usually regarded as a successful example of a regional organization among Third World countries, ASEAN, has studiously refrained from attempting to become a conventional security organization. Its members may have agreed on certain principles of state conduct, such as the unacceptability of military intervention by a regional state to change the government of a neighbour – that formed the basis for its diplomatic campaign against Vietnam's actions in Cambodia. But the governments do not necessarily feel confident about the long-term durability of their respective political systems, they do not share a common view about the principal security threats to the region, nor do they agree about the roles that external powers should play in Southeast Asia.

Not surprisingly, these divergences have combined to militate against the development of a regional consciousness comparable to that of the more homogeneous Europeans. Such regional consciousness that has emerged is of relatively recent origin and has been confined largely to the economic sphere, and then only in part. It has been articulated by elites within the worlds of business, academe and government. It has taken the form of a variety of trans-Pacific non-governmental or semi-governmental organizations that so far have been largely consultative in purpose. But, especially since the end of the Cold War, influential voices within the region have called for the upgrading of regional institutions so that they are both more comprehensive in membership and better able to address formally matters of security as well as of economics. This may be regarded as an open acknowledgement of the absence of such a facility so far.

Nevertheless, in surveying the evolution of the region into the world's most dynamic centre of economic growth and technological change, it is clear in retrospect how important the role of the United States has been in providing the security structure and economic environment that have made this possible. In the absence of a multilateral security treaty organization along the lines of NATO, the United States put in place in the 1950s a series of bilateral security treaties or their equivalents of sufficiently broad geographical scope as to provide for a series of military bases and facilities that made a Pacific Rim strategy militarily viable. The United States established treaties that have endured with Japan and South Korea in Northeast Asia, with the Philippines and Thailand (the Manila Pact) in Southeast Asia and with Australia and New Zealand (the effective membership of the latter has been in abeyance since 1985). This Pacific perimeter defence structure was further buttressed by the American bases in Guam and Hawaii, and the Philippines until 1992, and by its special arrangements with island groups in the central and southern Pacific (notably the Marshall Islands). These separate arrangements were overseen administratively by the commander-in-chief for the Pacific of the US Navy.

The result has been that while the United States perceived its strategic role in the Asia-Pacific area as part of a larger strategic rationale that was both global and regional in scope, its series of bilateral partners have tended to perceive their part in narrower parochial or self-interested terms. The latter have tended to judge the value of their strategic association with the United States mainly in terms of particular national interests or even in terms of those of the local holders of political power. Hence the frustration the United States experienced in the

1980s and early 1990s, in renegotiating its bases treaty with the Philippines or in finding a mutually acceptable arrangement with New Zealand over the question of disclosure of whether visiting American ships are carrying nuclear weapons. Since the end of the Cold War there has been widespread support within the region for the continued deployment of American forces in the west Pacific, which is seen as essential for maintaining stability in the region. Even China has refrained from calling for an American withdrawal – at least in the short term. But at the same time, there has been apprehension within the region that American domestic opinion may not support the deployment in the long term. Continuing trade disputes and criticism of America within the region, as part of the resistance to the perceived attempt to export American political values, have added new complexities to the strategic relationship.

From the perspective of international politics it is striking that the main convenient dividing point in the history of the region during the Cold War period should also be the main turning point in American policy towards the region. The transformation of the pattern of global alignments and the role of China in 1969–71, which changed the balance of power within the region, were interconnected with profound changes in American strategic policies, as marked by the 'Nixon doctrine' of 1969 that forswore further commitment of American ground forces to major combat on the Asian mainland and by the Sino-American alignment of 1971–72. These developments reflected both the escalation of China's disputes with its giant communist neighbour to the level of armed conflict and the ending of the military phase of America's policy of containment in Asia. This found institutional expression in the abolishment of the military structure of the Southeast Asian Treaty Organization (SEATO) in February 1974 and then the organization itself in June 1977. During the 1970s, in the Asia-Pacific, the congruence between ideological and strategic affinities was erased. Yet the American system of bilateral alliances survived the change, especially that with Japan. Even though the alliance with Taiwan had to be formally abrogated in 1979, a way was found through the domestic legislative mechanism of the Taiwan Relations Act to preserve much of the substance of the former treaty. Containment was still practised, but more indirectly through diplomacy and assisting third parties to resist the territorial expansion of Soviet power either by proxy, as through Vietnam in Indo-China, or directly, as in Afghanistan.

In addition to providing a militarily secure international environment for its allies and associates in the region through the exercise of hegemonic power, the United States also provided an international economic environment that has facilitated the remarkable growth of the economies of most of these friends. By opening its domestic markets and by applying liberal economic principles without demanding reciprocity (at least not until recent times), the United States made it possible for first Japan and then the East Asian NIEs to follow policies of rapid economic growth that combined various mixes of export orientation and import substitution. Certainly the United States has benefited from Asia-Pacific economic dynamism, but its benefits have become disproportionate to the costs. According to the *IMF Direction of Trade Statistics*, in 1985 the United States accounted for nearly 40 per cent of the value of the total trade of the East Asian countries, as compared to 15 per cent that was counted as trade amongst themselves. But even excluding America's trade with Japan, its total trade with Asia was valued at US$158.8 billion, and that involved a trade deficit of US$43.9 billion which was not far behind the trade deficit with Japan of US$52.5 billion. In 1980, however, according to the same IMF source, the United States had a trade deficit with Japan of US$12.2 billion and a trade *surplus* of US$1.5 billion with the other East Asian countries. Thus in the 1980s the American trade deficit with the East Asian countries as a whole leapt from just over US$10 billion to nearly US$100 billion. By 1993 the overall American deficit with Asia and Japan had grown to US$121.2 billion. Japan by contrast enjoyed a surplus with Asia and America with a combined value of US$104–15 billion.[8]

Although the seeds for the economic transformation of the region were sown earlier, it was not until the 1970s (in the case of Japan) and the 1980s (for the East Asian NIEs) that the region began to be recognized as a centre of economic growth and technological development of global significance. Unlike in the security realm, where the United States is still unquestionably the dominant (if not unchallenged) military power, American economic leadership in the region has long been contested by Japan. As early as 1965 a leading Japanese scholar graphically depicted Japan's envisioned role as the leader of a 'flying-geese formation' to characterize the future economic development of East and Southeast Asia. With Japan in the lead, economic dynamism would be diffused first to the NIEs, who in turn would be followed by some of the ASEAN countries and possibly China, Vietnam, North Korea, Burma and even the Soviet Union.[9] Yet even as Japan's trade with Asia has leaped in total value from US$7.9 billion in 1970 to US$49.5 billion in 1980 and to US$147.6 billion in 1989, it has always enjoyed a surplus. The trade surplus in 1989 came to US$17.6 billion and in 1993 to US$50.1 billion.[10] It is clear that although American trade may have declined as a proportion of overall Asian trade, access to its domestic markets on a non-reciprocal basis was still of great significance to the economic dynamism of the region in the 1990s.

Thus, in terms of the region as a whole, it is the United States that has provided the general security and other 'public goods' as its friends and allies have benefited while pursuing their more parochial concerns. For some time, Americans have been debating whether their country has been declining as a hegemonic power. But since the ending of the Cold War, governments, business elites and academics in East Asia have begun to question whether the United States will continue to provide the secure strategic and economic environments that have proved to be so advantageous to the countries in the region. Within the United States there is uncertainty about the character of the emerging post-Cold War period and the role that the United States should play now that it is effectively the only super-power left. There is also uncertainty about the United States continuing to pro-vide the economic 'public goods' in the Asia-Pacific, as it has done so far.

The economic success of the Western orientated countries in the region since the 1970s has doubtless contributed to stabilizing their political systems and to encouraging the development of more democratic forms of political representation. Yet in most instances the consolidation of statehood is too recent and the sources of conflict both within and between the states of the region too apparent for any complacency to emerge in this respect. Indeed these uncertainties contribute to the difficulties in developing regional security institutions.

This is true even in Southeast Asia, where the Association of Southeast Asian Nations (ASEAN) in 1992 marked its twenty-fifth anniversary as a generally acknowledged successful regional organization, especially in the Third World. Yet its members do not share a common strategic outlook. They differ in their assessments of the sources of threats to regional security and on the extent to which they should seek to exclude the external great powers. Moreover, even after three or four decades of independence the member states still find that communal problems, challenges from fundamental Islam and intra-mural disputes about borders and territory have been contained rather than solved.

Relations within the region are also complicated by historical legacies from different eras. The legacy of the colonial period still endures in many respects in Southeast Asia, long after the European powers were compelled to retreat from Asia. For example, at certain levels communications and social/educational ties with the former metropolitan powers are easier and more visible than those with neighbouring countries. The legacies of historical relations of even earlier eras continue to complicate more contemporary arrangements. This is most evident in the case of China, which is central to the concerns of the region as a whole. China's sheer size and the memory of its traditional assertion of superiority and its former claims to bestow legitimacy on local rulers sustain unease among its neighbours in the region. That memory has also contributed to giving a keen edge to the response within the region to the sponsorship by China's communist rulers of revolutionary insurgencies that challenged social order and the local regimes for nearly forty years after the end of the Pacific War. Not surprisingly, unease remains about the character of China's appeal to the ethnic Chinese residents in the region, who exercise an economic influence disproportionate to their relatively small numbers and who have become major investors in China. These concerns are exacerbated by China's territorial claims, especially in the South China Sea, where as recently as 1995 naval forces were deployed to advance them.

The ways in which traditional and contemporary sources of conflict can combine to accentuate problems may be seen from a brief consideration of the recent history of Indo-China, which has been the most persistent focus of major power conflict in the region. Long-standing enmities between some of the local and regional forces had been interrupted by the French colonial intervention in the nineteenth century. The series of wars that followed the Pacific War saw these ancient enmities become enmeshed with the external involvement of the two superpowers. At the risk of oversimplifying, it can be argued that the settlement of the Cambodian conflict as an international problem in the early 1990s only became possible once the more distant great powers disengaged, to leave the historically engaged neighbouring countries to accept a settlement based on the then-current distribution of power between them. Above all, once the Soviet Union was no longer able or willing to support Vietnam, the Vietnamese found that they could no longer sustain their position in Cambodia. Vietnam, which in 1986 had shifted its main priority to domestic economic reform and development, then sought to mend relations with China. These developments de-linked the Cambodian conflict from the global and regional rivalries that had hitherto blocked all attempts at a settlement. With the conflict localized, it became possible for the United Nations to tender its services in an attempt to reconcile the differences between the warring factions. Meanwhile there can be little doubt about the enhanced position of the regional 'victors' China and, up to a point, Thailand.

In Northeast Asia too, the legacies of the conflicts of previous centuries as well as of the Pacific War and the Cold War continue to shape the international relations of the region. Here, too, the resolution of long-term conflicts has in some, but not all, respects eased with the ending of the superpower confrontation. The disengagement of the major external sources of conflict has not in itself solved the conflicts of Korea, nor the territorial dispute between Russia and Japan, and especially not the China–Taiwan problem, but by being disentangled from the wider global conflict of the Cold War it has become possible to reduce the stakes of the conflicts and to introduce greater flexibility into their management.

The ending of the Cold War provides a convenient point to look back at the previous forty-five years to identify the underlying themes that have shaped the agenda of international politics in the Asia-Pacific region and to establish the points of junction and disjunction between the global, regional and local levels of politics noted earlier. But the ending of the Cold War has also ushered in a new era characterized less by a tangible sense of new order than by one of transition and uncertainty.

The ending of the bipolar divide between the United States and the Soviet Union has broken the basis of the linkage that used to enmesh some regional questions with global issues. Indeed, the character of what is of global concern has changed. For example, the potential conflict between the two Koreas has ceased to be regarded as a possible trigger that could ignite a third world war; rather it is now seen as being of local or, at most, of regional significance. But the possible acquisition of nuclear weapons by the North is perceived with alarm as an issue of global importance.

The world has become more complex and its lines of conflict more disparate. In retrospect the Cold War era provided the United States government with an organizing framework that bound together questions of global strategy with those of ideology, politics and even economics. Now that that framework has gone, it is proving to be much more difficult for Washington to develop a coherent strategy to address the new situation. It can no longer override domestic concerns and special interests by invoking the strategic imperatives of foreign policy. In fact, now that the global agenda has changed, it is the domestic arena that is claiming attention in the United States. These developments have raised new concerns within the Asia-Pacific as to whether the American public and Washington will have the political will to maintain current levels of forces in the region and to fulfil the commitments of the United States. As a result there is concern within the region that a new distribution of power may be in the process of emerging that may prove disruptive of the relative stability of the last decade.

The impact of the ending of the Cold War on the Asia-Pacific has been altogether different from that on Europe. The Asian communist regimes (with the exception of Mongolia – which in any case had many of the characteristics of an Eastern European satellite of the Soviet Union) have not collapsed. The East Asian economic 'miracle' continues to unfold as it has spread to the ASEAN countries and most spectacularly to China itself. But as China stands on the threshold of developing the economic weight to match its leaders' great power aspirations, new questions have arisen, or perhaps old questions have emerged afresh, about its capacity to survive as a unitary state. Meanwhile its weaker neighbours seek to draw China into closer engagement with the region, particularly through participation in the new regional organizations, the ARF and APEC.

This book will first provide a historical overview of the region as a whole as it has evolved since 1945. It will be subdivided chronologically so as to facilitate discussion of the possible links between local developments and changes in the balance of power at both regional and global levels. Subsequent chapters will analyse separately the interests and policies of the two global powers, the United States and the Soviet Union/Russia, as these have taken shape within the region. That will be followed by chapters on China and Japan, respectively, as the two major regional powers of global significance.

Notes

1 Cited by Bernard K. Gordon, 'Pacific Futures for the U.S.A.' in Lau Teik Soon and Leo Suryadinata (eds), *Moving into the Pacific Century: The Changing Regional Order* (Oxford: Heinemann, 1988), p.3.

2 The World Bank, *The East Asian Miracle: Economic Growth and Public Policy* (Oxford: Oxford University Press, 1993).

3 F.C. Jones, *Japan's New Order in East Asia: Its Rise and Fall 1937–45* (London: Oxford University Press, 1954); and Robert J.C. Butow, *Tojo and the Coming of War* (Princeton: Princeton University Press, 1961).

4 Interestingly, the Japanese government decreed immediately after the attack on Pearl Harbour in December 1941 that the term 'the Far East' (*kyokuto*), an 'obnoxious' reflection of the notion that 'England was the centre of the world', was no longer to be used, and that henceforth the war was to be known as that of 'Great East Asia' (*Daitoa*). See Christopher Thorne, *The Far Eastern War: States and Societies 1941–45* (London: Counterpoint, Unwin Paperbacks, 1986).

5 Michael Leifer, *ASEAN and the Security of South-East Asia* (London: Routledge, 1989), pp.17–51.

6 All figures are drawn from the *CIA World Factbook*.

7 This account of regional order is derived from accounts in Hedley Bull, *The Anarchical Society* (London: Macmillan, 1977), ch.3; Stanley Hoffman, *Primacy or World Order* (McGraw-Hill, 1978) chs 3–4; and Michael Leifer, 'The Balance of Power and

Regional Order' in Michael Leifer (ed.), *The Balance of Power in East Asia* (London: Macmillan, 1986). The question of order should be distinguished from that of regime, to which it is closely related, as the latter is usually related to principles and procedures as these apply to a particular issue area.

8 The range of the Japanese surplus arises from discrepancies in the IMF statistics between those listed for the US and those for Japan, see *IMF Direction of Trade Yearbook 1994.*

9 Kaname Akamatsu, cited by Takashi Inoguchi, 'Shaping and Sharing Pacific Dynamism' in Peter A. Gourevitch (ed.), *The Pacific Region: Challenges to Policy and Theory* (The Annals of the American Academy of Political Science, September 1989), p.48.

10 As before, these figures are drawn from the *IMF Direction of Trade Statistics Yearbooks.*

1 The impact of the Cold War and the struggles for independence, 1945–54

It was the advent of the Cold War in the late 1940s and early 1950s that brought about a junction in the Asia-Pacific between the international, regional and local dimensions of politics and military strategy. More precisely, it was the Korean War, begun in June 1950, that effectively integrated the Asia-Pacific into the Cold War system that had first emerged in Europe. But unlike the situation in Europe, where the Cold War divided the protagonists into two clearly defined camps of opposing ideological, economic and political systems separated by an 'iron curtain', the divisions in Asia were less clear cut and were still being contested long after they had been settled in Europe. Moreover, in Asia there also emerged a non-aligned dimension registered at the Asian–African Conference held in Bandung in 1955. The difference between Asia and Europe was also apparent from the way the Second World War was conducted in the two theatres, and from the different consequences of that war in each sector. The European war had been fought over established states by vast land armies, and ended in a division of Europe between the Soviet and Western victorious armies. The war in the Asia-Pacific was won essentially through American naval and air power culminating in the dropping of the two atomic bombs. This left a scramble for power in many parts of Asia involving both civil wars and struggles for independence against the returning colonial powers.

Although the Pacific War had provided a strategic rationale for treating the region as a whole, the Western allies came to treat Northeast and Southeast Asia separately. As the United States concentrated its forces on the assault on Japan itself, Britain was in effect entrusted with winning the war in Southeast Asia, with initial responsibility for Burma, Thailand, Malaya (including Singapore) and Sumatra. In July 1945, the rest of the Dutch East Indies, excluding the island of Timor, as well as Indo-China south of the 16th Parallel of latitude, were transferred to the Southeast Asia Command under Admiral Mountbatten. Indo-China north of the 16th Parallel was allocated to the China Command of Chiang Kai-shek, and the rest was designated as the Southwest Pacific Command.[1] This division of labour was to accentuate the differences between the two sub-regions of Northeast and Southeast Asia in the early years after the war, since the immediate agenda for the north centred on relations between the United States and the Soviet Union and the domestic evolutions of China and Japan, whereas that of the south turned on the struggles for independence with the returned colonial powers. As became evident from the American involvement in the struggles in Indo-China from the late 1940s, it was the advent of the Cold War that began to link the two sub-regions together from both global and local perspectives. It was only then that the results of local struggles for power or independence were regarded as having implications for the global distribution of power and influence. That provided a basis, on the one hand, for competing local elites to seek and to obtain external patronage and, on the other hand, for the external powers to extend such support for their own competitive advantages.

Northeast Asia

The immediate aftermath of the Pacific War was shaped by the understandings reached at the Yalta Conference, which in turn reflected the realities of American maritime hegemony in the Pacific and Soviet dominance of the landmass of Northeast Asia.[2] The result was a division into spheres of interest. The United States exercised predominance in the Pacific Ocean, including the Philippines, Okinawa and Japan. The Soviet Union regained Sakhalin and the Kuriles as well as obtaining rights in Manchurian railways and ports and gaining Chinese recognition of the independence of its protégé, the former Outer Mongolia. Headed by the British, the colonial rulers sought to restore their positions in Southeast Asia. China had been expected to emerge as a sovereign power and to join the other three great powers in establishing a trusteeship over Korea.[3] In the event, a trusteeship did not emerge in Korea. Instead a hasty agreement about the division of responsibility for accepting the Japanese surrender was concocted between the Americans and the Soviets which, to the agreeable surprise of the former, was observed unilaterally by the Soviet forces, who stopped at the 38th Parallel even though American forces had yet to arrive.[4]

The American view of international order was not confined to balance of power considerations, it also put a premium upon domestic stability in the form of democratic institutions within states.[5] The linchpin of Roosevelt's original post-war strategy in the Asia-Pacific was that a 'united and democratic China' would emerge capable of exercising decisive influence as one of the great powers in the kind of post-war order envisaged in his 'Four Freedoms' speech of January 1941 and in the Atlantic Charter, which he announced with Churchill in the August of that year. The Charter asserted such principles as denial of territorial aggrandizement, guarantee of the right of self-determination for all nations, creation of an open liberal economic system, and international cooperation to preserve peace and security. Although these principles were incorporated with Soviet agreement in the United Nations Charter at the San Francisco meeting in 1945, and despite Soviet attendance at the Bretton Woods meetings that agreed the framework for a world economy based on free trade, it became clear that the Soviet Union had no intention of following them in terms understood in the West. By 1946 the American disillusionment with Soviet behaviour in Poland was affecting American attitudes in the East.[6]

Nevertheless, the American disappointment with China's failure to live up to their wartime expectations coupled with the failure of the 1945–46 Marshall mission to avert a civil war did not lead the American administration to cast the rivalry between the nationalists and communists within the framework of the Cold War at that point.[7] The origins of the Cold War were in Europe, and that was the main focus of the attentions of both the Soviet Union and the United States. The Truman Doctrine of March 1947, which elevated the specific obligations being undertaken towards Greece and Turkey to a universal commitment to 'support free peoples who are resisting attempted subjugation by armed minorities or outside pressures', was in fact made some time after the Americans had begun to assist those two countries. As many have argued, the high moral tone and the universal character of the doctrine was directed as much at mobilizing the American public back home as it was aimed abroad. By this stage a good number of American problems stemmed from the absence of means to carry out the growing international commitments the US was undertaking. Immediately the war had ended, the US began a rapid and extensive demobilization of its armed forces. These had stood at 12 million at the end of the war with Germany, and had come down to 3 million by July 1946 and to 1.6 million a year later. Defence spending followed a similar trajectory. By 1945, the last year of war, it had reached US\$81.6 billion; in fiscal year 1946 it came down to US\$44.7 billion and in fiscal year 1947 it dropped to US\$13.1 billion.[8]

Just as the hoped-for cooperation with the Soviet Union was being replaced by confrontation, the American capacity to meet even the needs of Western Europe had diminished. The Truman Doctrine was designed at least in part to galvanize the American public. It was a factor in building support for the Marshall Plan for Europe and in providing further aid for Chiang Kai-shek. But the disappointment with China had already led to a reconsideration of the American interest in retaining forces in Korea south of the 38th Parallel. Indeed, by 1947–48 it had been decided to withdraw them. Meanwhile the United States had begun to regard Japan not only as a country that had to be encouraged to develop along liberal lines, but also as one that had to undergo reconstruction as a potential ally, and as a source of stability in Northeast Asia.[9]

Despite Soviet apprehensions, the United States government had no intention of intervening in the Chinese civil war. As the communist victory loomed the US government took the view that deep indigenous forces were at work and that the costs of intervention were unacceptably high and had little chance of success. Although there is evidence to show that Mao Zedong and Zhou Enlai on their side had hoped to cultivate relations with the United States, perhaps for economic reasons and to avoid becoming exclusively dependent upon the Soviet Union, nothing came of their private overtures. Leading US administration figures also hoped to wean the Chinese communists from Moscow along the path pioneered by Tito.[10] Whether or not such developments amounted to a 'lost chance', Sino-American relations diverged more and more markedly in the course of the nine months from the establishment of the PRC in October 1949 until the outbreak of the Korean War in June 1950. At home an anti-communist hysteria, sparked in part by the administration's own Cold War rhetoric and fanned by Senator McCarthy's campaign against so-called domestic traitors, including those in the State Department who were alleged to have contributed to the 'loss' of China, played a part in the difficulties in deciding upon foreign policy by rational calculations of measured interests. Meanwhile Mao in public encouraged hostility towards the United States, proclaimed his adherence to the Soviet Union in July when Liu Shaoqi was secretly sent to Moscow, and in December 1949 went himself to Moscow to negotiate an alliance that was eventually signed in February 1950.

Nevertheless the Truman administration had decided early in 1950 that US interests in Taiwan were not important enough to prevent its conquest by the Chinese communists. Even the Joint Chiefs of Staff, who recognized the damage that that would cause to American strategic interests, were unwilling to recommend military intervention because the limited American forces available might be needed for higher priority use elsewhere.[11] With the Yalta system having broken down in the Asia-Pacific because of the communist victory in China, US policy became less than consistent and coherent. Its policy of limited assistance to the Kuo Min Tang (KMT or Nationalist)· government 'pleased no one and gained nothing'.[12] In January 1950, as Mao was still embroiled in difficult negotiations with Stalin, first Truman on 5 January made it clear that the US would not defend Taiwan and then on 12 January Acheson stated at the National Press Club that the American defence perimeter in Asia ran from the Aleutians through Japan and Okinawa to the Philippines. Korea was not included among those listed as being of vital strategic importance to the US, instead it was said to be under UN protection.

The perimeter defence concept would have been badly flawed if indeed the PRC had taken over Taiwan. But had the US sought to defend Taiwan it would undoubtedly have ensured the enmity of the PRC by undermining its national aims of unifying China, thereby driving it still further towards the Soviet Union. The trouble was that the policies designed to serve the US administration's long-term policy goal of weaning China away from its Soviet ally were not in accord with its own short-term strategic interests. Being still disillusioned with the KMT but bound by a Republican congress to extend aid to Chiang Kai-shek, the administration still clung on to the hope that a separate Taiwan might emerge under different auspices.

Thus on the eve of the Korean War the US perimeter defence strategy involved a strong commitment to the defence of Japan and to upholding the liberal domestic system that was evolving there under the American aegis, and it also included Okinawa and, further south, the Philippines. But despite American aid to the Chiang Kai-shek regime in Taiwan and to the Syngman Rhee regime in South Korea, the American commitment to them was more qualified. Although there was some support for these regimes among Republicans in Washington, there was no fundamental disagreement among the leaders of the Truman administration that even though it was in American interests to uphold them the means to do so had been stretched very thin. The main American priority was Europe and care had to be taken to avoid being over-committed elsewhere. On the communist side, there was continued distrust between China and the Soviet Union despite the alliance between them. Nevertheless, both Mao and Stalin had given Kim Il-Sung the go-ahead to seek to reunify Korea by force. Yet it is still not clear how each had calculated the security interests involved. Clearly they had reason to believe that the Americans would not intervene, but they did not appear to have contingency plans ready in case they did.[13] Moscow was absent from the Security Council at the crucial time in June 1950, ostensibly in protest at the exclusion of the PRC from the UN. Western analysts have found no evidence to suggest that the Chinese were involved in the preparations for the war or that they intended to become involved in it.[14] The Soviet Union had played the major part in establishing and arming the Kim regime right up to late spring 1950, and it is possible that Stalin may have approved Kim's war plans with a view to increasing Soviet influence over China. Although Kim had effectively been put in place by the Soviet forces in 1945, the character of Kim's relations with Stalin remains unclear. How much of a free hand did he have? Was there any idea of tying in Kim's plans with Mao's plans to attack Taiwan? Despite the increased availability of archival material, many questions remain. But there can be little doubt that both sides regarded the existence of a friendly regime (which at that time could only have meant a communist one) on their Korean borders as vital to their respective securities. In that sense, Korea was more important to the Soviets than to the American side.

Although the Cold War had already begun to influence the international politics of the Asia-Pacific, as was demonstrated by the US despatch of aid to Indo-China in May 1950, the Korean War had the effect of drawing a sharp demarcation line in Northeast Asia between the communist countries on the one side and the so-called free world on the other that was to last for the next twenty years. The North Korean attack on the South across the 38th Parallel on 25 June 1950 may have been regarded by Kim Il-Sung as a national civil war to unite his artificially divided country, but in the international climate of the time, it was bound to have been seen as more than that. In Washington it was immediately regarded as a new instance of communist aggression and a test of Western resolve, especially after the success in countering the Soviet blockade of West Berlin a year earlier. The impact in Europe of the possible successful communist use of force in Asia was very great, and North Korea's sudden attack was an important element in the decision to establish a unified NATO command. The consequence in Asia was President Truman's immediate announcement that an economic embargo would be imposed on China and that the US Seventh Fleet would be interposed in the Taiwan Straits, thus preventing a pending Chinese communist attack upon the island. Truman's intention was to deny Taiwan as a potential base to the Soviet Union in the western Pacific.[15] The effect of the decision on Mao was to confirm his view that the Americans supported Chiang Kai-shek in the hope of invading the Chinese mainland to reverse the result of the Chinese civil war.[16] In retrospect the Chinese were to argue that this was the decisive turning point in their relations with the Americans.

However, it was the crossing of the 38th Parallel by the American-dominated UN forces in October 1950 (after their defeat of the forces of the North) and their approach to the Chinese border in total disregard of Chinese warnings to desist that led to military intervention by the Chinese. What was seen by the UN as a move towards uniting Korea was perceived by Mao as a threat to China's security and the survival of his newly established revolutionary regime. Local, regional and international political and security issues became enmeshed together in an apparent seamless web.

Instead of seeking to distinguish between primary and secondary strategic interests, the outbreak of the Korean War caused the Truman administration to define its interests in absolutist terms and to try to apply the strategic doctrine of containment in Northeast Asia as laid out in NSC-68 of 1949 – the first comprehensive attempt to extend Cold War strategic thinking to Asia. Following the European pattern a sharp geographic line was drawn on the map between two opposed systems whose security was ultimately guaranteed by each of the superpowers. The line ran between Japan and the USSR in the Sea of Japan, along the armistice line (roughly the 38th Parallel) between North and South Korea and through the Taiwan Straits between Taiwan (the Republic of China – ROC) and the Chinese mainland (PRC). The disposition of some of the offshore islands in the Straits was to become the ostensible cause of two major crises in the Cold War era. At the same time, it is important to recognize that the strategic divide that was underlined by a political and ideological bifurcation between the US and the USSR as global powers was mirrored not only by a regional divide, as described above, but by local ones in which both Korea and China were split into two separate states claiming exclusive jurisdiction of the whole country. The sharpness and immobility of the line drawn between 'East' and 'West' was paralleled by a stalemate in the civil war between the divided states. The competitive junction between the two global powers and their local allies had become very close indeed.

The Korean War itself may be regarded as being essentially a domestic or civil war that had unanticipated international consequences.[17] Despite the release of new source material in the last few years, the motives and calculations of the different communist leaders are still unclear. Both Kim Il-Sung of North Korea and Ho Chi Minh of Vietnam visited Moscow during the course of Mao's negotiations with Stalin. Kim obtained Stalin's approval to go to war and apparently that of Mao too, whose advice to Kim to pursue a more guerrilla-based strategy was ignored.[18] The veil of secrecy over Mao's relations with Stalin has been lifted to reveal extraordinary degrees of distrust. As Mao put it a dozen years later:

> after the victory of the revolution [Stalin] ... suspected China of being a Yugoslavia, and that I would be another Tito. ... When did Stalin begin to have confidence in us? It was at the time of the [Korean War] from the winter of 1950. He then came to believe that we were not Tito, not Yugoslavia.[19]

Whether by accident or by design, the Korean War was beneficial to Moscow in that it ruled out for a long time the possibility of an accommodation between Beijing and Washington.[20]

Despite the enormous destruction unleashed upon Korea and its people and the high rate of casualties of the opposing armies,[21] the Korean War is credited as the first limited war of the Cold War era in which the US and the USSR exercised calculated restraint so as to avoid its widening. Both sides, for example, connived in effect to suppress news of extensive clashes between the Soviet and American air forces.[22] It should be noted, however, that at the end the Eisenhower administration threatened to use nuclear weapons so as to bring to an end the armistice negotiations that had been dragging on for two years.

The Korean War also prompted the US to seek to include Japan in attempts to strengthen the 'free world' in the region. This involved preparing for the conclusion of a peace treaty and for tying Japan into some kind of regional alliance. The administration's special envoy, John Foster Dulles, who visited Japan in early 1951, was unable to persuade the Japanese to re-arm and settled instead for a policy of economic cooperation by which Japanese productive capacity would be used in support of the war effort. American ideas of establishing a regional Pacific pact also foundered on residual allied distrust of Japan and on differences between them. In the build-up to the peace treaty itself, the US signed a mutual defence treaty with the Philippines in August 1951, and one month later a similar treaty with Australia and New Zealand. The Japanese Peace Treaty was also signed in September in San Francisco. Japan and the US signed a mutual defence treaty and the following year the American occupation came to an end as Japan resumed full sovereignty.

Despite American efforts, the end result was a Cold War alignment in Northeast Asia very different from the one that emerged in Europe. Although the first hot war of the era had been fought in this part of the world, regional ties were relatively weak on both sides of the divide. On the Soviet side its dominance over Eastern Europe was not matched in Northeast Asia. It exercised influence but not control over North Korea, and the PRC was too big, independent and proud to be dominated in that way, especially as it had proved itself to be a major power on the battlefields of Korea, where for the first time in modern history Chinese forces had fought a modern Western army to a standstill. On the American side too there was no Asia-Pacific equivalent to the Marshall Plan, let alone NATO. Instead there were a series of primarily bilateral treaties across the Pacific.

Southeast Asia

The end of the Pacific War saw the return of the colonial powers to a very changed world. The legacy of the Japanese had been, first, to have shattered the myths of colonial white superiority and, second, to have accelerated the nationalist drive for independence. Three levels of foreign relations may be identified in the early evolution of the foreign relations of the states of Southeast Asia.

The process of acquiring independence and the character of the post-colonial settlement involved relations with former rulers. In some cases these endured in relative harmony well beyond the transfer of sovereignty. The second level involved local reactions to great power involvement in the region. The third involved intra-regional relations among the resident states.[23] More broadly their different roads to independence became embroiled in the wider struggles of international politics that centred on Cold War issues, and they greatly influenced the subsequent alignments and international roles of the new states.

The international aspects of the end of the Pacific War also contributed to shaping the subsequent development of independence in the resident states. The SEAC under British leadership lacked the resources to cope with the sudden and unexpected surrender of the Japanese forces in Southeast Asia. This led to delays in establishing a significant SEAC presence in the Dutch East Indies and French Indo-China in particular. Nationalist groups filled the vacuum, which led to armed confrontations as the Dutch and the French later returned in force. Indeed armed struggle that inevitably acquired external dimensions became a feature of the acquisition of independence in both territories. The impact of the communist victory in the Chinese civil war in the late 1940s was also widely felt in the region as an inspiration and source of support for insurgents and as a challenge to incumbent elites.

The Philippines became independent as a close associate of the United States and it was not until the US abandoned its bases there at the end of the Cold War that the Philippines began to move away from its highly ambivalent position that sought to balance its professed Asian identity with its dependence on America. This pattern was evident from the acquisition of independence. The US had promised independence even before the war and moved to implement it speedily once the war had ended. The Philippine Republic was inaugurated on 4 July 1946, but from the outset the Filipino elite accepted a dependency on the United States, to whom it was indebted for its continued dominance of the country. The American supreme commander, General Douglas McArthur, chose to overlook the collaborationist record of much of this elite, as the principal resistance movement to the Japanese was the communist-led Hukbalahap (People's Anti-Japanese Army). The United States contributed to the economic rehabilitation of the Philippines, but at the same time it insisted upon a trade act that benefited American agrarian and manufacturing interests. In March 1947 it was agreed that huge American bases would be installed on Filipino territory. By 1949 the communist-led Huks had turned to armed struggle against the corrupt ruling elite. This led to greater American military aid and to relative success in containing the insurgency. In January 1950 the American secretary of state, Dean Acheson, declared the Philippines to be part of America's strategic defence perimeter in the Pacific.

The Filipino elite has been called bi-national on account of its attachment to the US.[24] By virtue of geography and history the Philippines has been set somewhat apart from the other Southeast Asian countries. Compared to them, the historical influences of Indian and Chinese cultures have been relatively small.

There was no national centre or state before the Spanish conquest in the sixteenth century. Islam had spread from Borneo and from what is now Indonesia to the island of Luzon, but it was driven back south by the vigorous extension of Catholicism by the missionaries who accompanied the conquistadors. Having in effect created the Philippines as a state, the Spaniards also left their mark on the social structure, leaving behind a wealthy mestizo elite based on large rural estates who have come to dominate politics, as well as a legacy of extensive rural poverty. Not surprisingly, the Philippines has often been depicted as a piece of Latin America located offshore of East Asia. The newly independent country 'acquired a reputation [in Asia] for being a spokesman for American interests'. Indeed, right up until the closure of the American bases at the end of the Cold War, the Filipinos' sense of identification with Asia continued to be ambivalent. Notwithstanding shared linguistic and ethnic origins with their near neighbours, Indonesia and Malaysia, the Philippines remained somewhat aloof from their regional concerns. In 1963 it formed the Association of Southeast Asia (ASA) with Malaya and Thailand – the other two pro-Western states of the region – which soon foundered because of the Filipino claim to Sabah. The Philippines became involved in the Vietnam War under the influence of the United States. Its membership of the Association of Southeast Asian Nations (ASEAN) did not make a substantive difference initially, but over time the intra-regional dimension carried increasing weight in Filipino foreign policy. However, the Philippines remained the Asian state with the closest ties to the United States.[25]

Indonesia, by contrast, professed great attachment to what became known as non-alignment. This may be traced to the impact of the complex struggle for independence, when the great powers were found wanting, and to the Indonesian sense of an entitlement to exercise the leading position in Southeast Asia. Interestingly, despite the anti-communist outlook of the Indonesian army, there was a tendency among its senior officers to feel that they had much in common with their Vietnamese equivalents, because their respective struggles for independence involved anti-colonial armed struggle. In fact the Indonesian road to independence involved both armed struggle and diplomacy.

Indonesian independence was first declared on 17 August 1945, two days after the surrender of the Japanese. The latter had left behind a trained Indonesian military force and an active youth movement. The British arrived in September to be followed by the Dutch a month later to confront a mass movement. The Dutch established influence over the outer islands and attempted to crush the independence movement by two 'police actions'. By the time of the second in December 1948, the international political environment had changed to the advantage of the Indonesians. In the first two or three years after the Second World War, American sentiment in favour of national independence rather than old-world colonialism was tempered by the need to shore up the weakened West European countries and their fragile democracies against the perceived communist and Soviet threat. But by late 1948 a new dimension had entered the equation, as the impact of the Cold War began to be felt in Southeast Asia too. The Americans now began to fear that the appeal of communism to the peoples of

Asia would grow if the nationalists were continually to be frustrated in their rightful quest for independence. Moreover, the Americans took note of the crushing of the communist uprising in Mediun by the Indonesian Republican forces earlier in September 1948. The Dutch then came under increasing American pressure to concede. Paradoxically, it was the success of the second 'police action' in December that hastened their end. Amid a context in which the Indonesian army had begun a guerrilla campaign, a negotiated settlement was eventually reached and the Republic of the United States of Indonesia was formed, initially under UN auspices, in December 1949. These events reaffirmed the Indonesian attachment to independence, as in a bipolar world the Soviet Union had proved to be untrustworthy because of Mediun and the United States unreliable because of inconsistency.

This left two sets of tensions that were to dominate Indonesian politics and foreign relations for a long time thereafter. First, a tension developed between the army and the politicians; and second, a tension emerged between the efficacy of struggle and diplomacy in the conduct of foreign affairs. The army came to see itself as even more than the ultimate protector of the Indonesian state and, under President Sukarno's Guided Democracy, the army became part of the uneasy triumvirate in charge of the ship of state. In the end, after the failed 1965 coup, it eventually took over supreme power in 1966 under the leadership of General Suharto. Until his fall, Sukarno combined elements of both struggle and diplomacy in his assertive foreign policy. This was most evident in his successful campaign to annex West Irian (the former West New Guinea) in 1963 where he played the United States and the Soviet Union against each other and in the unsuccessful attempt to undermine the newly formed Malaysia in his campaign of *Konfrontasi* of 1963–66. Notwithstanding the diplomatic support of the United States in the struggle for independence, and even on the West Irian question, Indonesia became firmly wedded to the non-aligned position of Asian nationalists and indeed it became a leading exponent of it.[26]

In contrast to the Dutch in Indonesia and the French in Indo-China, the British sought to encourage Malaya on the road to independence, and indeed there was a Malay elite that was close to Britain and that espoused democratic values. But the British task was complicated by the consequences of having encouraged the settlement of migrant labour from China, particularly in the nineteenth and early twentieth centuries. By the outbreak of the Pacific War the Chinese and also Indian immigrants had come to account for nearly half the population. During the occupation the Japanese cultivated the resentful Malays at the expense of the Chinese, who had been greatly influenced by stories of the resistance of their kith and kin and fellow nationals to Japanese aggression in China itself. During the war the British supported the communist-led and Chinese-dominated resistance against the Japanese. Their support was in many ways similar to that of the Americans for the communist-led Vietnamese resistance to Japan at the same time.

After the war the British were unable to persuade the ethnic Malays of the virtues of a projected Malayan Union with equal citizenship for Chinese and

Indians, despite excluding the Chinese-dominated city of Singapore. It was rejected by the newly formed United Malays National Organization (UMNO) which dominated the alternative Federation of Malaya established in 1948. The Malayan Communist Party (MCP) with its constituencies among the Chinese communities found that its political effectiveness within the trade unions was being curtailed and it turned to armed struggle in June 1948. That insurrection also reflected the changing international circumstances associated with the beginnings of the Cold War and the inspiration of the pending victory of the communists in the civil war in China and of the armed struggle begun by the communist-led Vietminh against the French.

The British declared a state of emergency in June 1948. The Emergency lasted officially until 1960; a rump insurgency force continued to operate in the jungles of the Thai–Malay borders until the late 1980s. But the back of the insurgency was broken in the early 1950s after the resettlement of some half a million (Chinese) squatters on whose support the insurgents depended. The costs to the victorious side were nevertheless enormous. Against guerrillas, who at no stage numbered more than 8,000 men, were deployed 40,000 regular British and Commonwealth troops, 70,000 Malay police and some 200,000 home guards. But the Emergency itself led to the establishment of the Malayan Chinese Association (MCA) in February 1949, made up of anti-communist Chinese Chambers of Commerce and educated professionals. A pact between the two communal organizations UMNO and MCA at municipal elections in 1952 at the expense of a multiracial rival eventually paved the way to independence in 1957.[27]

The only country in Southeast Asia that did not experience colonialism, Thailand, nevertheless had to make difficult adjustments in order to adapt to post-war conditions. It chose a path of adhering closely to the United States, primarily because it was the dominant power and also because Thailand's regional interests coincided with the Cold War objectives of the United States in the area.

The military government, which came to power following a coup in 1932 that overthrew the absolute monarchy, accommodated to the power of Japan and allowed its armies transit to British-held Burma and Malaya. Immediately after the Japanese surrender a new Thai government, headed by a civilian member of the 1932 coup group who had led a wartime resistance to Japan, nullified the arrangements made with Japan and promised to return with compensation the territories the Japanese had granted the Thais from Burma and Malaya. The United States helped the Thai government, which was now headed by its former minister to Washington, to resist pressure for further concessions from Britain. At the end of complex diplomacy Thailand also gave up territories in Laos and Cambodia, and it was admitted to the United Nations at the end of 1946. Thailand has enjoyed a continuity of diplomatic style that goes back a long time in history.

Though it is often wrongly construed as one of neutrality, in fact it has always been a diplomacy which has been 'hard' towards small neighbours and 'soft' towards the dominant regional power: China before the Opium wars, then Britain, then Japan, and, particularly evident ever since 1954, the United States.[28]

Interestingly, even earlier Thailand had sent a contingent to participate in the Korean War, which contributed to securing benefaction from the United States. Thailand became a party to the 1954 Manila Pact with the US that secured a formal American commitment to come to the defence of the country, and Bangkok became the headquarters of SEATO.

Burma, one of the historic political centres in Southeast Asia, became a province of British India in the nineteenth century, which led to an inflow of immigrants from India. Burmese nationalism before the Pacific War had a distinctive anti-Indian flavour. In 1937 Burma was separated from India and given considerable control over domestic affairs. During the Japanese occupation it was granted nominal independence in 1943, but this proved to be illusory, and although the British return was welcomed in 1945 there was now impatience for independence. The leader of the nationalist movement, Aung San, was a former student leader who had been commander of the Japanese-sponsored Burmese National Army. The British offered independence within dominion status that in the end was rejected. Aung San, along with six of his colleagues in the cabinet, was assassinated in July 1947 before the formal transfer of power had been completed. Association with the Commonwealth had already been rejected and the Republic of the Union of Burma became formally independent in January 1948. But faced with ethnic rebellions and opposition from China's communist leaders, combined with a lack of interest in its security from Britain and the United States, the new Burmese government opted for a policy of what Michael Leifer has called 'non-offence', especially towards its giant neighbour to the north.[29] By the early 1950s it became active in voicing the concerns of Asian neutralism (in the Cold War) and it was one of the key Asian powers that met in Colombo to help convene the first Asian–African summit conference in Bandung in 1955.[30]

Vietnam was the most important country in Indo-China and its history after 1945 was dominated by the armed struggle for independence from France, led by the communist Vietminh, that began in 1946 and culminated in the Geneva Agreements on Indo-China of July 1954 that resulted in the recognition of the independence of Laos and Cambodia and of a communist North Vietnam and a non-communist South. These eight years of armed struggle, later known as the First Indo-China War, brought together the three main dimensions of conflict: the global, the regional and the local. It also began a process of international and regional conflict that was not to be concluded before the end of the Cold War itself. At this stage the conflict initially involved the intensely nationalistic and fervently communistic Vietminh against the returning French forces who had desperately and largely unavailingly sought to recruit a credible Vietnamese nationalistic alternative to the Vietminh. The two warring parties were soon to be backed by the victorious Chinese communists on the one side and by the

Americans on the other. American support became possible only after the Elysee Agreements of March 1949, which gave the Indo-Chinese states nominal independence.

Once the Vietminh in the North had secured access to Chinese communist support after the latter's domestic victory in 1949, the terms of the war turned remorselessly against the French. Up to that point the French forces had been in possession of most of the cities and towns in Vietnam, but had difficulty in controlling the rural areas. Thereafter the Vietminh were able to escalate their fighting capabilities from guerrilla to positional warfare. The French finally conceded that they should withdraw after their defeat at Dien Bien Phu in May 1954.[3] That surrender has been called 'the worst defeat any Western colonial power ever suffered on the battlefield at the hands of an Asian people'. The war which drew in the external powers became the primary agency that led to what has been called the internationalization of the problems of Southeast Asia. Within the context of the Cold War, it highlighted an American concern with the domestic conditions of the states of the area. It provided a framework for placing the domestic developments and the contending elites of the countries of the region within a Cold War syndrome that at its height joined them with the axis of international as well as regional conflict.

The Geneva conference

The Geneva Conference of 1954 which convened to address the Korean and Indo-Chinese issues may be seen as the benchmark that signalled the completion of the integration of East Asia into the Cold War system. It also confirmed China's great power status (even though John Foster Dulles is famously reputed at one point to have refused to shake the hand of Zhou Enlai). It affirmed the stalemate of the Korean armistice and it helped to end what turned out to be the First Indo-China War.

The Geneva Agreements of July 1954 effectively ended the French presence in Indo-China. They arranged a partition of Vietnam that, although provisional in principle, resulted in practice in a victorious communist regime in the North beyond the 17th Parallel and an insecure anti-communist regime in the South. The two were supposedly to be united through elections to be held two years thereafter. The Geneva settlement also called for an independent but neutral Cambodia and Laos. The Geneva Agreements satisfied the Chinese government by preventing an immediate American military intervention – which was one of the routes that Mao feared the Americans might follow in order to attack China itself.[32] Moreover, following the Korean War, the Chinese adopted a new diplomatic stance that favoured peaceful coexistence so as to be better able to concentrate on economic development at home and cultivate newly established Asian governments. The post-Stalin Soviet leaders also sought to reduce tensions with the Americans. That is why the two communist giants had combined to put pressure on the Vietnamese communists to give up ground they controlled below the 17th Parallel. Twenty-five years later, after the 1979 Chinese attack on

Vietnam, the Vietnamese leaders publicly revealed their anger at what they regarded as the Chinese betrayal at Geneva.[33]

The Americans too were displeased with the agreements and, together with the government of South Vietnam, they refused to accept the final declaration. The United States, however, did not block the Geneva settlement because of the position of its European allies, notably the British and the French, but neither did it wish to condone formally the communist victory. The American representative confined himself to declaring that his government would regard any attempt to upset the terms of the settlement by force as a threat to peace. Dulles himself regarded Geneva as confirming that 'the tide is running against us in the channel of [his] tough policy. If we are to continue to pursue it we shall lose many of our allies.'[34] By the middle of 1954 the Cold War had left its mark on Southeast as well as Northeast Asia. The Philippines and increasingly Thailand were closely tied to the United States. North Vietnam, as a communist state, belonged to the socialist camp and South Vietnam sought to consolidate its precarious statehood under American protection. The fragile states of Laos and Cambodia were nominally neutral by an agreement of the regional and external powers. Burma had perforce to choose inoffensive neutrality. Indonesia was increasingly identifying its independent course in what came to be called non-alignment. Malaya, which was still subject to the Emergency, had yet to be granted independence as its colonial ruler gradually asserted mastery of the one Cold war insurgency still active in the region. But it was clear that in the aftermath of independence that would not long be delayed, the Malay elite would lean to the British side.

More generally, the very different paths by which the countries of Southeast Asia acquired independent statehood were to have marked effects upon their subsequent political developments and upon their foreign relations. Some, especially Thailand and the divided Vietnam, could draw on traditions of national identity and statehood that long antedated the colonial era. However, others such as the Philippines, Malaysia and Indonesia were new successor states to the previous colonial order and although these too could draw on pre-colonial antecedents, this was true of only parts of the new states, such as the old trading principalities in parts of what is now Indonesia. Nation building for the very new states encompassed a wider task than the enormous problems of seeking to establish good governance. The conduct of foreign affairs became an essential part of the new nation building as it provided potent new symbols for evoking national unity.

Yet in many respects some of the profound challenges that confronted the older and the newly established states in the aftermath of independence were similar. In varying degrees, with the exception of the Indo-Chinese states they were led by Westernized elites with limited experience in government who had to deal with wide disparities in cultural and political traditions and with deep divisions between town and country. Their inadequate infant administrations had to tackle the still destructive remains of the war and to develop their national economies quite often against the legacies of one-sided economic development of the colonial period. The attempts by their leaders to strengthen national consciousness frequently met with only limited success when faced with ethnic, religious and local particularisms. Moreover none of the new states was free of border or territorial disputes. The rhetoric of Asian solidarity often failed to take into account the realities of differences within and between states, the limited capacities of governments and the paucity of the opportunities to cooperate to solve common problems. Moreover, none could really escape the patterns of alignments set by the Cold War.

Notes

1 Evelyn Colbert, *Southeast Asia in International Politics 1941–1956* (Ithaca: Cornell University Press, 1977), p.53.
2 For accounts of the Yalta Conference, see Diane Shaver Clemens, *Yalta* (New York: Oxford University Press, 1970); and Russell D. Buhite, *Decisions at Yalta: An Appraisal of Summit Diplomacy* (Wilmington: Scholarly Resources, 1986). For a considered judgement, see John Lewis Gaddis, *Russia, the Soviet Union and the United States* (New York: McGraw-Hill, 1990), pp.165–67; and, for a perspective from a Beijing-based political scientist, see Wang Jisi, 'An Appraisal of U.S. Policy toward China, 1945–55, and Its Aftermath' in Harry Harding and Yuan Ming (eds), *Sino-American Relations, 1945–1955* (Wilmington: Scholarly Resources, 1989), p.290.
3 See the discussion by Akira Iriye, 'Security and Stability in Northeast Asia: A Historical Overview' in Martin E. Weinstein (ed.), *Northeast Asian Security after Vietnam* (Urbana: University of Illinois Press, 1982), p.9.
4 See the accounts by Bruce Cummings, *The Origins of the Korean War*, 2 vols (Princeton: Princeton University Press, 1981 and 1990); and by Max Hastings, *The Korean War* (London: Michael Joseph, 1987).
5 See the parallel discussions in Iriye, 'A Historical Overview' (*op. cit.*), pp.3–5, 10–15. See also John Lewis Gaddis, 'Korea in American Politics, Strategy, and Diplomacy, 1945–50' in Yonosuke Nagai and Akira Iriye (eds), *The Origins of the Cold War in Asia* (Tokyo: University of Tokyo Press, 1977), pp.277–80.
6 Gaddis, 'Korea in American Politics … ' (*op. cit.*), p.278.
7 See the argument and citations by Aruga Tadashi, 'The United States and the Cold War' in Nagai and Iriye (eds), *The Origins of the Cold War in Asia* (*op. cit.*), p.78.
8 John Lewis Gaddis, *Strategies of Containment* (Oxford: Oxford University Press, 1982), p.23.
9 See the point made by the US Joint Strategic Survey Committee in April 1947 noted in Akira Iriye, 'Continuities in U.S.–Japanese Relations, 1941–49' in Nagai and Iriye (eds), *The Origins of the Cold War in Asia* (*op. cit.*), p.403. It should be recognized, however, that the entire thrust of Iriye's argument is to show that, until 1949, US policy in Asia operated within the pre-Cold War 'Yalta system'.
10 For discussion of these issues, see Dorothy Berg and Waldo Heinrichs, *Uncertain Years: Chinese American Relations 1947–1950* (New York: Columbia University Press, 1980); Nancy Bernkopf Tucker, *Patterns in the Dust: Chinese–American Relations and the Recognition Controversy, 1949–1950* (New York: Columbia University Press, 1983); and Steven M. Goldstein, 'Sino-American Relations, 1948–50: Lost Chance or No Chance?' in Harding and Yuan (eds), *Sino-American Relations, 1945–1955* (*op. cit.*), pp.119–42. For an analysis based on recently available Chinese sources, see Chen Jian, *China's Road to the Korean War: The Making of the Sino-American Confrontation* (New York: Columbia University Press, 1994), Part II. For a considered analysis of the position of the Truman administration, see John Lewis Gaddis, *The Long Peace: Inquiries into the History of the Cold War* (Oxford: Oxford University Press, 1987) ch.6.
11 Ralph N. Clough, *Island China* (Cambridge, MA: Harvard University Press, 1978).

12 Suzanne Pepper, 'The KMT-CCP conflict 1945–49' in John K. Fairbank and Albert Feuerwerker (eds), *The Cambridge History of China*, vol.13: *Republican China 1912–1949, Part 2* (Cambridge: Cambridge University Press 1986), p.786.

13 For an account of the Chinese side see Chen Jian, *China's Road … (op. cit.)*; and for an account of the Soviet side see Kathryn Weathersby, *Soviet Aims in Korea and the Origins of the Korean War, 1945–1950: New Evidence from Russian Archives* (Washington, DC: Cold War International History Project, Woodrow Wilson Center, Working Paper no.8, November 1993). See also her 'New Findings on the Korean War', *Cold War International History Project Bulletin* no.3 (Washington, DC: Woodrow Wilson Center, Fall 1993). All these are based on archival sources that only recently became available. It should be noted that the findings must be treated with caution, as access to the Russian archives is incomplete and Chinese documentation is still only available second hand through the writings of official Chinese scholars who have had access to the archives.

14 For more detailed discussion of the Soviet and Chinese positions, see chapters 6 and 7. For an account of the prevailing Western view of the Chinese role at the time, see Mineo Nakajima, 'Foreign Relations: From the Korean War to the Bandung Line' in Roderick MacFarquhar and John K. Fairbank (eds), *The Cambridge History of China*, vol.14: *The People's Republic, Part 1: The Emergence of Revolutionary China 1949–1965* (Cambridge University Press, 1987), pp.271–72. For the best account of Sino-Soviet relations at this time that is based on new archival materials and on the accounts of participants, see Sergei N. Goncharov, John W. Lewis and Xue Litai, *Uncertain Partners: Stalin, Mao, and the Korean War* (Stanford: Stanford University Press, 1993). See also the previous note.

15 Gaddis, 'Korea in American Politics … ' *(op. cit.)*, p.289.

16 Hao Yufan and Zhai Zhihai, 'China's Decision to Enter the Korean War: History Revisited', *The China Quarterly* 121 (March 1990), pp.94–115.

17 For accounts of the background to the Korean War, in addition to those cited in note 13, see Cummings, *The Origins of the Korean War (op. cit.)*; Max Hastings, *The Korean War (op. cit.)*; Rosemary Foot, *The Wrong War* (Ithaca: Cornell University Press, 1985); Allen S. Whiting, *China Crosses the Yalu: The Decision to Enter the Korean War* (Stanford: Stanford University Press, 1960).

18 See Hao and Zhai, 'China's Decision to Enter the Korean War' *(op. cit.)*. But Goncharov, Lewis and Xue (*Uncertain Partners (op. cit.)*, p.146) show that Mao could hardly have objected to Kim's proposed war because of fear of American intervention when he himself had secured a promise of Soviet support for his proposed invasion of Taiwan. He could hardly have expressed fears about American intervention in Korea without tacitly admitting to Stalin the likelihood of similar involvement in Taiwan, thereby jeopardizing his support.

19 Mao's speech of 24 September 1962 in Stuart Schram (ed.), *Mao Tse-tung Unrehearsed* (Harmondsworth: Penguin, 1974), p.191.

20 O.B. Borisov and B.T. Koloskov, *Sino-Soviet Relations 1945–1973: A Brief History* (Moscow: Mysl Publishers, 3rd supplemental edn, 1980), p.117.

21 According to Jon Halliday and Bruce Cummings, 2 million North Korean civilians and 500,000 soldiers and at least 1 million Chinese soldiers died on the communist side. They estimate that 1 million South Korean civilians died. See their *Korea: The Unknown War* (London: Viking, 1988), p.200. Max Hastings gives the following figures for the UN side: '1,319,000 Americans served in the Korean theatre, and 33,629 did not return. A further 105,785 were wounded. … The South Korean army lost 415,000 killed and 429,000 wounded.' The figures for the remaining thirteen states that sent combat forces were 3,063 killed and 11,817 wounded. See his *The Korean War* (London: Pan, 1988), p.407.

22 Jon Halliday, 'A Secret War', *Far Eastern Economic Review* (22 April 1993), pp.32–36.

23 Michael Leifer, *The Foreign Relations of New States* (Melbourne: Longman Australia, 1974) p.2. Much of the subsequent discussion of Southeast Asia in this chapter draws on chapters 1 and 2 of this book.

24 See the general argument of Alfred W. McCoy, 'The Philippines: Independence without Decolonisation' in Robin Jeffrey (ed.), *Asia – The Winning of Independence* (London: Macmillan, 1981), in particular pp.50–53.

25 Evelyn Colbert, *Southeast Asia in International Politics* (*op. cit.*), pp.90ff. See also D.G.E. Hall, *A History of South-East Asia* (London: Macmillan, 4th edn, 1981), pp.899–905; Milton Osborne, *Southeast Asia, An Introductory History* (Sydney: George Allen and Unwin, 1979), pp.44–46; and Peter Lyon, *War and Peace in South-East Asia* (Oxford University Press, 1969), pp.39–46.

26 This account relies on Lyon, *War and Peace ...* (*op. cit.*), pp.55–67; Anthony Reid, 'Indonesia: Revolution without Socialism' in Jeffrey (ed.), *Asia – The Winning of Independence* (*op. cit.*), especially pp.140–55; Osborne, *Southeast Asia* (*op. cit.*), pp.139–46; John R.W. Smail, 'Indonesia' in Mark Borthwick, *Pacific Century, The Emergence of Modern Pacific Asia* (Boulder: Westview Press, 1992), pp.230–33; and Michael Leifer, *Indonesia's Foreign Policy* (London: George Allen and Unwin, 1983).

27 This account has drawn mainly on Lee Kam Hing, 'Malaya: New States and Old Elites' in Jeffrey (ed.), *Asia – The Winning of Independence* (*op. cit.*), pp.213–57; and Milton Osborne, *Region of Revolt* (Australia: Pergamon Press, 1970), pp.71–82.

28 Lyon, *War and Peace ...* (*op. cit.*), p.34. This account has also drawn on Colbert, *Southeast Asia in International Politics* (*op. cit.*), p.90ff.; and Hall, *A History ...* (*op. cit.*), pp.896–98.

29 Leifer, *Foreign Relations ...* (*op. cit.*), p.14.

30 This account has relied mainly upon Lyon, *War and Peace ...* (*op. cit*), pp.46–55; and Hall, *A History ...* (*op. cit.*), pp.770–88, 878–85.

31 For an excellent account of the French experience, see Bernard B. Fall, *Street Without Joy: Indochina at War, 1946–54* (Harrisburg: Stackpole, 1961).

32 Hao and Zhai, 'China's Decision ... ' (*op. cit.*), p.106.

33 *Chinese Aggression Against Vietnam* (Hanoi: Foreign Languages Publishing House, 1979).

34 John Lewis Gaddis, *The Long Peace: Inquiries into the History of the Cold War* (Oxford: Oxford University Press, 1987), p.132, note 2.

2 The application of bipolarity, 1954–70

This was the period when international politics in the Asia-Pacific, as elsewhere in the world, was greatly shaped by the attempts of the United States and the Soviet Union to consolidate their respective sides of the Cold War as part of the management of the central balance of power between them. Although the alliance patterns in the Asia-Pacific were bilateral and much more volatile than in Europe – as attested by the collapse of the Sino-Soviet alliance into acrimony and bitter rivalry – they nevertheless reflected the essential bipolar character of international politics of the period. Most of the countries in the region were linked to one or other of the two superpowers, and the changing character of Soviet–American relations had a discernible impact upon the points of conflict and cooperation in the region.

Perhaps one of the most important ways in which the operation of bipolarity was distinctive in the Asia-Pacific during this period centred on the role of China. As a relatively independent strategic actor that had proved its entitlement to great power status in the Korean War, China moved from being a close ally of the Soviet Union in the early 1950s to become its most implacable adversary by the end of the 1960s. Indeed, for much of the 1960s it challenged both the superpowers simultaneously. Moreover, within the Asia-Pacific region itself China exercised considerable weight independently of all other powers. However, it was not until relations were opened with Washington at the beginning of the 1970s that the main features of a broader strategic triangle involving Beijing as well as Moscow and Washington became evident. Nevertheless, as we now know, the Eisenhower administration sought to drive a wedge between China and its Soviet ally by a policy of calculated toughness towards the former so as to increase pressure upon the alliance beyond breaking point.[1] The irony is that when that point was reached during the Kennedy and Johnson administrations, the United States became too focused on Vietnam to exploit it. Hence tripolarity did not fully emerge until 1971/1972 when Chairman Mao and President Nixon recognized their common interest in managing an augmented Soviet threat.

If the unity of the communist side of the bipolar divide in the Asia-Pacific was threatened by the nationalist sentiments of independent governments (and that included North Vietnam and to a degree North Korea as well as China[2]), the pro-Western side was also characterized by greater diversity than obtained in Europe. The Cold War rhetoric that characterized the application of the containment policy of the bipolar period was even less appropriate here than in Europe. Thus India – the world's largest democracy – enjoyed closer relations with the Soviet Union than with the United States. The Indian attachment to non-alignment stopped it from joining the Western alliance systems in the early years, especially as Pakistan became allied to the United States. Once the conflict with China deepened as a result of the border skirmish of 1959 and open warfare of 1962, India's links with the Soviet Union were correspondingly consolidated. The notion that the Cold War consisted of a conflict between the 'free world' and that of communist dictatorships did not accord with the situation elsewhere in Asia. Although the economies of the pro-Western states in East Asia were orientated towards the market, the majority were not ruled by 'free' democratic governments. Additionally, with the possible exception of Japan, most governments, especially in Southeast Asia, were fragile in their exercise of power and fearful of a variety of challenges to their survival. These came not only from communist insurgencies that exploited rural discontent, but also from ethnic unrest, disorders based on religious forces, and from separatist elements – all of which could be aided and abetted from the outside, and not necessarily by communist forces alone.[3]

Unlike the European theatre, the threat to the pro-Western side beyond Taiwan, Korea and to a degree Vietnam, was not on the whole one of conventional military assault. If the two superpowers tended to approach these regional and local preoccupations from the global perspectives of bipolarity, local elites and governments sought external support and even patronage with their own more parochial security interests in mind. The conjunction between the two worked best in the cases of Korea and Taiwan where the divisions of the Cold War and the respective civil wars coincided. But, as we shall see, even there the correspondence was less than complete. In Southeast Asia the conjunctions were on the whole less clear cut. Even in the case of Vietnam, where after 1954 the United States may be said to have had a global strategic interest in assisting the regime in the South to survive the threat from the North, it did not follow, as the prominent 'realists' Hans Morganthau and George Kennan pointed out at an early stage, that the American interest was so vital that the fall of the South would undermine its standing in the central balance with the Soviet Union. Moreover they also argued that American power could not substitute for effective government backed by popular support.[4]

The nationalist sentiments of the majority of the countries of the Asia-Pacific did not coincide with the Cold War cleavage. Many of the states had newly emerged from colonial or semi-colonial rule and were economically less well developed. Their leaders claimed to have much in common that transcended the East–West divide. Led by the five powers which met in Colombo in April 1954, many sought to establish a separate and distinctive international identity that was epitomized by the Asian and African Conference that met in Bandung in April 1955. Leaders of communist and anti-communist governments rubbed shoulders together in the name of Asian–African unity as they sought to register their own separate international agenda. Although conflicts of interest soon shattered its rhetoric of the solidarity of the 'Bandung spirit', the conference paved the way for the development of the non-aligned movement and other Third Worldist institutions. Yet, whatever their public protestations, governments faced with domestic or external challenges to their survival and to the national security of their states often turned for support to precisely the same external great power they were otherwise denouncing – usually the United States.

The actual balance of power between the Soviet Union and the United States was more uneven in the Asia-Pacific than in Europe. Despite its credentials as a Pacific power, the Soviet Union was much more of a European power. Its political, historic and cultural heartland was in Europe. The Soviet Far East was more of an outpost of empire. It was strategically important, but it was sparsely populated and of minor economic significance. Consequently, the Soviet economic impact on the region was restricted to its communist allies, possibly India and to a point Indonesia and Afghanistan.[5] As for the bulk of the Asia-Pacific, the significance of the Soviet Union was limited to strategic considerations. The United States, by contrast, bestrode the Pacific like a colossus. Until brought low by the war in Vietnam during the late 1960s, the United States exercised its hegemonic economic power with great self-confidence. It sponsored and oversaw the re-emergence of Japan and provided the favourable 'public goods' that facilitated the astonishing economic dynamism of the Pacific Rim. The means available to the United States to influence if not actually control international developments in the region far exceeded those available to the Soviet Union.

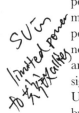

Accordingly, this chapter will first consider the application of the American strategy of containment before proceeding to discuss the attempt to establish Asian and African solidarity and the two offshore island crises in the Taiwan Straits that shaped the conduct of Sino-American relations. It will then turn to the communist side of the Cold War divide by examining the collapse of the Sino-Soviet alliance before evaluating the significance of the Second Indo-China War. It will conclude with an assessment of the impact of the development of bipolarity on the other points of conflict in the region.

The American strategy of containment in the Asia-Pacific

Containment became more than a strategy designed to limit the possible expansion of Soviet power – as was originally envisaged by George Kennan, who first coined the term.[6] It became inflated with the aim of stopping the expansion of communism wherever it seemed likely to spread. In much of the rhetoric of the American government, communism was seen as both monolithic and international, with its centre in Moscow. Arguably, in Europe this was very much one and the same thing, where the confrontation with Soviet power was more than a balance-of-power matter, as it constituted a clash between two incompatible systems. The military divide was bolstered by a clash of ideologies, by fundamental differences in running the economies and by radically different political systems. The dividing line between the two was soon tightly demarcated by heavily

U.S economic 帮助 封杀(围)这两个共产主义 communism

militarized borders. In Asia, however, the division was less clear cut and there was not the same correspondence between the spread of communism and the expansion of Soviet or Chinese power. Containment, as applied by the United States government, was not a doctrine that allowed for the greater subtlety and discrimination that Asian conditions required. Moreover, unlike the West European countries, few of the Asian states allied or associated with the United States could be described as democratic. Consequently, there was the danger that the United States' anti-communist crusade in the name of the free world could backfire if it were perceived to be carried out in support of an unpopular dictatorial regime.

There was an economic corollary to the strategy which involved the United States in extending massive economic assistance, in order to rehabilitate the economies of the 'free world' so as to strengthen the resilience of their societies against the appeals of communism. The Marshall Plan that was extended to facilitate the economic recovery of Western Europe had originally been offered to Europe as a whole, including the East, and it only became a keystone of containment after its rejection by Moscow in late 1947 and the communist coup in Czechoslovakia early in 1948. Although no such grand scheme was applied to Asia, the United States extended economic aid both in the form of investment and technical assistance and in the form of favourable trade policies. Japan was the main focus of attention. In the event, it became the principal economic beneficiary of the Korean War, as the provision of supplies to the Western war effort helped to re-establish Japanese industry. In general terms these policies played an important part in helping the reconstruction of South Korea and Taiwan, which contributed to ensuring the survival of the respective regimes. In Southeast Asia the situation was complicated by the political problems attendant upon nation building in newly independent states in the aftermath of colonial rule. The conditions of most of the states seemed so fragile that in the 1950s and 1960s, beginning with Eisenhower, successive American presidents persuaded themselves that were South Vietnam to 'fall' to communism, a domino effect would be created in which the rest of the states in Southeast Asia would also fall.[7]

The evolution of the American strategy of containment was of major significance in shaping the development of the Asia-Pacific as a whole. The doctrine of containment actually followed by the Truman administration owed more to the formulation of a document drawn under the leadership of Kennan's successor, Paul H. Nitze, than it did to the original view as articulated by the former. The Nitze version, known by its bureaucratic code name, NSC-68, 'derived its view of American interests primarily from its perception of the Soviet threat' which had the effect of denying the utility of distinguishing between those American interests that were peripheral and those that were vital. It went on to argue that American interests depended as much on the perception of power as on the reality of power itself. In other words, the balance of power depended as much upon appearances as upon rational calculation of strategic significance and advantage. If America 'even appeared to be losing ground to its adversaries, the effects could be much the same as if that loss had actually occurred'. The document also called in effect for America to ensure that it always negotiated with the

corollary
推论 引理

Soviet Union from a position of strength. The purpose of policy in Asia was to deny any further advances to communism in any form. Although the significance of nationalism even for communists was appreciated, it was nevertheless held that countries that came under communist sway necessarily followed a path of hostility towards the United States.[8] The application of the NSC-68 version of containment was prompted by the Korean War. That war was also significant, as it occasioned massive re-armament by the United States which led to the 'militarization of containment' that was to have profound consequences, especially in East Asia.[9]

The Eisenhower administration sought to improve upon the earlier containment policy, which it criticized for surrendering the initiative by being essentially a strategy of response. Its 'New Look' strategy was designed to seize the initiative and reduce costs by reacting to the adversary's 'challenges in ways that were calculated to apply to one's strengths against the other side's weaknesses, even if this meant shifting the nature and location of the confrontation'. Nuclear weapons were a key element in that strategy, but the strategy also involved building alliances, conducting psychological warfare, carrying out covert actions and, when appropriate, holding negotiations. The two concepts most readily associated with Secretary of State John Foster Dulles were nuclear 'brinkmanship' and 'massive retaliation'. Resort to them was threatened in the 1954 and 1958 crises over the offshore islands of Quemoy and Matsu, precisely because they could not be defended by conventional means. But had nuclear weapons been used, it would have been difficult to argue that the interests at stake really justified the resulting devastation or the risks of possible retaliation. Typically, Dulles argued that the issue at stake was Taiwanese morale. If Taiwan were lost, the security of the entire western Pacific would be damaged, and Southeast Asia would come under communist influence.

John Lewis Gaddis, the principal historian of containment, has faulted the Eisenhower administration, particularly for lacking confidence in its own supposed reliance upon the independence and nationalism of Third World countries. Accusing the administration of 'hyperactivity', he argued that the attempts to tie Third World governments into alliances coupled with unilateral security guarantees were overbearing and in reality unenforceable. Moreover, accusations about the 'immorality' of Third World 'neutralism' only made matters worse. Although the administration hoped to split China from the Soviet Union, no strategy had been devised for exploiting the consequences. As early as 1954, General Ridgway, who had succeeded MacArthur in Korea, had pointed out that that would require bringing 'Red China to a realization that its long range benefits derive from friendliness with America.' That was ruled out by Eisenhower himself on the grounds that the requisite diplomatic contacts were unacceptable, as they would pose problems with allies, destroy Chiang Kai-shek and be resisted by an American people still 'emotional' about China.[10]

The Kennedy administration, followed by that of Johnson, favoured a symmetrical rather than the asymmetrical response espoused by the previous administration. The earlier emphasis upon nuclear brinkmanship that entailed either inaction or a response that was wholly disproportionate to the original provocation was sharply criticized for lacking credibility. The new strategy of 'flexible response' called for an appropriate and careful response to any act of aggression, be it a limited or general war, conventional or nuclear, large or small. Top priority went to decreasing reliance upon nuclear weapons and to developing mobile forces capable of fighting and assisting allies in fighting different types of war. Accordingly, a much enhanced counter-insurgency capability was developed replete with so-called special forces so as to be able to counter wars of national liberation. At the same time, the Kennedy administration continued with the programme of acquiring a greater variety of nuclear weapons. Alongside the strategy of 'flexible response' came that of graduated response through carefully controlled escalation and crisis management. Ironically, given the outcome in Vietnam, the Kennedy administration also saw itself as favouring the forces for change and the new emergent classes in Third World countries.

Gaddis argues that the fundamental reason why the Kennedy and Johnson administrations regarded the 'loss' of such a small and distant country as South Vietnam in such catastrophic terms was because of their undifferentiated view of American security interests: 'They tended to view the American stake there as determined exclusively by threats and obligations. The security of the United States, indeed of the entire non-communist world, was thought to be imperilled wherever communist challenges came up against American guarantees.' There was an element of self-fulfilment in this since the more the policies towards Vietnam were upheld as necessary to safeguard credibility the more American credibility required those policies to be successful.

Furthermore, the employment of a supposedly calibrated ladder of escalating responses to persuade the other side to desist or to compromise could work only if there were a clear adversary who accepted that the other side were willing and able to escalate to a point that would be destructive of its key values. Since the escalatory responses in Vietnam were aimed at several targets (Hanoi and the Vietcong directly, Moscow and Beijing indirectly), and since the United States had long indicated that there were limits beyond which it would not go in the war, lest it bring in Chinese and Soviet forces, the strategy became ensnared in finding what Gaddis calls disparagingly 'some middle ground between the insanity of nuclear war and the humiliation of appeasement'. The very disproportionate character of the American commitment brought about its own undoing. Despite the huge American military presence, the communists carried out uprisings in the main cities of South Vietnam in early 1968. Although the communist 'Tet offensive' was eventually defeated, it became a political success as President Johnson threw in his hand by refusing to escalate further and by refusing to run for re-election. It fell to the new President Nixon to change the direction of American international politics, bringing means and ends into closer alignment and opening the way to cooperation with China and to détente with the Soviet Union.

In terms of actual policy, the Eisenhower administration attempted to consolidate its containment strategy in East Asia by concluding a series of treaties that aimed ultimately at establishing a multilateral arrangement that would bring together the various parties in a collective defence pact against communist expansion. The preambles of the American security treaties with the Philippines and ANZUS of 1951 and that with South Korea of 1953 all referred to the development of 'a more comprehensive system of regional security in the Pacific area'. In the spring of 1954 (i.e., coincidental with the Geneva Conference) and into the summer the United States was active in promoting a multilateral security pact for Southeast Asia that bore fruit of a kind in September in the signing of the Collective Defence Treaty for Southeast Asia – the Manila Pact. Formally speaking, the Southeast Asia Treaty Organization (SEATO) was established the following year in Bangkok. The United States, Britain, Australia, New Zealand, France, Thailand, Pakistan and the Philippines agreed to act together 'in accordance with [their] constitutional practices' to encounter an 'armed attack' if they could unanimously agree on its designation and they further agreed to consult if any signatory felt threatened. South Vietnam, Cambodia and Laos were not signatories, but the provisions of the treaty were extended to them gratuitously by a protocol attached to the treaty. The highly qualified security commitments of the Manila Pact and SEATO in particular compared unfavourably with the more explicit ones of NATO and of the bilateral pacts the United States had signed in the region.

In the event, SEATO did not provide a basis for the collective defence of South Vietnam. Moreover it was noticeable that even in its attenuated form, the Manila Pact did not attract other Asian members such as Indonesia, Burma, Ceylon (as it then was) or India. Asian non-alignment was already beginning to become a factor in international politics. Meanwhile Cambodia in 1955 rejected the gratuitous protection on offer as being inconsistent with its neutrality, and Laos was eventually excluded from it by the outcome of the Geneva Conference of 1962. Thus the underlying rationale of the Manila Pact had already been removed before it could be invoked in 1964. The Americans were left to intervene unilaterally.

The first Taiwan offshore island crisis of 1954–55

The People's Republic of China (PRC) nevertheless felt that in 1954 it had cause for alarm, especially as it became clear that a mutual defence treaty was in prospect between Washington and Taipei. That provided the occasion for the first offshore island crisis of 1954–55. It can be seen as an example of how local, national, regional and international issues were enmeshed. From Beijing's perspective the Taiwan problem not only involved the question of China's national security, but it also constituted the tail end of the uncompleted civil war and, above all, it was a question of sovereignty and territorial integrity. Taiwan was the last remaining province beyond Beijing's control, and there was fear that a treaty with the Americans that was linked to the other American allies would put Taiwan, with international endorsement, permanently beyond the reach of the PRC short of a world war.

By shelling the islands close to the Chinese shore Beijing was first declaring its determination to lay claim to Taiwan as well; second, it was implicitly warning off America's allies from the putative alliance; third, it was complicating the American position by compelling it to include the protection of those islands in its treaty commitment so as to make it more difficult to establish Taiwan as a separate entity; and finally, it was hoping to begin a dialogue with the United States so as to break out of the economic embargo and isolation imposed upon it by the United States. Taipei sought an American commitment that would both ensure it relative equality with America's other Asian allies and uphold its occupation of the offshore islands in the hope of an eventual return to the mainland to overthrow the communist regime. Constituting the Republic of China, the Chiang Kai-shek government saw itself as the legitimate representative of the whole of China and, as Chinese patriots, its leaders were unwilling to contemplate a separate Taiwan. Indeed one of the American concerns was that a collapse of morale 士气. on the island might cause the regime to make its own deal with Beijing. The American interest was to link Taiwan in the emerging security system of the Asia-Pacific and so complete the cordon of containment. To this end it did not wish its security commitments to be subject to military conflicts over islands where the PRC enjoyed overwhelming geographical advantage. Still less did it wish the crisis to lead to splits with allies.[11]

In the event, none of the other American security agreements in the region mentioned Taiwan, and the United States and the Republic of China (Taiwan) signed a mutual defence treaty on 2 December 1954, but it was carefully limited to the defence of Taiwan and the Pescadore (Penghu) Islands. On 29 January President Eisenhower signed the Formosa Resolution, passed by Congress, giving him the discretion to defend the offshore islands should he judge that necessary for the security of Taiwan itself. Meanwhile Eisenhower gave separate assurances to Chiang Kai-shek about the offshore islands of Quemoy and Matsu, but not about the more northerly Dazhen (Tachen) Islands which were evacuated and then promptly taken over by the PRC. That reassured Beijing, as it confirmed the statements emanating from Washington that President Eisenhower opposed any plans for invading the mainland. If the US was unwilling to support Taipei in holding on to outposts such as the Dazhens, it was unlikely to lend support to a beachhead on the mainland. At the same time and against its better judgement, the United States had in effect been manoeuvred into supporting Taipei's occupation of Quemoy and Matsu on the grounds that their loss would undermine the morale on Taiwan. But in truth, that suited both Beijing and Taipei at the time as it precluded the formal separation of Taiwan from the mainland. The outcome in the end was mixed for all sides. The United States was able to include Taiwan within its western Pacific security perimeter, but it had to give up on its hope of a collective defence system amid uncertainties about the character of its commitment to Quemoy and Matsu. In the process of reaching that point Washington had threatened the possible use of nuclear weapons and had given a practical demonstration of how points of no geopolitical significance to itself could influence its main interests. If the readiness 'to go to the brink' over such an issue was

Quemoy 金门. Matsu 马祖岛

designed to assure allies in principle of American resolve, in practice it frightened them off lest they be dragged into conflicts in which the general interest was not apparent.

The Bandung Conference of April 1955

In contrast to the group of countries that were to set up SEATO, Ceylon had earlier taken the initiative to bring together at Colombo the prime ministers of Burma, India, Indonesia, itself and Pakistan. Other than Pakistan they held that military pacts increased insecurity and they favoured Nehru's policy of 'neutralism'. This was defined in terms of the 'five principles of peaceful coexistence' agreed to by India and China in April 1954.[12] That agreement of the two great Asian powers was reached at a time when there was a prospect of an imminent American military intervention in Vietnam. A year later some thirty countries held the first ever conference of Asian and African nations in Bandung, Indonesia. They demonstrated their desire to be heard on matters of international affairs, especially on issues of peace and cooperation. The delegates talked loudly about affairs for which they had no responsibility, and in subdued tones about those, such as Korea, Vietnam and Kashmir, for which they did. They were divided about cooperation with the West and the communist countries. No bloc or permanent organization emerged from the meeting. It solved none of the questions on which the participants had conflicts of interest and it made little difference to the distribution of power. But it was of great symbolic significance as it for the first time articulated a Third World voice that was to become a growing feature in international politics thereafter. It provided an opportunity for leaders to meet who would otherwise have found it difficult to do so.

It also provided the occasion for China to establish what would now be called its Third World credentials.[13] In the not inconsiderable person of Zhou Enlai, Chinese diplomacy presented a more reasoned face to several leaders of anti-communist governments. He helped to convert Prince Sihanouk of Cambodia to accept the desirability of the neutral status of his country. The conference also provided the occasion for the signing of a nationality treaty with Indonesia. Reversing the old Republican or KMT position on the dual nationality status of overseas Chinese that had been the cause of constant friction with Southeast Asian governments, the new treaty in effect enjoined the Chinese residents to choose either Indonesian or Chinese nationality. The new approach was designed to mollify governments in the region more generally who had professed concern about the potential 'fifth column' aspects of their resident Chinese. In the event, the agreement was not ratified until 1960 and it meant that those traders who retained Chinese nationality became subject to laws that prohibited aliens from trading in rural areas. The PRC duly protested at these harsh laws, but in the interests of placating Indonesia, with whom the Chinese sought to be on good terms, the PRC undertook to repatriate those Chinese who wished to return to China. Some of the tens of thousands who were repatriated were descendants of migrants who had left China several generations before.[14] The episode demonstrated some of the difficulties of the Chinese position in seeking simultaneously to cultivate friendly relations with Southeast Asian governments and to protect the interests of resident Chinese nationals, for whom in any case the PRC was not well placed to offer practical assistance. Moreover, in practice neither the PRC nor the governments and peoples of Southeast Asia punctiliously observed the distinctions between the different nationality credentials of the Chinese resident in the area.

To return to the Bandung Conference, Zhou used the setting as a platform on which to demonstrate his government's 'reasonableness', especially in contrast to the position of the United States. He skilfully used the occasion to appeal for a dialogue with the United States that in effect brought the first Taiwan offshore crisis to an end. This led to an agreement to hold Sino-American talks at ambassadorial level in Geneva.

The 'Bandung spirit' soon evaporated. Local disputes between member states proved to be no easier to resolve. Thailand and the Philippines, whose leaders had apparently been impressed by Zhou Enlai's performance, still refused to recognize the PRC. Although the PRC had abandoned its earlier revolutionary approach in favour of a more conventional diplomacy, especially towards its Asian neighbours, profound problems remained. Although relations had improved with India, as indicated by their agreement of April 1954 by which India recognized Chinese sovereignty over Tibet (thereby giving up its residual interest in the region as the successor to the British Raj), there were still outstanding boundary questions and a more intangible sense of rivalry between the two major Asian powers with the different political visions embodied in their respective political systems. Indeed remaining boundary and territorial questions were problems that affected China's relations with all its neighbours. It became evident that these could raise deep problems when the negotiations with a compliant Burma took four or five years before eventually an agreement was reached, even though there was manifest goodwill on both sides. China's neighbours suspected that a newly reunified China would be influenced by the legacy of the more distant past when imperial China exercised a kind of superior overlordship over the other Asian rulers. The communist issue deepened the distrust: Beijing was seen as a supporter of local communist parties dedicated to the overthrow of the newly established and fragile regimes by subversion and by rural insurgencies. It was feared that China would seek to exploit domestic weakness and intra-regional disputes. Moreover the PRC's new approach towards the nationality of the millions of ethnic Chinese resident in Southeast Asia, welcome as it was, did not dispel the distrust about their potential as a fifth column; still less could it address the many communal problems they faced; and China's residual patrimonial attitudes suggested a responsibility that in reality it lacked the capacity to discharge. These misgivings about China intensified in 1958 when Chinese foreign policy shifted away from the moderation of Bandung towards a more militant revolutionary line, which was in part caused by the failure to improve relations with the United States.[15]

If some of the earlier hopes that a sense of Asian solidarity would promote a wider sense of community failed to materialize, the Bandung Conference was not without a lasting impact. It placed the Third World and its concerns firmly on the international agenda. It contributed to de-legitimizing colonialism and to widening the demands for independence. In foreign policy terms it was the precursor of the non-alignment movement. Although the separate visions and interests of the independent states and their leaders before too long undermined the 'spirit of Bandung', the conference marked the emergence of the Third World as a factor in international politics.

The second offshore island crisis of 1958

As in the previous crisis, the issue combined elements of local and international questions. In fact the second crisis may be said to have followed from the failure to solve the deeper problems inherent in the first. The price that the United States and China each demanded of the other for improving relations was making concessions regarding Taiwan that neither was in a position to make. The Sino-American Geneva talks had begun in August 1955 in a favourable international atmosphere. The treaty ending the military occupation and division of Austria had been signed in May and the four powers, the US, the USSR, Britain and France, had just concluded their summit meeting. But the Sino-American talks soon foundered on their irreconcilable positions. The Americans wanted Beijing to agree to renounce the use of force in the Taiwan area and the PRC wanted the Americans to agree to withdraw from the area. The only agreement they were able to reach was on the subject of citizens of each country held or detained by the other.

Over the next two years the Americans sought to consolidate the status quo and establish a *fait accompli* that would give Beijing no alternative but to accept international opinion that the situation was similar to Germany, Korea, Vietnam and even Ireland. By 1958, having failed to obtain a renunciation of force by Beijing *vis-à-vis* Taiwan and having succeeded in maintaining Taiwan's participation in numerous international fora, the United States suspended the talks. Angered by the breakdown of the link with the US that had been forged with such difficulty and having found that its policy of peaceful coexistence with Washington and Taipei had not turned out well, Beijing chose to take the initiative once again by generating a crisis on the offshore islands.

In the summer of 1958 Beijing began an orchestrated campaign over the Taiwan question that culminated in carefully considered bombardments of Quemoy in which days of intensive shelling would be followed by lighter shelling. The US Navy escorted Taipei supply ships to within three miles of the island. Having decided that the loss of Quemoy could lead to the loss of Taiwan, amid talk of the use of nuclear weapons, Eisenhower and Dulles issued a public warning to Beijing on 4 September. The following day Beijing stopped the shelling and on 6 September Zhou announced that the PRC would accept an American offer to resume talks. On 7 September the Soviet leader Khrushchev felt safe to

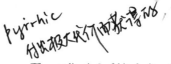

warn Eisenhower that an attack on the PRC would be considered as an attack on the Soviet Union. From 8 September until 6 October Beijing resumed intensive shelling and then announced a cease fire. On 25 October Beijing announced that it would resume shelling but only on odd days – a state of affairs that was to continue for the following twenty years.[16]

For Mao and Zhou Enlai the Taiwan problem had two aspects, an international one involving the United States, and a domestic one involving the KMT. Their consistent aim was to negotiate the removal of the former before proceeding to settle the latter. The offshore islands were never considered as a separate issue, rather they were thought of as a way of bringing pressure to bear on Washington over its Taiwan commitment as a whole. The fact that the exercise was never repeated suggests that Mao and his colleagues recognized that to do so might be counterproductive: Washington might be pressed to respond to international sentiment and to growing voices at home that the offshore islands were not worth the high stakes invested in them. In other words the danger from Beijing's perspective was that rather than being a peg to which the United States was tied in a noose (as Mao had once put it), the islands might be discarded and thus pave the way for a more formal separation of Taiwan from the mainland. From the perspective of Washington the successful management of the crisis proved something of a pyrrhic victory – at least for the strategy of nuclear brinkmanship that underlay it. The disproportionate response paved the way for the development of the new strategy of flexible response. But it left Taiwan firmly embedded within the American scheme of containment. It was not until that issue had been addressed between Beijing and Washington in 1971 that their bilateral dispute over Taiwan could be reconsidered in 1972.

The collapse of the Sino-Soviet alliance

The breakdown of the alliance was a complex and protracted affair that took about ten years to unravel from its beginnings in 1956. The Sino-Soviet alliance which had seemingly been cemented by the Korean War began to unfold as differences of interest began to emerge. Many factors played their part given their previous history, the vast differences of culture between them and the disparities in their socio-economic conditions. But as these had obtained when the alliance was first established, the most significant factors that occasioned the collapse of the alliance were those of international politics and strategy. As the senior ally, the Soviet Union could not allow China to place its global strategic interests in jeopardy. For its part, an independent China could not be expected to subordinate itself to the degree of compliance demanded by its Soviet ally. As the major communist powers, the character of their relations affected the character of the relations between the Soviet Union and the other communist states, as well as the character of the international communist movement as a whole. All these relations were expressed in ideological terms and, since ideology was at the heart of the legitimacy of Communist Party rule in both the Soviet Union and China, the legitimacy of the regimes in Moscow and Beijing was necessarily affected by their disagreement. That may explain why by the early 1960s both sets of leaders were condemning the other as traitors to the communist cause. Ultimately for Marxist–Leninists there could be only one correct view and no true comrade would persist in publicly putting forward a contrary view.[17]

At the heart of their dispute were their respective relationships with the United States. After establishing his authority as successor to Stalin, Khrushchev sought to diffuse some of the tension with the United States partly in order to carry out reforms at home, but primarily because of the unacceptable risks associated with nuclear weapons and the high costs of maintaining a military confrontation with the United States and its allies. To this end he sought to reach various understandings with the United States and declared an interest in preventing local wars and wars of national liberation from escalating into conflicts between East and West. Ironically, in the mid-1950s the Chinese leaders had also sought to diffuse tensions with the Americans because they wanted to concentrate upon economic development at home. But unlike their Soviet colleagues, Mao Zedong and Zhou Enlai found an obdurate Eisenhower administration that refused to respond in kind. As was noted earlier, Dulles took the view that the way to drive a wedge between the two communist giants was to keep up the pressure on China. Not only were the Chinese denied the diplomatic openings that became available to their Soviet colleagues, but they also found no evidence, as far as they were concerned, of the United States having developed more moderate or reasonable approaches as claimed by Khrushchev. Consequently the Chinese leaders found that the Soviet leaders tried to prevent them from standing up for what they regarded as their sovereign and irredentist rights and from supporting wars for national liberation in the Third World. For example, in 1959 Khrushchev publicly charged the Chinese leaders in Beijing with seeking 'to test the international stability by force'. For their part, the Soviet leaders were unwilling to allow the Chinese to determine the nature of Soviet dealings with America.

A major turning point was the refusal of the Soviet Union in 1959 to supply China with a sample atomic bomb. The logic of the situation in fact was for the United States and the Soviet Union to combine together to restrain China from developing its own nuclear weapons. Indeed that was one of the factors that led to the signing of the Test Ban Treaty in 1963. Undaunted, however, the Chinese tested their first device the following year.[18] Meanwhile the Soviet Union declared itself neutral in the border conflict that had reared up suddenly in 1959 between China and India. In 1960 it withdrew all its several thousands of experts from China. Taking their blueprints with them, they dealt the Chinese economy a severe blow at a time of low ebb as the country faced famine and economic downturn after the disastrous Great Leap Forward. By 1962 the Soviet Union was to be found alongside Britain and the United States in support of India after its humiliating defeat by China in their border war. Thereafter the Chinese and Soviet leaders took opposite positions on all the key international issues. In 1963 and 1964 the Chinese deepened the inter-state conflict when they publicly raised the issue of the 'unequal treaties' imposed by Tsarist Russia on the weak Qing Dynasty and other border disputes, which they argued had yet to be settled.

By this stage they had each condemned the other as betrayer
and of the interests of their own people. Not even the removal
1964 (which coincided to the day with the testing of China's first nuc.
changed the situation. Meanwhile Mao, having condemned the Soviet leade.
revisionists who had used state power to bring about a counter-revolution by
peaceful means, began to identify similar alleged revisionists alongside him in
China. This was to culminate in the Cultural Revolution. Clearly foreign and
domestic policies had become closely interconnected.

The impact of the collapse of the Sino-Soviet alliance on the international
politics of the rest of the Asia-Pacific was not immediately obvious. As observed
earlier, the United States, which had played a role in fomenting it, seemed to
have no plans to exploit it. The Kennedy and Johnson administrations took the
view that difficult though it was, they could do business with a post-revolutionary
Soviet leadership, but not with the revolutionary Chinese, whose aggressiveness
had to be stopped. It was only with the advent of Nixon and Kissinger that the
Americans took positive steps to take advantage of the conflict between the two
communist giants. Nevertheless the impact of the communist schism was real
enough. It divided the communist world on national lines, thus weakening
the general appeal of communism and its effectiveness as a force for change. The
conflict also provided greater opportunities for independent manoeuvre to the
smaller communist powers, which in the Asia-Pacific meant primarily North
Korea and North Vietnam. Although the Soviet Union in 1963 withdrew its
assistance from Vietnam, this was resumed after Khrushchev's ouster. Curiously,
the United States chose to start bombing North Vietnam in 1965 just as
the Soviet premier was visiting Hanoi to determine the character of Soviet
aid. The Soviet Union not only became the main supplier of advanced weaponry
to the North during the war with the United States, but it also began to reduce
Chinese influence in Vietnam. However, for reasons of geography and ethnicity
the communist parties of Southeast Asia (with the exception of the Philippines
until 1969) continued to accept Chinese patronage.

The most immediate impact of the Sino-Soviet dispute was felt in the Third
World, where the two competed for power and influence among the newly inde-
pendent countries and for the allegiance of the various liberation movements.
The dispute complicated the attempt to reconvene the Bandung Conference in
Algeria in 1965. China's greater militancy and its opposition to India may have
won it adherents among the more radical governments and movements, but
that served to alienate others, especially in Southeast Asia. The experience of
Indonesia is instructive in this regard.

The rise of President Sukarno from the mid-1950s and the progressive weakening of parliamentary government were accompanied by a more assertive
foreign policy that focused on the acquisition of West Irian (or Dutch
New Guinea) from the Netherlands, who had refused to include it in the transfer
of sovereignty in 1949. The failure to elicit full support from the still American-
dominated General Assembly of the United Nations resulted in the expropriation
of Dutch economic interests in Indonesia in late 1957. This tended to consolidate

the interests of Java and the central government against the outer islands. This was further confirmed by the government's declaration of an archipelagic principle on 13 December. That challenged American claims to rights of passage through the high sea. Accordingly, covert American aid was offered to a rebellion that broke out in early 1958, centred in Sulawesi and Sumatra. Britain, Taiwan and the Philippines were also seen as active in the rebel cause. The failure of the rebellion by the summer helped to bring about an uneasy coalition between President Sukarno as the country's leader, the army as the defender and upholder of national unity and the Communist Party, which could mobilize mass support. Thus although there was a temporary accommodation with America when it pressured Holland to give up West Irian, it soon petered out. Sukarno, meanwhile, had accepted Soviet and East European military aid. Indeed a degree of competition emerged between the two superpowers over cultivating the support of Indonesia.[19]

As Sukarno became more militant as a Third World leader he began to lean more to the Chinese side as the Sino-Soviet conflict unfolded. Sukarno's claims as a nationalist and anti-imperialist leader coalesced in his belligerent response to the proposal to establish Malaysia, triggered by a revolt in Brunei in December 1962. The armed confrontation (or *Konfrontasi*) that was countered by British and Commonwealth troops threatened to further subdivide Southeast Asia, as Sukarno responded by creating 'the axis of Djakarta–Phnom Penh–Hanoi–Peking–Pyongyang'.[20] Others identified a more modest but more sinister Sino-Indonesian axis. Close links were also established between the Indonesian and Chinese communist parties. This in turn heightened tensions between the Indonesian army on the one side and the communists and Sukarno on the other. In the event, an abortive coup attempt took place on 1 October 1965, which resulted in the deaths of six generals. Under the leadership of Major General Suharto the coup forces were overcome within two days. Whether or not the Chinese were involved in the coup in 1965, their influence in the country was eliminated and the limitation of their capacity to exercise power cruelly exposed as many tens of thousands of ethnic Chinese as well as alleged communists were killed. President Sukarno was finally removed from power in 1966 and General Suharto as the new leader was able to bring confrontation to an end. The following year the new relations with Malaysia were to form the core of the newly established ASEAN. This was immediately denounced by both Peking and Hanoi as a proto-imperialist organization. The divisions in the communist world had combined to cause losses for both the Soviet and Chinese sides. But these events also demonstrated the extent to which the fortunes of the external powers could be determined by the interplay of domestic forces in the smaller regional powers.

Sino-Soviet relations deteriorated still further during the Cultural Revolution that began in China in 1965/1966. That also prevented them from joining forces to assist Vietnam. The Chinese had rejected Soviet overtures to this effect, as Mao suspected that the ultimate Soviet purpose was to broker a deal with the United States to the detriment of China. Rejecting Soviet requests for an air corridor and for use of Chinese bases in the south, the Chinese reluctantly agreed to allow Soviet military aid to be sent through Chinese territory by train. Soviet military assistance soon exceeded that of the Chinese in both quantity and quality. In fact it was essential for Hanoi in combating American air power. By this stage the Soviet Union had begun to upgrade its military forces to the north of China. A security treaty was signed with the Mongolian People's Republic in 1966 that led to the stationing of Soviet forces in the south of the country. In 1967 China began to match the Soviet build-up in quantity if not quality. In 1968 the Chinese had a fright, with the Soviet invasion of Czechoslovakia and the proclamation of the Brezhnev Doctrine that allowed the Soviet Union the right to intervene in a socialist state to 'safeguard the revolution'. Interestingly, the North Vietnamese supported the Soviet rather than the Chinese position, while North Korea did not commit itself.

In March 1969 the Chinese instigated a limited conflict on one of the disputed riverine islands. After unsuccessful attempts to open negotiations, victorious Soviet sorties into Xinjiang and hints about a possible Soviet surgical nuclear strike eventually led to a meeting at Beijing airport between the Soviet premier, Kosygin, and Zhou Enlai in September, as the former returned from the funeral of Ho Chi Minh that both had attended in Hanoi. That diffused the immediate crisis.[21] The Chinese had sought to convince the Soviet Union that the PRC could be credibly defended on the basis of self-reliance. The Soviet side feared that an uncontrolled China could open a second front in addition to the main front in Europe. It additionally attempted to persuade the West that they shared a joint interest in restraining China and it continued to drop broad hints that it was contemplating a strike against Chinese nuclear targets. It was only then that Kissinger and President Nixon were alerted to the possible implications for the United States. The Sino-Soviet conflict had finally reached the point where the changes it had wrought to the fundamentals of the central balance of power during the Cold War became clear.

The Second Indo-China War

This war arose from the perception in Washington that a communist victory in the South, building upon the earlier victory in North Vietnam, would work to the advantage of its global adversary and that it would lead to the fall of the rest of Southeast Asia, to the enormous disadvantage of the West. Back in April 1954 President Eisenhower had claimed that all Southeast Asia was like a row of dominoes. If you knocked over the first one, what would happen to the last one was 'the certainty that it would go over very quickly'.[22]

In the late 1950s Hanoi re-activated the war through insurgency in the South, which consisted initially of a systematic campaign to assassinate local officials. The regime in the South that was led by the Catholic Ngo Dinh Diem and his brother Ngo Dinh Nhu had a narrow social base of support and it was destined never to succeed in generating a South Vietnamese nationalist ethos. Certainly they lacked the national authority of Ho Chi Minh and the communist movement that he led. The Diem regime was ineffective and it faced opposition from different social groups that it tried to suppress. In December 1960 the establishment of the National Front for the Liberation of South Vietnam (NLF) marked an important stage in the development of the armed struggle. The incoming Kennedy administration regarded the struggle as aggression from the North that initially was blamed on Moscow and then attributed to Beijing. The administration took the view that the Chinese had to be shown that wars of national liberation could be stopped and that the United States had to show its allies and friends in the Third World in particular that it stood by its commitments. It was this kind of thinking that the realists were to criticize, for its failure to distinguish peripheral from vital interests – even before American liberals attacked the moral basis for prosecuting the war.

The regime in the South was ineffective in carrying out the economic and socio-political programmes recommended by American advisers. The American government, however, persuaded itself that, in the words of Defense Secretary McNamara in June 1962 after his visit to Vietnam, 'every quantitive measurement we have shows we're winning this war'. In one of his last press conferences President Kennedy declared, 'Our goal is a stable government there, carrying on a struggle to maintain its national independence. We believe strongly in that. ... In my opinion for us to withdraw from that effort would mean a collapse not only of South Vietnam but Southeast Asia. So we are going to stay there.' Not long afterwards Diem and his brother were killed in a military coup of which the US government had prior knowledge. Three weeks later President Kennedy was assassinated in November 1963 and Lyndon Johnson became president. Under his direction, the United States armed forces replaced the South Vietnamese army as the main combat troops. The attempt to compel the North to negotiate through a graduated escalation of bombing backfired. The United States misunderstood the commitment of the communists to the nationalist cause and that bombing, as shown by the bombing of Nazi Germany in the Second World War, would stiffen resistance, especially of a dictatorship. In 1968, as a result of the Tet offensive and its impact within the United States, President Johnson decided that he could continue no longer. By that stage the United States had 525,000 troops in Vietnam. It took another five years before an agreement was reached with North Vietnam in 1973 on American withdrawal and a political settlement, and a further two years before the final American humiliation as the Northern army reunified Vietnam by force in April 1975. By that stage, however, the Sino-American rapprochement had long destroyed the original American rationale for containing China in Vietnam.

The war had also embroiled the other two weaker countries of Indo-China, Laos and Cambodia, whose neutrality had supposedly been established by the Geneva Agreements. Indeed that of Laos had been reconfirmed by an additional Geneva Conference in 1962. Of the two, Laos had developed less of a national identity and statehood. Its fortunes were very much the by-play of external forces. The main figures and even elements of the military were dependent upon external patrons within the region and at times even beyond the region. The most powerful politically and militarily were the Pathet Lao who were very much in effect a provincial branch of the Vietnamese communists. Although other regional interests were also engaged, it was in keeping with Hanoi's strategic perspectives that its interests should predominate, especially as the supply routes to the south (the Ho Chi Minh Trail) ran through Laos. Consequently, the victory of the communist forces there followed closely on the tails of those of Vietnam.

Although Vietnamese interests were broadly similar in Cambodia, through which the Ho Chi Minh Trail also ran, Cambodia was more developed politically and more coherent nationally than Laos. One of the keystones of Cambodian nationalism was resentment against the Vietnamese for having encroached upon their once strong and extensive kingdom. The Mekong Delta of South Vietnam was once Cambodian land and there were still ethnic Khmers resident there. But events in Cambodia too were shaped by the war in Vietnam. Prince Sihanouk manoeuvred to retain neutrality for his country by conceding territorial access to the Vietcong, which served as the pretext for his overthrow in 1970 by a rightist military coup which set up a fragile and oppressive administration. The Vietnamese communists then acted to crush the Cambodian army, so enabling the extremist indigenous Khmer Rouge to expand its power, ultimately seizing Phnom Penh in 1975.

The Second Indo-China War is usually considered to have been an unmitigated disaster for the United States. It was America's first defeat in a major war and the repercussions of the failure still resonate at home more than twenty-five years later as a constraint against committing American troops to foreign combat. The war also resulted in a sense of America's relative decline, especially as the Soviet Union, after its experience in the Cuban missile crisis, had taken the opportunity to narrow substantially the gap with the United States in nuclear and conventional power. But the extent of the damage can be exaggerated. Although SEATO was shown to be a broken reed and, unlike during the Korean War, the European allies stayed at home, regional allies such as Australia, New Zealand, the Philippines, South Korea and Thailand did contribute forces in one form or another. Arguably, the United States also missed opportunities to exploit the Sino-Soviet rift, but the war divided the two communist powers still further, even though they both had to assist the North. There can be little doubt that the conflict took on a momentum of its own as its original objectives were overtaken by the mechanics of prosecuting the war. The roots of the Vietcong insurgency were traced to Moscow and by 1964 they were located in Beijing,[23] but by 1965 Moscow assistance was being sought to put pressure on Hanoi and by 1966 tacit understandings were reached with the Chinese on how to limit the war from escalating into a Sino-American one.[24] In the end the larger strategic purposes of the war got lost altogether as Washington aligned with Beijing and pursued détente with Moscow.

A positive lesson was soon learned from the war: that American resources were not unlimited. A chastened President Nixon announced in Guam in July 1969 a new security doctrine for the United States in Asia. Henceforth its allies would be expected to do the bulk of the ground fighting while the Americans would contribute with their navy and air force from offshore, as well as with military supplies and military training. Within the region it can be argued that the defeat in Vietnam marked the beginning of gnawing uncertainties about the durability of American capacity and will to deploy, when needed, countervailing power. Yet, as seen from the perspective of the 1990s, it is difficult to point to long-term damage to American interests in the Asia-Pacific. No dominoes fell beyond Indo-China and most of America's allies prospered, leaving America still as the dominant force in the region, while a socialist Vietnam embraced free-market economics.

The impact elsewhere in Pacific Asia

The acute polarities of the Cold War ensured that the status quo in Northeast Asia was not challenged during the 1950s and 1960s. The stalemate of the Korean War had resulted in a local settlement that was endorsed by the great powers. No matter that both North and South regarded it as no more than provisional, neither could challenge the division of the country without the support of the external powers. Since that division did not challenge their interests sufficiently to warrant a resumption of the war, a stand-off ensued that was directly comparable to the one between East and West in Europe. The North was able to sustain its independence by taking advantage of the Sino-Soviet rift, but each had too much to lose by challenging the status quo to allow its interests to be tied to the North's war chariot. For its part the South did not have its confidence in the American commitment tested until the changes wrought by the Sino-American rapprochement and its own economic revival. That left both North and South to focus on domestic reconstruction amid the costs of sustaining a high degree of military preparedness. Although both were dictatorships, the communist North was tighter and more pervasive in its control of society and the economy as its leader, Kim Il-Sung, consolidated its grip. The South Korean dictator, Syngman Rhee, by contrast, had to allow for parliamentary politics. His attempts to subvert them eventually brought him down after student disturbances in 1960. A brief period of rule by a democratically elected government that was badly divided and ineffective was ended by a military coup a year later that brought Park Chung Hee to power for another eighteen years.

Japan's position as the key nodal point of American strategy and economic concerns in the Asia-Pacific was not seriously challenged by either the Soviet Union or China. As part of its policy of accommodation towards the West in 1955/1956, the Soviet Union initiated talks with Japan also. This culminated in mutual recognition and in Japan's entry to the United Nations. But no agreement was reached on the groups of four islands adjacent to Hokkaido still occupied by the Soviet Union. Consequently, they were unable to agree upon a peace settlement. This left Japan firmly in the American camp. Although the Japanese found ways to trade with the PRC (contrary to the American embargo), that too did not affect the country's international position. By focusing upon economic development Japan was able to emerge by the end of the 1960s as one of the world's leading economic powers.

There were few vital interests at stake for the two superpowers in Southeast Asia. This was also largely true for the two major regional powers, China and Japan. Under these less restrictive circumstances, the more fluid geopolitical conditions of Southeast Asia allowed for a greater degree of change to take place. As we saw in the previous chapter, the states of Southeast Asia, with the exception of Thailand, had all experienced European colonial rule. That, together with the manner of their emancipation, had a profound effect upon their subsequent identities as states. These identities in turn shaped both their domestic politics and their foreign relations. Indeed the two have been closely linked from the perspective of international politics. The internal and external politics of the states of Southeast Asia were closely interlinked. Whether considering the question of treating an ethnic minority such as the Chinese, or assessing the importance of Islam as a political influence, or indeed even examining the question of the territorial claims of states, it is not always clear whether the external dimensions are derived from the domestic political arena or vice versa. It should also be recognized that although the major external powers in this period may not have identified vital interests for which they were prepared to fight major wars, this did not mean that they lacked interest in the region. Indeed, at times they showed willingness even to intervene in support of territorial claims and disaffected elite groups. With these broad considerations in mind, the international history of each of the main states will be surveyed briefly.

The Philippines, as previously noted, has been described as 'being simultaneously a kind of detached bit of [Latin America], an East Asian offshore island, the occasional and uncertain champion of an embryonic community of South-east Asian states, and indubitably a part of the Malay world'.[25] The central pillar in its foreign relations continued to be the manifold connection with the United States, which in addition to the alliance and the military bases also included pervasive American commerce and culture. Filipino troops were deployed in Vietnam and American airfields were used, albeit not for bombing. The sense of dependence has also evoked a certain anti-American rhetoric in Filipino nationalism and a concurrent search for ways to assert a Southeast Asian identity and to find endorsement within the region for such an identity. Essentially the Philippines has been self-absorbed with its own problems, such as the continued rumblings of the Huk insurgency, and the discontent of the Muslim minority in the south centred on the island of Mindanao. But the overwhelming problem has stemmed from a political system that has been strong on the rhetoric of democracy and weak on orderly governance, which consequently has been unable or unwilling to address the economic, social and administrative difficulties that have existed since independence. Its relations with its Southeast Asian neighbours have been somewhat guarded, despite institutionalized regional links, notably that of the Association of Southeast Asian Nations, but also the two ill-fated regional associations that preceded it. In addition to the degree of distance from neighbours caused by their separate identities and the Filipino ties with the United States, the Philippines' claim to Sabah, which was incorporated within the Malaysian Federation, created problems too, even though it was not pursued with much vigour.

Thailand is on the whole more homogeneous than most of the other Southeast Asian states, with around 90 per cent of the population identifying themselves as ethnic Thais, as Buddhist and as Thai speakers. The traditional concern with the threat from Burma abated in the post-independence period as the Burmese state became tied down by its various domestic insurgencies. But Thailand has been troubled to the east. There was periodic fear of subversion through Thai-speaking Laos in the 1950s and 1960s, partly because of suspected Chinese influence through their road-building activities in the north and partly through a Vietnamese-inspired communization of Laos. Accordingly, the Thais supported the so-called right-wing Lao leaders and they felt vindicated when their suspicions that the 1962 Geneva Agreement on Laos would work out in favour of the Vietnamese were confirmed. Part of the problem from a Thai perspective was the vulnerability of their adjacent northeast provinces, which were relatively neglected. Meanwhile traditional Thai–Khmer animosities were exacerbated by complaints about the way in which Khmer and Thai minorities were treated in each other's countries. Essentially Thai governments thought of Cambodia as an unreliable buffer against Vietnam. To the south, the Malay-speaking areas of Thailand's Kra peninsula have posed problems less because of possible separatism than as a base for insurgency and cross-border smuggling. Here there has been more cooperation with Malaysia to quell the troubles, rather than the eruption of discord over possible irredentism. The alliance with the United States was crucial as much for the Thai military in enhancing its domestic political primacy as in sustaining Thailand's international position. But it has been an alliance that served Thai interests too; and it proved to be no barrier to Thailand's active pursuit of schemes for regional intergovernmental cooperation.

Malaysia, whose official religion is constitutionally defined as Islam, has been troubled by its ethnic mix, which even after the expulsion of Singapore in 1965 (see below), was made up of some 45 per cent Malay, 35 per cent Chinese, 10 per cent Indian and a further 10 per cent from elsewhere. It was formed as a federation in 1963 to include the two states of Sarawak and Sabah in northern Borneo, Singapore, and the peninsular, Malaya itself. Brunei was originally proposed as a member, but in the end it did not join. The Federation was seen as a means of divesting remaining British colonial possessions in Borneo and using them to counterbalance the Chinese population of Singapore. Its formation brought to a head a number of factors that have been central to Malaysia's domestic and international concerns. The communal problems between Malays and Chinese are both domestic and external issues of great complexity. As elsewhere in the region, the Chinese are resented both because of their command over much of the commerce and because of their preservation of their distinctive ways of life with their ties to the Chinese homeland. They are also regarded as the beneficiaries of the colonial era. As Muslims, the Malays are subject to the twin pressures of asserting their Islamism and of temporizing that in order to accommodate the Chinese and Indians in their midst. Even the Islamic world in Malaysia is divided between the more tolerant and those of a more fundamentalist persuasion. Not surprisingly, communal conflict has been a continual spectre and indeed, in 1969, when the establishment Alliance Party incorporating members of both communities did less well in the elections than expected, severe rioting broke out. The subsequent regrouping of the 'grand coalition' implemented a 'New Economic Policy' which allocated a greater share of the nation's wealth to the Malays, whose cultural heritage was to be better protected and whose advancement was to underpin political dominance with economic control. These events had an extensive impact upon the region, as they drew attention both to the inability of Chinese governments in either Beijing or Taipei to protect the overseas Chinese and to their economic significance in each of the countries in the region.

Similarly, the challenge of a more assertive Islam within the Malay community may be seen as simultaneously a domestic matter for the less fundamentalist UMNO leadership and as a regional and/or international one that affected the wider world of Malay culture, especially after the 1967 Arab–Israeli war and the Israeli control of the holy places. In fact pan-Malay solidarity (with anti-Chinese undertones) had been briefly fanned in 1963, with the short-lived formation of Maphilindo – an acronym comprising Malaya, the Philippines and Indonesia. But its development was aborted by the establishment of Malaysia only a few weeks later. The two initial challenges to its legitimacy by the Philippines and Indonesia respectively may have abated soon, but they too may be seen as illustrative of wider problems. The Philippines' claim to Sabah has been a continual reminder that Malaysia's territorial integrity cannot be taken for granted. The Indonesian denunciation of Malaysia as a neocolonial entity and its political, economic and military confrontation (*Konfrontasi*) of the Federation from 1963 to 1966 highlighted contradictory elements in the Malaysian international posture. Its defence and economic interests placed it within the Western camp, but its changing regional interests and domestic predispositions involved a degree of unease with that. Hence Malaysia sought membership of the non-aligned movement not long after.

Ethnic tension resulted in the expulsion of Singapore from the Federation within two years. The question of regional identity arose towards the end of *Konfrontasi* in late 1965, when the Malaysian government began to cultivate relations with Indonesia and to distance itself from Britain despite its having defended the Federation along with Australia and New Zealand military. At the same time, however, the Malaysian government made a number of gestures favourable to the United States. Kuala Lumpur, for example, was the only Asian capital that President Johnson visited in 1966 that was not a co-belligerent in Vietnam. Against that, however, there were countervailing regional associations, notably those that led to the establishment of the Association of Southeast Asian Nations (ASEAN) in 1967. Signifying a new understanding between Malaysia and Indonesia, its five member governments committed themselves to strengthening their economic and social stability so as to prevent external interference and to accept the temporary character of foreign bases which were not used to interfere with other states in the region.

Indonesia, which is made up of more than 13,000 islands, of which 1,000 are inhabited, has been subject to a sense of weakness and vulnerability arising from social and geographical fragmentation and to a sense of what Michael Leifer has called an 'entitlement' to play a leading role in the management of regional order in Southeast Asia.[26] In the first decade after independence the state successfully overcame challenges to its integrity. In particular, in 1958 it overcame an armed revolt based on several major islands that had a degree of assistance from external forces including the United States. The vociferous objection to external interference that has been a marked feature of successive Indonesian governments should not obscure the fact that American diplomatic pressure was instrumental in ultimately gaining independence from the Dutch in 1949 and in recovering what came to be called Irian Jaya (the former Dutch New Guinea). In both instances it proved possible to use Cold War factors to Indonesian advantage. The circumstances of the first occasion were discussed in the previous chapter. The Irian Jaya case was facilitated in part 'by Sukarno's ability to use Soviet arms transfers to persuade the government of the United States of the political utility of persuading, in turn, the Netherlands government to revise its adamant opposition to transferring the territory to Indonesia'.[27]

In Indonesia too, there was a close correspondence between domestic and external policies. The period of parliamentary democracy 1950–59 saw a commitment to an 'independent and active' foreign policy which involved non-alignment as part of a policy designed to cater to a national mood that was still shaped by the experience of the national revolution or struggle for independence. But it also 'served as a way of sustaining domestic priorities designed to overcome economic, social and administrative shortcomings'.[28] However, it was with the advent of the period of 'Guided Democracy' under the leadership of President Sukarno that the linkage became even more evident. Sukarno balanced two incompatible coalitions, first, with the more conservative armed forces and second, with the Communist Party (PKI). The former provided physical power and the latter a mass base. Their incompatibility led to the avoidance of taking critical decisions on domestic policy. Foreign policy issues which evoked a nationalist response had the great virtue of providing Sukarno with 'great freedom of political manoeuvre without arousing domestic discord'.[29] His confrontationalist style against the West, depicted as the 'old established forces' ever anxious to thwart and obstruct the 'new emerging forces' such as Indonesia, was most evident in the campaign to acquire West Irian (Irian Jaya) from the Dutch and in the armed confrontation with Malaysia as a creature of neocolonialism after its creation in 1963.

With the collapse of Guided Democracy after the abortive coup of 1965, the new government of General Suharto established a new domestic order that soon found expression in a different approach to foreign policy. While still upholding the long-standing goals of abjuring military alliances and asserting pre-eminence in the affairs of the Southeast Asian region, the new government abandoned the leftist-style rhetoric of Sukarno for a growing association with the Western industrialized states. Relations immediately soured with Beijing as it was openly accused of being implicated in the 1965 coup. This accentuated the impression of a new pro-Western tilt that was only slightly mollified by the retention of correct relations with the Soviet Union. The ending of the confrontation with Malaysia resulted in a situation in which the five governments of Southeast Asia who were interested in regional cooperation were sufficiently like-minded to combine that with the exercise of reconciliation with Indonesia. Thus on 8 August 1967 in Bangkok, the Association of Southeast Asian Nations (ASEAN), comprising Indonesia, Malaysia, Singapore, Thailand and the Philippines, came into being. Since the last two were allied to the United States and were involved in the American war effort in Vietnam, which was then at its height, and in order to minimize communist and non-aligned possible suspicions about its orientation, the main emphasis was placed on ASEAN's role to facilitate cooperation in economic, social and cultural matters. The goal of encouraging peace and stability in the region was given less public attention, but it was considered to be of the utmost importance. The extent to which this was done, however, did reflect long-standing Indonesian perspectives. Thus the members committed themselves to strengthen the economic and social stability of the region and to preserve their national identities and security from 'external interference in any form and manifestation'. They also affirmed the temporary character of foreign bases that could remain only with 'expressed concurrence' of the host countries and with the proviso that they did not subvert countries within the region.[30]

Singapore, as a city state made up predominantly of ethnic Chinese, was acutely conscious under its leader, Lee Kuan Yew, of its vulnerability given its geopolitical location between Malaysia and Indonesia. This was particularly true after its expulsion from the Malaysian Federation in August 1965. It had reason to fear both Sukarno's *Konfrontasi* and the profuse expressions of pan-Malay solidarity after its end. Accordingly, it welcomed both the formation of ASEAN in 1967 and the decision to form the Five Power Defence Arrangements by the British Conservative government on its coming to power in 1970 by way of recompense for the British decision to retreat militarily from East of Suez. The agreement committed Britain, Australia and New Zealand to maintain a modest defence presence in both Malaysia and Singapore. Singapore has sometimes taken high-profile positions that would not always be welcome to its vastly larger neighbours as a way of securing their proper respect. Moreover, unlike perhaps either Malaysia or Indonesia, Singapore has a geostrategic interest in encouraging rather than discouraging the presence of external great powers in the seas of the region. Such is the Singaporean concern about being absorbed by its neighbours that its defence posture has been likened to that of a poisonous shrimp that draws attention to itself by its brilliance as a warning to potential predators about the terrible pains that would follow from swallowing it.

This period of bipolarity began with an assertive American attempt to consolidate the containment of communism in East Asia and ended with the United States in a more chastened mood after its travails in Vietnam. The heady days of the Eisenhower and Kennedy administrations interpreted every gain to a supposedly monolithic international communist movement as something to be denied in principle rather than something to be responded to in terms of variable geopolitical significance. But one of the first decisions of the Nixon presidency in 1969 was to limit American military interventions in East Asia to air and naval power alone. Meanwhile the Sino-Soviet rift which the West had anticipated in the late 1940s and early 1950s duly took place, but the West was ill placed to exploit it until after the debacle in Vietnam, when Kissinger and Nixon appreciated the geopolitical significance of the rift. Also, a stalemate developed in Northeast Asia, while in Southeast Asia the United States got bogged down in Vietnam. As China turned inwards during the Cultural Revolution the other Southeast Asian states were able after the fall of Indonesia's President Sukarno to contain their differences and various disputes by establishing a regional association. Although more modest in its scope, the more pragmatic orientation of ASEAN ensured it a longer and more effective lifespan than did the more trumpeted declarations of Asian and African solidarity, as epitomized by the Bandung Conference. However, the established bipolar character of containment in Asia had run its course as the deeper significance of the emergence of China as a separate centre of power was to emerge in the course of the pending Sino-American rapprochement.

Notes

1 Gordon H. Chang, *Friends and Enemies: The United States, China, and the Soviet Union, 1948–1972* (Stanford: Stanford University Press, 1990); and John Lewis Gaddis, *The United States and the End of the Cold War: Implications, Reconsiderations, Provocations* (Oxford: Oxford University Press, 1992).

2 Donald S. Zagoria, *Vietnam Triangle: Moscow, Peking, Hanoi* (New York: Pegasus, 1967).

3 Much of this is captured in a book written at the end of the period under review. See Milton Osborne, *Region of Revolt, Focus on Southeast Asia* (Australia: Pergamon Press, 1970).

4 See George F. Kennan, *Memoirs, 1950–1963* (New York: Pantheon, 1983), pp.58–59; and Hans J. Morganthau, 'Politics among the Nations: The Struggle for Power and Peace' (New York: McGraw-Hill Inc, 6th edn, revised by Kenneth W. Thompson, 1985).

5 For an account that draws a sharp distinction between Soviet economic relations with Asian communist countries and the majority of the other East Asian countries, see Ed A. Hewett and Herbert S. Levine, 'The Soviet Union's Economic Relations in Asia' in Donald S. Zagoria (ed.), *Soviet Policy in East Asia* (A Council on Foreign Relations Book, New Haven and London: Yale University Press, 1982), pp.201–28.

6 For an authoritative account of Kennan's ideas, see John Lewis Gaddis, *Strategies of Containment* (Oxford: Oxford University Press, 1982), chs 2–3.

7 Cited in Stephen E. Ambrose, *The Rise to Globalism: American Foreign Policy Since 1938* (London: Penguin, 6th rev. edn, 1991), pp.142–43.

8 This account draws upon Gaddis, *Strategies of Containment* (*op. cit.*), ch.4, and the quotations are from pages 98 and 103, respectively.

9 Martin Borthwick, *Pacific Century* (Boulder: Westview Press, 1992), p.394.

10 Gaddis, *Strategies of Containment* (*op. cit.*), chs 5–6. The quotation from Ridgway is on page 195.

11 This and the following paragraph have benefited from the excellent analysis by Thomas E. Stolper, *China, Taiwan and the Off-Shore Islands* (New York: M.E. Sharpe, 1985).

12 These were: respect for territorial integrity and sovereignty; non-aggression; non-interference in internal affairs; equality and mutual benefit; and peaceful coexistence.

13 For accounts, see G.H. Jansen, *Nonalignment and the Afro-Asian States* (New York: Praeger, 1966); George McT. Kahin, *The Asian-African Conference* (Ithaca: Cornell University Press, 1956); and Peter Lyon, *Neutralism* (Leicester: Leicester University Press, 1963).

14 Stephen A. Fitzgerald, *China and the Overseas Chinese: A Study of Peking's Changing Policy* (Cambridge: Cambridge University Press, 1973).

15 For accounts of Chinese policies in Southeast Asia, see Jay Taylor, *China and Southeast Asia: Peking's Relations with Revolutionary Movements* (New York: Praeger, expanded and updated edn, 1976); and Melvin Gurtov, *China and Southeast Asia – The Politics of Survival* (Lexington, MA: D.C. Heath & Co., 1971).

16 This account relies strongly on Stolper, *China, Taiwan and the Off-Shore Islands* (*op. cit.*), ch.VIII.

17 The advent of new archival material and the significance of new perspectives since the end of the Cold War have deepened knowledge of the Sino-Soviet conflict. The most notable book to have been published so far is Sergei N. Goncharov, John W. Lewis and Xue Litai, *Uncertain Partners: Stalin, Mao and the Korean War* (Stanford: Stanford University Press, 1993) which has transformed understanding of the establishment of the Sino-Soviet alliance and the beginnings of the Korean War. Nevertheless, the best books that treat the breakdown of the relationship remain Donald S. Zagoria, *The Sino-Soviet Conflict 1956–1961* (Princeton: Princeton University Press, 1962); and John Gittings, *Survey of the Sino-Soviet Dispute* (Oxford: Oxford University Press, 1969).

18 For the most complete account of China's development of nuclear weapons, see John Wilson Lewis and Xue Litai, *China Builds the Bomb* (Stanford: Stanford University Press, 1988).

19 See Michael Leifer, *Indonesia's Foreign Policy* (London: George Allen and Unwin, for the Royal International Institute of International Affairs, 1983), pp.45–53.

20 *Ibid.*, p.105.

21 For detailed accounts and analysis, see Thomas Robinson, *The Sino-Soviet Border Dispute* (Santa Monica: The Rand Corporation, 1970); and Gerald Segal, *Defending China* (Oxford: Oxford University Press, 1985), ch.10.

22 See note 7.

23 Gaddis, *Strategies of Containment* (*op. cit.*), p.249–50.

24 See the discussion in Allen S. Whiting, *The Chinese Calculus of Deterrence* (Ann Arbor: University of Michigan Press, 1975).

25 Peter Lyon, *War and Peace in South-East Asia* (London: Oxford University Press, for The Royal Institute of International Affairs, 1969), p.46.

26 Leifer, *Indonesia's Foreign Policy* (*op. cit.*), p.xiv.

27 *Ibid.*, pp.67–68.

28 *Ibid.*, p.29.

29 *Ibid.*, p.55.

30 For further readings on Indonesia, see Franklin B. Weinstein, *Indonesian Foreign Policy and the Dilemma of Dependence*, (Ithaca: Cornell University Press, 1976); Michael Leifer, *Indonesia's Foreign Policy* (*op. cit.*); J.A.C. Mackie, *Konfrontasi: The Indonesia-Malaysia Dispute, 1963–1966* (Kuala Lumpur: Oxford University Press, 1974); and Peter Polumka, *Indonesia's Future and South-East Asia* (London: International Institute for Strategic Studies, Adelphi Papers no.104, 1974).

3   The period of tripolarity, 1971–89

The structure of the international system during this period has often been depicted as a strategic triangle comprising the United States, the Soviet Union and China. There is some merit in this view, but it should not be exaggerated.[1] China did not carry the same strategic weight as the other two and its impact on global configurations of power was still quite limited. The essentials of the Cold War between Moscow and Washington and the centrality of the strategic balance between the two superpowers and their allies remained in place. The principal change that occurred was that China became more openly recognized as a complicating factor in the conduct of American–Soviet relations, especially in East Asia where its influence was more evident. Henry Kissinger's surprise visit to Beijing in July 1971, which may be said to have formally ushered in this new phase in international politics, did not suddenly elevate China to superpower status. Unlike either of the superpowers, China's military reach continued to be limited to areas adjacent to its land borders. It lagged far behind in military technology and its economy was not yet of global significance. What gave a new salience to China's significance was the new strategic weight the Soviet Union had gained as a result of its sustained military build-up while the United States had been bogged down in Vietnam. Now that the Soviet Union had 'caught up' with the United States, the China factor acquired a new importance.

China's international strategic importance stemmed first from the fact that alone of the other countries in the world it claimed to be able to defend itself from either of the superpowers, who in turn had gone to great lengths to contain Chinese power; and second from its independent diplomatic stance as demonstrated by its shift from alliance with the Soviet Union to revolutionary isolationism and now to an alignment with the United States. China also benefited from its geographical location and its perceived potential. But China's elevation into the diplomacy of tripolarity also stemmed from the importance the two superpowers accorded the country in their conduct of relations with each other. That, however, did not alter the fact that the dominant strategic relationship in world affairs was still that of the United States and the Soviet Union. The key pillars of the Cold War remained in place throughout this period and these emanated from the confrontation in Europe where the Chinese impact was not great.[2] The Soviet leaders regarded themselves as representatives of the fellow superpower, with whom the Americans had to deal over serious issues. As Brezhnev once put it, Nixon went 'to Peking for banquets but to Moscow to do business'.[3]

Each of the parties to the strategic triangle perceived it differently and changed their policies over time. The Chinese, whose principal foreign policy concerns to date could be described as seeking to manoeuvre between the two superpowers in order to preserve China's independence, opened to America in order to better contain the Soviet Union. Later, however, the Chinese shifted to a more independent position as the Soviet threat declined and as the Reagan administration no longer seemed to need the Chinese counterweight as much as its predecessors. Kissinger and Nixon, as the architects of the new structure of international relations, saw it less as a means of bringing unrelenting pressure on one party by the other two than as a means of bringing about a balance or equilibrium in which the Soviet leaders would see it to be in their interests to act with restraint.[4] Their successors, however, argued as to whether it would be possible to rein in a Soviet Union that had not acted with 'restraint' by supplying sophisticated weaponry to China – what became known as playing the 'China card'. The issue was finally settled by the Reagan administration's huge military build-up, which made the Chinese role almost redundant.[5] The Soviet leaders, who had less room for manoeuvre in the triangle than the other two, first emphasized their significance to the Americans as a fellow superpower, only to later describe the Chinese as extreme 'anti-Soviets' who had got the Americans on side, and finally to end up in a position in which they sought to cultivate relations with the Chinese partly in order to limit American unilateralism.[6]

Even within the Asia-Pacific, the effect of tripolarity was not to change the fundamental pattern of alliances involving the United States and the Soviet Union but rather to change the position and relations of China. Thus American alliances with South Korea, Japan, the Philippines, Thailand and so on all held, as did the Soviet alliances with Mongolia, North Korea and North Vietnam (soon to be a reunified Vietnam). Even the one American international alliance that was ended – that with Taiwan – was soon renewed through domestic American legislation in the form of the Taiwan Relations Act. As against that, China's relations in the region changed radically, notably in Southeast Asia where relations were soon established with former adversaries Malaysia, the Philippines and Thailand, but deteriorated rapidly with its former ally Vietnam. Moreover the underlying strategic enmity between the United States and the Soviet Union was complicated in the Asia-Pacific by a Sino-Soviet conflict that was particularly intense in the 1970s and whose influence was still apparent for much of the 1980s.

The period of tripolarity may be divided roughly into two: from 1971 until 1979, when the United States still sought détente with the Soviet Union and when Sino-Soviet relations continued to be marked by deep enmity; and from 1980 to 1989, which was characterized initially by greater enmity between the United States and the Soviet Union and a slow improvement in Sino-Soviet relations that by the late 1980s ended in a more balanced relationship between the three powers, culminating in the normalization of Sino-Soviet relations and the ending of the Cold War. As seen from the more mechanistic view of the strategic triangle, the United States was favoured by the 'pivot' position during the first period as it alone enjoyed good relations with the other two, who in turn sought to cultivate Washington against the other rival. But it was principally China who became the 'pivot' in the second period as it benefited from the deterioration of relations between the other two and was accordingly cultivated by them. However, tripolarity was only one of the elements that shaped relations between the three great powers. Other factors must also be taken into account such as strategic developments, questions of ideology, changes in the domestic political circumstances in each of their societies and the impact of developments elsewhere. Nevertheless the periodization also accords with other important developments. The year 1979 was a turning point in many ways, as it was then that China launched its brief incursion into Vietnam. The Soviet Union later invaded Afghanistan which led the United States to adopt a more confrontationist policy towards the Soviet Union. It was also the year in which China's new policies of economic reform and openness began to take shape and in which the United States and China commenced a new period of normalized relations.

Tripolarity phase I, 1971–79: the problems of détente

Tripolarity, according to its chief exponent, Henry Kissinger, was meant not only to serve American interests, but also to promote the goal of equilibrium among the main powers and thus serve the general interest. The United States seemingly enjoyed the key position of being the 'pivot', as it could deal directly with the other two while they in turn froze each other out in bitter confrontation.

But the immediate effect of Henry Kissinger's visit to Beijing in July 1971 was to serve China's interest by accelerating the return of the People's Republic of China to full participatory membership of the international community. That autumn the UN General Assembly voted overwhelmingly to expel the Republic of China (i.e., Taiwan) and replace it with the PRC. The general trend of improving state relations with the PRC reached a high tide as nearly all states rushed to normalize relations with Beijing. But the startling diplomatic success of the Americans in establishing a strategic alignment with the Chinese, according to Kissinger's own account, was followed not by immediate conciliatory moves by the Soviet Union, but by Moscow's encouragement of India to act boldly in facilitating the break-up of Pakistan, a staunch ally of the PRC. After signing a treaty with the Soviet Union in August 1971, the Indian government assisted the rebellion in East Pakistan in seceding and in establishing the state of Bangladesh. According to Kissinger, only American pressure (including the so-called 'tilt to Pakistan') prevented India with Soviet connivance from proceeding to capture the whole of Kashmir and in the process destroying the remaining Pakistani army and bringing about the dismemberment of West Pakistan. That in turn would have left China vulnerable and it could possibly have undermined the Nixon/ Kissinger initiative to establish a new and necessary balance of power.[7] It is clear even from this self-serving account that the opening to China did not automatically result in more 'restrained Soviet behaviour' and it also pointed up that the weakness of China could make it a liability for the United States under certain circumstances as well as an asset under others.

In fact, from the outset each of the powers not only understood tripolarity differently but they also experienced the pressures of tripolarity in different ways. This arose in part from the lack of symmetry among the three powers and in part because of the ways in which domestic factors interacted with the external pressures. Thus China's relative weakness made it court the United States in the first place against the perceived threat of the Soviet Union. But ideological rivalry with the Soviet Union which went to the heart of the legitimacy of Mao and his Cultural Revolution intensified his hostility towards the country and, at least in the eyes of his Soviet adversaries, precluded any prospect of an accommodation until his death. Thus for most of the 1970s China's leaders sought in vain to establish an international coalition to confront the Soviet Union and openly derided the American development of détente with the Soviet Union as appeasement. The Soviet leaders were so convinced that Mao personally was at the heart of Chinese hostility towards them that they put out feelers towards the Chinese after Mao's death in 1976. In the event, it was not until Deng Xiaoping had gained ascendancy in Beijing in late 1978 and jettisoned much of Mao's ideological legacy that China's leaders were in a position to explore the prospects for improved relations.

The Soviet leaders during this period focused almost entirely on their relations with the United States, with whom they felt that a broad strategic parity had been achieved that was only marginally affected by the Chinese factor. As long as the Soviet leaders thought that the United States sought détente and stability they concluded that the Americans would resist Chinese efforts to transform the dynamics of tripolarity into an anti-Soviet united front. Only when the United States abandoned détente in President Carter's last year did the Soviet leaders believe that Washington had combined with Beijing against them. In other words, even then the Soviet leaders saw tripolarity as a function of bipolar relations between Moscow and Washington. It was not until 1982, when the Soviet Union was bogged down in Afghanistan and demonstrably in a weakening position compared to the United States, which was engaged in a rapid military build-up, that the Soviet leaders responded positively to earlier Chinese initiatives to improve relations.

The United States' leaders, and Henry Kissinger in particular, consciously sought to exploit the dynamics of triangular diplomacy. Yet it is not easy to identify what specific tangible gains the United States achieved in its dealings with the Soviet Union, either in the arms control negotiations or in the attempts to constrain Soviet activism in the Third World. Indeed, it can be argued that Soviet activism was in part triggered by concern about the China factor. Furthermore, it has been argued persuasively that the intensification of the Soviet military build-up to the north of China in the mid-1970s threatened American strategic interests too.[8] Moreover, during the Nixon and Ford administrations, when Kissinger played a major role in shaping foreign policy, the American efforts to consolidate détente with the Soviet Union were made at the expense of exciting suspicion in China's leaders.

Following the departure of Kissinger in 1976, the main effect of tripolarity seemed to be to excite divisions between American decision makers. The Carter administration consciously sought to pursue a more idealist foreign policy, but it felt the pressure of tripolarity through divisions within the administration about whether or not to use the threat of arming China as a means of restraining aggressive Soviet behaviour. The arguments between Secretary of State Vance and National Security Adviser Brzezinski were continued into the next administration, as exemplified by the contrast between Secretary of State Haig and his successor, Shultz. Haig went so far as to argue that China 'may be the most important country in the world' for American security interests.[9] For Shultz, China was little more than an important regional power, albeit of great potential, that was constrained by its communist system and, as far as Asia was concerned, for him 'the centrepiece ha[d] always been Japan'.[10] The issue was finally settled as a result of the changing balance of power in favour of the United States, which had the effect of reducing China's potential strategic significance.

The regional impact

The transformation of China's position in the central balance between the United States and the Soviet Union may have had less impact on the global bipolar system than was previously thought, but it certainly had an immediate effect on the Asia-Pacific region. From being a target for American containment policies, China had become a partner in alignment with the United States. Moreover, the Sino-Soviet enmity that had hitherto been confined to the ideological realm and to direct bilateral confrontations was now to become more readily apparent in the region as a whole. Given the significance of China for all the countries in the region, the political, security and economic consequences were both immediate and far reaching.

The first to feel the impact was Taiwan. Hitherto, it had been one of the key cornerstones of American global strategy. It was at the centre of the American containment strategy in Asia and, in particular, of the confrontation with Chinese communism. For the Chinese too, Taiwan had been seen as being of key significance in America's geopolitical strategy, and as one of the critical points from which an invasion of the mainland might have been launched. Henceforth, from the perspective of Beijing, Taiwan returned to being a problem of sovereignty and Chinese unity. It was important, but not a pressing issue that threatened the survival of the state, and it was at best a secondary problem in Sino-American relations. Its significance had changed as the Sino-American international geopolitical alignment had changed. This was confirmed by the famous Shanghai Communiqué of February 1972, signed by US President Nixon and the PRC premier, Zhou Enlai, which as Kissinger rightly claims, 'was not about Taiwan or bilateral exchanges, but about international order'.[11] Interestingly, the terms of the communiqué were to allow America alone of all the Western countries to maintain full diplomatic relations and a security treaty with Taiwan while simultaneously maintaining a quasi-embassy in Beijing. Even when relations were normalized between Washington and Beijing in January 1979, Washington was still able to insist on its interest in a peaceful resolution of the Beijing–Taipei dispute and on its intention to continue to sell arms to the island. Although the United States had to abrogate its defence treaty with Taiwan (technically, the Republic of China), the Taiwan Relations Act of the US Congress, signed by the president in April 1979, committed the US to maintain a capacity to 'resist any resort to force … that would jeopardize the security … of the people on Taiwan'. Much as this was resented by Beijing, it did not stop the Chinese leaders from cultivating the United States as a strategic partner, nor from seeking to deepen economic and other relations with the US.

The Taiwan issue had in effect become a bilateral issue between the peoples on both sides of the Taiwan Strait, with the United States as the guarantor that the issue would not be settled by force. The formal position of the PRC did not change until relations were normalized in January 1979. At that point the Beijing leaders dropped their harsh threat to 'liberate' Taiwan in favour of a milder offer of 're-unification', to be based on the granting of what on paper was a considerable degree of autonomy. The threat to use force was retained, according to Deng Xiaoping, lest the island ally itself with the Soviet Union, declare independence or prolong matters unduly. The government in Taipei rejected the blandishments of Beijing, as it was buttressed by Taiwan's economic success and promises of American support. Little changed until the second half of the 1980s, when the development of economic ties across the Strait and the beginnings of democracy on the island introduced important new factors into cross-Strait relations.

Japan also reacted smartly to the dramatic news of the American opening to China by accelerating its own moves to normalize relations with its giant neighbour. But it was not before the Japanese had replaced the relatively right-wing Eishiro Sato, who had links with the Kuomintang in Taiwan, with Kakuei Tanaka as prime minister that the Chinese agreed to establish diplomatic relations in September 1972. The American *démarche* came as a shock to the Japanese – another soon followed with a major change in American economic policy of surcharging imports and ending the trade of dollars at a fixed price for gold. It was, to say the least, disconcerting for a country that had hitherto been regarded as America's most important ally in Asia to find that its democratic friend, economic partner and strategic associate had suddenly sought an alignment with communist China, Japan's giant neighbour, and until that point, their joint protagonist, without even informing Tokyo in advance. Indeed such was the fascination of China for Henry Kissinger that Mao 'went so far as to advise [him] to make sure that when he visited Asia [he] spend as much time in Tokyo as in Peking'.[12] It was as if Mao and Zhou Enlai appreciated the significance of the US alliance with Japan as a constraint upon the Soviet Union and as the bedrock of strategic stability in East Asia better than Nixon and Kissinger. Indeed, according to Kissinger the Chinese leaders never sought to play off Japan and the US against each other.[13]

Japan was therefore able to develop relations with the PRC without encountering international pressures or constraints except for those emanating from the Soviet Union. Thus Japan normalized relations with the PRC amid a piece of creative diplomacy by which it was able to maintain diplomatic relations with Taiwan in all but name.[14] The PRC, like its predecessor the ROC, waved aside potential claims to reparations then estimated to be worth US$50 billion.[15] Disputes about the sovereignty of the Senkaku (or in Chinese, Diaoyutai) Islands were put aside by joint agreement, and within three years agreements were reached about fishing, navigation and communication matters as both sides deepened their economic relations.

Until 1978, Sino-Japanese relations were conducted almost entirely as simple bilateral matters, sheltering as they did under the Japanese security alliance with the United States that the Chinese also regarded as a stabilizing factor. The issue that raised larger regional and international questions was the signing of a peace treaty. The Soviet Union was also anxious to sign such a treaty with Japan, and at the same time it was concerned by Chinese attempts to persuade Japan to sign a treaty that *inter alia* expressed opposition to 'hegemony', which was widely regarded as a Chinese code word for the Soviet Union. However, Soviet–Japanese negotiations broke down on Soviet refusal to acknowledge even the legitimacy of the Japanese right to dispute ownership of the four islands to the north of Japan. Soviet diplomacy was judged to be overbearing, and that paved the way for the Chinese to obtain Japanese agreement to sign a Treaty of Peace and Friendship in August 1978 with them instead. To assuage Japanese sentiments the Chinese agreed that opposition to hegemony should be mentioned in the preamble rather than being dealt with in a separate clause. They also accepted the wording that the treaty was not directed against any third party.

It was nevertheless the Soviet factor that brought Sino-Japanese relations back into the maelstrom of international and regional politics. In the Soviet perception, the United States had already adopted a more pronounced anti-Soviet position in the course of the visit to China in May 1978 by Z. Brzezinski, President Carter's national security adviser,[16] and now the Sino-Japanese treaty contributed to the Soviet sense of isolation and encirclement. In the view of the Soviet leaders, they were now confronted in East Asia by an alignment of the most populous, the most economically successful and the most powerful states (i.e., China, Japan and the United States). That may well have played a part in the Soviet decision to support Vietnam in its conquest of Cambodia in late 1978 and in its own invasion of Afghanistan a year later. The Sino-Japanese treaty also contributed to emboldening the Chinese to mount their attack on Vietnam in early 1979. Whether or not Japan's leaders appreciated the larger significance of their treaty with the PRC, Sino-Japanese relations were necessarily a part of the international dimensions of the Asia-Pacific region and could not be seen or understood primarily through the prism of bilateral relations, important though they were for both countries. Nevertheless Sino-Japanese relations always had dimensions that could only be understood in a bilateral context.[17]

Interestingly, the situation on the Korean peninsula was not greatly altered by the change in Sino-American relations. The North felt that its capacity to pursue an independent course had been considerably limited as it saw its two giant neighbours and allies separately seek détente with its principal enemy, the United States. In 1972 it made a gesture towards opening talks with the South and it began to purchase industrial plants and other forms of advanced technology from the smaller capitalist countries. However, little came of these cautious beginnings and the North was left in default of loan repayments to a number of countries. It was not until the latter half of the 1980s that the impact of the Gorbachev changes in the Soviet Union and the primacy of economics in China's foreign policy began to make a difference to the international dimensions of the Korean divide between North and South.

The 1970s were still marked by the North having worse relations with the Soviet Union than with China. Although the Soviet Union no longer sought to control the North, it nevertheless sought to constrain it from possible adventurous acts that might embarrass the Soviet Union in its relations with the United States, in what was still one of the world's most dangerous trouble spots. Unlike in the case of Vietnam, the opportunity to recruit North Korea to the Soviet side because of China's alleged 'defection' to America simply did not arise. The Koreans did not regard the Chinese as a long-standing historical threat to their independence, nor could the Soviet Union assist the North in achieving nationalist aims of unification without considerable risk to its own national security interests. On the contrary, these Soviet concerns led its leaders to dilute their support for the claims of the North to be the only sovereign body with the legitimate right to rule the whole of the Korean peninsula. Instead they suggested to the North that the model of the two Germanys should be applied to Korea.

The Chinese, by contrast, quickly apologized for the excesses of the Cultural Revolution, and Zhou Enlai's visit in 1970 assured Kim of Chinese acceptance of the sole legitimacy of the North. At that point he shared the Northern view that the danger of Japanese militarism was once again evident. China's new relations with the United States that began only a year later entailed a certain cooling of relations. The two allies also began to differ on the alleged menace of Japan, and by 1978 the Chinese had signed a treaty with Japan. Nevertheless the North continued to tilt towards China without cutting off links with the Soviet Union. This may be seen from the North's criticism of the Vietnamese invasion of Cambodia and its corresponding silence about the Chinese attack on Vietnam. Not surprisingly, in this period the Chinese rather than the Soviets were the principal suppliers of weaponry to the North.[18]

The South was principally concerned about the depth and durability of the American defence commitment in Korea. Indeed that had been a primary consideration in the deployment of 50,000 combat troops to fight in South Vietnam in response to President Johnson's request for international support for the American war effort. The Nixon and Ford administrations were careful to give assurances of continued support to South Korea after the opening to China and in the course of the stages of the American withdrawal from South Vietnam, culminating in the final debacle of 1975. However, the anxieties that were raised the following year by the incoming Carter administration because of the campaign pledge to withdraw American forces from South Korea were not completely assuaged, even though President Carter was soon persuaded to change his mind.[19] These considerations were not a function of tripolarity, but rather they arose from the impact on the United States of its disastrous experience in Vietnam and from different assessments of principally Soviet behaviour. In other words, the Korean situation continued to be dominated by the Cold War considerations associated with the bipolar system, even though that system itself had weakened. The reason for the persistence of the stalemate stemmed from the mutual hostilities of North and South supported by the external powers, rather than primarily from the external powers themselves.

The impact of the Sino-American rapprochement and the emergence of tripolarity was immediate and far reaching in Southeast Asia. America's new relations with China coupled with the pursuit of détente with the Soviet Union removed the last vestiges of the original strategic purposes for the American intervention in Vietnam. The potential success of the North could no longer be seen as a victory by proxy for the geopolitical interests of the Chinese communists. Nevertheless the American process of withdrawal was prolonged, principally because of the perceived need to withdraw 'with honour' in order to sustain America's credibility as an ally and to assuage domestic forces. To this end the United States sought to use the linkage with the Soviet Union to bring pressure to bear upon North Vietnam and to persuade the Soviet Union that it should act with restraint in international affairs if détente was to work as a basis for international order. In the event, the negotiations with the North dragged on in a context in which it was by no means apparent that Moscow could dictate to Hanoi or that Hanoi could determine Soviet reactions.

Meanwhile the repercussions of the Sino-American alignment were bringing about new divisions and realignments in Indo-China that were to culminate in the Third Indo-China War. The new challenges from the changes in the region's international environment had the effect of transforming the Association of Southeast Asian Nations (ASEAN) into a more cohesive diplomatic community. These changes must be set within a wider context than that of the emergence of tripolarity alone. The British had decided in January 1968 to accelerate the timetable of their military disengagement from East of Suez. Three months later a Soviet naval flotilla made its first appearance in the Indian Ocean, which was soon to be seen as the harbinger of a more active Soviet naval presence in that part of the world. In March that year, after the Tet offensive by the Vietnamese communists, President Johnson's decision not to seek re-election and to pursue a solution by negotiation was seen as a decisive turning point in acknowledging the limits of American power. This was confirmed when, to the manifest unease of America's Asian allies, the recently elected President Nixon stated in Guam in July 1969 that the United States was no longer prepared to undertake principal combat roles in their defence. The American opening to China was seen therefore as indicating a new role in the region for China. It was also to pave the way for introducing the Sino-Soviet conflict as an additional interposition in the region.

The impact of these changes was felt deepest in Indo-China. This was not immediately apparent, as China's leaders sought to assuage Vietnamese fears of Chinese betrayal. Chinese aid continued to flow and Chinese diplomatic support for North Vietnam remained formally correct. But the North Vietnamese, who were already reliant upon the Soviet Union for the supply of advanced weaponry and had reason to fear Chinese attempts to subordinate Vietnamese interests to their own, leaned still further towards the Soviet side. In January 1973 the Americans and the North Vietnamese finally signed agreements in Paris that confirmed the final American military withdrawals. Two years later, in April 1975, the North swiftly overran a demoralized South. Meanwhile the Chinese took the opportunity in 1974 to seize by force the remaining part of the Paracel Islands occupied by the South. These islands in the South China Sea are claimed by both China and Vietnam, and the Chinese opportunistic seizure further added to the growing enmity between Hanoi and Beijing that was still largely concealed behind a veil of diplomatic niceties. However, the American debacle in Indo-China exacerbated Chinese fears of a Soviet attempt to fill the vacuum left by the departing American forces.

The critical point of division between China and Vietnam centred upon Cambodia. April 1975 also witnessed the final victory of the Khmer Rouge in their capture of Phnom Penh from the forces of Lon Nol, whose pro-Western army had ousted Prince Sihanouk five years earlier. The virulent anti-Vietnamese nationalism of the Khmer Rouge served Chinese interests as it denied Vietnam the opportunity of dominating the whole of Indo-China. But the prospects of finding a basis of accommodation between the competing parties did not materialize, as the Khmer Rouge initiated a series of provocative assaults along the borders with Vietnam. These in turn heightened Vietnamese fears about Chinese attempts to limit their independence. Emboldened by its closer links with the Soviet Union, the government in Hanoi which had experienced difficulties in imposing the command economy upon the South took measures in 1978 to encourage the ethnic Chinese (who, as elsewhere in Southeast Asia, dominated much of the local commerce) to leave. There also emerged a conjunction of interests between the Soviet desire to constrain China and the Vietnamese security objectives of removing the Khmer Rouge challenge and defying Chinese attempts to prevent the Vietnamese from asserting their claims to exercise special influence over Indo-China as a whole.

By the end of 1978 the international, regional and local lines of conflict had combined to bring about the Third Indo-China War. Backed by membership of COMECON in June and by a formal friendship treaty with the Soviet Union in November, the Vietnamese invaded Cambodia on 25 December, captured Phnom Penh on 7 January, and imposed a regime of their choice. The Khmer Rouge forces retreated as guerrillas to hideouts, primarily near the borders with Thailand. The Chinese, having signed a treaty with Japan in the summer and after agreeing to normalize relations with the United States in December 1978, followed up with visits by Deng Xiaoping himself to both Washington and Tokyo in which he vowed to 'teach Vietnam a lesson'. Despite obtaining less than enthusiastic backing, the Chinese launched an attack on 17 February 1979 into northern Vietnam, ostensibly because of border violations. Three weeks later the Chinese troops were withdrawn after inflicting considerable damage, but not before their limitations as a fighting force had been exposed by the Vietnamese. This then resulted in a stalemate that lasted ten years, in which an internationally isolated Vietnam was dependent upon the Soviet Union to sustain its dominant position in Cambodia while being confronted on the margins by resistance forces that enjoyed international legitimacy and the support of China, the United States and the ASEAN countries.[20]

The impact of these international and regional changes to the security environment of the ASEAN countries was to facilitate their emergence as a more cohesive diplomatic body after first highlighting some of their different security perspectives. Their first response to the new international position of China illustrated these divisions. In 1971, under pressure from the US State Department to resist the PRC's claim to the China seat, the Philippines acquiesced in the interests of its American alliance; Thailand and even non-aligned Indonesia abstained; but Malaysia and Singapore voted in favour of the PRC. Singapore was concerned about the sentiments of its majority community; and the Malaysian government sought to find an accommodation with Beijing so as 'to demonstrate to the country's resident Chinese community and to its insurgent Communist Party that its legitimacy was recognized and endorsed by its counterpart in Beijing'.[21] In fact this was the origin of the initiative to declare Southeast Asia a Zone of Peace, Freedom and Neutrality (ZOPFAN). As first conceived, Malaysia sought formal neutralization to be guaranteed by the external powers including the PRC. But at Indonesia's insistence, all reference to external guarantees was removed and the resulting declaration of November 1971 specifically called for recognition and respect for a ZOPFAN that would be 'free from any form or manner of interference by outside powers'.[22]

In 1974 Malaysia became the first ASEAN country to recognize the PRC. Thailand and the Philippines followed suit a year later but not until after the victories of the revolutionaries in Cambodia and Vietnam. Indeed, the victories fundamentally changed the regional security environment of ASEAN. The American debacle in Vietnam raised doubts about its residuary security role in Southeast Asia, at a time when the relatively conservative governments of ASEAN suddenly found themselves directly confronted by triumphant revolutionary regimes to the north. In response a summit was held in February 1976 that sought to affirm the purpose of the association as a body primarily concerned with internal security and of its vision for an attainment of a regional order that emphasized the peaceful settlement of disputes. It held out the prospect of the socialist Indo-Chinese states becoming associated with ASEAN through a 'Treaty of Amity and Cooperation'.

As the new lines of conflict emerged between Cambodia and Vietnam, China and Vietnam, and China and the Soviet Union, the ASEAN countries found themselves being courted in 1978 by the two sets of disputants. Vietnam's invasion and occupation of Cambodia proved to be the turning point. By imposing by force on a recalcitrant neighbour a government of their own choosing, the Vietnamese had violated a fundamental tenet that held ASEAN together. But perhaps more to the point, they challenged the immediate national security interests of Thailand. As the frontline state, Thai interests predominated in shaping the ASEAN response. However, they did not entirely override the long-standing tendency among ASEAN members, especially Malaysia and Indonesia, to regard China as the long-term threat to the region and to see Vietnam as something of a buffer against the spread of Chinese influence. Thus the ASEAN response was to avoid condemning Vietnam while at the same time refusing to accept the legitimacy of the new government in Phnom Penh. Accordingly, recognition continued to be granted to the previous government and state of the Khmer Rouge – regardless of the latter's gruesome record.

The result was a situation in which Thailand in effect forged an alliance with China, alongside its existing formal alliance with the United States, that emboldened it to confront Vietnam by helping the Chinese in particular to assist the remnant Khmer Rouge and other resistance forces lodged in sanctuaries along the porous Thai border with Cambodia. Vietnam, aided by the Soviet Union, maintained an army of occupation in Cambodia that was able to provide relative security for its puppet government to build a degree of administrative effectiveness. However, Vietnam was unable to wipe out the resistance forces without risking a potentially wider conflict with Thailand. Meanwhile ASEAN played an effective diplomatic role in orchestrating the isolation of Vietnam, especially at the United Nations. ASEAN lacked the necessary military muscle or corporate solidarity to change the stalemate. For example, a resolute Vietnam saw no reason to respond sympathetically to Malaysian and Indonesian attempts to draw it into a diplomatic settlement. The stalemate was only broken ten years after the initial invasion, when the Soviet Union was no longer able to continue to supply Vietnam with the material it needed to prosecute the war and underpin its economy.

Tripolarity phase II, 1980–89: from confrontation to the end of the Cold War

The Soviet invasion of Afghanistan at the end of 1979 ended whatever remaining interest the Carter administration still had in détente. The president's complaint that his opposite in the Kremlin had 'lied' to him was symptomatic of the view that the Soviet Union was not a responsible treaty partner. As a result, in his last year as president, Carter initiated a significant rebuilding of American military power that was to be carried to great lengths by his successor, President Reagan, with whom the policy was to be identified. The deterioration in relations with the Soviet Union also had an effect on American policy towards China. President Carter authorized the export to China of 'non-lethal' military equipment, including advanced computers and other high technology products.[23]

From a Soviet perspective, the politics of the strategic triangle had already changed more than a year earlier, when in May 1978 Carter's national security adviser, Z. Brzezinski, had openly indicated an American tilt towards China.[24] But the American response to Afghanistan was such as to persuade the Soviet leaders that it was no longer a question of triangular politics, but one of a growing direct confrontation of the Soviet Union by the United States.[25] The Soviet position in the Asia-Pacific had worsened considerably. It was faced by a hostile coalition of Japan, China and the United States, with the latter now embarked on a huge military build-up. Additionally its major ally, Vietnam, was also isolated and required considerable economic and military support. Lacking also in extensive economic relations in the region as well as being diplomatically isolated because of the double effect of the invasions of Cambodia and Afghanistan, the Soviet Union possessed only military power with which to advance its interests. Having become bogged down in Afghanistan and with its ally stalemated in Cambodia, there was no clear avenue that was open to the Soviet leaders to translate their military power into political advantage, especially as the United States had embarked on a course of a rapid military build-up. The opportunities for reaching new understandings on the basis of détente had gone.

As perhaps the most skilful practitioners of realpolitik, the Chinese sensed the Soviet predicament at an early stage.[26] In April 1979 the Chinese proposed the resumption of talks with the Soviet Union, ostensibly in accordance with the terms of the long defunct thirty-year treaty of 1950. Having consolidated their relations with the United States, the Chinese may have been emboldened by the lack of a Soviet move to defend the Vietnamese ally when it was under attack from themselves. The Chinese initiative may also have been a portent of the Chinese diplomacy of seeking a favourable and peaceful international environment in which to pursue the priorities of domestic economic development. Ideology was ceasing to be a problem between the two sides as the Chinese had begun to dismantle much of Mao's ideological legacy. Sino-Soviet talks began in September, but were then suspended by the Chinese after the Soviet invasion of Afghanistan. However, the domestic economic imperatives in China were such that there was a steady push to improve relations with the Soviet Union. Before long a succession of cultural, scientific and other kinds of delegation visited each country. Trade began to pick up. The Soviet Union had responded in kind in 1981 and in March 1982 Brezhnev delivered a speech in Tashkent aimed primarily at a Chinese audience, in which he stated for the first time in nearly twenty years that in the view of the Kremlin China was a socialist country.[27]

From the perspective of China's leaders, and Deng Xiaoping in particular, the new opening to the Soviet Union was important as it reduced tension and perhaps added some leverage to China's dealings with the United States. But it was the relationship with America that was vital. America was the key to the opening of China to the international economy; it was still the centre and powerhouse of high technology in the world; and its forces provided the kind of strategic stability in the Asia-Pacific that had proved beneficial to China. The declaration of an 'independent foreign policy' at the CCP Congress in September 1982 should not be taken at face value. It did not mean that China had placed itself in the middle ground between the two superpowers. China still tilted strongly towards the United States on the important strategic questions. Thus, throughout the 1980s the American intelligence monitoring facility for observing Soviet missile tests in Central Asia remained in place in Xinjiang. The PRC and the US continued to pursue parallel policies in Cambodia and Afghanistan where they each supported the resistance forces and kept up the pressure on Vietnam and the Soviet Union respectively. Certainly irritations grew in Sino-American relations. The Taiwan issue was a problem in the first two years of the Reagan administration and the Americans were displeased by Chinese criticisms of American behaviour in the Middle East and Central America, but the Chinese were more circumspect closer to home.[28]

In fact, by the end of 1982 the pattern of triangular relations had begun to change because of changes in the underlying distribution of power between the protagonists, rather than because of any mechanistic properties of the triangle itself. The huge American military build-up coupled with the adverse Soviet strategic position was the key. As noted earlier, George Shultz, who replaced Alexander Haig as the American secretary of state in August 1982, reflected some of the implications of this by according Japan a higher priority in US policies in Asia. Essentially, the US no longer needed China in order to deal with the Soviet strategic challenge. Interestingly, Deng Xiaoping was careful to insist that there could be no consummation of Sino-Soviet relations before the Soviet Union had made the concessions of removing the three famous 'obstacles' – ending Soviet support for Vietnam in Cambodia, withdrawing the Soviet occupation forces from Afghanistan, and reducing the Soviet military threat on the Chinese border. These obstacles did not prevent distinct improvements in Sino-Soviet relations over the course of the decade, but they did signify to the Americans that the Chinese were not in danger of realigning with the Soviet Union. Meanwhile the Reagan administration had retreated from Reagan's declared intention, during the election campaign, of restoring state relations with Taiwan. But it withstood Chinese threats to downgrade relations over the question of advanced arms sales to Taiwan. Nevertheless a new modus vivendi was reached between Washington and Beijing after the Americans agreed to increase high-tech transfers to China. In practice, however, the Americans had begun to downgrade China's significance in the management of strategic relations with the Soviet Union.[29]

The unravelling of the Cold War and the end of the 'triangle'

The economic stagnation of the Soviet Union had become evident even before Brezhnev's death. But the full scale of the problem did not become clear until the accession of Gorbachev in 1985. The Soviet economy was declining and general living conditions were deteriorating, more closely resembling those of a Third World rather than an advanced industrial country. The economy had been badly skewed in favour of the military. Gorbachev and his team of reformers recognized that there was a foreign policy dimension to this sorry state of affairs and initiated a new policy, under the guise of 'New Thinking', that sought to reverse the excessive reliance that had been put upon military force.[30]

It soon became evident that Gorbachev's first foreign policy priority was to manage relations with the West. In fact the new Soviet approach seemed to be to disentangle itself from costly regional conflicts in the Third World so as to focus more clearly on bilateral security issues with the United States. In the process, China was becoming marginalized in the management of security relations between the two superpowers. Thus China played little or no part in the negotiations that led to Soviet consent in the Intermediate Nuclear Force (INF) agreement of December 1987 to eliminate all of its SS-20 missiles, including those in Asia. Similarly, China was not a party to the international agreement of 1988 by which the Soviet Union pledged to withdraw all its armed forces from Afghanistan. Yet China was a major beneficiary of both.[31]

In two major speeches in Vladivostok in 1986 and Krasnoyarsk in 1988, Gorbachev addressed a number of Chinese concerns. He accepted in principle the Chinese claim that their riverine borders in Northeast Asia followed the middle of the main channel (the Thalweg Principle) rather than the Chinese bank, as had previously been asserted since Tsarist times. He also promised unilaterally to withdraw some Soviet forces from Mongolia and Afghanistan and to negotiate a reduction of forces along the Sino-Soviet border. Additionally, he pledged to withdraw from Cam Ranh Bay, but he argued that that should be tied to an American withdrawal from Subic Bay in the Philippines. More to the point, from a Chinese point of view, Gorbachev began to cut Soviet assistance to Vietnam, after having indicated that he would not allow Soviet obligations to that country to stand in the way of his larger objective of improving relations with China. By late 1988 he had agreed to press Vietnam to withdraw unconditionally from Cambodia and announced the unilateral reduction of more than a quarter of a million Soviet troops from Asia. The Vietnamese then declared that all their forces would be withdrawn from Cambodia by September 1989, irrespective of a Cambodian settlement. This paved the way for what was termed the 'normalization' of Sino-Soviet relations through a visit to Beijing by Gorbachev himself in May 1989. As an indication of how great the change in strategic relations had become, the American side positively welcomed the event, as symbolized by a visit to Beijing by President Bush himself three months earlier. The Sino-Soviet summit, which was overshadowed by the Tiananmen demonstrations, did nothing to harm Sino-American relations. It took place at a time of improved Soviet–American relations, and neither the Chinese nor the Soviet leaders wanted to put at risk their respective relations with the United States.[32]

At that point the impact of huge domestic upheavals took over. The unprecedented demonstrations in Tiananmen Square that culminated in the massacre of civilians by the Chinese People's Liberation Army on 4 June not only threw Sino-American relations into crisis, but they also appalled Gorbachev and prevented any further substantive developments in Sino-Soviet relations. These events were followed in the autumn by the sudden collapse of the communist regimes in Eastern Europe, starting with East Germany and the breach of the

Berlin Wall, which has been taken as the symbolic event that marked the end of the Cold War. Collectively, these events also signified the final end of the strategic triangle. The apparent collapse of Sino-American relations was not accompanied by an improvement in Sino-Soviet relations and, in any case, the United States and the Soviet Union had embarked on a closer relationship based on entirely new terms, by which the Americans lent their support to Gorbachev and his reform programme while he in turn ceased to oppose American foreign policy initiatives. In short, the Cold War between the two superpowers was over.

The regional impact

The Korean peninsula at first experienced a heightening of tension in the early 1980s, before the accession of Gorbachev changed the course of Soviet policy. From 1985 onwards the impact of the Soviet 'New Thinking' coupled with the priority the Chinese gave to economics paved the way for the transformation of the foreign relations of the two Koreas. By the time of the end of the Cold War, South Korea had successfully developed its 'northern policy' of cultivating relations with China and the Soviet Union, and it was clearly only a matter of time before full recognition and diplomatic relations would be established. Although that in itself would not necessarily bring about a settlement of the Korean question, it would disengage it from the conflict of the superpowers.

Such an outcome was far from obvious in the early 1980s. The continued build-up of Soviet naval power in the Pacific had accentuated the importance of its nuclear strategic forces in the Sea of Okhotsk that were targeted on the United States and the means to defend them with advanced weaponry. This in turn raised concern in the American forces in the Far East and in South Korea. That was the context in which the South acquired advanced military aircraft from the US. The North, possessing only the relatively obsolescent Chinese aircraft and troubled by China's relations with the United States, turned to the Soviet Union. At that point the more conservative Chernenko had succeeded Andropov as the Soviet leader. During his brief rule he presided over a cooling of relations with China that was marked *inter alia* by gaining access to North Korean ports for the Soviet Pacific Fleet and by establishing rights to overfly Korean territory, thus gaining better intelligence about Manchuria. The Soviet Union also supplied North Korea with more advanced aircraft and related weapons systems. The breakthrough in their relations was symbolized by Kim Il-Sung's first official visit to Moscow for more than twenty years in May 1984.[33]

With the accession of Gorbachev in March 1985 the pattern began to change. The commitment to reform at home and the development of a foreign policy based on 'New Thinking' inclined the Soviet Union to find ways of disengaging from regional conflicts, to reach arms control agreements with the United States and to improve relations with China. This immediately reduced the scope for North Korea to play off its two giant allies against each other. The Chinese meanwhile had begun to develop economic relations with the South by using the route through Hong Kong. By 1987 their indirect trade was valued at three times that of China's trade with the North. The Soviet Union had also indicated an interest in cultivating ties with the South. To the dismay of the North, both attended the 1988 Olympic Games in Seoul.

Unlike the situation at the end of the 1960s, the South Korean economy now far outshone that of the North. In 1984 the GDP of the South stood at US$83.2 billion, more than double the North's US$39.9 billion.[34] Constrained by the reduction of support from its two giant neighbours and confronted by a South whose economy was technologically more advanced and whose rate of growth continued to outstrip its own, the North attempted in a small way to open its own economy to the capitalist world along lines pioneered by the Chinese. But it found its options severely circumscribed as it was both unwilling to reform its domestic economy and unable to pay outstanding debts to Western countries remaining from its last attempt to acquire Western technology, more than a decade earlier in 1973–74. Thus the impact of the changed relations between the superpowers and of China's economic-based foreign policy was to reduce the significance of the Korean peninsula in the management of global strategic relations. This in turn left the North as an isolated Stalinist state at a disadvantage with the South, which by this stage had become one of East Asia's 'little tigers' – a 'newly industrializing country' (NIC). These conditions paved the way for the beginning of a dialogue between the two Koreas. But the basis of the divide between the two as sole claimants for legitimacy for Korea as a whole remained.

Japan was little affected, either by the decline or by the re-emergence of détente. Unlike the West Europeans, the Japanese neither attempted to pursue a separate path of improved relations with the Soviet Union, nor entertained the same kind of concerns about the reliability of the American security guarantee. The Japanese public opposition in 1982 to the Soviet deployment of SS-20s in the Far East had less to do with any fears about the possible 'de-coupling' of the United States from Japan and 'had more to do with hurt national pride at having been left out of East–West arms deliberations'.[35] This was illustrative of those countries that were separately allied to the United States, primary among whom was Japan, who having consolidated its new statehood and attained considerable economic success, went on to develop a sense of patriotic pride and a national assertiveness that found expression in a degree of resentment against what were regarded as the overbearing demands of the United States. From the American point of view, it was considered only proper that these countries should shoulder more of the defence burden under these more propitious circumstances. Hence Japan came under increasing pressure from the United States. Japan did indeed become more active in using economic and diplomatic instruments that in many ways paralleled American strategic policies, and by the end of the 1980s Japan had agreed to undertake responsibility for protecting the seas within a thousand-mile radius of Tokyo. But part of the problem was that, unlike in the case of NATO, there was no regional security arrangement that bound the various allies with the United States in a common approach to the region. Consequently, anything that went beyond Japan's immediate security concerns as understood in Tokyo was in fact resisted.

Perhaps more than the United States, Japan had a special interest in promoting trade and economic development in East Asia as a way of encouraging political stability. For reasons of geography the region was more important to Japanese security than it was to that of the United States. As the constraints of bipolarity diminished, it was to be expected that the differences in emphasis between the United States and Japan should become more evident. As we shall see, Japan was the most reluctant of the G-7 countries to apply sanctions against China after the Tiananmen killings, and it was the first to rescind them.

As the significance of bipolarity declined, long-standing trading problems between Japan and the United States acquired more salience. The yawning trade gap in Japan's favour, which continued to grow despite the oil shocks of the 1970s, became a source of deepening recriminations between the two sides. Having encouraged the development of the Japanese economy during the Cold War period, in part by allowing exceptionally favourable terms of trade that did not involve reciprocity, the United States throughout the 1980s was continually engaged in a vain struggle against some of its consequences. It was one thing for an American president to play down the issue during the period of high confrontation with the Soviet Union, but it was quite another when that confrontation began to abate in the second half of the 1980s. However, the full significance of the reduced tolerance of the United States was not to become clear until the Cold War was well and truly over.

The weakening of the significance of bipolarity set the context for a remarkable transformation of Taiwan. In the late 1980s it embarked upon the road of democratization at home and developing economic relations with mainland China across the Straits (primarily through Hong Kong). This was the product of a particular combination of international, regional and domestic factors that in their own way illustrate the dynamic qualities of the interactions of international politics in the region. As we have seen, China's leaders had already perceived by the mid-1980s that the threat from the Soviet Union had abated, and they had accordingly placed an even higher priority on economics in their foreign relations. This led to a remarkable growth in China's economic relations with South Korea – which, of course, had its own reasons for improving relations with the giant ally of North Korea. At the same time Hong Kong was developing ever closer economic ties with neighbouring Guangdong Province – a trend that was intensified by the Sino-British agreement in 1984 to revert sovereignty of the colony to China in 1997. Sino-American ties had settled considerably after the irritations of the early 1980s, so that the Taiwan issue was no longer prominent on their agenda.

Taiwan had already reacted to some of these changes by agreeing to participate in several international institutions alongside the representatives of the PRC, even though this required dropping the official name of the Republic of China. For example, its athletes participated in the 1984 Olympic Games under the rubric of 'Chinese Taipei'. That neatly bypassed the question as to whether it was a rival claimant to the legitimacy of the Chinese state or merely a Chinese province. These changes to the external environment of Taiwan coincided with domestic developments that made continuation of the status quo increasingly untenable. Kuomintang authoritarian rule was subject to increasing challenges from a growing middle class that was the product of the successful economic development of the island. There was a need for a generational change in many of the political institutions, notably the legislature, as many of the original main-landers who came with Chiang Kai-shek in the late 1940s were incapacitated by advanced age. There was a perceived need to broaden the social bases of the ruling institutions by incorporating more of the local Taiwanese. The proclaimed positions that sustained Kuomintang rule were losing legitimacy, and the abso-lutely negative response to the appeals from the mainland for greater contact across the Straits carried less support. Moreover, there was a fear that Taiwan would lose its competitive economic position in the rapidly changing Asia-Pacific economy and miss out on the opportunities presented by the opening up of the Chinese economy. Fortunately for Taiwan, the respected Chiang Ching-kuo (Chiang Kai-shek's son and heir) was still at the helm to initiate the beginnings of the transition to democracy and the opening to China.[36]

International concerns in Southeast Asia centred primarily on the Cambodian question. Here too the developments that were later to make a settlement possible should be understood as flowing from the interactions of international, regional and local political developments. The new détente between the Soviet Union and the United States that was manifested by the arms control agreement of 1987 and the agreement by the Soviet Union in 1988 to withdraw from Afghanistan, the priority that Gorbachev attached to improving relations with China, and the constraints that were imposed by his domestic reform agenda and the foreign policy based on 'New Thinking', were incompatible with continuing to extend to Vietnam the economic and military assistance that alone made it possible for Vietnam to maintain forces of occupation in Cambodia. Meanwhile at its Sixth Party Congress in December 1986, Vietnam's leaders committed themselves to replace the conventional socialist economic model with a programme of renova-tion (Doi Moi), as economic failure was damaging the legitimacy of the regime, but they still upheld their 'special' relations with Laos and Cambodia.[37] After the limits to Soviet aid were made clear in 1988, Vietnam announced in April 1989 that it would withdraw its forces from Cambodia in September. This effectively removed Cambodia from being a critical issue in either Soviet–American or Sino-Soviet relations. That, however, still left unresolved the competition between Vietnam and China for a balance of power in Indo-China favourable to their respective interests. That had found expression in their support for opposing sides in the Cambodian civil war. In 1987 and 1988 the Vietnamese attempted in vain to reach a negotiated settlement that would have excluded the Chinese and ostracized the Khmer Rouge (the faction that had enjoyed Chinese support as the most effective and most determined opponent of Vietnam). But it was not until the Vietnamese sought to make their peace with the Chinese in 1989 and 1990 and deferred to China's right to broker a deal among the indigenous Cambodian factions that the way was opened for reaching a settlement. Vietnam had found that it 'could no longer reconcile imperative economic reforms with the preservation of its hegemony over Cambodia'.[38] This reduced the significance of Cambodia as a critical issue in regional affairs.

Although ASEAN was active as a diplomatic community in isolating Vietnam and in maintaining international support for the Cambodian resistance, it was not critical to determining the outcome of the conflict. Indonesia did join with France as co-chair of an international conference on Cambodia, which met first in July 1989 in Paris with the other ASEAN countries participating. But the arrangements for power sharing within Cambodia proved elusive at that stage. That problem could only be addressed after the contest between China and Vietnam had been settled in favour of the former. A final agreement on power sharing arrangements was not reached before the end of the Cold War.[39]

Notes

1 Considerable differences exist in the scholarly literature about the character and significance of the strategic triangle. Compare, for example, Steven I. Levine, 'China's Foreign Policy in the Strategic Triangle' in June Dryer (ed.), *Chinese Defense and Foreign Policy* (New York: Paragon House, 1988), which tends to discount China's significance, with Thomas W. Robinson, 'On the Further Evolution of the Strategic Triangle', and Lowell Dittmer, 'The Strategic Triangle: A Critical Review', both in Ilpyong Kim (ed.), *The Strategic Triangle: China, the United States and the Soviet Union* (New York: Paragon House, 1987). There have also been attempts to apply game theory or mechanistic principle to explain the operational dynamics of the triangle. See for example, Gerald Segal, *The Great Power Triangle* (London: Macmillan, 1982); Lowell Dittmer, 'The Strategic Triangle' (*op. cit.*) and his earlier 'The Strategic Triangle: An Elementary Game Theoretical Analysis', *World Politics* (July 1981), pp.485–515. For a retrospective account of the complexities of the relationships, see Robert Ross (ed.), *China, the United States, and the Soviet Union: Tripolarity and Policy Making in the Cold War* (New York and London: M.E. Sharpe, 1993).
2 See Lawrence Freedman, 'The Triangle in Western Europe' in Gerald Segal (ed.), *The China Factor: Peking and the Superpowers* (London: Croom Helm, 1982), pp.105–25.
3 Henry Kissinger, *The White House Years* (London: Weidenfeld & Nicholson and Michael Joseph, 1979), p.836.
4 *Ibid.*, p.764.
5 Banning N. Garret and Bonnie S. Glaser, 'From Nixon to Reagan: China's Changing Role in American Strategy' in Kenneth A. Oye et al. (eds), *Eagle Resurgent? The Reagan Era in American Foreign Policy* (Boston: Little Brown, 1987).
6 Robert Legvold, 'Sino-Soviet Relations: The American Factor' in Ross (ed.), *China, The United States and the Soviet Union* (*op. cit.*), especially pp.66–80.
7 See Kissinger's account of the Indo-Pakistan crisis in his *The White House Years* (*op. cit.*), pp.843–918 (especially pp.913–18).
8 Stephen Sestanovich, 'U.S. Policy Toward the Soviet Union, 1970–90: The Impact of China' in Ross (ed.), *China, the United States, and the Soviet Union* (*op. cit.*), especially pp.134–35.
9 Alexander M. Haig Jr, *Caveat: Realism, Reagan, and Foreign Policy* (New York: Macmillan, 1984), p.194.
10 George P. Shultz, *Turmoil and Triumph: My Years as Secretary of State* (New York: Charles Scribner's Sons, 1993), p.173.
11 Kissinger, *The White House Years* (*op. cit.*), p.1086.
12 *Ibid.*, p.1089.
13 *Ibid.*, p.1090.

14 David N. Rowe, *Informal 'Diplomatic Relations': The Case of Japan and the Republic of China, 1972–74* (Hamden, CT: Shoe String Press, 1975).

15 Chae-Jin Lee, *China and Japan, New Economic Diplomacy* (Stanford: Hoover Institution Press: Stanford University, 1974) p.10.

16 Legvold, 'Sino-Soviet Relations' (*op. cit.*), pp.69–70.

17 For the best account of these, see Allen S. Whiting, *China Eyes Japan* (Berkeley: University of California Press, 1989). See also Laura Newby, *Sino-Japanese Relations: China's Perspective* (London: Routledge, for the Royal Institute of International affairs, 1988).

18 For a clear account of the North's relations with its two giant neighbours, see Ralph N. Clough, 'The Soviet Union and the Two Koreas' in Donald S. Zagoria (ed.), *Soviet Policy in East Asia* (A Council on Foreign Relations Book, New Haven: Yale University Press, 1982), pp.175–200.

19 Nam Joo Hong, *America's Commitment to the Security of South Korea: The First Decade of the Nixon Doctrine* (Cambridge: Cambridge University Press, 1986).

20 For accounts of the origins and development of the Third Indo-China War, see David W.P. Elliot (ed.), *The Third Indo-China Conflict* (Boulder: Westview Press, 1981); Grant Evans and Kevin Rowley, *Red Brotherhood at War* (London: Verso, 1984); Nayan Chanda, *Brother Enemy: The War After the War* (San Diego: Harcourt Brace Jovanovich, 1986); and Robert S. Ross, *The Indochina Tangle; China's Vietnam Policy, 1975–1979* (New York: Colombia University Press, 1988).

21 Michael Leifer, *ASEAN and the Security of South-East Asia* (London and New York: Routledge, 1989), p.55.

22 *Ibid.*, pp.147–50.

23 For details, see Harry Harding, *A Fragile Relationship: The United States and China since 1972* (Washington, DC: The Brookings Institution, 1992), pp.91–94.

24 Legvold, 'Sino-Soviet Relations' (*op. cit.*), pp.69–70.

25 *Ibid.*, pp.76–80.

26 Kissinger described them as 'the most unsentimental practitioners of balance-of-power politics I have encountered' (*The White House Years* (*op. cit.*), pp.1087–88).

27 For accounts of Sino-Soviet relations, see Chi Su, 'The Strategic Triangle and China's Soviet Policy' in Ross (ed.), *China, the United States and the Soviet Union* (*op. cit.*), pp.39–61; Gerald Segal, *Sino-Soviet Relations After Mao* (London: International Institute of Strategic Studies, Adelphi Papers no.202, 1985); Guocang Huan, 'Sino-Soviet Relations' in Yufan Hao and Guocang Huan (eds), *The Chinese View of the World* (New York: Pantheon, 1989); and Thomas G. Hart, *Sino-Soviet Relations: Re-Examining the Prospects for Normalization* (Hants: Gower, 1987).

28 For the best and most detailed account of Sino-American relations in this period that nevertheless tends to exaggerate the depths of the troughs, see Harry Harding, *A Fragile Relationship* (*op. cit.*), chs 3–6.

29 Robert S. Ross, 'U.S. Policy Towards China: The Strategic Context and the Policy-Making Process' in Ross (ed.), *China, the United States, and the Soviet Union* (*op. cit.*), pp.169–71.

30 For a compelling contemporary analysis, see Sewern Bialer, *The Soviet Paradox: External Expansion, Internal Decline* (New York: Vintage Books, 1986).

31 See the accounts of the two sets of negotiations in *Strategic Survey 1987–88* and *Strategic Survey 1988–89* (London: International Institute of Strategic Studies, 1988 and 1989).

32 For accounts, see Harding, *A Fragile Relationship* (*op. cit.*), pp.174–80; Steven M. Goldstein, 'Diplomacy amid Protest: The Sino-Soviet Summit', *Problems of Communism* 38 (September–October 1989), pp.49–71; and Herbert J. Ellison, 'Soviet–Chinese Relations: The Experience of Two Decades' in Ross (ed.), *China, the United States, and the Soviet Union* (*op. cit.*), pp.93–121.

33 For accounts, see Yufan Hao, 'China and the Korean Peninsula' in Yufan Hao and Guocang Huan (eds), *The Chinese View of the World* (New York: Pantheon, 1989),

especially pp.181–84; and, more generally, Gerald Segal, *The Soviet Union and the Pacific* (London: Unwin Hyman, for the Royal Institute of International Affairs, 1990), ch.5; and Douglas T. Stuart (ed.), *Security Within the Pacific Rim* (Hants: Gower, for the International Institute for Strategic Studies, 1987), relevant chapters.

34 Yufan Hao, 'China and the Korean Peninsula' (*op. cit.*), p.187.

35 Reinhard Drifte, 'Japan's Relations with the East Asia-Pacific Region' in Stuart (ed.), *Security Within the Asia Pacific Rim (op. cit.*), p.26.

36 For accounts of the transformation of Taiwan, see Peter R. Moody, *Political Change on Taiwan* (New York: Praeger, 1992); Simon Long, *Taiwan: China's Last Frontier* (London: Macmillan, 1991); Tun-jen Cheng and Stephen Haggard (eds), *Political Change in Taiwan* (Boulder and London: Lynne Rienner, 1992); and Denis Fred Simon and Michael Ying-mao Kau (eds), *Taiwan: Beyond the Economic Miracle* (London and New York: M.E. Sharpe, 1992).

37 Michael Leifer and John Phipps, 'Vietnam and Doi Moi: Domestic and International Dimensions of Reform' (London: Royal Institute of International Affairs, Discussion Paper no.35, June 1991).

38 Michael Leifer, 'Power-Sharing and Peacemaking in Cambodia?' in *SAIS REVIEW* (winter–spring 1992), p.148. The analysis in this paragraph draws considerably from this article.

39 For a succinct account see Michael Leifer, *Dictionary of the Modern Politics of South-East Asia* (London: Routledge, 1995), pp.12–14.

Part II

The policies of the great powers

The foreign policies of the major powers have contributed greatly to shaping the international politics of the Asia-Pacific. This is especially true of the United States, which has dominated the region since 1945 by its military and economic power. The United States and the Soviet Union (until its demise and replacement by Russia), as the two superpowers, determined much of the structure of international politics as a whole and, therefore, the external environment of the region. As integral members of the region they also contributed to its development in their own right. Since the nineteenth century, when Russia and the United States consolidated their presences on the northwestern and eastern shores of the Pacific Ocean respectively, they have been active members of the Asia-Pacific region, which in turn has contributed to enlarging the scope of their identities and focus of operations as states. Although the extent of their engagement and commitments in the region may have varied over time, total withdrawal or neglect has never been a practicable option. For the United States in particular, East Asia has been seen as the only major economic and strategic powerhouse to rival Europe in importance. Correspondingly, it has also been regarded as a source of threat at the opposite extremity of a shared ocean.

4 The United States and the Asia-Pacific

The conduct of American foreign policy towards the Asia-Pacific since 1945 has been shaped by the complex interplay between global priorities and regional interests. As the world's leading power in the second half of the twentieth century, the United States has tended to cast its policies in terms of global visions and strategies. The significance attached to East Asia should be considered not only in terms of the historical evolution of American relations with that part of the world, but also with reference to its place within the broader international context of America's foreign relations. Relations with particular regions and countries may have their own distinctive features, but ultimately, the extent of American engagement has been determined by the place allotted to them within the larger scope of American priorities as a whole.

American policies in the immediate aftermath of the Second World War were shaped by the desire to build a better world, formed in part by the perceived lessons of that war and of what had led up to it. The war itself was seen as an integral whole. In the words of President F.D. Roosevelt, it was 'a single world conflict that required a global strategy of self defence'.[1] The war brought to the fore the tension in the balance of priorities to be attached to the Atlantic and Pacific dimensions of America's geopolitical interests that has continued ever since. Even though the Atlanticists won the day then, and in the persons of Dean Acheson and George Kennan they continued to shape priorities after the war, the global significance of East Asia was not overlooked. To the surprise of Churchill, Roosevelt insisted in 1943 on China being elevated to one of the 'Big Five' in the future United Nations. After the war Japan figured prominently in the State Department's thinking on global economic reconstruction and as one of the centres that the emerging policy of containment had to defend.[2]

The domestic sources

The determination of American global and regional strategies derive from domestic as well as international factors. The former include the influence of ideas about American identity and purpose, and the impact of the divergent influences on foreign policy that derive from the diffusion of political power within the country.

As many have noted, the sense of 'American exceptionalism' that is central to American views of their country's identity has had a profound effect on American dealings with the world outside.[3] The idea that, by virtue of its special claims as a nation founded on the basis of liberty, the United States exercises particular responsibilities to act as a beacon to others, or indeed, more actively, to uphold and to promote liberty elsewhere, has had a marked effect on its foreign relations. Realists of the distinction of Hans Morganthau and Henry Kissinger have noted with disapproval how this has resulted in both a tendency to retreat into an isolationism that deliberately avoids 'entanglement' (to use President Washington's loaded term) with the flawed old world of European power politics and a tendency to engage in an undifferentiated globalism that in the name of idealist principles seeks to make the world a better place in the American image.[4] Others have argued that American foreign policy has exhibited a tension between its professed ideals and its general balance-of-power principle of preventing the emergence of a centre able to exercise a predominance of power in either Western Europe or Eastern Asia.[5] Still others have drawn attention to ideological elements that have sustained American attitudes toward other countries, such as a sense of superiority, race consciousness and democratization.[6] Related, but different, forms of analysis focus on cultural dimensions of American foreign policy, particularly as they contrast with those in Asia.[7]

In practice American policy towards East Asia has been characterized by contradictions and inconsistencies. But it is clear particularly in retrospect that American ideals, however imperfectly applied, contributed to the development of myths about the conduct of relations, especially with China, Japan and the Philippines, that have had a profound influence on the conduct of policy. Since most of the rest of Asia was subject to European colonial rule until after the Pacific War, the United States had few opportunities to develop relations there, let alone to cultivate myths about those countries. American policies towards China in the nineteenth century and in the first half of the twentieth century have been suffused with self-serving myths, to the effect that they have been imbued with noble purposes of upholding the Chinese state against external aggression and of transforming it for the good – i.e., in the direction of Christianity, the free market and democracy. The reality was much more complex, with America involved in great power politics and its business people engaged in commerce – perhaps not too dissimilar from the more self-avowedly imperialist Britain.[8] American policy towards Japan in the 1930s did not reflect Theodore Roosevelt's principle that his country would necessarily oppose any who would be 'top dog' in Asia. Isolationism was applied in Pacific Asia as it was in Atlantic Europe. Pious American rhetoric about self-determination and democratization was in conflict with the reality of imperial rule in the Philippines after its acquisition in 1898. Although a process of self-determination was begun early on and a date was set for the attainment of independence in the mid-1930s, the actual context was one that was imbued with neocolonialism.[9] Nevertheless the ideals and the myths to which they gave rise were important elements in the conduct of American policies towards these countries in the second half of the twentieth century.

The impact of the actual process of American foreign policy-making and implementation has contributed to shaping policy in a number of ways. As the American separation of powers is more complete than in the European parliamentary systems, American presidents have to share power with legislators who tend to have narrower policy agendas. Moreover the legislature (i.e., Congress) is able to make independent contributions to foreign relations – often to the dismay of the executive. For example, it is in Congress that the more isolationist and protectionist tendencies have been traditionally evident, most famously in the rejection of America's participation in the League of Nations, despite the role of President Wilson as one of its chief architects. Congress also served as the base for McCarthyism in the early 1950s, which undoubtedly deepened the ideological chasm of the early stages of the Cold War, and as the focus for the promotion of protectionist interests in the latter part of the twentieth century that have complicated still further the conduct of relations with Japan. Interestingly, Congress has also been the main fulcrum for the advancement of idealist impulses such as those associated with human rights.

Given that the president, unlike, say, British prime ministers, cannot command majorities in the legislature, he has had to exercise powers of persuasion, which has resulted both in what Americans have called pork-barrel politics (offering or withholding Federal favours to Congressional districts) and in reaching over the heads of Congress to appeal directly to the American people. The former has tended to distort policy by making provisions for special interests, and the latter has often given policy statements a populist and, at times, a crusading character. The tendency of American presidents to appeal to their people in broad crusading terms can be seen in the way the key doctrine of containment was articulated by President Truman in the apocalyptic terms of universalist rhetoric rather than in the more graduated terms of its progenitor, George Kennan.[10]

The diffusion of political power in the American political system and the apparent, if often real, discontinuities between successive presidents has frequently accentuated inter-bureaucratic rivalries and pitted the interests of incoming presidents against established networks of bureaucracy, Congress and others in Washington. It was concern with the convergence of interests between elements in the Department of Defense, Congress and the defence-related industries that caused President Eisenhower to warn his fellow Americans shortly before leaving office in 1959 against the dangers of what he called 'the military industrial complex'. In the case of President Nixon and his principal foreign policy lieutenant, Henry Kissinger, this led to the cultivation of secret so-called back channels in order to circumvent the conventional diplomatic and Congressional processes. Kissinger subsequently complained about the legalism and bureaucratism inherent in the conduct of America's foreign relations that he believed frustrated the practice of foreign policy according to the true national interest and in line with the principles of the balance of power.[11] Although no government with its attendant ministries and bureaucracies can be said to be entirely monolithic or free from the problems of 'bureaucratic politics', the American political system provides an environment that is more conducive for its operation than most.[12]

The principal effect on relations with Asia has been to accentuate the difficulties of Asian governments in discerning the key elements of policy amongst the different voices often articulated in Washington.

More than in most democracies, American foreign policy making has allowed considerable room for the influence of public opinion. Perhaps the clearest examples can be drawn from the Vietnam War. It was the loss of public support for further escalation as shown in opinion polls and in the results of the New Hampshire primary that led President Johnson to announce in March 1968 the end of that policy and his refusal to stand for election for a second term. Interestingly, the available evidence at the time of his announcement showed that the North Vietnamese and their Vietcong allies had been crushed by the military response to their Tet offensive. Thereafter it became an article of faith in Washington that the United States would not be able to engage in *prolonged* warfare because it would not be supported by public opinion.[13]

Interest groups also tend to exercise more influence on American foreign relations than is generally true of other democracies. The business or corporate sector has traditionally exercised influence both in the sense of advocating particular policies and in the more high-minded purpose of supplying leading personnel from the private sector to hold high positions in the public bureaucracy.[14] At different times businessmen have successfully pressed their special concerns and/or ideological outlooks on the conduct of American policy in Asia. Thus business interests contributed to the 'open door' policies of the last decade of the nineteenth century and to the virulent anti-communism that informed policy towards the People's Republic of China in the first twenty years of its existence.[15] More recently, they were apparently influential in persuading President Clinton to disassociate his concern for human rights from his decision to renew the Most Favoured Nation treatment to China, by which its exports to the US were subject to the same tariffs as the lowest offered to others.

Neither the tradition of American idealism nor the process of its foreign policy making allow for the conduct of diplomacy in the often secret, unemotional and professional way associated with traditional Europe. Not surprisingly, it has often disappointed realists for whom 'the proper sphere of foreign policy' is the 'middle ground of subtle distinctions, complex choices, and precarious manipulations'.[16] Since 1945 (and indeed for the hundred years before that), American policies towards the Asia-Pacific in general and some of its key countries, such as China or Japan in particular, have not been conducted in such measured ways. It is only by reference to these complex domestic factors as well as the external influences that it is possible to understand the evolution of American relations with the region since 1945.

Containment in the Asia-Pacific

The doctrine of containment was fashioned primarily with the Soviet Union and Soviet communism in mind. Its origins were in Europe and indeed it was in Europe where its principles were best applied and where its ultimate purpose of bringing about the collapse of the communist system was eventually achieved. But since containment was expressed in moral and universal terms it evoked a Manichean view of a world divided between two opposing systems, which soon became the reality in Europe, where a very real 'iron curtain' sharply demarcated borders separating the two camps. It was an approach to understanding the world that came to be broadly accepted in the United States. Thus, despite the Vietnam debacle and the soul-searching to which it gave rise, American public opinion supported the long-term policy of opposition to the Soviet Union.

As it was a way of understanding the world rather than a strategy that related means to ends, containment in practice encompassed a number of different strategies in the course of the forty-odd years in which it served as the fundamental basis for American foreign policy.

Being a universal doctrine, containment was extended from Europe to the Asia-Pacific, but with very different results. Being more diverse, the Asia-Pacific could not be divided by a tangible iron curtain that separated two tightly bound sets of military alliance systems buttressed by competing ideologies, socio-economic and political systems. Yet it was in Asia that the United States fought the two major wars of containment, which ended by almost undermining the cohesion of American society. It was in Asia that the United States had to balance some of the contradictions of containment, such as propping up dictatorial and fragile regimes in the name of upholding democracy against communism, or expending enormous costs in areas of relatively low strategic priority in terms of America's global position so as to demonstrate commitment to allies, only to see this allow the principal adversary (the Soviet Union) to improve its strategic standing as a result. Yet, by the end of the Cold War, containment in Asia could nevertheless be described as a success: America has remained the predominant power; all its allies (with the exception of South Vietnam) have consolidated their statehood and prospered economically; and even its adversaries (or former adversaries) have embraced the market economy. Certainly many problems remain and new ones have emerged – not least the difficulties in understanding the post-Cold War situation and in devising a coherent and consistent strategy for the new era.

The beginning

American thinking about the new order after the Second World War was built upon the Atlantic Charter of 1941. This distinguished between the 'aggressor nations' (Germany, Japan and Italy) who were to be permanently disarmed and the 'peace loving nations' who would gradually reduce their force levels. The key element in the American vision of the post-war order was that the main allies (including the Soviet Union) who fought the war against the aggressors would work together to create a better world. At this stage President Roosevelt envisaged that China would become the major power in Asia as it revitalized through close association with the United States. In 1944 a series of international conferences were held under the American aegis to forge agreement for the new character of the post-war world. These led to the establishment of the United Nations and to the creation of a liberal international economic and financial system named after the location of the conference at Bretton Woods. Conferences were also held on the subjects of food and agriculture and on how to provide relief and rehabilitation. At this stage, if there was a degree of friction, it was with Britain (rather than the Soviet Union) since, as part of his 'four freedoms' that underpinned the American vision, Roosevelt expected the Europeans to allow their colonies to proceed towards self-determination and independence. This was anathema to Churchill, who made it clear with specific reference to Hong Kong that 'nothing would be taken away from England without war'.[17] He also distrusted the American idealist approach to Stalin, preferring instead to treat him on the basis of traditional power politics. Although the American expectations of a new cooperative international order were soon dashed by the Cold War, important elements of this idealist vision remained to shape future developments of international relations, including the Asia-Pacific region.

The ending of the war in the Pacific, however, provided evidence of how in practice American idealism was tempered by considerations of power. At Yalta in February 1945 Roosevelt behaved in the mould of classic colonial big-power practices. Not only did he make secret concessions to Stalin at China's expense by agreeing to allow the Soviet Union exclusive rights in Manchuria (including the use of a naval base) despite the absence of Chinese representation there, but he also undertook to persuade Chiang Kai-shek to accept them. Having made these concessions in order to get the Soviet Union to join in the war against Japan and indeed having agreed at Yalta that the Soviet Union would be one of the four occupying powers, the United States in the end defeated Japan largely by its own efforts (including the use of the atom bomb), and in effect denied the Soviet Union a significant role in the occupation of Japan.

Considerations of power could also be expressed in the language of idealism and universalism. Not long after China was plunged into civil war in 1946, the new American president declared in effect the beginning of the policy of containment, in what became known from March 1947 as the Truman Doctrine. In taking over from a weakened Britain the support of Greece and Turkey so as to halt a possible Soviet advance on the Mediterranean, Truman explained American purposes in the universal terms of a policy 'to support free peoples who are resisting attempted subjugation by armed minorities or by outside pressures'. He depicted the new state of the world as a struggle between two ways of life, with America obliged to defend democracy from its oppressive enemy. This was of course the language of morality rather than of strategy. Arguably the two coincided in Europe, but in Asia matters were less clear cut.

The United States had tried but failed to mediate in the Chinese civil war, and it became clear that China would not play the role in the post-war international order as originally conceived in Washington. Attention in the State Department was already shifting to the desirability of rehabilitating the Japanese economy as part of the general programme of reconstructing the economies of Western Europe. This was less a Cold War issue than a matter of averting a damaging worldwide recession threatened by the enormous imbalance between American exports to the rest of the world and its imports. At the same time Japan, in con-tradistinction to China, was seen as an economic centre of potential significance in altering the world balance of power. As in the case of occupied Germany, the State Department began to argue in late 1946 to early 1947 in favour of repla-cing the policy of punishment with one of rehabilitation. The relaunching of the economies of Germany and Japan was seen as essential if 'the free areas of Europe and Asia' were to 'function vigorously and healthily'.[18] By mid-1947 the American occupation policy in Japan had begun to change emphasis from seeking to eliminate the vestiges of the past that were associated with militarism and the capacity to prepare for making war towards encouraging economic development and political stability. The constitution that had been developed by the Americans, with its famous Article Nine that renounced war, was modified in practice to allow for what were called 'self-defence forces'. The huge economic conglomerates, the Zaibatsus, such as Toshiba and Mitsubishi, began to be dis-cretely encouraged; and the forces of the left found the policies of the American occupation distinctly less friendly.[19]

American policy in Southeast Asia in the early years after the war was torn between promoting the independence of colonies from their European masters and recognizing the need to avoid undermining fragile European allies. At the same time its treatment of its own colony of the Philippines hardly served as an edifying model of how independence should be granted. The United States moved rapidly to grant independence to the Philippines in 1946, but it did so on terms that were favourable to American economic interests. For example, American firms were granted 'equal rights' with Filipinos in the exploitation of the natural resources of the country. Furthermore, American strategic interests were protected the following year by the Military Bases Agreement, by which the United States leased for ninety-nine years twenty-three bases with full jurisdic-tion.[20] With regard to Indonesia, the United States took the view that the Dutch could not sustain their rule there by force, however successful they might be in the short term. Moreover, by late 1948 the United States was less concerned about the fragility of Holland itself. After the Indonesian Republicans had defeated the armed challenge of the radical and communist forces in Mediun in September 1948, the United States needed little persuasion to support the Indonesian nationalists. American pressure was successfully applied to per-suade the Dutch to concede independence in 1949.[21] In Indo-China, however, the United States did not put similar pressure on the French. The problem from an American perspective was that the effective nationalist resistance to the French was led by the communist Vietminh.

Elsewhere in East Asia the United States had made no preparations for the future of Korea after the defeat of Japan, beyond some vague ideas about placing the country under an international trusteeship. In the event, a hastily contrived agreement was reached with the Russians that, for the purposes of occupation, the peninsula be divided between them at the 38th Parallel. The Red Army stopped at the Parallel in early August 1945, even though it was nearly a month before the first American contingent arrived. This indicated that at this point neither side regarded Korea as being of particular strategic significance. With great difficulty, the Americans tried to build a democratic state in the South under the leadership of the autocratic Syngman Rhee. In 1947 the US referred the matter to the United Nations, who supervised elections in the South. The North refused to accept the UN role. Syngman Rhee was duly elected and the Republic of Korea was inaugurated in August 1948, and he proceeded to consolidate his rule through a ruthless dictatorship. In September 1948 the Democratic People's Republic of Korea was established in the North after a series of communist-style elections that had begun almost two years earlier. The last Soviet forces were withdrawn in March 1949 and the Americans, whose armed forces were still overstretched after the massive demobilization after the Second World War, followed suit in June. Despite some misgivings in the Pentagon and the State Department about what had been done in the American name, it was felt that the best had been made of a bad job.[22]

Even the communist victory in China in October 1949 was not seen entirely within the prism of the Cold War and containment. The theme of the American government's white paper was that the communist success was the result of deep-seated upheavals within the country. It hardly fitted the purpose of the Truman Doctrine of supporting 'free peoples who are resisting attempted subjugation by armed minorities or by outside pressures'. In his letter of transmittal to Congress, Acheson seemingly contradicted his department's argument by asserting that China had come under the control of the Kremlin. But that representation was part of a larger purpose, or strategy, of seeking to bring about a split between the two communist giants by playing on Chinese nationalist sentiments. It was envisaged that the historical legacy of Russian imperialism combined with the Soviet incapacity to meet Chinese needs of external economic support would lead to a rift. Such thinking at this stage implied a more flexible approach than that ordinarily associated with containment. Indeed, the American government was even prepared to contemplate the conquest of Taiwan and the defeat of Chiang Kai-shek and his remnant forces by the Chinese communists. There was also the prospect that the United States would recognize the People's Republic of China before long.[23] Acheson also played on the theme of Sino-Soviet national differences in his speech of 12 January 1950, while Mao Zedong was negotiating a new partnership in Moscow.[24]

American strategy in the Asia-Pacific at this stage in January 1950, as outlined by Truman and Acheson, envisaged a perimeter defence stretching from the Aleutian Islands in the north, reaching through Japan and the Philippines down to Australia and New Zealand in the south, but excluding Korea. These were the areas of the highest priority.[25] Acheson did not altogether ignore South Korea, however, as he argued that its defence would be based on collective security through the United Nations.[26] Moreover, Cold War calculations were very much in evidence in American approaches towards the region, even if not yet expressed in terms of containment. For example, despite misgivings, the United States recognized the fragile and less than independent Indo-Chinese states as 'independent states within the French Union', both because it sought to bolster the French government itself and because it feared the consequences for the rest of Southeast Asia of a communist victory by Ho Chi Minh, especially after the victory of the communists in China.[27]

It was the attack of North Korea upon the South on 25 June 1950 that brought the full application of containment to the Asia-Pacific. The attack provided the point at which American global and regional perspectives were joined. The end of the Berlin blockade in May 1949 was thought to have stabilized matters in Europe, but since then the Soviet Union had broken the American monopoly by testing an atomic bomb in August and the Chinese communists had declared their victory in October. Notwithstanding Acheson's attempts to sow dissension between them, Mao and Stalin concluded their treaty of alliance in February 1950. The surprise attack was seen as a turning point, 'Communism has passed beyond the use of subversion to conquer independent nations and will now use armed invasion and war.'[28] Within two days of the invasion Truman had ordered American air and naval forces into action in Korea and announced that the navy would be interposed between Taiwan and the Chinese mainland. He also sent American military advisers to assist the French war in Indo-China.

In effect, the strategy of the maritime defensive perimeter, which distinguished between greater and lesser priorities, was cast aside in favour of the containment strategy of seeking to deny the communist forces any further advances, wherever they might occur. Although sound strategic reasons could have been advanced for denying the North victory in Korea in order to safeguard Japan and for denying Taiwan to the communist Chinese in order to secure American naval predominance in the west Pacific, these were not the reasons given for the American intervention. The key document that defined American strategy for containment was NSC-68, which had been submitted to President Truman and formally approved by him in September 1950. In the words of its principal architect:

> the underlying conflict ... were [*sic*] far more fundamental than disagreements over specific interests, *inter alia*, control over geography, ports, oceans, raw materials, or even respect, prestige, renown or position in the eyes of history ... the contest was not one of competition over specific national interests; it had an absolute ideological quality about it, which, from the Soviet side, did not permit compromise.[29]

The adoption of NSC-68 led to a massive increase in American defence spending, rising from US$13.1 billion in 1950 to US$22.5 billion and then US$44.0 billion in 1951 and 1952 respectively.[30] It also accelerated the supply of direct American assistance to the French forces fighting the Vietminh in Indo-China. But as far as the conduct of the Korean War was concerned, after the Chinese intervention destroyed the hopes of total victory over the North, containment resulted in a rather minimalist strategy of seeking to restore the status quo ante, as if to do more might provoke the enlargement of the war to begin a third world war. A more flexibly conceived national strategy might have suggested different options.[31] The immediate effect of the Korean War and the strategy of containment was an attempt to draw a demarcation line between the countries controlled by the communists and the rest of the Asia-Pacific. This included the attempt to establish an economic embargo against China even more severe than the one that applied against the Soviet Union.

The application of containment: Northeast Asia

If the American intervention in the Korean War was the first instance of the application of containment in the Asia-Pacific, the thinking that underlay the doctrine also shaped the conduct of the war. American war aims were limited in the sense that they did not want to widen the war to attack mainland China lest they draw in the Soviet Union and lead to a general world war. This was an objective shared by the other side. So all sides combined to keep secret the American bombing of Manchuria and the Soviet piloting of many of the fighter jets on the communist side. The aim was to punish aggression but not to roll back communism. An early indication of this was Truman's refusal to accept MacArthur's suggestion that a contingent of nationalist troops be included in the allied forces.

And, when the opportunity presented itself after the sweeping victory of the Inchon landings, Washington pressed ahead towards the border with China in order to take over the North. But following the Chinese intervention, the US objectives were confined to restoring the status quo ante. The Korean War, indeed, was seen at the time as America's first limited war, and as such it embodied the concept of containment.[32]

The Korean War gave further impetus to the policy of reconstruction in Japan. It accelerated the drive towards ending the occupation, signing a peace treaty and establishing a military alliance. Japan would gain full independence, in return for establishing a small 'self-defence' army and for signing a ten-year (renewable) agreement allowing the continuance of American bases in Japan and Okinawa. The peace treaty provided the occasion for the US to conclude separate treaties with the Philippines, and trilaterally with Australia and New Zealand. Ostensibly they sought reassurance against a resurgence by Japan. The details of reparations were left to be settled at a later stage, but the Americans made it clear to disappointed allies that these would have to be tempered so as not to cripple the country. John Foster Dulles, the leading American negotiator, pointed out to the Japanese prime minister, Yoshida, 'the great utility of the reparations clause in creating employment in Japan through processing foreign materials'.[33] Of the Asian countries, India and Burma refused to attend the peace conference in San Francisco in September 1951 and neither of the two claimants to represent China was invited. The Soviet Union attended, but withdrew and did not sign. Although the treaty left it to an independent Japan to decide with which China it would deal, political opinion within the United States made it clear that recognition of communist China would be unacceptable. The famous letter handed by Yoshida to the American ambassador on 24 December 1951 (i.e., before Japan had technically become sovereign) stated that Japan would conclude a treaty with nationalist China.

Japan, it was clear, was to become the core base of America's arc of containment in the Asia-Pacific. The Americans provided military security and facilitated the economic reconstruction of the country. Boosted by the Korean War, the Japanese economy benefited from access to American loans and to the American market while protecting Japanese industries at home. As Dulles had predicted, Japanese industry also profited from the forms of reparation in Southeast Asia. The Americans also went to great lengths to cement ties with Japan and to squash latent and not so latent neutralist tendencies. Thus, as secretary of state, Dulles was also instrumental in persuading the Japanese to reject the Soviet offer of a peace treaty in 1956. The Soviet Union had offered to settle the dispute over four islands to the north of Japan, seized at the end of the war as a notional part of the Kurile chain, by ceding claims to sovereignty over the two closest to Hokkaido. Dulles said that if Japan were to recognize the Soviet title to the other two islands the United States would ask that Okinawa be confirmed as American territory. He feared that the Japanese might be tempted by Soviet blandishments to separate Japan from the United States by going on to offer the country some kind of neutral status.[34]

In 1960, despite considerable domestic opposition, the Japanese government signed a security treaty with the United States. But such was the intensity of the dissent that President Eisenhower cancelled a projected visit to mark the occasion.

The election of President Eisenhower had brought in an administration determined to take a more assertive approach towards the communists compared to the earlier policy of containment, which was regarded as too passive. At the same time it was determined to reduce military spending and to translate America's nuclear superiority into effective diplomatic gains. This gave rise to the 'New Look' strategy. The first instance of this approach in the Asia-Pacific was the use of the threat of atomic weapons to end the awful military stalemate and bring the prolonged armistice negotiations in Korea to a rapid conclusion in 1953.[35] The armistice also highlighted the difficulties of the United States in dealing with recalcitrant allies in whose interests presumably containment was carried out. The Syngman Rhee government (regarded by many inside and outside the American government as a nasty dictatorship) was opposed to it and was only bought off by promises of aid and by a treaty-based guarantee of its military security from the United States. None of America's other allies wished to be associated with the treaty.

The issue of Taiwan raised more complex problems. At stake was not so much the American commitment to the defence of Taiwan island itself, but some of the islands just offshore from the mainland. These above all symbolized for Chiang Kai-shek his indissoluble link to the mainland, over which he claimed rightful title and to which he had vowed to return to vanquish the communists. As these were less readily defensible they were a thorn in the side of America, which in the end came to prefer an arrangement by which Taiwan might be fully separated from China proper. In the course of the first offshore island crisis in 1954–55, the

Americans persuaded the nationalists to withdraw from the more northerly Dazhen (or Tachen) group of islands, but the nationalists dug in their heels over Quemoy and Matsu, which were immediately opposite Taiwan by the coast of Fujian Province. Although Washington regarded the islands as inconsequential in themselves, their continued possession was seen as vital to nationalist morale. In March 1955 the Eisenhower administration publicly and privately raised the prospect of using atomic bombs against China. This led Beijing to decide to develop an independent nuclear capability.[36] Eventually the matter was diffused by China's Premier Zhou Enlai's offer to negotiate, which he made while attending the first Asian-African conference in Bandung of April 1955. The crisis as a whole had the effect of confirming the reluctance of America's other allies in the Asia-Pacific to join it in signing a mutual defence treaty with the Republic of China (i.e., Taiwan). Consequently, the United States alone signed a mutual defence treaty with the Republic of China in December 1954.

As for China itself, the Eisenhower administration continued the policy of containment and isolation. The Geneva Agreements for Indo-China of 1954 were regarded as a setback for the West rather than a basis on which new relations could be developed. A publicly hostile stance that refused to acknowledge conciliatory gestures by Zhou Enlai in 1955 and 1956 on the grounds of high principled opposition to international communism was privately explained as being designed to wean China away from the Soviet Union. Picking up on the approach of Acheson in the first nine months after the victory of the Chinese communists in 1949, Dulles claimed to be driving a wedge between the two communist giants by making the Chinese demand economic and strategic assistance from the Russians that was beyond the capacity and will of the Soviet Union to give.[37] Thus, from 1956 to 1960 the Eisenhower administration evinced a readiness to develop contacts and explore the prospects for negotiations with the Soviet Union that it specifically denied the Chinese. The Soviet invasion of Hungary in 1956 and its initiation of a crisis over Berlin in 1958 did little to erase the view in Washington evoked by Khrushchev's speeches of 1956, which denounced Stalin and called for a new spirit of peaceful coexistence, that the Soviet leader was a potential partner for negotiations. Notwithstanding Zhou Enlai's conciliatory gestures, which continued through into 1956, Dulles took a tough line of rejecting contact through, for example, the exchange of journalists. Indeed, in a speech in early 1957 in San Francisco, he denounced the Chinese communists for still being puppets of the Russians, when the American intelligence agencies knew that this was very far from the truth.

The second offshore island crisis of 1958 once again raised the issue in Washington of whether their defence was integral to the defence of Taiwan. Once again, the conclusion was that the islands could not be given up without undermining the morale and hence the survival of the nationalist regime. Once again, the possible use of nuclear weapons against the mainland was openly discussed in Washington. In the event, the Chinese side 'blinked first' and the crisis came off the boil. It has been persuasively argued that, as a result of the diplomacy of the Korean War and the conduct of the two offshore island crises, the

American and Communist Chinese governments developed a pattern of inter-action that suggested they had come to understand how to conduct their hostile relations in ways that would not lead to war.[38] But, as in the Truman adminis-tration before it and in the Kennedy and Johnson administrations that were to follow, the Chinese communists were regarded as the primary instigators of what was seen as Vietnamese communist aggression in Indo-China.

These developments took place within a context in which American strategic thinking was responding to the changing circumstances of Soviet nuclear power and the strategic equation between the two superpowers. As the Soviet Union acquired missiles capable of hitting continental USA in the late 1950s, so the rationale of 'massive retaliation' and limited nuclear warfare lost credibility as instruments for American foreign policy. Moreover, as the futility of a nuclear war became apparent, American thinking turned to how to meet the challenge of a variety of possible communist points of expansion from local wars to wars of national liberation in what is now called the Third World. The former was to lead to the strategy of flexible response as articulated by the Kennedy adminis-tration. The latter resulted in a Third World strategy that was designed to enhance 'nation building' and to stop the seemingly invincible communist guer-rilla strategy through what was called 'counter-insurgency warfare'.[39]

Indeed, with the advent of the Kennedy administration, the Chinese commu-nists under Mao's leadership were seen as more dangerous foes than the Russians. Especially after the Cuban missile crisis, when détente was developed with the Soviet Union, the Chinese communists were regarded as still being led by first generation revolutionaries who were imbued with a fanaticism that was not sus-ceptible to rational counter-argument. Their Soviet equivalents, however, belonging to the third generation of leaders since the revolution, were thought to be more 'rational'. Moreover, the Soviet Union was said to have learned from experience that its conventional and nuclear military forces could not hope to prevail against the United States without bringing about the annihilation of both sides. Accordingly, it was thought to be prepared to reach understandings with the United States. The Chinese, by contrast, according to the Kennedy adminis-tration, had still to learn that their 'people's war' strategy was not invincible.

By this time, however, it was no longer a question of driving 'wedges' between Moscow and Beijing, it was rather an issue for the Kennedy of the 'new frontier' (who according to his inaugural address was willing to 'pay any price, bear any burden ... in the defence of liberty') of winning the decisive battle against com-munist guerrilla warfare and thus winning the Cold War. At this time American military academies altered their curricula to focus on counter-insurgency warfare, with Mao's writings forming important texts. Kennedy averred to a French offi-cial in 1963: 'The Chinese are perfectly prepared, because of their lower value of human life to lose hundreds of millions [of people] if necessary ... to carry out their militant and aggressive policies.'[40] After the Cuban missile crisis Kennedy went so far as to instruct his special ambassador to sound out Khrushchev about his views about destroying China's incipient nuclear facilities.[41] Indeed, much of the point of the 1963 Test Ban Treaty was to suggest that Washington and

Moscow would work together to prevent the proliferation of nuclear weapons. In other words they would cooperate together to try to prevent China from becoming a nuclear power. By this time the idea of the 'wedge' as a means to wean China away from the Soviet Union was no longer uppermost in the minds of administration officials. Ironically, of course, this was at the high point of the Sino-Soviet split, and it seemed as if the Americans shared the Soviet view of the Chinese. Interestingly, the Americans and Soviet leaders simultaneously sided with India against China in their brief border war of October/November 1962 (i.e., immediately after the Cuban missile crisis).

In one sense President Kennedy had modified the American view of the Chinese communist claim to represent Chinese sovereignty. He no longer accepted the fiction that Taiwan represented all of China. His administration, however, wanted the communist Chinese state 'to modify its aggressive stance and behaviour and recognize *de facto* the existence of an independent Taiwan'.[42] Since that had become the core issue dividing the PRC and the US, both in the sense of challenging the unity of the state and in the strategic sense of the island being a point from which attacks against the mainland might be launched, it could be construed as even more challenging than the previous position, which simply preferred one version of China to the other. By the time of the accession of President Kennedy, the number of states recognizing communist as opposed to nationalist China was increasing and was due to increase still further as more Third World countries achieved independence. Consequently, it was purely a question of time before the communists would prevail in terms of numbers and gain recognition at the United Nations instead of the nationalists. Accordingly, the new Kennedy position threatened to remove that prospect. The fact that Chiang Kai-shek of Taiwan objected even more strongly meant that Kennedy's approach did not become official policy. But, not surprisingly, the Chinese communists regarded Kennedy as even more dangerous than his predecessor. Indeed, they dubbed him the 'tiger with a smiling face'. The view of the Chinese communists as the ultimate menace was so deep rooted among Kennedy's people that in 1965 Dean Rusk attacked an article by the Chinese defence minister, Lin Biao, on 'people's war' as a Chinese version of Hitler's *Mein Kampf*. In fact, far from being an exhortation to expansion, the article indicated that the Chinese would not intervene in the Vietnam War and that it advised Hanoi to scale down its conduct.[43]

Both the Kennedy and Johnson administrations were committed to a view of the world that was still recognizably the one that had underpinned NSC-68 ten to fifteen years earlier. Namely that the communist challenge was universal and that it had to be met in the spirit of a zero-sum game where a victory for one side was necessarily a loss for the other. Consequently, were the US to sustain the 'loss' of a small and distant country such as Vietnam, the credibility of all its commitments would be undermined. As Secretary of State Dean Rusk put it in 1965, 'the integrity of the U.S. commitment is the principal pillar of peace throughout the world. If that commitment becomes unreliable the communist world would draw conclusions that would lead to our ruin and almost certainly to a catastrophic war'.[44] This was to be the primary reason advanced for the American intervention in Vietnam, but initially it was explained as necessary to stop the Chinese communists, who were said to be behind the Vietnamese communists.

By 1966 American attitudes towards how best to deal with communist China were beginning to change. In 1965 a tied vote in the UN General Assembly on the question of who represented China meant that for the first time the Americans failed to obtain a majority in favour of the nationalists on Taiwan. The Senate Foreign Relations Committee held hearings on China in 1966 and the establishment China experts favoured a change to 'containment without isolation'. Although the administration was still worried about a possible backlash because of the public's presumed residual sense of grievance over the 'loss of China', attitudes changed there too. Anxious to avoid a Chinese intervention on the Korean model, the administration limited its escalations in Vietnam so as not to provoke the Chinese. This had the effect of providing a modus vivendi between the two sides, despite the ferocity of the rhetoric directed against each other.[45] Nixon's famous *Foreign Affairs* article of October 1967, which held out the prospect for a new relationship with China, was not considered to be highly exceptional at the time.

In other words, by 1966/1967 American attitudes towards China had developed significantly. The wisdom of seeking to isolate a state with a quarter of the world's population that since its nuclear test of October 1964 had become a nuclear power and that was clearly an independent actor of some significance on the world stage no longer made sense, especially as it had quite evidently broken away from the Soviet Union. However, this did not mean that containment was no longer applicable, as the country was still perceived as a dangerous adversary in Asia and as a fomenter of revolution elsewhere in the Third World.

The application of containment: Southeast Asia

American historical relations with Southeast Asia were largely confined to the Philippines, to whom it granted independence of a kind in 1946. Even the final settlement of the Pacific War in this part of the Asia-Pacific was left primarily to the European allies – essentially the British – who restored their colonial rule. Britain, however, moved speedily to concede to demands for Burmese and Indian independence. Britain and France also gave in to American pressure for the international rehabilitation of Thailand, a wartime ally of Japan. Yet the American impulse to press the Europeans to grant independence was tempered by the need to avoid undermining the prestige and standing of the fragile governments at home in Europe. General De Gaulle pronounced upon the significance of the issue in August 1946: 'United with the overseas territories which she opened to civilization, France is a great power. Without these territories she would be in danger of no longer being one.'[46] The Americans in fact stood gingerly aside until their approach became infused with Cold War thinking. It was the fear of communism that drew the United States into active engagement in the area.

The British attempt to crush the communists in the course of the Malayan emergency that began in June 1948 was watched with concern. But what gave rise to alarm was the French struggle with the Vietminh in Indo-China, particularly after the communist success in China in 1949, which opened the Sino-Vietnamese border to a massive influx of Chinese military assistance. Unlike Indonesia, where there was a non-communist authority to whom the Americans pressed the Dutch to concede, the main nationalist movement in Indo-China was the communist-dominated Vietminh. With considerable misgivings the Americans and also the British recognized the French-imposed government of the Emperor Bao Dai as one of the associated states of the French Union that was set up in November 1949, and tried in vain to persuade the French to concede more to Bao Dai so as to establish him with some nationalist credentials. After the (communist) Democratic Republic of Vietnam gained the recognition first of the PRC and then of the USSR in January 1950, the American definition of the significance of Indo-China grew, as did their readiness to be committed there.

First the State Department in February and then the Joint Chiefs of Staff in April 1950 sounded the alarm as to the possible consequences of the fall of Indo-China to the communists. They anticipated that Burma and Thailand would also succumb, to be followed by Malaya and the whole of Southeast Asia. That would jeopardize the American defence perimeter, allow the Chinese and the Soviets access to resources that could change the balance of power and, by denying Asian markets and materials to Japan, could damage its relations with the United States.[47] Here lay the origins of the domino theory, beloved of Eisenhower and his successors, that if Vietnam fell so would all the rest. Although the Southeast Asian mainland was still not seen as sufficiently important in terms of stretched American global commitments to justify direct intervention, economic assistance was extended to the French in May. The outbreak of the Korean War in June 1950 provided the rationale for sending military as well as economic aid to the French. The latter steadily increased, until by 1954 the United States was paying for more than 80 per cent of the French war effort.

The Geneva Conference of 1954 that settled the First Indo-China War was regarded by Dulles as a defeat for the West. The partitioning of Vietnam meant the establishment of not only a new communist state in Asia, but one that was the most powerful among the now four Indo-Chinese states. The conference had also brought out into the open Anglo-American differences on how to treat communist China. Within two months the United States took steps to bolster the security of the region against further communist gains with the Manila Treaty of September 1954, which led to the establishment of the Southeast Asia Treaty Organization (SEATO). Despite its obvious weaknesses in having failed to elicit Asian support beyond Thailand, the Philippines and Pakistan (to whom the United States was already closely linked) and in obligating its members to a less than binding military commitment to each other's defence, it provided a mechanism for extending a commitment to Cambodia, Laos and South Vietnam without their assuming treaty obligations themselves. It served the American purpose of enhancing its deterrent position in Southeast Asia without committing it to increasing its military deployments. Southeast Asia continued to be regarded as a region of lesser strategic priority.[48]

During the remainder of the 1950s the United States sent military advisors to Laos, South Vietnam and Thailand. Existing military missions in the Philippines and elsewhere were enlarged. Lacking in sympathy for Asian neutralism or non-alignment, the Eisenhower administration tended to see these manifestations of Asian nationalism as helpful to the communist menace. Indonesia used this concern adroitly in eliciting American pressure on the Dutch to relinquish West Irian, which they eventually did in 1963. Previously, the United States had become involved in regional revolts in Indonesia in 1958, as Dulles was persuaded that they were rebelling against growing communist influence in Jakarta. But on being informed that the Indonesian army which was putting down the rebellion was staunchly anti-communist, Dulles quickly changed tack.[49]

North Vietnam began its attempt to reunify the country through unleashing guerrilla warfare in the South and through the formation of the National Liberation Front of South Vietnam in 1960. This involved the development of a supply route that went south first via Laos and later included Cambodia – the so-called Ho Chi Minh Trail. The role of its eastern uplands gave strategic significance to Laos, as competing external patrons sought to uphold their candidates for control of its government. As Eisenhower prepared to leave office he strongly recommended to the incoming Kennedy that he take a stand on Laos, as it was the linchpin domino. Its fall to communism would be followed by Cambodia, South Vietnam, and probably Thailand and Burma.[50] The critical juncture in Laos was reached in 1961, when a civil war had broken out and the neutralist and Pathet Lao (who were virtually an adjunct of the Vietnamese communists) sides were being supplied by Soviet airlifts while the rightists were backed by Thailand and the CIA. Being reluctant to intervene after the American Cuban debacle at the Bay of Pigs, it was only the following year in May 1962 after the despatch of 6,000 marines to neighbouring Thailand that the United States was able to secure an agreement at a conference convened in Geneva for the formal neutralization of the country and the withdrawal of all foreign troops. Laotian neutrality was ostensibly preserved, but in practice several thousand Vietnamese military personnel remained, ensuring that the trail to South Vietnam would be kept open.[51]

Imbued with the activist approach symbolized by the evocation of the myth of the 'New Frontier', the Kennedy administration developed a theory of modernization and nation building that together with counterinsurgency warfare was directed towards defeating the communist strategy of revolutionary guerrilla wars or wars of national liberation that both Moscow and Beijing were pledged to support. This was seen as fitting in with the new general strategic doctrine of flexible response, which was regarded as more credible than that of massive retaliation, given that the Soviet Union was thought to have acquired the capability to strike continental America with nuclear weapons. Consequently, the Kennedy administration placed much emphasis on political reform in the South as well as on seeking to build up the South Vietnamese army. Dissatisfied with the authoritarian style of President Diem, the United States encouraged his over-throw. But his assassination on 1 November 1963 led to a succession of coups by generals that had the effect of undermining what little authority had been enjoyed by the unlamented Diem. America was in effect faced with the choice of cutting its losses and reconciling itself to the eventual victory of the communists or becoming more deeply and directly involved in the fighting. Kennedy himself was assassinated later that November. He had prevaricated over the choice and his former associates are divided as to which path he would have chosen.

His successor, President Johnson, decided to intervene with combat troops, and in March 1965 he began a sustained bombing campaign against the North with the morale of the South very much in mind. Ironically, in view of the later anti-war movement, the American commitment at this juncture enjoyed considerable public support. Moreover, it was principally the realists, such as Walter Lippmann and Hans Morganthau, who opposed the war at this stage as a dere-liction of American strategic priorities. As in Korea, the Americans sought to limit the war, but this time that meant avoiding a military confrontation with China as well as with the Soviet Union. As a result it was decided not to invade North Vietnam, nor to bomb southern China. The American strategy was geared to graduated escalation, by which the bombing of the North was increased in intensity step by step. Meanwhile ground forces in the South were increased rapidly in the vain hope of pressing Hanoi to concede that it could not win so as to negotiate a settlement that would guarantee the survival of the South. Within three years American forces had been increased to nearly 550,000.

The war showed no signs of coming to a conclusion, and much of it was televised and beamed into people's homes. It became unpopular and the dis-content it evoked tended to merge with America's domestic woes, leading to major riots in several cities. A foreign policy could not be sustained for long against such domestic opposition. Thus it was the Tet offensive of the communists at the end of January 1968 that proved the turning point. Although their urban uprising was eventually crushed, the early communist successes in the main cities including Saigon that were shown on television suggested that the American task was hopeless. President Johnson turned down a request from his commander in the field, General Westmoreland, for an additional 200,000 troops and announced in March 1968 after the New Hampshire primary that he was calling a halt to the bombing and that he would not seek a new term in office. This in effect brought to an end that stage of containment when the United States acted as if its resources were limitless and as if it could oppose the further expansion of communist power wherever it might arise.

President Johnson's legacy in foreign affairs included not only the huge Vietnam problem, but importantly also a strained but working relationship with the Soviet Union. Building upon the momentum of the 1963 Test Ban Treaty, various other arms-control agreements were agreed, including the 1968 Nuclear Non-Proliferation Treaty. Despite their differences, both superpowers in the end sought to restrain their allies in the Middle East War of 1967; and Johnson acquiesced in the Soviet invasion of Czechoslovakia even as he sought to limit

Soviet pressure on the more independent communist countries, Rumania and Yugoslavia. Johnson had even tried to elicit Soviet help in reaching agreement with Vietnam during the course of his summit meeting with the Soviet Premier Kosygin in Glassboro in June 1967. Johnson claimed to be following a two track policy of thwarting communist aggression in Vietnam on the one hand and showing on the other that 'there was an alternative to confrontation' through the creation of 'a climate in which nations of the East and West could begin co-operating to find solutions to their worst problems'.[52] The Chinese were not a party to the latter. Indeed they thought, not entirely without reason, that such cooperation that did exist in American relations with the Soviet Union was directed against them.

American policy in the period of tripolarity

The advent of President Nixon and his close foreign affairs collaborator, Henry Kissinger, brought fresh perspectives to what they regarded as the problem of managing global order. Nixon soon accepted that great as American power still was – indeed no other country disposed of remotely comparable military, eco-nomic or technological resources – it could no longer seek to dictate the character of international order by its own efforts alone. The first practical indication of the new approach was Nixon's informal briefing to the press during a stopover in Guam in July 1969. In what became known as the Nixon Doctrine he pledged to maintain all existing treaty commitments and the shield of nuclear deterrence, but called upon any victim of other types of aggression to assume the responsibility for providing manpower for its defence, while the United States would provide training, weapons and offshore assistance through air and sea forces. This pro-vided the rationale for the 'Vietnamization' of the war – that is the withdrawal of American ground troops and their replacement by the forces of the South Vietnamese army. However, this was not thought of as a simple withdrawal, such as when the French finally called it a day and withdrew from Algeria. The American withdrawal was considered within the larger context of America's global strategic responsibilities. It was considered essential that America's cred-ibility as a provider of security and international order should not be under-mined by a defeat at the periphery of superpower contention, where it had committed so much force, treasure and prestige – hence the concept of 'peace with honour'. The Nixon administration claimed that the doctrine provided a new kind of flexibility that was absent from earlier doctrines of containment. Others, however, noted what seemed to be a contradiction between maintaining the same commitments as before while providing fewer capabilities with which to meet them.[53]

The China factor came into view early on in the Nixon administration. According to Kissinger it was the 1969 Sino-Soviet border conflict and the attendant Soviet soundings as to how America would react in the event of a Soviet attack upon China's nuclear installations that first alerted them to the strategic significance of China for the United States and for their vision of international order. This prompted the secret diplomacy that finally resulted in Henry Kissinger's path-breaking visit to Beijing in July 1971. Kissinger regarded the end of 1969 as the beginning of the triangular diplomacy with the communist world. As he later explained, 'We moved toward China not to expiate liberal guilt over our China policy of the late 1940s but to shape a global equilibrium.'[54]

Kissinger's visit to Beijing in July 1971 was arranged in secret through the good offices of Pakistan. The immediate response of the shocked Soviet leadership, according to Kissinger, was to sign a treaty of friendship with India on 9 August 1971. This was at a time when the Pakistani army was engaged in the suppression of widespread civil unrest in East Pakistan, where a momentum was building up for secession. In Kissinger's view the treaty and the subsequent Indian assistance to the secession of Bangladesh was an opportunity for the Soviet Union 'to demonstrate Chinese impotence and to humiliate a friend of both China and the United States'.[55] As if to demonstrate that the score had been evened somewhat, it was on the day after the signing of the treaty with India that President Brezhnev issued the formal invitation to President Nixon for a summit meeting in Moscow in May or June 1972 (i.e., after the Beijing summit due in February). The United States then sent a naval task force to the Gulf of Bengal as part of executing its famous so-called tilt towards Pakistan. According to Kissinger, Zhou Enlai joined him in believing that the United States had indeed saved West Pakistan.[56]

The episode may be seen as setting the tone for what was later called US–Chinese 'parallelism'. Within a context of complementary local, regional and global interests, the two states acted separately, but in the knowledge of the other's actions, to support a joint ally – in this case Pakistan. But the episode also masked a fundamental difference between the two sides that was to haunt the development of their relations and to cause divisions within subsequent American administrations. Mao and Zhou Enlai sought a united front against the Soviet Union and therefore wanted the United States to take an unyielding confrontationist approach towards it. Nixon and Kissinger, however, still sought détente with the Soviet Union in order to draw it into their vision of global equilibrium.

By virtue of China's relative weakness and vulnerability to Soviet military power, questions of national security were uppermost in the concerns of China's leaders. They came to suspect that Kissinger's interest in détente would encourage him to concede too much to the Soviet Union and that the result would be some kind of superpower condominium. Moreover, as the weaker power, China was always in danger of being used as a tactical pawn by the United States to 'buy' agreements with the Soviet Union at China's expense. By the mid-1970s, after SALT I, the Vladivostok agreement of December 1974, grain sales, technology transfer and the Helsinki accords of mid-1975, Mao complained that Washington had 'stood on China's shoulders' to reach agreements with Moscow.[57]

In the aftermath of the Kissinger and Nixon visits, Mao and Zhou Enlai abandoned their opposition to America's alliances in the Asia-Pacific. Thus Mao came to appreciate the significance of the Tokyo–Washington axis and even chided Kissinger at one point for not spending as much time in Tokyo as he did in Beijing. Mao and Zhou Enlai also tacitly supported the US military presence in the Philippines, Thailand and even South Korea. Moreover, although they could not say so publicly, the two Chinese leaders also shared an interest with Washington in seeking to forestall a humiliating US exit from Vietnam. The formula on Taiwan in the Shanghai Communiqué of 1972, whereby the United States avoided taking a position on the status of Taiwan, satisfied Mao to the extent that he had subordinated the Taiwan issue to larger strategic concerns. Indeed, alone of all the countries in the world, the United States for most of the 1970s was able to maintain its embassy for China in Taipei and continue its security treaty with Taiwan as the Republic of China while its leaders enjoyed close relations with those in Beijing.

Despite Nixon's initial apprehensions, his opening to China and his subsequent visit evoked a mood of euphoria in the United States. The reaction of America's Asian allies was positive, but more guarded. Japan felt subject to two Nixon shocks. The first was that it had not been informed in advance, let alone consulted, about the rapprochement with China; and the second was the almost simultaneous announcement of the withdrawal of the US dollar from the gold standard. American unilateralism on matters of such intrinsic importance to its most significant Asian ally was profoundly unsettling. But at least the way was open for Japan to develop its own relations with China. Essentially the United States left its allies to make their own adjustments to China, although it assured them of the continuation of its existing commitments.

The triangular policy of Nixon and Kissinger that also characterized the brief Ford administration (in which Kissinger was secretary of state) was predicated on avoiding taking sides and on maintaining good relations with both the Soviet Union and China, so as to promote their vision of an international order by which all the major powers would agree to act with restraint and not challenge the status quo by resort to violence, directly or indirectly. Since the Soviet Union was the only other true global power, the main thrust of the policy was directed towards it. Triangular diplomacy, from the American perspective, was primarily directed at restraining the Soviet Union, because China's global reach was limited and the likelihood of it re-engaging with its former ally (at least in this period) was remote. Building on relations of adversarial partnership with the Soviet Union begun by Kennedy and Johnson, Nixon and Kissinger espoused a policy of détente, by which they hoped to persuade the Soviet leadership of their common interest in basing international order on the balance of power – or, to use Kissinger's phrase, 'global equilibrium'. Central to this policy was the doctrine of linkage, according to which all major events should be seen as interconnected. It meant that progress in one area of interest to the US, say Vietnam, could be made conditional on progress in another of interest to the Soviet Union, say the Middle East, trade, or arms limitation. Above all it was meant to induce the Soviet Union to act with 'restraint'. In other words, the Soviet Union was not to sponsor the further expansion of communism. This could be seen as but another version of containment.

There were several problems with this strategy. For example, certain of these areas, such as arms control, might have an intrinsic importance in themselves that should not be made conditional on other matters. Similarly, it gave rise to a tendency to see the world as still dominated by the two superpowers, even though both Nixon and Kissinger were on record as seeing the emergence of a more complex multipolar world. Perhaps more damagingly, such an approach called for carefully calibrated policies that could not be sustained given the diffusion of power within the American political process. By 1974, for example, the administration's capacity to use trade with the Soviet Union for linkage purposes was constrained by the Jackson–Vanik amendment that required the Soviet Union to allow open emigration as a condition for normalizing trade. Opposition in Congress and in the State Department constrained Kissinger from acting as he would have wished over Angola in 1975. Moreover, the Kissinger approach antagonized the liberals, on the one hand, with its ill-concealed disdain for their moral concerns and, on the other hand, it simultaneously opened itself to criticism from the right for institutionalizing a process by which the Soviet Union made gains while the United States accepted a less than superior strategic position.

The immediate issue for the United States for the duration of the Nixon administration, however, was to manage the withdrawal from Vietnam with 'honour'. In the event, an agreement for a ceasefire and for the withdrawal of the remaining American forces was reached with Hanoi in January 1973 after both sides had failed to achieve a decisive advantage in the war. The agreement also called for the return and accounting of prisoners (an issue that subsequently was to be an obstacle to the normalization of American relations with Vietnam for more than twenty years), continuation of American military and economic aid to the South whose political future was to be left to be settled by elections and, finally, an American offer of economic assistance to the North. According to Kissinger the American constraint on Hanoi was the recourse to bombing, but once this was denied by Congress and once Nixon had become enfeebled by Watergate, the way was open for Hanoi to attack the South with impunity.[58] Be that as it may, the Northern offensive in March 1975 succeeded rapidly and Saigon fell on 29 April amid ignominious scenes as the last American helicopters fled the embassy. American forces had been withdrawn two years earlier, but the trauma of defeat was deep and long lasting, especially at home.

In the Asia-Pacific, however, the impact of the American debacle was less severe. Both Cambodia and Laos also fell to communist forces. Although it was not known at the time, the former was fanatically anti-Vietnamese, and no other dominoes fell. Thailand endured, as did the other pro-Western states of Southeast Asia, and the American position in the western Pacific was little affected. Indeed, nearly ten years before, communism had been eliminated from Indonesia. Arguably the Soviet Union, as the principal supporter and arms supplier of Vietnam, benefited. It had taken the opportunity of the American concentration on the Vietnam War to augment its naval capabilities, and its Pacific Fleet, which had become the largest in the Soviet navy, gave the Soviet Union a significant capacity to project force in the region.[59] But in the process it brought into play its conflict with China and the incipient conflict between China and Vietnam, which had been revived from 1971 – albeit behind the scenes. Thus despite its humiliation in 1975 and its virtual military disengagement from Southeast Asia (with the exception of its important bases in the Philippines), by virtue of the Third Indo-China War that began in Cambodia in 1978/1979 and the Soviet invasion of Afghanistan in December 1979, the United States in the end did not have to pay a significant price in the region for its failings.

By this stage President Carter was in office. His administration's early initiatives in Asia did not inspire confidence in its strategic sense of purpose. Although the Carter administration sought to apply tripolarity in a different way from the two previous administrations, which stood accused of abandoning American values, it failed to develop a clear sense of priorities that could be understood by its two major communist interlocutors. Arising out of the Soviet obligations to observe human rights that were incurred by the Helsinki agreements of 1975, the Carter administration emphasized human rights issues in the conduct of relations with the Soviet Union. That antagonized the Soviet leaders, who saw it as a ploy to undermine their government, and it delayed progress in negotiating further arms-limitation agreements until it was too late. Additionally, the administration agonized openly about whether to treat the two communist giants equally and about whether to play the China card by supplying it with arms and by deepening relations whenever the Soviet Union was judged to have behaved aggressively. Unlike Moscow, Beijing was not required to show greater respect for human rights, but, to their intense embarrassment, some of the governments of America's Asian allies were not spared. More disquieting was the early insistence on removing the 50,000 American troops still based in South Korea, even though President Carter was soon dissuaded from such a unilateral and potentially destabilizing exercise. Sending an emissary to Vietnam to initiate diplomatic contact was seen within the region as reflecting a domestic American agenda of purging the guilt about policy towards the erstwhile enemy, rather than being the result of a newly thought out strategy. With a new and not fully settled leadership in Beijing that sought an unyielding approach to the Soviet Union rather than to make compromises on Taiwan, the visit there by Secretary of State Vance in August 1977 to explore the prospects for normalizing relations did not proceed well.[60]

The sharpening of tensions between China and Vietnam in 1978 brought to a head incipient divisions in the Carter administration, between those led by the National Security Adviser, Z. Brzezinski, who sought a more confrontationist approach towards the Soviet Union and who also favoured closer relations with China, and those headed by the Secretary of State, C. Vance, who sought to renew détente with the Soviet Union and to maintain an even balance between the two. Although there was agreement about the desirability of normalizing relations with China, there were also those who wanted to normalize relations with Vietnam. Meanwhile the administration encouraged Japan in August 1978 to sign a peace and friendship treaty with China, despite the anti-hegemony clause (which was generally seen as being aimed at the Soviet Union).

Soviet attempts to intimidate Japan had backfired. As the tension deepened between China and Vietnam and its Soviet ally, the Carter administration found in Deng Xiaoping (who had just consolidated his supremacy) a leader who was willing to make the necessary compromises to establish full diplomatic relations with China. This also meant, in effect, the end of attempts to establish diplomatic relations with Vietnam.

The normalization of relations with China involved ending official relations with Taiwan, withdrawing remaining troops and terminating the security treaty. But an understanding was reached that while Beijing would not renounce the use of force, the United States would continue to sell arms to Taiwan. This was followed up in April 1979 by domestic American legislation, known as the Taiwan Relations Act, that was enacted against Carter's wishes, obliging the Executive to regard any use of force against Taiwan as a threat to the security of the western Pacific and as of 'great concern' to the US.[61]

The establishment of formal diplomatic relations with the PRC was followed in January by a highly successful visit by the Chinese leader Deng Xiaoping to the United States, in the course of which he openly vowed to 'teach Vietnam a lesson' for its invasion of Cambodia in December 1978 with Soviet support. An embarrassed Carter administration neither supported nor fully and openly opposed Deng. The limited Chinese incursion into Vietnam of February–March 1979 was followed by an unofficial alignment with Washington. In April 1979 China accepted the installation in Xinjiang of electronic listening devices to monitor Soviet rocketry that had been displaced by the Khomeini revolution in Iran. In January 1980, Defense Secretary Brown visited Beijing in the aftermath of the Soviet invasion of Afghanistan and began a policy of exporting to China advanced military technology of a non-lethal character. Before the year was out, China and the United States had established 'parallel' policies on Cambodia and Afghanistan. As separate allies of both Thailand and Pakistan, they supported them in different ways and also supplied arms to the Cambodian and Afghan resistance fighters operating with the assistance of the two respective allies. The two also worked together to deny the Cambodian seat at the UN to the Vietnamese-installed government in Phnom Penh and to isolate Vietnam both economically and politically. More broadly at this time, 'on issue after issue' – from the unity of NATO to the strengthening of the Association of Southeast Asian Nations – Peking's position came to resemble that of the United States.[62]

The accession of the Reagan administration did not fundamentally change the coordinated 'parallel' policies pursued with China with regard to Cambodia and Afghanistan, but nevertheless the character of Sino-American relations changed. Several factors accounted for this. President Reagan himself offended Beijing by his early rhetoric that called for upgrading American relations with Taiwan. Perhaps more importantly, the Reagan strategy of a massive rebuilding of American nuclear and conventional forces coupled with a more robust approach to the Soviet Union meant that by the summer of 1982 Washington no longer put so much emphasis on tripolarity as a means for restraining Soviet behaviour. If China had become less important to the United States, China had also gained a greater degree of diplomatic manoeuvre, as it had less cause to fear Soviet aggression. Additionally, with the Soviet Union bogged down in Afghanistan, the Chinese could afford to take the 'sting' out of relations with the Soviet Union. Consequently the Chinese began to move to what they called at the Twelfth Communist Party Congress in September 1982 an 'independent foreign policy', according to which China would 'never attach itself to a big power or a group of powers'.

A series of incidents took place by which the Chinese sought to test the character of the American commitment to them. This brought out the last conflict within an American administration about the significance of the China card. On this occasion it was Secretary of State Alexander Haig who argued about the intrinsic strategic significance of China for the United States against a more general trend to devalue China's significance as both a trading and a strategic partner. His replacement by George Shultz in June 1982 brought about a more sober reassessment of the significance of China. It was thought that China was decades away from becoming a global power and, in view of the different cultures and strategic perspectives, Shultz warned in March 1983 that Sino-American relations would inevitably be characterized by 'frustrations and problems'. Pride of place in American policy should belong to Japan. Henceforth China loomed smaller in American strategic calculations than at any time since the original rapprochement more than ten years earlier.[63] Interestingly, as mutual expectations were reduced, the United States developed its best working relations with China in the remaining years of the Reagan presidency. Certainly there was American disquiet about Chinese arms sales to Iran and Iraq in the course of their war, but essentially their 'parallel' partnership over Cambodia and Afghanistan continued until the 1988/1989 agreements with the Soviet Union brought the issues to an end as matters of global concern. Moreover, trade and other relations with China developed well despite the differences between the two societies. Indeed popular opinion within the United States chose to believe that the economic reforms in China were leading the country in a more liberal direction.

American relations with its formal allies in the 1970s and 1980s underwent important changes, despite the fact that the United States remained the fundamental provider of regional security. Although the Nixon Doctrine and the subsequent American debacle in Vietnam raised doubts about the extent to which the United States would be prepared to intervene militarily to uphold its commitments, on the whole these doubts did not give rise to major problems. These arose largely in response to the growing economic power of first, and most notably, Japan and then of the other Pacific Rim countries that by the mid-1980s came to be regarded as newly industrializing countries or economies (NICs or NIEs). In many respects their economic achievements may be regarded as a product of the success of America's post-war policies. By providing military security, investment and privileged access to the domestic American market without demanding equal reciprocity, successive American administrations had provided them with unusually favourable opportunities to develop.

Three problems arose, especially with Japan after its rapid economic growth elevated it to the world's third (or perhaps even second) largest economy in the early 1970s. First, from the late 1960s Japan developed a large and growing trade surplus with the United States, and as it grew so did American discontent. Second, the United States became dissatisfied with Japan as a 'free-rider' and demanded that it contribute more to regional security. Third, Japan began to recognize that in some respects its interests diverged from its American ally, and with the growth of the Japanese economy came a sense of pride and self-assertiveness that tended to resent American pressure to accommodate to what were seen as particular American rather than common concerns. In many ways these problems were exacerbated in the 1980s as a result not only of the huge American trade deficit, but also of the massive budget deficit that arose from the Reagan administration's vast expenditure on defence. A good part of the latter was financed by Japanese investment.

Two decades of constant trade friction were capped in 1987 by the American imposition of trade sanctions for the first time. In fact, as both sides recognized, their two giant economies were interdependent, but one was conscious of its vulnerability as a resource-poor country whose interests did not always coincide with those of its long-term protector, and the other felt that it could no longer sustain a vast trade imbalance that was considered to have been obtained through unfair practices, especially since the American economy had lost its hegemonic character. These problems were exacerbated by the cultural divide between the two countries.[64] Their incipient conflict was contained, however, by their over-riding interest in not challenging the basis of their security alliance and by the recognition of the mutual dependence of their economies. As long as the Cold War lasted, it served to prevent recurrent disputes from escalating to challenge the fundamental ties between the two allies.

Notes

1 Cited in James C. Thomson Jr, Peter W. Stanley and John Curtis Perry, *Sentimental Imperialists: The American Experience in East Asia* (New York: Harper & Row, 1981), p.192.
2 For the accounts of Acheson, see Ronald L. McGlothlen, *Controlling the Waves: Dean Acheson and U.S. Foreign Policy in Asia* (New York: W.W. Norton & Co.,1993), pp.26–40; and for those of Kennan, see John Lewis Gaddis, *Strategies of Containment* (Oxford: Oxford University Press, 1982), pp.76–79.
3 For a sustained, if unsympathetic, account, see Christopher Coker, *Reflections on American Foreign Policy Since 1949* (London: Pinter, 1989).
4 See Hans J. Morganthau, *A New Foreign Policy for the United States* (London: Pall Mall, 1969), p.15; and more generally, Henry Kissinger, *Diplomacy* (New York: Simon and Schuster, 1994), which contrasts unfavourably American idealism with traditional European statecraft.
5 See, for example, Bernard H. Gordon, *New Directions for American Policy in Asia* (London and New York: Routledge, 1990), p.7; and President Theodore Roosevelt, who in 1903 stated that America must oppose any who would be 'top dog' in Asia, cited in Lau Teik Soon and Leo Suryadinata (eds), *Moving into the Pacific Century: The Changing Regional Order* (Oxford: Heinemann, 1988), p.3. See also John Lewis Gaddis,

'The Modern World: World War I to 1984' in Michael P. Hamilton (ed.), *American Character and Foreign Policy* (Grand Rapids, MI: William B. Eerdmans Publishing Co., 1986), p.38.

6 Michael H. Hunt, *Ideology and U.S. Foreign Policy* (New Haven: Yale University Press, 1987).

7 Perhaps the most notable writer on this theme is Akira Iriye. See in particular Iriye (ed.), *Mutual Images: Essays in American-Japanese Relations* (Cambridge, MA: Harvard University Press, 1975). See also Warren I. Cohen, *America's Response to China: A History of Sino-American Relations* (New York: Columbia University Press, 3rd edn, 1990).

8 See W.I. Cohen, *America's Response to China (op. cit.)*; Michael H. Hunt, *The Making of a Special Relationship: The United States and China to 1914* (New York: Columbia University Press, 1983); and John K. Fairbank, *The United States and China* (Cambridge, MA: Harvard University Press, 4th edn, 1983).

9 Thomson *et al.*, *Sentimental Imperialists (op. cit.)*, ch.8, pp.106–33.

10 Gaddis, *Strategies of Containment (op. cit.)*, especially pp.51–53.

11 There are many examples in his *The White House Years* (London: Weidenfeld & Nicolson, 1979) and *Years of Upheaval* (London: Michael Joseph, 1982). But his discussion of the opening to China brings out very well his irritation with the bureaucratic ways of the State Department in outlining agendas based on long-established issues and in determining their priorities through institutional bargaining. These he felt obstructed the diplomacy based on changes in the balance of power. Consequently, his secret diplomacy tended to bypass the State Department altogether. See *The White House Years*, ch.XVIII, pp.684–732.

12 The classic, but perhaps exaggerated and much disputed, account is that of Graham T. Allison, *Essence of Decision: Explaining the Cuban Missile Crisis* (Boston: Little Brown, 1971).

13 For general accounts of the significance of public opinion, see James N. Rosenau, *Public Opinion and Foreign Policy: An Operational Formulation* (New York: Random House, 1961), ch.4. See also Charles W. Kegley Jr and Eugene R. Wittkopf, *American Foreign Policy: Pattern and Process* (New York: St Martin's Press, 1991), ch.9. For a more historical survey, see Melvin Small, 'Public Opinion' in Hogan *et al.*, *Explaining the History of American Foreign Relations* (Cambridge: Cambridge University Press, 1991), pp.165–76.

14 Michael J. Hogan, 'Corporatism' in Hogan *et al.*, *Explaining the History of American Foreign Relations (op. cit.)*, pp.226–36.

15 Thomas J. McCormack, *China Market: America's Quest for Informal Empire, 1893–1901* (Chicago: Chicago University Press, 1967); and Stanley Bachrack, *The Committee of One Million: 'China Lobby' Politics, 1953–1971* (New York: Columbia University Press, 1976).

16 Morganthau, *A New Foreign Policy … (op. cit.)*, p.15.

17 William R. Louis, *Imperialism at Bay* (Oxford: Oxford University Press, 1978), p.285.

18 Dean Acheson, *Present at the Creation* (New York: W.W. Norton & Co., 1969 [reissued in 1987]), p.229. For the broader significance attached to Japan, see Gaddis, *Strategies of Containment (op. cit.)*, ch.3; and Ronald L. McGlothlen, *Controlling the Waves: Dean Acheson and U.S. Foreign Policy in Asia* (New York: W.W. Norton & Co., 1993), ch.2.

19 W.G. Beasley, *The Modern History of Japan* (London: Pall Mall, 3rd edn, 1981).

20 For a critical account, see Frank H. Golay, *The Philippines, Public Policy and National Economic Development* (Ithaca: Cornell University Press, 1961).

21 Michael Leifer, *Indonesia's Foreign Policy* (London: George Allen and Unwin, 1983), pp.19–26.

22 For a critical account, see Bruce Cummings, *The Origins of the Korean War*, 2 vols. (Princeton: Princeton University Press, 1990). For a careful historian's analysis, see Peter Lowe, *The Origins of the Korean War* (London: Longman, 1986). On the demobilization, see Gaddis, *Strategies of Containment (op. cit.)*, p.23.

23 Nancy Bernkopf Tucker, *Patterns in the Dust: Chinese–American Relations and the Recognition Controversy* (New York: Columbia University Press, 1983).
24 For an account of the impact of the speech on Mao and Stalin, see Sergei N. Goncharov, John W. Lewis and Xue Litai, *Uncertain Partners: Stalin, Mao, and the Korean War* (Stanford: Stanford University Press, 1993), pp.101–4.
25 As Kissinger has pointed out, these were the precise terms which General Douglas MacArthur, then Commander of America's Pacific Forces, had used in public in March 1949 to define the 'line of defense' (Kissinger, *Diplomacy* (*op. cit.*), p.475).
26 Bruce Cummings, *The Origins of the Korean War* (*op. cit.*), vol.2, pp.423–28, argues that it was understood by all concerned that South Korea was included in the defence perimeter. Michael Schaller, *Douglas MacArthur: The Far Eastern General* (Oxford: Oxford University Press, 1989), pp.161, 163, 172; and John Merril, *Korea: The Peninsular Origins of the War* (Newark: University of Delaware Press, 1989), pp.166–67, argue to the contrary that Korea was excluded. Goncharov *et al.*, *Uncertain Partners* (*op. cit.*), pp.141–42 presents evidence that the North Koreans told the Soviets in the spring of 1950 that the Americans would not intervene, but that Stalin was not altogether convinced.
27 Evelyn Colbert, *Southeast Asia in International Politics, 1941–1956* (Ithaca: Cornell University Press, 1977), pp.204–8.
28 Truman statement of 27 June 1950, cited in *ibid.*, p.477.
29 Paul H. Nitze, 'Grand Strategy Then and Now: NSC-68 and its Lessons for the Future', *Strategic Review* 22, 1 (Winter 1994), pp.16–17.
30 See 'Appendix' in Gaddis, *Strategies of Containment* (*op. cit.*), p.359, where he gives the percentages of GNP allocated to defence for the three years as 4.6, 6.9 and 12.7 respectively.
31 Kissinger argues the case very strongly in his *Diplomacy* (*op. cit.*), ch.19.
32 David Rees, *Korea: The Limited War* (London: Hamish Hamilton, 1964). For recent accounts of the war, see Max Hastings, *The Korean War* (London: Michael Joseph, 1987); and Jon Halliday and Bruce Cummings, *Korea: The Unknown War* (London: Viking Penguin, 1988).
33 Acheson, *Present at the Creation* (*op. cit.*), p.544.
34 Kimura Hiroshi and K.O. Sarkisov, 'Japan and the Soviet Role in East Asia' in Warren I. Cohen and Akira Iriye (eds), *The Great Powers in East Asia 1953–1960* (New York: Columbia University Press, 1990), pp.165–67.
35 Although the Americans thought that the threat had been instrumental in effecting an agreement, Chinese researchers forty years later have tended to play down its significance. See Rosemary Foot, 'Nuclear Coercion and the Ending of the Korean Conflict', *International Security* 13, 3 (Winter 1988/1989); and Zhang Shu Guang, *Deterrence and Strategic Culture: Chinese–American Confrontations, 1949–1958* (Ithaca: Cornell University Press, 1992), p.133.
36 Nancy Bernkopf Tucker, *Taiwan, Hong Kong, and the United States: Uncertain Friendships* (New York: Twayne Publishers, Macmillan Publishing Co., 1994), p.41.
37 Gordon H. Chang, *Friends and Enemies: The United States, China, and the Soviet Union, 1948–1972* (Stanford: Stanford University Press, 1990).
38 J.H. Kalicki, *The Pattern of Sino-American Crises: Political–Military Interactions in the 1950s* (Cambridge: Cambridge University Press, 1975).
39 For a succinct and skilful analysis of the evolution of American strategic thinking, see Robert S. Litwak, *Detente and the Nixon Doctrine* (Cambridge: Cambridge University Press, 1984), ch.1, 'America as the Night-Watchman State 1947–68', pp.11–47.
40 Cited by Walter LaFeber, *The American Age: U.S. Foreign Policy at Home and Abroad, 1750 to the Present* (New York: W.W. Norton & Co., 2nd edn, 1994), p.593.
41 *Ibid.*, p.593. The irony of this should be noted, since it was precisely the prospect of such an exercise by the Soviet Union that was to alert Kissinger and Nixon six years later to the advantages to the United States of preventing such an exercise.

42 W.W. Rostow, cited in Gaddis, *Strategies of Containment* (*op. cit.*), p.231.
43 Harry Harding and Melvin Gurtov, *The Purge of Luo Jui-ch'ing: The Politics of Chinese Strategic Planning* (Santa Monica: Rand Corporation, R-548-PR, 1971)
44 Gaddis, *Strategies of Containment* (*op. cit.*), p.240.
45 Allen S. Whiting, *The Chinese Calculus of Deterrence* (Ann Arbor: University of Michigan Press, 1975), pp.170–95.
46 Cited in Evelyn Colbert, *Southeast Asia* ... (*op. cit.*), p.205.
47 Colbert, *Southeast Asia* ... (*op. cit.*), p.204.
48 Gary R. Hess, 'The American Search for Stability in Southeast Asia: The SEATO Structure of Containment' in Cohen and Iriye (eds), *The Great Powers* ... (*op. cit.*), pp.272–95; and Colbert, Southeast Asia ... (*op. cit.*), ch.11.
49 Michael Leifer, *Indonesia's Foreign Policy* (*op. cit.*), pp.50–51.
50 Dwight D. Eisenhower, *Waging Peace: The White House Years, 1956–1961* (New York: Doubleday, 1965), p.607.
51 For a succinct analysis, see Michael Leifer, *The Foreign Relations of New States* (Melbourne: Longman Australia, 1974), pp.79–80. See also Kissinger, *Diplomacy* (*op. cit.*), pp.645–47, for an argument that American idealism and the remoteness of the country in the American consciousness prevented the US from fighting successfully with a relatively small intervention force to stop the war in the South from erupting.
52 Lyndon B. Johnson, *The Vantage Point: Perspectives of the Presidency, 1963–1969* (New York: Holt, Reinhart and Winston, 1971).
53 See the discussion in Litwak, *Detente and the Nixon Doctrine* (*op. cit.*), chs 3–4.
54 Henry Kissinger, *The White House Years* (*op. cit.*), p.192. See also chapter 6 for his account of the 'First Steps Toward China'.
55 Kissinger, *The White House Years* (*op. cit.*), p.867.
56 *Ibid.*, p.913.
57 Michel Oksenberg, 'A Decade of Sino-American Relations', *Foreign Affairs* 61, 1 (Fall 1982), p.180.
58 See chapter 27 in Kissinger, *Diplomacy* (*op. cit.*), pp.674–702 and p.692 in particular.
59 For a balanced discussion of the strengths and weaknesses of the Soviet position, see Paul F. Langer, 'Soviet Military Power in Asia' in Donald Zagoria (ed.), *Soviet Policy in East Asia* (New Haven: Yale University Press, for the Council on Foreign Relations, 1982), pp.255–82.
60 Oksenberg, 'A Decade ... ' (*op. cit.*), p.183.
61 Harry Harding, *A Fragile Relationship: The United States and China Since 1972* (Washington, DC: The Brookings Institution, 1992), p.86 and, more generally, ch.3. See also Tucker, *Taiwan, Hong Kong, and the United States* (*op. cit.*), pp.132–40.
62 *Ibid.*, p.94.
63 *Ibid.*, p.136. 'Political Protectionism in the Pacific' (London: International Institute for Strategic Studies, *Adelphi Papers* no.228, Spring 1988. For divergent views of US–Japanese relations on these matters, see Kathleen Newland (ed.), *The International Relations of Japan* (Basingstoke: Macmillan, 1990); Takeshi Inoguchi and Daniel I. Okamoto (eds), *The Political Economy of Japan*, Vol.2 (Stanford: Stanford University Press, 1988); Edward J. Lincoln, *Japan's Unequal Trade* (Washington, DC: The Brookings Institution, 1990); and Roger Buckley, *US–Japan Alliance Diplomacy, 1945–1990* (Cambridge: Cambridge University Press, 1992).

5 The Soviet Union/Russia and the Asia-Pacific

The Soviet Union and the new Russia will be treated together, but in sequence. If the Soviet Union was a global power, the new Russia is more of a regional power. The demise of the Soviet Union in 1991 and its replacement by Russia have fundamentally changed the character of the relations between the Eurasian state and the countries of the Asia-Pacific, as has indeed happened even more strikingly elsewhere in the world. In addition to the loss of the capabilities of a superpower, another significant change was the abandonment of communism and the concomitant claim to lead a worldwide communist movement. Nevertheless, there are important continuities. First, it is important to recognize that despite its universalist communist pretensions, a Russian imprint on Soviet conduct was always evident, even though its depth may have been disputed.[1] Second, and by the same token, the Soviet legacy is evident in many respects even as the leaders of the new Russia grope towards a different future. Importantly, the new Russia has been regarded internationally in some respects as the heir of the Soviet Union. For example, it assumed without question the permanent Soviet seat on the UN Security Council. And, like the Soviet Union before it, the new Russia still aspires to be recognized as a global power alongside the United States. In this respect Russia still disposes of a nuclear arsenal of superpower dimensions and its military industries can still produce advanced weapons systems.

The new Russia has also inherited the borders of the former Soviet Union, except, of course, where these were taken over by the new states formed from the old Soviet Republics. In the Asia-Pacific, broadly defined, these include the five Central Asian Republics of Turkmenistan, Uzbekistan, Tajikistan, Kyrgyzstan and Kazakhstan. The last three together with Russia share a border with China's Xinjiang Autonomous Region, and accordingly impinge directly on the narrower definition of the Asia-Pacific used in this book. All five states are members of the Commonwealth of Independent States (CIS), with Russia as the key member. Those bordering China negotiate remaining border issues collectively, which in practice tends to mean that the new Russia has inherited most of the old border and territorial disputes of the former Soviet Union, which it itself had inherited from Tsarist Russia.

Despite the loss of vast tracts of land to the former Soviet Republics, Russia is still the world's largest state, stretching across the vast Eurasian landmass from the

Baltic to the Pacific. In that respect, both the Soviet Union and Russia have tended to regard the Far East as an outpost, a point of vulnerability to be defended, rather than a gateway to the Asia-Pacific – even though the rhetoric of Presidents Gorbachev and Yeltsin may have suggested otherwise.

The conduct of Soviet policy towards the Asia-Pacific since 1945 has been shaped by the competing priorities of global, regional and domestic security and ideological concerns. Ideological concerns, as understood here, do not refer only to the doctrinal matters of Marxism–Leninism, but rather to the practical consequences at home and abroad that arose from the claim by successive Soviet leaders to be at the head of a worldwide communist movement. Global issues centred primarily on the strategic relationship with the United States and regional ones focused primarily upon China, Japan, Korea and Vietnam.

Domestic concerns about the region arose largely as a consequence of the vast geographical expanse of the Soviet Union. This contributed to a sense of insecurity, at one level, about the thinly populated Russian Far East that was supplied by the Trans-Siberian Railway and by sea via the Indian Ocean, both of which were vulnerable to interdiction in wartime. Indeed, it was the tyranny of distance that caused the Russian explorers and traders to retreat from northern California in the first half of the nineteenth century and the government to sell Alaska to the United States in 1867.[2] The wars fought with Japan in the first half of the twentieth century for dominance in Korea, Manchuria and Inner Asia established a linkage between defeat abroad and upheaval at home, and they also came to illustrate the strategic necessity of avoiding having to fight a war on two fronts. That historical legacy, combined with the Soviet goal of matching and perhaps exceeding the United States in military terms as a fellow superpower, found expression in an over-militarized approach in the Far East.

At perhaps deeper levels, the distant Russian outposts in the Far East illustrated ambiguities about the sense of identity of this vast Eurasian state. The uneasy suspension between East Asia and Western Europe has led Russian people, as Dostoevsky noted, to be regarded as Europeans in Asia and as Asiatics in Europe.[3] It has been argued persuasively that 'the Soviet far east is an extension of European Russia into Asia'.[4] Although three-quarters of the Soviet Union lay in Asia and about 30 per cent of the Soviet population lived in its Asian lands, the Soviet Union neither considered itself nor was it considered by others to be Asian. It was not invited to the first Asian and African conference in Bandung in 1955, nor did it evince any desire to attend. When it sought to attend the abortive follow-up conference ten years later in Algeria, it did so mainly in order to spike the guns of its Chinese adversaries. At most, Soviets and Russians have thought of themselves as Eurasians. Any Asian identity that was claimed was done for political advantage, as for example when Stalin greeted a visiting Japanese foreign minister in 1941 with the toast: 'You are an Asiatic, so am I.'[5] The Soviet Union has been rightly described as 'a power in East Asia but not an East Asian power'.[6] Pacific Russia has not been integrated into the region. With the exception of the decade of the special relationship with China in the 1950s, the economic links with East Asia have been of minimal significance. Since the break with China, trade with Pacific Asia has averaged out at between 5 and 10 per cent of total Soviet trade, and with the exception of the Asian communist countries Soviet trade accounted for a negligible proportion of that of individual Asian countries.[7]

The absence of significant economic and political intercourse with the countries of the region meant that once the conflict with China emerged in the 1960s, Soviet policy in East Asia became excessively reliant on military means.

Ideological and institutional influences on policy

The Soviet Union came into existence as a result of the Bolshevik Revolution, and despite its many changes it bore the marks of its birth right up to its demise nearly seventy-five years later. Perhaps the most important of these was the absolute rule by the highly centralized Communist Party, which was subject to no state law, constrained only by its evolving customary practices and legitimized by its ideology. The party's role in principle was to construct the socio-economic basis for socialism and communism at home and to promote the expansion of other revolutions abroad. In practice, however, the legacy of Lenin – the founding father – was ambiguous, as the revolution had bequeathed a state as well as a new international movement. Very early on, with the Treaty of Brest-Litovsk of 1918, it was decided to put the interests of preserving the nascent state before the prospects of extending the revolution. Moreover, after the civil war and the defeat of the allied intervention in 1921, it was argued that the revolutionary state could coexist with the hostile capitalist states which encircled it because of the implacable rivalries between them.

In other words, the Leninist legacy in foreign affairs was ambiguous in at least two respects: first, the Soviet leadership, being in command of both party and state, was charged with promoting revolution abroad through leading foreign communist parties whose interests at critical moments could be sacrificed for those of the Soviet state; and second, the state leaders were enjoined to exploit divisions between other states in order to ensure the survival of the Soviet Union and coexist with them while simultaneously seeking to undermine them through their communist parties.[8]

A further legacy from the Leninist era was a view of the relations of the Soviet Communist Party state with the nationalist movements in the colonies and semi-colonies of Asia and, by extension, Africa. Seen as the weak link of imperialism, it was the Soviet obligation to assist their struggles for independence, even though they might be led by representatives of their upper and middle classes, as this was seen as weakening the metropolitan capitalist states and hastening the revolutionary process there. In addition to giving rise to another layer of ambiguity in adjusting the priorities of immediate Soviet state interests and those of the independence movements, it also raised problems of adjusting both of those interests to those of communist parties in Asia. Thus even Lenin found it expedient to turn a blind eye to the persecution of local communists in order to cultivate relations with Kemal Ataturk, the radical nationalist leader of Turkey.[9]

Adam Ulam, perhaps the most notable Western interpreter of Soviet foreign policy, has argued that some of the very qualities that brought the Bolsheviks to power also served to handicap them: 'Extreme suspiciousness of every movement and every government not fully sharing their ideology and an underestimation of the staying power of Western countries, and a view of international politics as consisting mainly of the clash of economic and military interests.'[10] With the advent of Stalin, these traits were emphasized still further. Under his personal dictatorship the doctrine of 'socialism in one country', which had emerged earlier to deal with the disappointment of the failure of revolutions elsewhere in Europe, was now interpreted as requiring the total subordination of communist parties everywhere to the needs of the Soviet state, whose security interests were defined exclusively in accordance with the astute, but paranoid, outlook of one man. But not even he was able dominate the Chinese Communist Party, so that the incipient contradiction of seeking both to encourage and to control the Chinese comrades remained to haunt both him and his successors after the Second World War. 'Socialism in one country' acquired an even more autarchic character when, through his programme of forced collectivization of agriculture and national industrialization begun under the First Five Year Plan in 1928, Stalin also created an economic system that clearly cut off the Soviet Union from the international (capitalist) economy. Moreover, the terror and the climate of distrust that it nurtured at home had a corresponding effect in heightening suspicion of the outside world.

With regard to foreign policy, Stalin consistently argued that the Soviet Union faced an encirclement by capitalist powers with whom war at some stage was inevitable and yet that in the short term it was possible to live in peaceful coexistence with these powers by taking advantage of their irresolvable rivalries. This left it open to the Soviet leader to make temporary alliances and to practice balance of power politics. This in fact characterized his policies in the 1930s that culminated in the Nazi–Soviet Pact in 1939. The wartime alliance with Britain and America did not lead Stalin to share Roosevelt's internationalist outlook. And, as the conferences of Teheran and Yalta were to show, what Stalin practised was traditional power politics in order to promote the survival and development of Soviet goals as he understood them. Thus in East Asia he sought the restitution of Russian borders and privileges going back to the nineteenth century and the establishment of buffer zones around the Soviet Union that he could dominate.

The countries of East Europe and North Korea emerged as communist states closely modelled on and tightly controlled by the Soviet Union – in practice by Stalin. In theory the socialist camp was bound by the principles of socialist internationalism – allegedly a higher form of relationship than those obtained between the Western allies. Tito's Yugoslavia refused to accept Stalin's control, was expelled from the camp in 1948, and went on to develop a form of nationalist communism that was to complicate the Soviet Union's relations with its East European satellites thereafter. With the establishment of a communist regime in China an even greater challenge was posed to Soviet control of the socialist camp.

The Soviet leadership of the socialist camp and the international communist movement, it is clear, was a source of both strength and weakness. Under Stalin's leadership it provided strategic depth and a source of inspiration that communism could spread under a single banner and thus face the future with confidence, especially as the Soviet form of industrialization had supposedly been vindicated by the triumph of the war against Germany. At the same time leadership of the communist world carried the seeds of weakness as the Soviet Union was necessarily obliged to maintain the new communist regimes and underwrite their security, while all the time being vulnerable to the emergence of nationalist challenges that could question the authority and the universal validity of that leadership which was expressed in ideological terms. Even the great Stalin had been challenged by Tito. As would be seen, it was one thing for him to shrug off the challenge, but it was to be beyond his successors in the end. The ideological challenge that China was to present augmented those of strategy, politics and other points of difference. Stalin's successors would also find that the price of leadership of the socialist camp was to have to tend to the demands of far-flung members such as Vietnam and Cuba in ways that did not always accord with their sense of Soviet interests. Moreover, as many have pointed out, it was easier to have relations with non-communist India than communist China and easier to manage a neutral buffer state such as Finland than a fellow communist one such as Poland, Hungary or Czechoslovakia.

With the death of Stalin, no one man was able thereafter to exercise total dominance over the Soviet party and state, and it became possible to identify different interests and personalities exercising influence over policy. Indeed, bureaucratic interests became sufficiently evident for scholars to speculate about the extent to which policy making was subject to bargaining between the major organizations of state.[11] Although first Khrushchev and then Brezhnev were the principal leaders in their day, the ouster of the first in 1964 by his erstwhile colleagues and the general conservatism of the latter suggested more of an oligarchy. Meanwhile the diversity of Soviet industrial society became more evident. Although remaining a dictatorship, the Soviet Union gradually acquired authoritarian, as opposed to totalitarian, characteristics. The machinery of political repression was still in operation, but debates and differences of opinion were more freely aired, and in time a more subtle view of international relations gradually took root.[12] By the same process ideology lost its vitality and cohesiveness, while still remaining the core of the legitimacy for the rule of the Communist Party of the Soviet Union (CPSU).[13]

By the end of the Brezhnev era Soviet foreign policy had become greatly militarized, in the sense that, as its economy stagnated and the appeal of ideology declined, much of the exercise of Soviet foreign relations depended on the direct or indirect use of armed force. That was the only arena in which the Soviet Union could be counted as a superpower rival to the United States. Undoubtedly that contributed to the growing influence of the military in Soviet life, where the military industrial complex is now said to have accounted for 40 per cent of the Soviet GDP. But this did not mean that the military had come to dominate decision-making or that the Communist Party had lost its grip on the leadership.[14]

With the accession of Gorbachev in 1985 and his reformist agenda, foreign policy came to reflect more the domestic priorities of those reforms which were in turn a reaction to the deep-seated systemic crisis prevalent in the Soviet Union. At the same time, by seeking cooperation with the international community, Gorbachev and the new personnel whom he had advanced sought to encourage the process of open reform at home. By initiating the processes of demilitarization and de-ideologization in the interests of domestic reform, he initiated policies that led to the acceptance of asymmetrical arms control agreements and the withdrawal of Soviet forces and support from regional conflicts elsewhere.[15] They also contributed to endorsing the principle of self-determination, even for socialist states, which led to the collapse of communism in Eastern Europe and the independence of the Baltic States. These developments have generally been seen as the result of restructuring from above rather than as a response to unstoppable pressures from below. Yet, in turn, the reforms unleashed a plurality and confusion of forces that accelerated the process of disintegration. Perhaps the key problem was that the economic reform at home only succeeded in undermining the existing inefficient but functioning economic system, with the result that the only domestic return for the policies of demilitarization and closer integration with the Western world was economic chaos and the loss of support from potential domestic constituencies. By the summer of 1991 time had run out for both Gorbachev and the Soviet Union. The result in the Far East of the general process of demilitarization and disintegration was the emasculation of Russia as a significant great power in the Asia-Pacific.

Stalin's power politics in East Asia, 1945–53

The terms of the Yalta agreements of February 1945 made clear Stalin's fundamental security objectives in the Far East. By seeking to retain effective control over Outer Mongolia (the Mongolian People's Republic), restore the rights and territories lost to Japan in 1904 and re-establish the extra-territorial rights exercised by Tsarist Russia in Manchuria, Stalin aimed at enlarging the buffer zone on the Soviet periphery and gaining access to warm-water ports. As he explained to the nationalist Chinese foreign minister, who had come to negotiate a treaty of friendship and alliance later that summer, 'in the past, Russia wanted an alliance with Japan in order to break up China. Now we want an alliance with China to curb Japan.'[16] Before the treaty was signed on 14 August, the United States had dropped the atom bomb on Hiroshima that in effect obviated the American need for Soviet intervention on which the agreement to Stalin's terms had been based. Stalin hastily declared war on Japan and launched a rapid offensive against the Japanese forces in Manchuria and Korea. This not only ensured Soviet control of Manchuria, but also guaranteed Soviet dominance of Korea north of the 38th Parallel, as agreed with the United States earlier in August 1945.[17]

At the end of the Pacific War Chiang Kai-shek's government sought an alliance with Moscow, principally to ensure Soviet recognition and to limit the cooperation between Soviet and Chinese communist forces in Manchuria. At this point Stalin calculated that the communists could not win a civil war with the nationalists, and he was greatly concerned about the implications for Soviet national interests of the American commitment to the nationalists. Indeed, part of his reason for establishing a buffer zone across northern China was to make provision against a China that would be linked to America in ways envisaged by Roosevelt's wartime planners. Hence he urged Mao to put aside armed struggle and enter a coalition government with Chiang Kai-shek. It was not until the autumn of 1947, when the military position shifted in favour of the Chinese communists, that Stalin accepted Mao's claims that the communists would win and that the Americans would not be able to stop them. Indeed, in January 1948 when Stalin made his famous admission to Milovan Djilas that he had been proved wrong by the Chinese communists, he also noted that China was different from Greece and that America, 'the strongest state in the world', would never let the communists win.[18]

Stalin's calculations took into account the global balance and especially the situation in Europe. He refused to recognize the Democratic Republic of Vietnam as proclaimed by Ho Chi Minh in September 1945. Even though Ho had proved to be a trustworthy agent of the Comintern, Stalin's European priorities made him assign a higher priority to helping the communists in France gain entry into the coalition government. With the outbreak of the Cold War, Stalin insisted that the East European states reject the offer of Marshall aid. The ever suspicious Stalin began to tighten his personal dominance of the 'socialist camp' in Europe through extensive purges of so-called cosmopolitans and others. This was also related to the confrontation with Tito and his expulsion from the socialist camp. Mao and the Chinese could not be treated in the same way. China was simply too big and the independent national character of its revolution as led by Mao was too well established.

This did not mean, however, granting the Chinese communists a free hand. After the establishment of the People's Republic of China in October 1949, Mao went to Moscow to negotiate a new treaty of alliance. He arrived on 16 December and he did not return to Chinese soil until 27 February 1950. Over the two months of hard bargaining Stalin succeeded in holding on to most of the gains he had claimed at Yalta and in the 1945 treaty with the nationalist government. But he also had to accept the burden of agreeing to come to China's assistance in the event of an attack by Japan 'or any state allied with her and thus being in a state of war'. The latter qualification was to prove its importance in the Korean War and other Sino-American military engagements. Stalin may have disappointed his new Chinese allies with the paltriness of his economic assistance, limited to the value of US$300 million spread over five years, but he pleased them with his secret military assistance.[19]

Stalin greatly embarrassed Mao by insisting on an 'Additional Agreement' by which the Chinese had to agree to forbid citizens from third-party countries from residing or undertaking any economic activities in Manchuria or Xinjiang. Apparently, Stalin had in mind to insist on the exclusion of Americans in particular from all parts of China, but eventually he settled for these bordering provinces, the effect of which was to limit any foreign economic influence there to the Soviet Union alone. The only precedents for this were the unequal treaties of the imperialist era. The Chinese leaders had to swallow this bitter pill the day after they had, together with Stalin, repudiated Acheson's accusations that Stalin had special designs on these territories. The pill was not sweetened by the inclusion of the Soviet Far East and Central Asia in the zones denied to third parties, as that ban was already in place. No wonder the protocol was kept secret for forty years. Mao's bitterness was apparent when in 1958 he referred to these provinces as Soviet colonies.[20]

As for broader Asian concerns, Stalin was keen to designate China as having primary responsibility for the further expansion of communism there without at the same time conceding that Mao had made independent contributions of universal significance to the treasure trove of Marxism–Leninism. In this way China could be a kind of buffer to absorb such retaliation as the Americans might choose to carry out without the Soviets conceding to Mao a leading role (albeit of a lesser kind) in the international communist movement. This was signalled in the order in which the two communist giants recognized the Democratic Republic of Vietnam in January 1950. China was first on 18 January and the Soviet Union followed almost two weeks later. During this time, of course, Mao was still in Moscow. Interestingly, Ho Chi Minh visited Moscow while Mao was there, but Kim Il-Sung did not.

Throughout the early post-war years, Kim was wholly dependent on Moscow, and North Korea can be justly called a Soviet satellite.[21] The Soviet Union also extended more military aid to the North in the late 1940s and early 1950s than to Mao's armed forces during the same period. Despite the good personal relations between the Chinese and North Korean leaders, the lead-up to the war was determined almost exclusively by Stalin and Kim until a few months before the attack by the North. Kim had been pressing Stalin as early as 1949 for permission to unify the country by force. Attempts to ignite a takeover of the South by guerrilla warfare had failed. But Kim nevertheless hoped for a successful uprising once his troops had broken through the defences of the South. He claimed that a swift victory would ensue. Stalin, however, was concerned with the wider picture. He once told Kim that 'the Americans will never agree to be thrown out of [Korea and] lose their reputation as a great power'. But Stalin did not dismiss the possibility and consulted Mao. After all it was China, in Stalin's calculations, that would have to bear the brunt of any failures. Apparently, Mao first thought that the Americans would intervene, only to backtrack on this view later. In any event Stalin continued to prevaricate. When Kim visited him in April, Stalin stressed his preoccupation with the situation in the West and urged him to consult Mao, as he had 'a good understanding of Oriental matters'. In effect Stalin had consented, subject to Mao's approval. But Mao had been manoeuvred into a situation where he could not disapprove. Having obtained Stalin's promise of support for an invasion of Taiwan, Mao could hardly warn against the prospect of American intervention in Korea without inviting Stalin to draw similar conclusions about Taiwan. According to Chinese scholars, Mao, not surprisingly, urged Kim to rely upon guerrilla warfare.[22] But Kim followed his own course with Soviet assistance.

Stalin's objectives were mixed. Locally, he hoped to expand his buffer zone in Asia. From a regional perspective, by dominating the Korean peninsula he could expect to bring pressure to bear upon Japan that would limit its utility to the United States; moreover, he could also expect to widen the rift between Mao and the United States. Indeed, were Kim to fail, as indeed was the case, China and America could be expected to be engaged in hostilities, thereby drawing a line between them. From a more global strategic perspective America was bound to become more engaged in Asia – hopefully at the expense of its engagement in Europe – whether as a result of a humiliating loss or as a result of taking on a commitment in Korea. On the face of it the calculating Stalin had everything to gain and nothing to lose, whatever the outcome.

In the event, Stalin's gains were mixed. The reaction of the Western allies in Europe – the key geopolitical centre between East and West – was to consolidate the newly established NATO with an integrated command structure. Moreover, the American intervention led to a huge re-armament programme enabling the United States to be engaged militarily in Asia without reducing its deployments in Europe. Japan became even more tightly locked into the American alliance network. China, however, became more estranged from the United States and, in Stalin's terms, more trustworthy. But China had also proved itself in war to be a great power in its own right, and it was a China whose leaders had acquired new grievances against the Soviet Union. Right to the end Soviet interests were put ahead of those of China, even in Korea, where the terms for beginning truce negotiations in 1951 as initiated by Moscow included neither the issue of Taiwan nor China's entry into the UN.[23] It has been suggested that in his last year Stalin began to soften his confrontationist approach in Europe and to recognize that the newly independent post-colonial states were a new factor in world politics.[24] His death in March 1953 left the issue to be explored by his successors.

Peaceful coexistence and the Asia-Pacific, 1953–71

The policies of Stalin's successors towards the Asia-Pacific can only be understood within the context of Moscow's larger concerns. The death of the great tyrant meant that the harsher aspects of Soviet totalitarian rule had to be relaxed both at home and within the socialist camp. It also meant that China could no longer be circumscribed within the confines of limited economic assistance and the Korean stalemate. Beyond that, the Soviet advances in nuclear weaponry and the means of delivery were narrowing the gap with the United States and thereby leading to a situation in which understandings had to be reached if a disastrous nuclear war was to be averted. Further afield the significance of the newly emerging Third World countries was gradually making itself felt.

The response of the Soviet leaders to these challenges may be subsumed within the concept of peaceful coexistence. As redefined by Khrushchev it went beyond the terms set out by Lenin and Stalin to mean a long-term policy based on the recognition that the advent of the nuclear balance of terror ruled out the notion of a war between the socialist and capitalist camps, let alone the thesis that such a war was inevitable. Since the antagonism between the two camps remained, this called for a precarious combination of conflict and cooperation. It also meant that the Soviet Union would have to ensure that it achieved strategic parity with the United States so as to allow the momentum of what was termed 'the correlation of forces' (i.e., the sum total of economic, military and political factors) to work out in favour of the Soviet side. In other words, peaceful coexistence meant peaceful competition. Moreover, that was understood to operate not only between the two camps, but also within the capitalist countries, where it was argued that a peaceful transition to communist rule would now be feasible under the new conditions. Clearly the promotion of violent revolution in the countries of the West risked undermining the prospect of developing peaceful competitive relations with their governments.

Within the socialist camp peaceful coexistence, as understood by the Soviet leaders, meant that its members could enjoy considerable autonomy under Soviet leadership. In practice, however, the upheavals in Poland and Hungary in 1956 and in Czechoslovakia in 1968 showed that this was an elusive formula to follow and only Soviet intervention or the threat of intervention kept the integrity of the camp intact. Socialist internationalism was interpreted as allowing the Soviet Union to intervene to uphold the essence of the fruits of socialism as understood by its leaders. But the corollary was that the Soviet Union had to expend precious economic resources in support of these countries. Those that were beyond the effective reach of Soviet military intervention such as Cuba, Vietnam or North Korea were able to use the concept of socialist internationalism to obtain material assistance and security guarantees.

As applied to the Third World the new approach allowed the Soviet Union to promote itself as the 'natural ally' of those countries whose leaders professed to being opposed to imperialism and the West as well as to promote wars of national liberation against colonial rulers. This was soon extended to mean that, with Soviet support, Third World countries under the right sort of revolutionary leadership could transform themselves in time into fully fledged socialist countries.

The three dimensions of peaceful coexistence were linked and may be seen as having required precarious balances to be drawn in each sphere as well as between them. Matters were aggravated by the vehement opposition of the Chinese from the late 1950s onwards. Sensing that Khrushchev's attempts to establish a modus vivendi with the United States would require the subordination of their interests and aspirations to those of the Soviet Union, China's leaders and Mao in particular began by opposing his policies. But given the character of relations between communist states, Mao soon raised their differences into an ideological dispute. He went on to accuse the Soviet leaders of turning their backs on Marxism–Leninism and becoming in effect 'New Tsars'. Mao used the same ideological critique to attack those he regarded as his domestic opponents, so that the Cultural Revolution that began in 1966 was suffused with anti-Sovietism. By 1969 armed conflict had taken place on their borders, and amid ill-concealed threats of a possible Soviet attack upon China's nuclear installations, Beijing opened its doors to Washington, thus fulfilling one of Moscow's worst nightmares. The immediate response to Stalin's death from an uneasy collective leadership was to agree to the armistice in Korea and to continue to put greatest emphasis upon their European strategic interests. Consequently, during the Geneva Conference in June 1954 they joined with the Chinese in pressuring Ho Chi Minh to accept the division of the country at the 17th Parallel, principally because the Soviet Union was keen to support the then French government, which was opposed to West German entry into the European Defence Community. But now the Soviet leaders had to deal with a more assertive China. After the conference the Chinese Premier, Zhou Enlai, toured Eastern Europe (hitherto a strict Soviet preserve) in a manner befitting a leader of an independent major power. From there he visited India and Burma and together with their leaders declared the Five Principles of Peaceful Coexistence, which from a Soviet point of view implied either a kind of 'Asia for Asians' approach that excluded them or a claim that the Chinese could make independent ideological innovations of universal significance without reference to them.

In September Khrushchev, the first secretary of the CPSU and the effective if not unchallengeable leader, headed a delegation to China. As his own, perhaps self-serving, account showed, it was an uneasy occasion in which mutual distrust was evident behind the scenes, but withheld from public view.[25] All the Soviet special privileges in China – the last of the old imperialist-style foreign concessions – came to an end, including Port Arthur (Lushun) and Dairen (Dalian), despite the 1950 agreement reaffirmed in 1952 that the withdrawal would await a peace treaty with Japan. Agreements were also reached to extend Soviet economic assistance to China that, together with earlier ones, were to provide the basis on which Chinese industrialization could take off. The divisions and uncertainties in the Kremlin had certainly increased China's leverage.

However, Sino-Soviet divisions were apparent in Asia. While the Chinese pursued their own course at Bandung, the Soviet leaders cultivated separate relations with India. In February 1955 a substantial aid agreement was reached, and in June Prime Minister Nehru was lavishly received in Moscow. Unlike the Chinese, the Soviets could offer significant aid to Third World countries and also show that they could compete in this area with the United States. At the end of the year Khrushchev visited India, where he sided with his hosts over Kashmir. Pakistan, which had formally allied itself with the United States, was told that relations could improve when it returned to an 'independent' policy. The Soviet Union was building 'influence by intervening in a regional quarrel on behalf of the party engaged in struggle against 'imperialism and its lackeys'.[26] But it was also establishing a separate and close relationship with the biggest Asian power other than China.

The year 1955 was a time of substantial thawing of Soviet external relations. In addition to developing new policies towards Third World countries, a naval base was evacuated in Finland, Soviet troops withdrawn from Austria and the neutralization of the country within the Western economic framework was agreed. More remarkably, the Soviet leaders made their peace with Tito on bended knee. However, as the Geneva Conference of the big four demonstrated, only the 'atmospherics', but not the substance, of East–West relations had improved.[27] An exploration of relations with Japan was begun that culminated in a joint declaration in October 1956 that marked the restoration of diplomatic relations and stipulated *inter alia* that two of the four disputed islands would be returned to Japan upon conclusion of a peace treaty.[28] The underlying Soviet objective was to weaken Japan's ties with the United States. Interestingly, in subsequent years Soviet leaders went so far as to deny the existence of a territorial dispute. It was not until the accession of Gorbachev that the issue was once again openly recognized.

The culmination of the thaw was Khrushchev's enunciation of a new doctrine of peaceful coexistence and his denunciation of Stalin at the Twentieth CPSU Congress in February 1956. As we have seen, these were to prove explosive in their consequences, at first within Eastern Europe and then later in relations with China. Although Sino-Soviet differences were apparent at the conference of the ruling communist parties convened in Moscow in 1957, the somewhat chastened Khrushchev promised to assist the Chinese in the development of an atomic bomb. The promise was rescinded in 1959. In 1958 Khrushchev floated the idea of holding a summit meeting on the Middle East to which he suggested that India be invited without even mentioning China. After a visit to China the idea was dropped. The Chinese later charged Khrushchev with failing to support them during the Taiwan offshore island crisis of 1958 until the high danger mark had passed. In 1959, as Khrushchev was preparing to visit President Eisenhower, trouble erupted on the Sino-Indian border and, to the chagrin of the Chinese, Khrushchev had a statement of regret issued in which both sides were treated as equals, rather than following the customary practice of siding with a fellow socialist country. In April 1960 the Chinese finally went public with their complaints and accusations.

This brought out into the open that Soviet policy in the Asia-Pacific was designed not only to counter the American policy of containment, but also to compete for influence with China. During the 1950s and the early 1960s the North Koreans and the Vietnamese took care to avoid taking sides while sympathizing in practice with the Chinese. Much as they needed access to the more advanced Soviet weaponry, their interests required a harder rather than a softer line to be taken with Washington. Khrushchev, for his part, did not want any crisis or confrontation that might be caused by what he regarded as their intransigence or belligerence to damage his approach to Washington. Consequently, Khrushchev's reaction to the Laos crisis of 1961/1962 was to wash his hands of Indo-China. It was only after his ouster in 1964 that the new Soviet leaders returned. In fact, Premier Kosygin was visiting Hanoi in February 1965 when the Americans began to bomb the country.

The American intervention in Vietnam worked out well for the Soviet Union. In strategic terms it engulfed the United States in a massive outpouring of resources that weakened it both at home and abroad. It provided a breathing space for the Soviet Union to 'catch up' with America in nuclear weaponry and in the development of its navy. In diplomatic terms the Soviet Union gained from the American difficulties with its allies and from the condemnation of the non-aligned. It also gained from being solicited for its good offices to negotiate a set-tlement. Although it was unable to win over the Chinese for 'united action' in Vietnam, in a curious way the Soviet Union benefited from that too. Since the USSR alone could provide the advanced weaponry necessary to counter the US bombing, the Chinese could be painted into a corner as putting their interests ahead of their responsibilities to Vietnam. And no amount of Chinese rhetoric could dispel Vietnamese doubts that Mao had gained an understanding from the Americans that they would not extend the war to China, before unleashing the Cultural Revolution at home. Interestingly, it was the same reassurance that the Americans would keep the war limited that enabled the Soviet Union to benefit at so little cost to itself.

As far as non-communist Asia was concerned, the Soviet leaders continued and deepened their support for India, which became perhaps the best ally of the Soviet Union. The new Soviet leaders manoeuvred cleverly in the 1965 war between India and Pakistan. They helped India shrug off the rather clumsy ulti-matum from China and were able to offer their good offices to both sides in brokering the Tashkent agreement the following year. Khrushchev also attempted to cultivate relations with Indonesia. President Sukarno visited Moscow in 1956 and Khrushchev reciprocated in 1960. Considerable arms were sold and Moscow lent its support to Sukarno's campaign to obtain West Irian from the Dutch. In the event, Sukarno may be said to have used the Soviet support and weaponry to elicit sufficient American pressure on the Dutch to yield. When the Sino-Soviet conflict surfaced it suited Sukarno to side with the Chinese on ideological grounds, and this was confirmed when he initiated the campaign of *Konfrontasi* against the establishment of Malaysia in 1963. The Soviet Union had to accept the 'loss' of a country which at one point it had supplied with amounts of advanced weaponry that in the non-communist world were exceeded only by Egypt and India.[29]

The Soviet leaders were to draw quiet satisfaction from the failure of the 1965 coup, the demise of the pro-Chinese Communist Party of Indonesia (PKI) – notwithstanding the bloody massacre of hundreds of thousands of their members and of local ethnic Chinese – and the sidelining of Sukarno himself. Thereafter the Soviet leaders tried to develop businesslike relations with Singapore, Malaysia itself and Suharto's Indonesia. But the Soviet role was minor, as it was not significant economically, and these countries were essentially pro-Western, as became clear with the negative Soviet response to the formation of ASEAN in 1967. Nevertheless, it served President Suharto's claims to be non-aligned to have relations with the Soviet Union, even though in practice that did little to affect the fundamental pro-Western stance of his government.

It may be worth noting that with regard to Japan the Soviet Union did little to encourage its government to loosen ties with the United States. The possible concession on the disputed islands that was envisaged in 1956 receded from view as Soviet leaders began to insist that the matter had been settled and that there was nothing to discuss. Instead Soviet statements tended to take a threatening tone, especially as their Pacific Fleet gained in substance. It is nevertheless important to recognize that its deployments had as much to do with the strategic relationship with the United States as with regional issues.[30]

The launching of the Cultural Revolution in 1966 seems to have been judged by the Soviet leaders as requiring a military response. A defence treaty was signed with the Mongolian People's Republic, leading initially to the stationing there of two Soviet divisions and air support forces in 1967. By 1970 the number of Soviet ground divisions opposite China grew to thirty-three from the eighteen deployed in 1965.[31] Soviet diplomats sounded out how the West might respond to a Soviet strike against China's nuclear facilities. The Chinese initiated hostilities on the riverine border in March 1969, to which the Soviet Union responded with superior force three weeks later. But it was not until a successful incursion by a Soviet column took place in Xinjiang that the Chinese eventually agreed to begin talks. In 1969 Brezhnev also launched a scheme for establishing a collective security system in Asia. But this was seen as so obviously directed against China that not even India responded positively. Soviet pressure, however, proved in the end to be counterproductive as it brought about precisely what had been feared all along in Moscow – a rapprochement between Beijing and Washington.

The impact of tripolarity, 1971–89

It is important to recognize at the outset that at 'a fundamental level, Soviet perceptions of the triangle turned out to be far more a function of the state of U.S.–Soviet relations than perceptions of U.S.–Soviet relations were a creature of the triangle'.[32] In other words, important though China was, the central concern of Soviet foreign policy remained the United States. This was obviously true of the larger international strategic situation and of relations in such crucial areas as Europe and the Middle East.

But even here, until Sino-Soviet relations began to improve from about 1980 onwards, the Soviet leaders were anxious lest the heretical and implacable Chinese should adversely influence American attitudes towards détente. It has also been argued that an unstated reason for the Soviet Union to retain something of a numerical advantage in some of the categories of weapons agreed with the Americans in the Strategic Arms Limitation Talks was to cope with the nascent and growing Chinese nuclear capabilities.[33] From a Soviet perspective, the significance of China during the period of tripolarity may be seen in two separate phases. In the course of the first phase that lasted until 1979, the Chinese were regarded as the main source of anti-Soviet hostility, seeking to push the United States from the path of détente towards confrontation; in the second phase from 1980 until about 1987/1988, the role was reversed as Washington was cast in the role of seeking to restrain Beijing from reaching an accommodation with Moscow.[34]

Whatever the case elsewhere, the relations with China and the impact of tripolarity were at the heart of Soviet policy in the Asia-Pacific. Indeed, the first Soviet response to Kissinger's surprise visit to Beijing in July 1971 was to bolster the Indian position and show up the underlying weakness of China in its incapacity to assist its Pakistani ally during its hour of need as the civil conflict in East Pakistan threatened to dismember the country. A treaty was signed with India in August obliging the two parties to consult in the event of war. Although Kosygin urged Mrs Gandhi not to intervene, the Soviet Union provided substantial quantities of arms and gave unstinted support to India in the United Nations when it overran East Pakistan in December. The United States then claimed to have saved West Pakistan by sending a carrier force to the Bay of Bengal. The Pakistani prime minister, Z. Bhutto, then visited Moscow in March 1972 to normalize relations, leading to the Simla Agreement of July 1972, by which the Soviet Union persuaded India and Pakistan to re-establish relations. The realities of Soviet power had prevailed over the Sino-American arraignment, and even their ally Pakistan had to defer to Soviet power to extricate itself from the threat of further dismemberment.[35] From a longer-term perspective the Soviet leaders hoped that the alliance with India would serve their larger purpose of containing China. But it is generally thought that 1971 was the high point of Indo-Soviet relations. Thereafter relations remained close, but India proved reluctant to align itself fully with subsequent Soviet policy in the region.

The Soviet approach to Japan, which on the face of it looked promising in the early 1970s, was to end badly from the Soviet point of view. Far from being able to build on the détente established with the United States, and on the Japanese desire to maintain equidistance between China and the Soviet Union coupled with a Japanese interest in exploring the commercial possibilities of investing in Siberia, the Soviet leaders succeeded only in alienating Tokyo and in driving it towards closer relations with Beijing while cementing its ties with Washington. Following the normalization of relations between Tokyo and Beijing in September 1972, the Japanese prime minister, Tanaka, visited Moscow the following year – the first such high-level visit for seventeen years. While Brezhnev pressed for the joint development of Siberia, Tanaka pressed for the return of the 'Northern Territories'. The resulting communiqué was ambiguous at best, but it did call for further negotiations towards a peace treaty (which by implication would have to deal with the issue in one way or another). By the time these were initiated, Moscow had objected in February 1975 to the mentioning of an 'anti-hegemony' clause in the proposed peace treaty between China and Japan. Soviet leaders continued their objections and also proposed that a treaty of good neighbourliness be signed with them in lieu of a peace treaty – thereby shelving the territorial issue, whose existence Foreign Minister Gromyko was denying by the summer.

In an attempt to employ coercive diplomacy the Soviet Union began to increase the movements of its much enhanced air and naval forces to the north of Hokkaido. Even at this point, the Japanese foreign minister, Miyazawa, sought to restore some flexibility to the Japanese relationship between its two giant neighbours, by criticizing Chinese visitors in July 1976 for commenting adversely on the Soviet refusal to return the territories. This brought him even more openly into the Sino-Soviet crossfire. By this point the Soviet side had been emboldened by the 1975 Helsinki agreements, which ratified the Soviet-imposed borders in Eastern Europe. Other matters soon intervened, including the defection of a Soviet pilot with his top secret MIG-25 and the Soviet unilateral extension of its territorial waters by 200 miles, thus deepening the territorial and fisheries disputes with Japan. Meanwhile the Soviet side had raised so many difficulties over the question of Japanese cooperation in the exploitation of resources in Siberia that Japanese companies lost interest. In the end the Soviet side sought to compel the Japanese to drop their insistence on a peace treaty in favour of a treaty of good neighbourliness. Amid military exercises in the Northern Territories on an unprecedented scale, Moscow warned Japan against signing a peace treaty with China. Japanese public opinion, never well disposed towards the Soviet Union, became distinctly hostile, and under pressure from the United States the Japanese government duly signed the Treaty of Peace and Friendship with China on 12 August 1978. Far from manoeuvring cleverly to take advantage of the differences that existed between the other three great powers of the Asia-Pacific, Soviet diplomacy and heavy handed attempts to use its new found military power in the region only brought them together. By the end of 1978 the Soviet Union faced a hostile alignment of China, the United States and Japan.[36]

Various explanations have been advanced for the peculiar rigidity of the Soviet treatment of Japan. Some have argued that the obsessive Soviet anxieties about China blinded their leaders to the possibilities of flexible manoeuvre.[37] Others have argued that the problem lay in the deep-seated feelings of hostility and resentment in Russian attitudes towards Japan, which saw concessions in terms of a loss of prestige, rather than as an opportunity to strike a bargain.[38] It has also been suggested that, beginning in the early 1970s, the Kurile Islands acquired a new strategic significance as a critical line of defence to protect the Soviet sub-marine-based second strike capability that was located in the Sea of Okhotsk.[39] Perhaps it was a mix of all three combined with a Soviet desire to have a clear quid pro quo in the sense of tangibly separating Japan from the United States in the 1950s or from China in the 1970s.

The Soviet tendency in the 1970s to use its greater military power and especially its naval forces to promote and establish regimes to its liking in parts of Africa and the Middle East had contributed to the souring of relations with the United States and to the decay of détente. That had doubtless weakened the position of those such as Secretary of State Vance in the Carter administration who stressed the importance of reaching arms control agreements with the Soviet Union and maintaining a policy of even-handedness between it and China. In the Soviet view it was the visit to China by the American national security adviser, Z. Brzezinski, in May 1978 that marked the turning point towards the hard-line approach favoured by China.[40] By this stage it was clear that Sino-Vietnamese relations had substantially deteriorated, as the Chinese had publicly accused the Vietnamese of seeking regional hegemony and the Vietnamese had encouraged tens of thousands of ethnic Chinese to leave. The Soviet response was to heighten the differences and assist Vietnam in its plans to force out the troublesome Chinese-supported Khmer Rouge government from Cambodia and impose an alternative more to their liking. In June Vietnam was admitted to the Moscow-dominated Council for Mutual Economic Assistance (CMEA or Comecon) and in November a treaty was signed similar to that signed with India before its attack upon East Pakistan.

As if to demonstrate contempt for Chinese power despite the normalization of Sino-American relations announced on 16 December 1978, Vietnamese forces armed by the Soviet Union invaded Cambodia on 25 December, driving the Khmer Rouge to enclaves near the Thai border. Following a successful tour of the United States Deng Xiaoping ordered an attack upon Vietnam in February 1979. Although from a strictly military point of view the war went badly for the Chinese and could be said to have vindicated the military prowess of Vietnam and its backer the Soviet Union, from a strategic point of view the Chinese rammed home a geopolitical message that made the military costs acceptable to them. It soon became apparent that the international and diplomatic consequences were disastrous for the Soviet Union, especially in the Asia-Pacific. Vietnam became as much a liability as a strategic asset. Although the Soviet navy gained access to the former American bases in Vietnam, the Soviet Union and its ally were effectively isolated in the region. Continued Chinese pressure was allied to an economic embargo orchestrated by the United States and Japan and by a diplomatic campaign led by the ASEAN countries that ostracized Vietnam internationally and denied legitimacy to the regime it had imposed in Cambodia. The final blow was the Soviet intervention in Afghanistan in December 1979, in which Soviet forces enabled their beleaguered candidate to take over power, only to face the prolonged resistance of the Afghan Mujahedin. By 1980 the Soviet Union faced in effect a hostile coalition of all the countries in the Asia-Pacific save Vietnam and the indeterminate North Korea. Even India was less than supportive.

Paradoxically, the Soviet nadir in the early 1980s proved to be a turning point. Relations with the Chinese began to improve. As the Chinese reacted to a change in the balance of forces, with the Soviet Union bogged down and isolated and the United States set on the path of rearmament and determined opposition to the Soviet Union, the Chinese were ready to distance themselves from the US and explore openings to Moscow. This was assisted by the Chinese appreciation of the depth of the economic difficulties of the Soviet Union and by ideological changes associated with the Chinese reforms begun in December 1978 that involved the abandonment of the Maoist ideology of class struggle. New difficulties had also emerged in Sino-American relations. Brezhnev made a few moves to improve relations and left a legacy on which his successors could build.[41]

The main breakthrough occurred under the leadership of Gorbachev. But the higher priority that Soviet leaders habitually attached to relations with the

West was evident, as Gorbachev turned to the Asia-Pacific only in 1986. In two keynote speeches in Vladivostok in July 1986 and Krasnayorsk in September 1988, Gorbachev in effect acknowledged that past Soviet policy had been a series of costly failures. Seeing the normalization of relations with China as the key to developing better relations in East Asia and to participating in the economic dynamism of the region, Gorbachev made a series of unilateral concessions to the Chinese. These included accepting the Chinese argument that their river borders followed the centre of the main current rather than the line of the Chinese bank (the ostensible cause of the 1969 conflict) and making unilateral troop withdrawals from Mongolia and the Russian Far East. Initially, he sought to maintain ties with the Asian communist states, but the Chinese insisted that the Soviet Union withdraw from Afghanistan and above all stop its military assistance to Vietnam as well as cut back still further its force levels to the north of China as preconditions for normalization. Finally, in 1988, under severe economic pressure at home and from the Americans abroad, Gorbachev withdrew from these 'gains' of the late 1970s and early 1980s. The road then opened for Gorbachev's visit to Beijing in May 1989 to normalize relations. The visit itself was overshadowed by the demonstrations in Tiananmen Square, but nevertheless a deal was struck over Cambodia which endorsed a trend that was already evident in the winding down of Soviet aid to Vietnam. In the event, the suppression of the students in Beijing a month later opened yet another gulf between the Soviet and Chinese leaders. Although both sides maintained correct relations at the state level, the collapse of communism in Eastern Europe further widened the divide between the two sides.[42]

Gorbachev also sought to open the Soviet Far East to the economies of the Asia-Pacific, to develop multilateral approaches to addressing security problems and to improve relations with the countries of ASEAN. The Soviet Union squared the circle in the Security Council of avoiding offending either the ASEAN countries or its ally Vietnam, by ensuring that it was not a party to the settlement of the Cambodian conflict. Gorbachev, however, failed to address the question of Japan's claims to the Northern Territories until his domestic position was too weak, so that his 1991 visit to Tokyo failed in its basic objective of establishing good relations, despite the signing of some fifteen agreements. While Gorbachev felt that the territorial issue could only be negotiated once Japan had agreed to join with its Western partners in granting aid and favourable terms for the conduct of economic relations, his Japanese hosts held on to the view that nothing could be done before the territorial issue was settled. Moreover, the Soviet Far East lacked the necessary infrastructure of communications, appropriate institutions and so on, to appeal to Japanese companies or to enable the Soviet Union to participate actively in the economy of the region. Having withdrawn its military assistance to Vietnam and having offered no support to its ally in its military engagement with the Chinese over the Spratlys in 1988, the Soviet Union shrunk to insignificance in Southeast Asia. The only clear return for Gorbachev's policies in the Asia-Pacific was the cultivation of relations with South Korea. Unable and unwilling to continue supporting the economy and military of the North, he responded to the *Nord Politik* of the South. Unlike the other countries of the region, the South had very good reasons to cultivate economic ties with the Soviet Union. It was a blow to the North and diminished the security threat and, correspondingly, it enhanced the legitimacy and the freedom of diplomatic manoeuvre for the South. Their improved relations led to normalization as the two presidents met in the United States in June 1991.[43]

Notes

1 For a discussion with reference to differing schools of thought, see Alexander Dallin, 'The Domestic Sources of Soviet Foreign Policy' in Seweryn Bialer (ed.), *The Domestic Context of Soviet Foreign Policy* (Boulder: Westview Press, 1981), pp.335–408 and, in particular, pp.354–56.

2 For a brief account of the latter, see Gerald Segal, *The Soviet Union and the Pacific* (London: Unwin Hyman, 1990), pp.15–23.

3 Cited in John J. Stephan, 'Asia in the Soviet Conception' in Donald S. Zagoria (ed.), *Soviet Policy in East Asia* (New Haven: Yale University Press, 1982), p.35.

4 Malcolm Mackintosh, 'Soviet Attitudes Towards East Asia' in Gerald Segal (ed.), *The Soviet Union and East Asia* (London: Heinemann, 1983), p.7.

5 Stephan, 'Asia in the Soviet Conception' in Zagoria (ed.), *Soviet Policy in East Asia* (*op. cit.*), p.36.

6 Segal (ed.), *The Soviet Union and East Asia* (*op. cit.*), p.1.

7 Ed A. Herbert and Herbert S. Levine, 'The Soviet Union's Economic Relations in Asia' in Zagoria (ed.), *Soviet Policy in East Asia* (*op. cit.*), p.202, see also the chapter as a whole, pp.201–28; and Segal (ed.), *The Soviet Union and the Pacific* (*op. cit.*), p.136, see also his chapter 'The Economic dimension', pp.136–85.

8 Among the many accounts that may be usefully consulted, see Adam Ulam, *Expansion and Coexistence: Soviet Foreign Policy, 1917–73* (New York: Praeger, 2nd edn, 3rd imprint, 1976), chs II–III, pp.31–125; and Alfred G. Meyer, *Leninism* (Cambridge, MA: Harvard University Press, 1957).

9 Helene Carrere d'Encausse and Stuart R. Schram, *Marxism in Asia* (London: Allen Lane/Penguin, 1969), pp.40–41.

10 Ulam, *Expansion and Coexistence* (*op. cit.*), p.22.

11 See in particular G.H. Skilling and F. Griffiths, *Interest Groups in Soviet Politics* (Princeton: Princeton University Press, 1971); Erik P. Hoffmann and Frederic J. Fleron Jr (eds), *The Conduct of Soviet Foreign Policy* (Chicago: Aldine/Atherton, 1971); Bialer (ed.) *The Domestic Context of Soviet Foreign Policy* (*op. cit.*); and Jiri Valenta and William Potter, *Soviet Decision-Making for National Security* (London: Allen and Unwin, 1984).

12 Margot Light, *The Soviet Theory of International Relations* (Brighton, Wheatsheaf, 1988) and Allen Lynch, *The Soviet Study of International Relations* (Cambridge: Cambridge University Press, 1987).

13 See the general argument of Joseph L. Nogee and Robert H. Donaldson, *Soviet Foreign Policy Since World War II* (Pergamon Press, 1988), chs 2–3, pp.10–62.

14 Michael MccGwire, *Military Objectives in Soviet Foreign Policy* (Washington, DC: The Brookings Institution, 1987).

15 Michael MccGwire, *Perestroika and National Security* (Washington, DC: The Brookings Institution, 1991).

16 *Ibid.*, p.3.

17 Max Hastings, *The Korean War* (London: Pan, 1988), pp.15–16.

18 *Ibid.*, p.24.

19 For contemporary evidence of Chinese disappointment, see John Gittings, 'The Origins of Chinese Foreign Policy' in David Horowitz (ed.), *Containment and Revolution*

(Boston: Beacon Press,1967), pp.207–8. For an account (based on Chinese materials recently made available) of the extensive military assistance following Liu Shaoqi's secret visit to Moscow in August 1949 that was increased still further after Mao's visit, see Chen Jian, *China's Road to the Korean War* (New York: Columbia University Press 1994), pp.77, 84. Chen also states that these new materials suggest that China's leaders were eminently satisfied with the character and volume of all Soviet aid. He found no evidence of disappointment. But it should be noted that this is based on selective research materials gleaned from Chinese researchers, rather than from first-hand access to the Chinese archives.

20 For a fascinating and detailed account of the negotiations and the attitudes of both sides, see Sergei N. Goncharov, John W. Lewis and Xue Litai, *Uncertain Partners: Stalin, Mao, and the Korean War* (Stanford: Stanford University Press, 1993), chs 3–4, pp.76–129. For the quote by Mao, see Stuart R. Schram (ed.), *Mao Tse-tung Unrehearsed* (London: Penguin, 1974), pp.101–2.

21 Goncharov *et al.*, *Uncertain Partners* (*op. cit.*), p.131. The subsequent account of Moscow's role in the Korean War relies heavily on chapters 5–6 of this book.

22 Hao Yufan and Zhai Zhihai, 'China's Decision to Enter the Korean War: History Revisited', *The China Quarterly* 121 (March 1990).

23 Ulam, *Expansion and Coexistence* (*op. cit.*), pp.533–34

24 Marshall D. Shulman, *Stalin's Foreign Policy Reappraised* (Cambridge, MA: Harvard University Press, 1963). For a conflicting view, see Robert C. Tucker, *The Soviet Political Mind* (New York: W.W. Norton & Co., revised edn, 1973).

25 *Khrushchev Remembers*, vol.1, translated by Strobe Talbot (London: First Sphere Books, 1971), ch.18, pp.424–40; and vol.2 (London: Penguin Books, 1977), ch.11, pp.282–343.

26 Nogee and Donaldson *Soviet Foreign Policy* ... (*op. cit.*), p.180.

27 *Ibid.*, pp.114–17. See also Ulam, *Expansion and Coexistence* (*op. cit.*), pp.566–69.

28 For a detailed examination of the history and complexity of the competing claims to what the Japanese call the 'Northern Territories' or 'Islands', see John J. Stephan, *The Kurile Islands: Russo-Japanese Frontier in the Pacific* (Oxford: Clarendon Press, 1974).

29 Michael Leifer, *Indonesia's Foreign Policy* (London: George Allen and Unwin, 1983), pp.62–69.

30 Paul F. Langer, 'Soviet Military Power in Asia' in Zagoria (ed.), *Soviet Policy in East Asia* (*op. cit.*), p.258.

31 Lawrence Freedman, 'The Military Dimension of Soviet Policy' in Segal (ed.), *The Soviet Union in East Asia* (*op. cit.*), p.93.

32 Robert Legvold, 'Sino-Soviet Relations: The U.S. Factor' in Robert S. Ross (ed.), *China, The United States, and the Soviet Union: Tripolarity and Policy Making in the Cold War* (New York: M.E. Sharpe, 1993), p.78.

33 Adam Ulam, *Dangerous Relations: The Soviet Union in World Politics, 1970–1982* (Oxford: Oxford University Press, 1983), pp.75–77, 245–47.

34 Legvold, 'Sino-Soviet Relations' (*op. cit.*), p.76.

35 This account has drawn on Robert H. Donaldson, *Soviet Policy Towards India: Ideology and Strategy* (Cambridge, MA: Harvard University Press, 1974), especially pp.225–34.

36 For a detailed account of the relevant Soviet–Japanese diplomacy, see Fuji Kamiya, 'The Northern Territories: 130 Years of Japanese Talks with Czarist Russia and the Soviet Union' in Zagoria (ed.), *The Soviet Union in East Asia* (*op. cit.*), especially pp.134–45.

37 This is a point made repeatedly by Adam Ulam. See, for example, *Dangerous Relations* (*op. cit.*), p.153, 245–46.

38 Jonathan Haslam, 'The Pattern of Soviet-Relations Since World War II' in Tsuyoshi Hasegawa, Jonathan Haslam and Andrew C. Kuchins (eds), *Russia and Japan: An Unresolved Dilemma Between Distant Neighbours* (Berkeley: University of California Press, 1993).

39 See, for example, Michael MccGwire, 'A New Trend in Soviet Naval Developments', *International Defense Review* 13, 5 (June 1980). This has been disputed by Haslam (see note 36).

40 Legvold, 'Sino-Soviet Relations' (*op. cit.*), pp.69–70.

41 For an account of the specific steps taken to improve relations see Gerald Segal, *Sino-Soviet Relations After Mao* (London: International Institute for Strategic Studies, Adelphi Papers no.202, 1985).

42 For a comprehensive account of the lead up to the summit with Deng Xiaoping, see Steven M. Goldstein, 'Diplomacy Amid Protest: The Sino-Soviet Summit', *Problems of Communism* (September–October 1989). For an account of policy towards China in the Gorbachev years, see Charles E. Ziegler, *Foreign Policy and East Asia: Learning and Adaptation in the Gorbachev Era* (Cambridge: Cambridge University Press, 1993); and for an account of policy towards Southeast Asia, see Leszek Buszynski, *Gorbachev and Southeast Asia* (London: Routledge, 1992). For a broader evaluation, see Robert A. Scalapino, 'Russia's Role in Asia: Trends and Prospects' in Hasegawa *et al.* (eds), *Russia and Japan* (*op. cit.*).

43 For details, see Amy Rauenhorst Goldman, 'The Dynamics of a New Asia: The Politics of Russian–Korean Relations' in Hasegawa *et al.* (eds), *Russia and Japan* (*op. cit.*), pp. 243–75; and Ziegler, *Foreign Policy and East Asia* (*op. cit.*), ch.6, pp.108–27.

6 China and the Asia-Pacific

If the United States and the Soviet Union (until its replacement by the less significant Russia) may be described as global powers with a regional interest in the Asia-Pacific, China may be understood as a regional power with global influence.[1] China's principal security interests are largely concentrated in the Asia-Pacific, and its capacity to project power is limited in the main to that region. But the most important threats to its security as perceived by successive Chinese leaders came from one or other of the superpowers, and for the first forty years of its existence the PRC treated its security problems within the region as a function of its relations with the two superpowers. The predominance of the superpowers in the Chinese perspective necessarily gave China's regional concerns a global orientation. Indeed, in the 1980s it was persuasively argued that China did not even have a regional policy as such.[2] It is only since the end of the Cold War that China's leaders have developed policies that recognize that the future security and prosperity of their country requires the cultivation of close relations with the Asia-Pacific as a whole and with its neighbours in particular. This regional orientation does not mean that China's leaders have ceased to think of their country in global terms, but it is a recognition of the centrality of the region to the Chinese economy and of the importance of the fast-growing Chinese economy to the region itself. Despite the continuing economic troubles that began in July 1997, the Asia-Pacific region is still regarded as a major economic centre alongside those of Europe and North America, and China's growing weight within the region serves to enhance its global significance too. However, China's emergence as a rising power has raised new problems as it challenges the existing distribution of power based on American predominance, and it poses new problems for its smaller neighbours who seek to engage their giant neighbour in multilateral institutions in the hope of mitigating its potentially destabilizing policies.

In addition to the strategic factors, China's claims to be considered as a power of global significance arise perhaps most strongly from its historical legacy of centrality. But these have also been enhanced by the international recognition they have received. China is the only Third World country to be one of the Permanent Five (P5) members of the UN Security Council. By virtue of the country's size and independent revolutionary achievements, China was the only serious rival to the Soviet Union's leadership of the international communist movement.

Finally, even China's home-grown distinction of being the world's most populous country, the heir to one of the world's great civilizations, with a history of continuous statehood reaching back for more than 2,000 years, has been recognized in the special respect accorded it by diplomatic envoys from all over the world. As a result China's leaders have tended to claim a leading global role that their country's capabilities do not yet allow them to exercise. The leaders of the PRC have consistently argued that they have a right to be heard on every major problem in the world. It has been argued, not unjustifiably, that 'without first having acquired the reach of a global power, China acts as if it has already become a world power'.[3]

China's conduct within the Asia-Pacific must be understood against the backdrop of a complex series of factors including its historical legacy, its projection of a multiple international identity and its search for modernity and great-power status, as well as the series of interactions with the superpowers and neighbouring countries. China's international relations must be seen as inherently dynamic and unsettled, as they reflect the imperatives of domestic renewal and the yearning to achieve the genuine standing as a country of the first rank in terms of cultural and scientific achievement as well as in economics and power politics. Meanwhile China's leaders think of their country as one that has yet to recover from the consequences of the humiliations visited upon it by the imperialists in the hundred years from the 1840s to the 1940s. Thus even as China has become increasingly integrated with the international economy and indeed within the Asia-Pacific region, these old grievances continue to be of current significance.

From a geographical point of view China extends beyond the confines of the Asia-Pacific as followed in this book. China not only faces the Pacific, but it also looks into Inner Asia and borders on the Indian Subcontinent. In fact, traditionally China has been a continental power. The centre of gravity of China was inland. Historically it has always been threatened by conquest from the north. Until the advent of the Europeans China had not been challenged from the sea. Despite the fact that considerable commerce took place and that the danger of piracy was ever present, the Chinese authorities traditionally thought of the sea as a barrier rather than a gateway. China, the Central Kingdom, was described as the land 'within the four seas'. Indeed, the Chinese authorities found it difficult to understand at first that the conquering Westerners who had come by sea in the nineteenth century, nominally to seek trade, were fundamentally different from foreigners from Central Asia who also sought trading privileges.[4] One of the problems that contemporary Chinese are experiencing is having to shift from a continental to a maritime orientation. In other words it can be argued that, despite China's traditional dominance of East Asia, it is only in the contemporary period that China is becoming a full member of the Asia-Pacific.

The imprint of history

Contrary to the myth of a timeless unchanging imperial system, China's international history is varied and offers a number of different models for contemporary Chinese. Michael Hunt has drawn attention to at least two imperial styles and to what he has called 'a multiplicity of traditions'. These have involved:

> virtual political hegemony and cultural supremacy over much of Asia as well as repeated subjugation and internecine strife. They hold up many models of statecraft, from the lofty imperial style to shrewd Machiavellian cunning. They teach the use of brute force, of trade and cultural exchange, of secret diplomacy and alliances, of compromise and even collaboration with conquerors.[5]

All of these except perhaps the first and the last have been on display in one form or another in the international behaviour of the People's Republic of China.

Indeed much of the PRC's approach to the outside world may be seen as an attempt to recapture the past glory that, in the views of its leaders, had been mercilessly destroyed by the West and by Japan in the course of China's century of shame and humiliation from the 1840s to the 1940s. This yearning for greatness should not necessarily be seen as a drive to expand aggressively at the expense of others. But rather it should be understood as a desire to re-establish China's stature as a centre of civilization, which until modern times was superior in terms of culture and technology. The modern world challenged China not only in terms of power, but also in terms of civilization. Accordingly, it was not enough for the Chinese simply to try to catch up with Western military technology, but their society had to be transformed. This set up a tension between seeking to modernize, so as to be sufficiently strong and prosperous to prevent a repetition of the humiliating defeats of the nineteenth century, and striving to preserve a distinct Chinese cultural identity. The first calls for integrating with the foreign modern world and the second demands resistance to its alleged malevolent external influences. The tension finds expression in China's attachment to a fierce sense of independence that has made the PRC such a difficult ally down the years. In many ways this relates to anxieties of the Qing and even of the previous dynasty about the possible destabilizing effects upon Chinese society and ways of thought that contact with foreigners and foreign societies might engender. This, of course, has been even truer for the communist leadership of the PRC.

The definition of China's sovereign territory is also associated with the problem of interpreting the legacy of the past. The PRC, like the Republic before it, was established both as a break from the past and as a successor to that past. Although new revolutionary beginnings were proclaimed in domestic and foreign affairs, China's sovereign territory was defined in terms of succession to the Qing. This raised ambiguities about claims to certain territories. In 1936 Mao Zedong (in company with leading Chinese nationalists) went so far as to lay claim to the Mongolian People's Republic and call a former tributary state, Korea, a former Chinese colony, and he proceeded to claim that the Mohammedan and Tibetan peoples would join a future Chinese federation. Tibet at that point was technically under Chinese suzerainty, although in practice it was independent.[6] The more extravagant claims were dropped from the formal agenda after the establishment of the PRC in 1949. Henceforth there was no question of self-determination being applied to any of the peoples living within the then-designated Chinese territory or indeed to peoples in territories claimed to be Chinese, such as Taiwan or Hong Kong. In time, it led to the assertion that all the diverse ethnic peoples who lived within China's borders belonged to the 'Chinese family' and had always done so. This had the effect of claiming that members of the same ethnicity who lived on one side of the border were regarded as Chinese and on the other side as alien. It had strange consequences for the writing of earlier history, as wars between Chinese armies and nomadic outsiders now had to be treated on many occasions as civil wars.[7] Since all of its borders were said to be the product of unequal treaties imposed by the imperialists, not only did they all have to be renegotiated, but doubts were raised as to whether the Chinese might subsequently lay claims to 'lost lands'. In 1964 Mao deliberately raised the spectre of claiming vast tracts of eastern Siberia in the course of the dispute with the Soviet Union.[8]

More generally, there are traditions regarding the conduct of foreign relations that have left their imprint on contemporary practice. Prominent among these is the practice of centrality – being the 'central actor in international dealings, with considerable autonomy'. The Qing characteristically dealt with different peoples in disparate ways using separate bureaucracies. No conceivable links existed between the Qing's southern neighbours and those to the north, so that Qing China 'had no natural allies and no permanent enemies, but a complex of mutually separable relationships with its neighbours'.[9] In the century of 'shame and humiliation' China's leaders found themselves confronting the foreign powers, in effect as a group. Accordingly, China's leaders have sought to regain freedom of manoeuvre and initiative by dealing with foreign powers individually rather than as a unit. In fact, the PRC may be said to have displayed a remarkable aptitude as the weaker power in upholding independence by the politics of manoeuvre between the two superpowers. Strange as it may have seemed in the West, one of the abiding fears of Mao and his successors from the 1960s until the demise of the Soviet Union in 1991 was that the two superpowers might establish a condominium. At the same time, Chinese traditions of rewarding materially the bearers of tribute and lesser rulers who acknowledged their legitimizing majesty have found parallels in modern times, as the PRC has acted (albeit not consistently) as a benefactor of lesser states and clients.[10]

The historical experience of the communist-led revolution and the impact of Mao's strategic thinking, which used to loom large in accounts of underlying influences that shaped the conduct of China's foreign policy, loom less large from the perspective of the 1990s. But it would be a mistake to overlook that altogether, especially as, for the first fifteen years of economic reform and openness, China's foreign policy was still determined in the last resort by Deng Xiaoping and fellow founding fathers of the party, the army and the state. As long as Communist Party rule continues in China, its historical experiences will necessarily be influential. Ideology may not carry the same weight that it once did, but it cannot be disavowed and it still finds expression in the residual but persistent need to somehow differentiate 'socialist' China from the external 'capitalist' world. The United Front may no longer dominate Chinese approaches to international relationships, but aspects of its approach may still be seen in policies towards Hong Kong and Taiwan 'compatriots' and even towards 'overseas Chinese'. The influence of Mao's doctrines of people's war may have declined in the armed forces and, since the end of the threat from the north, they are no longer important as a deterrent factor. Nevertheless, as long as the Chinese armies lag behind the modernity of others, Mao's doctrines will not be completely abandoned and the experience of triumphing in the revolution against superior and more modern forces will still contribute to the self-confidence of China's rulers.

Historical cultural influences have shaped Chinese foreign policy making in several ways. As in the past, foreign relations in general have been regarded as extraordinarily sensitive, and they have been subjected to tight central control. Indeed, decision-making has been dominated by first Mao Zedong and then Deng Xiaoping. Although Deng has not exercised the total dominance of his predecessor, he has nevertheless made the key decisions on the most important issues. As a result of the economic reforms and the policy of openness since 1978, the number of groups and institutions involved in foreign relations has greatly expanded and it is possible to identify a growing influence being exercised by discrete groups such as the military, economic and regional interests, and perhaps even elite opinion as registered by experts.[11] Nevertheless, Mao and Deng have exercised personal power almost like latter-day emperors. Indeed, it can be argued that they have enjoyed still greater power as they have been less restrained by custom and ritual. This has facilitated the PRC's remarkable capacity to change alliances and move in new directions.

As presented by China's leaders, the transformations that have taken place in their foreign relations are nothing more than wise adaptations to changing international circumstances. The external world has always been portrayed as being in flux. Far from damaging the standing of a leader, the adaptability works to enhance the esteem with which his statesmanship is held. The moral tone of Chinese insistence on principles reflects a political culture that has long prized 'ethics more than the law, moral consensus more than judicial process and benevolent government more than checks and balances'.[12] In contrast with the Western penchant for the legalist approach, the Chinese prefer more broadly worded agreements that leave ambiguities for time to solve. Despite their formal adherence to Marxism–Leninism, China's leaders' views of international relations have been state-centred and concerned with behaviour and relationships rather than with underlying socio-economic structures. The critical question that has determined Chinese views of a given state has tended to centre on its relations with China and its stance towards China's principal enemy. Until the end of the Cold War this largely depended on China's relations with Washington and Moscow. Since these could change quickly and abruptly, Chinese behaviour towards other countries could seem puzzling and Machiavellian. However, as seen from China, its leaders were acting responsibly and morally. Indeed, most Chinese 'principled' pronouncements on world affairs invoke a moral tone, with pretensions to moral leadership. Alongside this has been a suspicion of entangling alliances and of multilateral commitments that, in binding China, are regarded as restricting its capacity for independent manoeuvre. As many have noted, even when China's leaders championed the cause of the Third World they stood aloof rather than join any Third World international groups.[13]

Finally, these experiences may explain the extraordinary tenacity with which China's leaders have held on to the traditional Western sense of inviolable sovereignty. But it is also important to recognize that the Leninist tradition and the lessons of the revolutionary warfare that brought the communists to power also made them the most astute practitioners of balance-of-power politics. They perceived this not just in the classical Western sense of calculating the distribution of power and acting accordingly. Nor did they quite follow the Soviet way of seeking to identify the correlation of forces that purported to take into account more than just the straightforward military factors. Instead they tended to understand power relations as a dynamic process in which it was important to appreciate the momentum of change. Thus their capture of the changing balance in Soviet–American relations on the eve of their famous rapprochement with the United States in 1971 was described as the Soviet Union being on the offence and the United States on the defence (Sugong Meishou).

The PRC's relations in the Asia-Pacific

The unification of China under a new and vigorous government was bound to present problems of adjustment to the countries of the Asia-Pacific. It was not clear how its historical assertions of centrality would be addressed in the very different modern world. Similarly, there was uncertainty as to how particular disputes over territory and borders as well as the legacy of the colonial era would be handled. How would the new China relate to the newly independent states and their regimes? What would be the relations between the new China and the overseas Chinese? These more particular concerns became inextricably linked for the first forty years after 1949 by the impact of the Cold War and by China's changing conflictual relations with the two global powers. The end of the Cold War has raised new issues about adapting to China's economic integration within the region and its rising power at a time of increasing doubts about the durability of the American military commitment to East Asia.

The evolution of the relations with the Asia-Pacific are best treated chronologically, in order to demonstrate the significance of China's relations with the two superpowers.

Opposition to the United States, 1949–69

The alliance with the Soviet Union, 1950–58

The alliance, whose details have been outlined in the previous chapter, tied the PRC into an uneasy dependence on the Soviet Union. Born of necessity and joined under conditions of distrust, the alliance provided Mao with a security treaty against an attack by the United States, in return for which he had to recognize the independence of Mongolia and to concede a whole set of special privileges for the Soviet Union in Manchuria and Xinjiang, more even than that exacted by the Tsars. Such hopes that the PRC leaders may have entertained about conquering Taiwan were shattered by the American decision to protect the island immediately upon hearing of the attack by North Korea upon the South. Having been manoeuvred into agreeing to Kim Il-Sung's plans to annex the South by force, Mao found that he had to intervene to support the North once the American-led UN forces crossed into the North and approached the Chinese border. He prevailed over doubting colleagues on the grounds that the incipient challenge to China's security and the survival of the revolution had to be met. That, together with the economic embargo announced by Truman, at the same time as the decision to protect Taiwan, placed China in the forefront of the Cold War in Asia as the main target for American isolation and containment, which was to last for the next twenty years.

The Korean War proved to be the first modern war in which Chinese armies were able to withstand the might of Western forces of superior firepower. That not only enhanced the PRC's prestige as a great power, but it endorsed its arrival as a regional power of considerable potency. This became evident after Stalin's death had paved the way for reaching an armistice agreement in Korea that then led to the convening of the Geneva Conference from April to July 1954 on both Korea and Indo-China. The PRC played a major role at the conference. By this time, the Chinese had detected a more relaxed international climate and were keen to encourage it, so as to be able to focus upon their own programme of industrialization. The death of Stalin had brought forth a weaker Soviet leadership that not only gave up the special privileges exacted by Stalin, but was willing to provide the PRC with sufficient economic assistance to launch the First Five Year Plan. Consequently, the Chinese at Geneva put pressure on the Vietnamese communists to withdraw from considerable areas they had occupied in the South back to the 17th Parallel and to allow Laos and Cambodia to become neutral. The Vietnamese communists neither forgot nor forgave the Chinese for forcing them to yield, so as to enable a potentially viable anti-communist state to emerge in the South. They saw it as part of a long-standing historical tendency of the Chinese to demand deference from them and to prevent them from attaining their rightful dominance of what came to be called Indo-China.

Moreover, the seeds of the territorial dispute with Vietnam and others over the sets of islands in the South China Sea were sown early in the 1950s, and it became clear that when it came to the question of sovereign claims, the composition or strength of the government concerned made little difference. In May 1950 a reported remark by President Quirino of the Philippines about the dangers to his country's security that would arise from the occupation of the Spratlys by 'an enemy', was angrily denounced in Beijing, which then took the opportunity to assert its claims. A more formal claim was put forward in 1951 by Zhou Enlai to all four major sets of islands in the South China Sea, in response to the draft peace treaty with Japan. The Vietnamese delegation, represented by the Bao Dai government, at the San Francisco Peace Conference to which neither of the Chinese governments was invited, took the opportunity to state Vietnam's claims to the Paracel and the Spratly Islands.[14] Little of substance happened at this time, especially as the Chinese side lacked the capacity to enforce its claims.

As elsewhere, the PRC also softened its approach to Japan. Jettisoning its earlier calls upon the Japanese Communist Party to confront the Americans, the PRC responded to Prime Minister Yoshida's interest in resuming economic ties in a small way in 1952. A Sino-Soviet joint approach in October 1954 raised the tempo to allow also for people-to-people diplomacy. But, unlike the Soviet Union, the PRC was unable to press ahead towards normalization because of Tokyo's recognition of Taipei. And it was that link that was publicized by the first ever visit to Taiwan by a Japanese prime minister, Kishi Nobusuke, in the different atmosphere of 1957 that led to a downgrading of relations the following year.

The PRC's new stance was also reflected in its approach to the newly independent states of Asia. In the first flush of the victory of the revolution, Mao had claimed that two years after achieving independence the people of India were still living 'under the yoke of imperialism and its collaborators'.[15] By 1951 that approach had been set aside and in 1954 the PRC signed a treaty about Tibet with India, whose preamble listed rules for international conduct that were later to be proclaimed as the Five Principles of Peaceful Coexistence.[16] The more moderate approach caused the Colombo powers to invite China to the first Asian-African Conference that was held in Bandung, Indonesia, in April 1955.

Meanwhile, Beijing had begun to praise the virtues of neutralism in Asia. Zhou Enlai cultivated the delegates from the other twenty-eight countries in Bandung, including representatives of America's allies such as the Philippines, Thailand and Pakistan. He had a major impact on Prince Sihanouk and subsequent Cambodian foreign policy by convincing him that non-alignment offered the best safeguard for Cambodia's security against neighbouring historical antagonists, both of whom were allied to the United States.[17]

It would have required more than Zhou's moderation, welcome as it was, to assuage concerns about China within Southeast Asia. It had been noted that the earlier revolutionary approach was being downplayed, rather than abandoned. The Chinese had earlier broadcast their support for communist insurgencies in Southeast Asia and their new tendency to argue that state relations were separate from Communist Party relations if anything only served to accentuate the suspicions of many of its neighbours. A further set of problems arose from the position of the so-called overseas Chinese, who generally dominated commercial activities in Southeast Asia. Their cultural and often familial ties to China often excited suspicion, which China's patrimonial attitude as expressed from time to time did little to dispel. In 1954 the PRC redefined citizenship within its new constitution, as a result of which Chinese living abroad were no longer automatically regarded as citizens of the PRC. They were encouraged to choose either local nationality or that of the PRC. If the latter, they were forbidden to participate in local politics. A practical example of the new policy was the treaty signed with Indonesia in April 1955, after the Bandung Conference. Ethnic Chinese residents of Indonesia who had not acquired citizenship were given the right to choose between the two nationalities within two years. But domestic opposition delayed ratification of the treaty for years, and discriminatory legislation was nevertheless passed in 1958.[18]

Ethnic Chinese were subject to much local animosity arising out of their dominant positions in the local economies, a sentiment that was fuelled by nationalist resentment at their role during the colonial era. They were also vulnerable to rapacious officials. The advent of the PRC raised suspicions about their fundamental loyalties. The PRC leaders were not always sensitive to their predicament, as from time to time they tended to refer to them all as fellow descendants of the Yellow Emperor. Yet, as the patrimonial power, the PRC was often at a loss to help them. Matters were not helped by the fact that some of the local insurgent Communist Party membership, such as that of Malaya, was made up primarily of ethnic Chinese. Thus, upon independence in 1957, the Federal Government of Malaya concluded a defence treaty with Britain and it shunned polite noises from Beijing. Nevertheless it carefully avoided establishing military ties with the United States and it stayed out of SEATO. Neither Thailand nor the Philippines were persuaded to open relations with Beijing. Yet the main effort of Beijing during the Bandung years was directed in the vain attempt to persuade these countries to forgo their alliances with the West in favour of better relations with their fellow Asians in Beijing.[19] Perhaps China's best relationship in Southeast Asia in this period was with Burma. It was the first regional state to establish diplomatic relations and its foreign policy adhered closely to the practice of non-alignment.

The moderate Chinese approach began to change in 1957, in large part because the United States had not responded positively to the PRC's overtures. These had not been entirely disingenuous, as the Chinese had probed American reactions over the Taiwan issue in 1954 by occupying some of the islands south of Shanghai, leading to the so-called first offshore island crisis. It was diffused dramatically by Zhou Enlai's diplomacy in Bandung, but the resultant Sino-American ambassadorial meetings in Geneva soon ended in a stalemate because of the impasse over Taiwan. Meanwhile, the American response to the Geneva Conference had been to tighten up its series of alliances, including the Manila Treaty and a security pact with Taiwan (technically, the Republic of China). In fact part of the reason for the PRC's pressure on the offshore islands was to warn off other governments from participating in the pact. The American readiness to deal with Moscow was not matched by a similar attitude towards Beijing. In 1957 the PRC reacted angrily to the news of the American deployment of nuclear-tipped missiles on Taiwan. The change was also caused by the deterioration in Sino-Soviet relations arising out of Khrushchev's handling of de-Stalinization, what was regarded as his mismanagement of Eastern Europe and his readiness to compromise with the United States, when Mao in particular felt that it was necessary to take a sharp approach. Despite these differences the Soviet Union agreed in late 1957 to assist the PRC in developing nuclear weapons.

By 1958 the strains in Sino-Soviet relations came to a head, in part because of Mao's anxieties about his country's psychological as well as material dependency on the Soviet Union, combined with the deep-seated differences over international strategy.[20] In April Khrushchev had proposed negotiating a nuclear test ban with the Americans that aroused Chinese resentment at this apparent move against their acquiring a nuclear capability. At a crucial meeting in the summer, Mao summarily rejected Khrushchev's suggestion to establish a joint fleet together, with joint naval and air communications facilities in China.[21] Not long after that meeting, Mao initiated the second offshore island crisis by bombarding Quemoy in the apparent expectation of forcing the Taiwan garrison to surrender 'without an American response, thereby demonstrating to Khrushchev Peking's resolve, Washington's impotence, and Moscow's irrelevance'.[22] But Mao had to back down, having in the process cemented the American commitment to the offshore islands as well as Taiwan itself. This had the effect of 'freezing' the situation until Sino-American relations were normalized twenty years later.

Self-reliance and opposition to both superpowers, 1959–69

Sino-Soviet relations on the whole continued to deteriorate. An exasperated Khrushchev withdrew the offer of nuclear assistance in 1959 and in 1960 finally withdrew altogether the Soviet experts who had been assisting in China's development. The latter was timed to inflict maximum damage, as China was suffering from one of the greatest man-inflicted famines in history as a consequence of the Mao-inspired Great Leap Forward. Although Mao withdrew from the forefront of policy making for a while, he began to make his return in 1962, not only with renewed emphasis on radicalism and self-reliance, but also with a claim that the Soviet leaders had abandoned the true path of socialism in favour of revisionism – a danger that Mao was soon to make clear existed in China too, in his view. This meant in effect that in Mao's opinion there was no room for compromise, either at home or abroad. Not all of his colleagues agreed, but Mao's views prevailed and they were to culminate in the destructive Cultural Revolution. What had happened in the Soviet Union, according to Mao, could happen in China too. The link between domestic foes and the external threat, therefore, was even more insidious and dangerous in the Soviet case, as it reached into all sections of the Communist Party. The domestic groups that were linked to the American threat were the intellectuals and former capitalists, who by comparison were more easily dealt with as outsiders to the citadel of power. For Mao the Soviet problem went beyond the issue of its approach to the United States.[23]

Despite Beijing's militant rhetoric, its responses to developments in Southeast Asia in the late 1950s and early 1960s suggested a preference for cautious diplomacy over revolutionary violence.[24] This was true of China's responses to what it regarded as adverse developments in the domestic security arrangements and/or diplomacy of Laos, Cambodia, Thailand and Burma, where its principal goal was to dissuade countries from pursuing policies hostile to it, particularly in association with the United States.[25] The approach to India, however, was different. As a major regional power that was a leader of the non-alignment movement and one of the most prominent leaders of the Third World, it challenged the Chinese confrontationist approach to the two superpowers. Nehru's close association with the arch-'revisionist' Tito only made matters worse from Mao's point of view. The Tibetan uprising in March 1959 led to the Dalai Lama's flight to India and disputes about the border led to small-scale fighting later that year. Khrushchev did not side publicly with China as was his duty towards a fellow socialist state. This paved the way for a more intensive border war in 1962 when, in response to India's 'forward policy' in what was then called the North Eastern Frontier Agency, the Chinese, claiming a desire to 'teach India a lesson', inflicted a humiliating defeat upon the Indian army. This contrasted with relatively generous border agreements that China reached with Burma and Nepal. Indeed, China found it easier to establish enduring relationships with smaller avowedly neutralist countries such as Burma and Cambodia. The effect of the war was to damage India's international prestige, to seal a close relationship between India and the Soviet Union, and to deepen Sino-Pakistani ties.[26]

The rise of Sukarno in Indonesia and his effective dominance over foreign policy provided the opportunity for the PRC to develop a relationship that had seemed to be going badly awry only a year earlier. The Chinese in 1959 had protested angrily at the way in which the Indonesian army carried out a government decree that in effect prohibited Chinese from engaging in retail trade outside of the main cities. The Chinese government went so far as to arrange the transport of tens of thousands of the traders to China. At one point the Chinese foreign minister was said to have warned his Indonesian counterpart, who had come to Beijing to settle matters by diplomacy, that 'if Indonesia did not rescind its anti-Chinese measures, Peking would call on the Singapore Chinese to launch a trade boycott to bring Indonesia economically to its knees'.[27] In the event, mindful of a possible Soviet interest in exploiting the issue as Khrushchev visited Jakarta in February 1960, the PRC backed down, only to find that it was fortunate in the rise of Sukarno. Given his emphasis on the significance of the so-called new emerging forces, the relatively conservative image of the Soviet Union that emerged from the public polemics of the Sino-Soviet dispute made Sukarno favour China after the success of the West Irian campaign in late 1962 and the onset of his campaign of confrontation with Malaysia in early 1963. When Sukarno withdrew in pique from the United Nations in 1965 and threatened to establish an alternative body he found a ready response in Beijing.

From a Chinese perspective all went well until the abortive coup of 1965. The Indonesian army claimed that the PRC was implicated. Members of the Indonesian Communist Party and ethnic Chinese were then slaughtered in their hundreds of thousands, as the PRC was powerless to help them. The new order of General Suharto had no place for relations with China and, amid the early chaos of the Cultural Revolution, all relations were severed in 1967. As suddenly as warm relations had begun, so they were ended. The volatility of apparent ideological partnerships in the Third World stemmed from the highly personalistic character of many of their governments, as the Chinese discovered from their dealings in Africa in attempts to replace the Soviet Union as the true supporter of anti-imperialism and national liberation.

Relations with Japan remained of a different order. There was a residual sense of guilt in Japan about its conduct in the war in China, especially as many regarded China as an important source in the development of Japanese culture and there were elements within Japan that did not wish to be cut off from China. Additionally, certain business interests sought economic relations. The PRC was interested not only in weakening the American trade embargo, but also in developing wider relations with Japan in the hope of weakening its ties with Taiwan and the United States. In 1962 the semi-official Memorandum Trade Agreement was signed in Beijing. In 1964 Mao, in an interview with Japanese journalists, caused considerable anger in Moscow as he declared that the southern Kuriles along with many other territories had been unjustly acquired by the Soviet Union. This was at a point when Mao had developed a view that the smaller and medium capitalist countries belonged to a special intermediate zone between the two superpowers, implying that they should find common cause with China. France, under the presidency of De Gaulle, recognized the PRC in 1964. But Mao was unable to make a similar breakthrough with Japan, and in the end little came of his initiative.[28]

Mao's central concerns lay with asserting self-reliance and opposing the two superpowers, whom he argued tended to collude against China, even though their interests were fundamentally antagonistic. At the heart of their collusion, in his view, was their opposition to China's acquisition of nuclear weapons. China's first nuclear test took place in October 1964, and for a time it alarmed both the Soviet Union and the United States. Mao was so exercised by the threat of war from the north as well as from the east that he ordered, at tremendous cost, that a third front of defence and military related industries be developed in the mountainous redoubt of Sichuan, deep in the interior.[29] However, the American intervention in Vietnam, which had been prompted initially by concerns to contain China and to disprove the effectiveness of Maoist revolutionary warfare, proved to be a turning point. The United States, seeking to limit the war to prevent a rerun of the Korean War, did not invade the north, but confined its ground fighting to the south and attacked the north only from the air and the sea. This meant that the Soviet Union, as well as China, was drawn in to coming to the defence of a fellow socialist country. But far from bringing the two communist giants together, the war divided them still further as Mao rejected the Soviet proposal for united action. Meanwhile, a tacit understanding was reached with the United States that its forces would not invade the north or attack China and that China would not directly enter the war. That understanding had been reached in part as a result of the Chinese demonstration of discrete commitment by helping to arm the North Vietnamese and by the visible, but unpublicized, deployment of Chinese troops in the north.[30] Once convinced that there would not be a repeat of Korea, Mao unleashed the Cultural Revolution, which was designed to sweep away his domestic Soviet-style 'revisionist' opponents and establish a new revolutionary political culture for the country. The spillover into foreign affairs was disastrous in the short term as it alienated many of the Asian countries that had previously been cultivated on geopolitical grounds, including Burma, Cambodia and North Korea.

Alarmed by the new militancy of the Chinese and perhaps also responding to Mao's 1964 challenge to Moscow on the territorial issue, the Soviet Union began to upgrade its armed forces along the lengthy border with China. Perhaps mindful of the claims on Mongolia that Mao had raised with Khrushchev in 1954, despite having recognized its independence four years earlier, the Soviet Union signed a defence treaty with Mongolia in 1966 and by the following year had stationed several divisions there. The growing tension and pressure from the militarily superior Soviet forces led the Chinese to attack one of the disputed islands in the Ussuri River on the Manchurian border in March 1969. The Soviet response, which involved penetrations across the border into Xinjiang, eventually compelled the Chinese to negotiate in September.[31]

At this time Soviet officials began to sound out discretely how the West might react if the Soviet Union were to attack China's nuclear installations. The high stakes with which Mao had been playing in confronting both the superpowers had finally reached the ultimate crisis. The various attempts to find counter-weights in the Third World and among the smaller capitalist powers had failed. The attempts to signal to the United States in the autumn of 1968 that the PRC wished to resume the dialogue in the wake of the Soviet invasion of Czechoslovakia had gone unheeded. From that point, however, the PRC broke away from its self-inflicted isolationist stance to encourage a new wave of diplomatic recognition by many countries, including those from the West. It was not until 1969, as a result of the fighting, that President Nixon and his national security adviser, Kissinger, responded. Meanwhile, if Beijing had been pleased by the Nixon Doctrine, which acknowledged that the United States would no longer commit land forces to fight wars in Asia, it was less pleased by the US–Japan agreement about the reversion of Okinawa, which included Japanese claims that its security interests included South Korea and Taiwan.

The management of tripolarity, 1970–89

The tilt to America to counter Soviet encirclement, 1970–81

The Sino-American rapprochement, which constituted a watershed in the Cold War, involved several understandings and agreements of global, regional and more local consequence. From a global perspective it loosened still further the bonds of bipolarity by adding a tripolar dimension. Although China was not a global power, it did affect the global balance. China had gained American support against (Soviet) 'hegemony' and had elicited a promise that Washington would not collude with Moscow against Beijing. Beyond that, the PRC's international standing was enhanced when in October 1971 it took over the China seat at the United Nations, including permanent membership of the Security Council. The American proposal to allow for a dual membership including the ROC (i.e., Taiwan) was defeated. At a regional level the Chinese reached an understanding about Japan that made them appreciate that the retention of the American security treaty with Japan was preferable from their point of view to a Japan that in fending for itself might experience a resurgence of the very militarism that the Chinese professed to fear. At the same time, Mao and Zhou indicated to Nixon and Kissinger that they did not pose a threat to Japan or South Korea. The Taiwan issue became localized in the sense that up until then it had been at the centre of the Sino-American confrontation and one of the key points of the geostrategic line of containment. As specified in the Shanghai Communiqué signed by Nixon and Zhou in February 1972, the Americans in effect agreed to 'one China but not now' and the Chinese in effect acquiesced in a continued American diplomatic and military presence on the island, at least for the time being.[32] The visit by Nixon to Beijing had a wider symbolic significance. It was striking that there was no question of Mao visiting Washington and it was as if a powerful barbarian leader was making amends for previous hostility by deferring to the emperor in Beijing.

At the same time, China's role within the region was transformed. It now looked forward to developing relations with all of the allies of America and the West, who had hitherto been parties to security treaties of which the PRC had been the target. The axis of conflict had changed. The principal one in the region had become that between China and the Soviet Union, although that operated within a global framework that continued to centre on the United States and the Soviet Union.

However, unlike the PRC's relations with most of the countries in the world, its relations with its pro-Western neighbours that involved immediate local and regional security issues took longer to normalize. They had been divided over the UN vote on China's membership, but the PRC sought to improve relations with all of them.[33] The slight delay with Japan was of China's making, essentially to make a point about Taiwan. Not only had Prime Minister Sato signed the Okinawa agreement extending Japan's security interests to include South Korea and Taiwan, but he had personally shown public partiality to the nationalist government there. Consequently, the Chinese delayed allowing the Japanese to establish diplomatic relations until they acquired a different prime minister. After the accession of Tanaka in 1972, relations were then speedily normalized.

Elsewhere in Pacific Asia, matters moved more slowly. The North Vietnamese understandably felt betrayed. Ten years later the Vietnamese foreign minister, Nguyen Co Thach, said that Mao had told his prime minister, Phan Van Dong, that

> his broom was not long enough to sweep Taiwan clean and ours was not long enough to get the Americans out of South Vietnam. He wanted to

halt reunification and force us to recognize the puppet regime in the South. He had sacrificed Vietnam for the sake of the United States.[34]

Not for the first time did the Vietnamese communists feel that their interests were being sold out in the interests of their great-power neighbour. Not surprisingly, they turned even more strikingly to the Soviet Union. But, just as the PRC could not at this point disavow the Vietnamese struggle without losing prestige and credibility, so the North Vietnamese could not afford openly to repudiate the PRC. Only in 1974, after the Paris agreements, but before enforced unification when the Chinese acquired by force that part of the Paracel island group held by the South, was some of the bitterness of the North made public.

The ASEAN countries were slow to respond to China's new international position and to its more positive appraisal of their association. Not only was there the long-standing problem of the overseas Chinese, but they still distrusted China for its links with the communist insurgents in their countries. As late as 1 October 1974, the PRC's National Day, Zhou Enlai gave pride of place to communist leaders from Southeast Asia.[35] Moreover, the Chinese continued to allow broadcasts by insurgent communist parties such as the 'Voice of the Malayan Revolution' to emanate from Yunnan Province. The pressures from the Cultural Revolution were still fresh and the memory of China's long historical shadow had far from faded. The fact that China's best relations in Southeast Asia had been based on a kind of deference from the relatively small and vulnerable neutral Burma and Sihanouk's Cambodia hardly commended it in the eyes of the ASEAN countries. The PRC had been loud in its condemnation of ASEAN as an agent of the imperialist West until 1968, and although Beijing changed its declaratory approach two years later, it was still regarded with suspicion. The Malaysian and Indonesian political and military elites in particular saw the PRC as the long-term threat to their country's independence. When eventually recognition came it was out of self-interest, rather than because of any change in the configurations of great-power relations. The ASEAN countries may be said to have benefited from these in the general scheme of things. Thus, in 1974 the Malaysian government recognized the PRC, in the expectation that this would be of assistance in handling problems with the relatively large ethnic Chinese community that accounted for 35 per cent of Malaysia's population. The Philippines followed suit over a year later, while also extending relations to the Soviet Union, thereby demonstrating a symbolic even-handedness rather than acquiescence to the Chinese approach. Thailand also extended recognition in 1975, mainly because of the communist Vietnamese success and the need to find a counterbalance now that the Americans were on their way out of Vietnam. Indonesia, however, refused to follow suit as the PRC was still held responsible for the coup of 1965 and the armed forces were resistant to any PRC diplomatic presence that might complicate their lucrative arrangements with local Chinese businesses. As a predominantly ethnic Chinese city, located between Malaysia and Indonesia, Singapore prudently announced that it would not recognize the PRC before Indonesia. But Prime Minister Lee Kuan Yew nevertheless visited Beijing in 1976.[36]

The communist victories in Indo-China and America's final ignominious departure from Saigon in April 1975 brought to the fore the Sino-Soviet conflict as the principal great-power conflict in Southeast Asia. The Chinese became increasingly shrill in their warnings to the countries of the area about letting in the Soviet wolf through the back door as the American tiger was leaving through the front. Earlier Chinese worries that Kissinger, in Mao's words, was 'climbing on [China's] shoulders to reach Moscow' were now tinged with alarm. Not only was the Chinese alignment with the United States being used in order to establish détente with the Soviet Union, but in the Chinese view the Americans and the Europeans were making concessions to the Russians by, for example, recognizing the borders they had imposed in Eastern Europe. The Chinese feared that this would leave them even more exposed to Soviet power, as indicated perhaps by their over-vigorous pronouncements that China was secure and that it was the West that was in danger. In any event, by 1977 a pattern had emerged by which China was in an alignment with the United States and was the principal supporter of the anti-Vietnamese Khmer Rouge regime in Cambodia, while the reunified Vietnam exercised dominance over Laos and was backed by the Soviet Union.

By 1978 matters had reached the stage by which the Vietnamese and the Chinese were competing for the support of the ASEAN states. Vietnam reversed its earlier hostility to ASEAN and its Zone of Peace proposal for regional order; and the Chinese, for their part, claimed to have watered down their support for the local communist parties and implied that the only reason for supporting them at all was fear that the alternative was to have them sponsored by Vietnam and the Soviet Union, whose aggressive ambitions knew no bounds. In the spring the Vietnamese began to 'encourage' the resident ethnic Chinese to leave in the hundreds of thousands amid rumours of an impending war. They not only fled northwards to China, but when that route was closed they embarked on often unseaworthy boats across the South China Sea. Many perished and many ended up in adjacent countries as unwanted refugees. Not only did this deepen Sino-Vietnamese enmity, but it also touched on the raw nerves of the overseas Chinese question, which affected the ASEAN countries as well as China. Meanwhile the cross-border attacks by the ultra-nationalist Khmer Rouge into Vietnam in particular eventually caused the latter to attack Cambodia and impose by force a regime to its liking in late January 1979.[37] The Chinese government had long objected to what they regarded as attempts by Vietnam to assert dominance over the whole of Indo-China, especially with the backing of a hostile superpower. But the anger of China's leaders was intensified by the perception of Vietnamese ingratitude for extensive Chinese assistance over nearly thirty years.[38]

The Vietnamese invasion had been preceded by a hasty re-enforcement of power alignments by both sides. In May Carter's national security adviser, Brzezinski, visited Beijing and pleased his hosts with his much tougher approach to the Soviet Union than that exhibited by Secretary of State Vance in August 1977. In June Vietnam was admitted to the Soviet-dominated Council for Mutual Economic Assistance (CMEA). In August the Chinese, who had begun to complain about encirclement, at last reached agreement with Japan about a peace treaty that included a reference to anti-hegemonism (the key concept aimed at the Soviet Union). In early November Vietnam signed a treaty with the Soviet Union that was very similar to the Indo-Soviet treaty agreed prior to the Indian attack on what was then East Pakistan. Although earlier in the year the United States had been toying with the prospect of establishing relations with Vietnam, on 16 December the Chinese and American governments finally agreed to establish diplomatic relations. Taiwan, which had been the stumbling block hitherto, was settled in a way that ostensibly met Beijing's long-standing terms involving the cessation of all official American relations, the abrogation of the security treaty and the withdrawal of all military personnel without the Chinese agreeing in turn to resolve the issue only by peaceful terms; the Chinese nevertheless accepted that the Americans were to continue to sell arms to Taiwan – albeit in a limited way that would eventually come to an end. The upshot was that Taiwan would continue to be able to defend itself against possible mainland attack for the foreseeable future and therefore it would be able to retain its de facto independence from Beijing. Although elements in the Beijing leadership were not happy with this aspect of the normalization agreement, Deng Xiaoping's insistence prevailed. He wanted to secure American acquiescence in his plan to 'teach Vietnam a lesson'.[39]

The Chinese duly attacked across the border with Vietnam in February and, after five weeks in which they destroyed much of the infrastructure of the adjoining provinces, they withdrew. The inadequacies of China's forces and of its military doctrine were badly exposed and they failed to divert Vietnamese forces from Cambodia. But the alternative of acquiescing in Vietnam's destruction of a client regime and its assertion of dominance in Indo-China would have damaged China's prestige and its great-power pretensions and exposed it as something of a paper tiger before the Soviet Union and its proxy. Moreover, the Chinese did in fact teach the Vietnamese a lesson in geopolitics in the sense that, unlike their former adversaries, France and the United States, or indeed their then ally, the Soviet Union, China was a constant presence as a more powerful neighbour. In the event, the United States led Japan in imposing an effective economic embargo on Vietnam, and the ASEAN countries promoted an effective diplomatic opposition to Vietnam in the United Nations and the Third World. This was intensified after the Soviet invasion of Afghanistan in December 1979. That led to a tacit strategic partnership with the United States, described euphemistically as the pursuit of parallel actions. Without publicity, each in its own way was allied to the front-line states of Thailand and Pakistan respectively and each gave military assistance. Each in its own way supported the resistance fighters in Cambodia and Afghanistan and each supported the relevant international embargoes and diplomatic opposition.

Interestingly, it was at this point that the Chinese began to explore an opening to the Soviet Union. The first initiative was made in 1979 after their withdrawal from Vietnam, when the Chinese called for talks that were neatly pegged to the expiry of their long-defunct 1950 treaty. These were then put off because of the

Soviet invasion of Afghanistan, but once the dust had settled somewhat in 1981, the Chinese again signalled that they sought to improve relations.[40] In the Chinese view the momentum of strategic advantage had begun to swing away from the Soviet Union and there was no longer the pressing need for the Chinese to tilt so heavily towards the Americans. The fact that the incoming Reagan administration touched on a number of matters of great irritation to the Chinese accelerated the process by which the Chinese sought to distance themselves from the United States.

The independent foreign policy, 1982–89

The new policy was given added weight by being declared at the Twelfth Party Congress in September 1982. The general secretary, Hu Yaobang, explained that henceforth China would follow an independent foreign policy in the conduct of its relations with the United States and the Soviet Union and that China would eschew alliances as these might limit the country's capacity to exercise independent initiative and damage relations with third parties. The United States too was now said to behave in hegemonic fashion, and the Chinese reserved the right to criticize such actions in the Middle East, Central America and elsewhere. The new declaratory policy enabled the Chinese side once again to place itself at the forefront of Third World concerns and to assume a posture more congruent with its sense of its international identity and dignity.

In practice China continued to pursue parallel political and military policies with the United States over Cambodia and Afghanistan. Moreover, the American intelligence facilities to monitor Soviet missile and related activities that were transferred to Xinjiang from Iran after the fall of the Shah continued to operate uninterrupted throughout this period. Nevertheless, the new policy of independence should not be dismissed as having been of purely declaratory significance. It served three fundamental purposes. It provided a basis for gradually improving relations with the Soviet Union which substantially increased the Chinese sphere for independent manoeuvre. Second, it reflected the major ideological changes that had taken place in China, which now defined economic development as the highest priority and repudiated Mao's emphasis on class struggle. Finally, the new policy more explicitly served the new approach by Deng Xiaoping that called for economic reform at home and openness to the international economy abroad on the basis of adherence to Communist Party rule.

China's leaders tended to define their new approach in general and global terms rather than with specific reference to the Asia-Pacific region. But it was here that the policy came into effect. Thus in 1984 and 1985, as the Chinese determined that the prospects for a world war had finally receded, Deng Xiaoping singled out 'peace and development' as the 'two really great issues confronting the world today'. While noting that peace centred on East–West relations, he suggested that development involved North–South relations and that the latter was the key. China, he said, would be truly non-aligned with regard to East–West relations, where it would oppose hegemonic behaviour. In North–South relations,

he claimed, China supported dialogue and encouraged South–South cooperation.[41] A further indication of the PRC's more relaxed view of its strategic
environment was evident from the change in the strategic guidance given to the
armed forces that took place in the spring of 1985. Instead of being instructed to
prepare for an 'early, major, and nuclear war', the Chinese military were directed
to focus their preparations for conducting local, limited wars around China's
borders, which were seen as the most likely form of conflict in the foreseeable
future.[42]

In practice, however, China's policies were directed almost entirely towards the
region. Sheltered from concern about the possible Soviet threat by the American
determination under the aegis of President Reagan to face down the Soviet
Union from a position of military strength, the Chinese were able to centre their
foreign policy on economic development. The policies of seeking modernization
through economic reform and opening to the international economy that were
begun in December 1978 had profound international implications. Although they
were temporarily eclipsed by the brief war with Vietnam, the international
implications of the policies of modernization called for a greater interdependence
with the international economy and the pursuit of policies of accommodation
with the West and the East Asian market economies in particular.

Relations with the United States were unaffected by the openly stated policy
of the newly appointed secretary of state, George Shultz, to anchor America's
policies in Asia on Japan rather than China as advocated by his predecessor,
Alexander Haig. In fact, Sino-American relations enjoyed perhaps their most
constructive and trouble-free period from the end of 1982 until the Tiananmen
killings in 1989.[43] As for the Soviet Union, the question became not whether
relations would improve, but rather when and under what terms they would
be normalized. Deng insisted that they could only take place once the deployment
of Soviet forces had been substantially scaled-down in the north (including
Mongolia); the intervention forces withdrawn from Afghanistan; and above all,
the Soviet support that enabled Vietnam to continue to occupy Cambodia had
come to an end. Meanwhile Sino-Soviet trade began to pick-up, border talks
were resumed and exchanges between middle-level officials occurred.

Against this background China's economic interests began to play an increasingly important role in the conduct of foreign policy and enhanced the significance of relations with countries of the Asia-Pacific. Not surprisingly, the
relationship with Japan prospered, but perhaps not as much as might have been
expected. Although relations were formally correct and both sides professed
friendship and interdependence, there were elements of distrust, resentment and
even fear that each side felt towards the other. The Chinese felt entitled to special
treatment as they had renounced claims to reparations in 1972, and yet they
complained that Japanese companies held back somewhat from investing in
China and were less generous in transferring technology than, say, the Americans.
They also found it unacceptable that certain senior Japanese officials from
time-to-time denied the aggressiveness and brutality of Japan's armies during the
Pacific War. Such occasions were used to warn against the re-emergence of

militarism – in other words, the resurgence of a militarily powerful Japan. The Japanese in turn resented Chinese strictures and what they regarded as attempts to interfere in domestic Japanese politics.[44]

Economic interests were to the fore in the development for the first time of relations with South Korea from 1985 onwards. Initially operating through Hong Kong, economic ties expanded quickly and soon involved dealings between officials. The improvements in Sino-Soviet relations had reduced the capacity of North Korea to exercise countervailing pressure on China. In 1984, during the short reign of the more conservative and ailing Chernenko in the Soviet Union, in return for advanced weaponry Soviet surveillance planes were allowed access to Korean airspace, the better to monitor China's forces, and Soviet ships visited North Korean ports. With the accession of Gorbachev these arrangements came to an end. By that point, however, the Chinese no longer felt obligated to the North, still less would they allow the North to exercise a veto of their relations with the South. By this time South Korea had begun a deliberate policy of cultivating the North's communist allies. China's economic-centred policies enabled it to respond, thereby beginning the process of eroding the last remnants of the Cold War.

Similar interests and flexibility were in evidence as the Chinese on the mainland responded positively to the beginnings of economic relations, initiated unofficially from Taiwan in the second half of the 1980s. Again these were directed through Hong Kong. By 1987 Taiwanese residents were allowed to visit the mainland. This in turn led to the development of what has been called 'Greater China', involving a complicated economic nexus that brought together the economies of Taiwan, Hong Kong and the Chinese provinces of Guangdong and Fujian.[45] The new approach by the Deng leadership had also facilitated the negotiation of an agreement in 1984 for the reversion of Hong Kong to Chinese sovereignty thirteen years later on terms that guaranteed the continuation of the Hong Kong way of life for a further fifty years. For China's leaders, and Deng Xiaoping in particular, the prize was the restoration of sovereignty over this prime symbol of the humiliation of their country in the nineteenth century. Although it was important to do so under conditions that would allow the territory to continue to be prosperous and stable so that it could continue to play a key role in the modernization of the country, Deng showed at one point in the negotiations that if necessary that could be sacrificed as long as the proper terms of sovereignty were not infringed.[46]

The economic imprint on China's foreign policy was also evident in Southeast Asia, where the strategic configurations of Indo-China had precedence. Throughout most of the 1980s a stalemate had evolved on the Cambodian issue. Vietnam was unable to wipe out totally the forces resisting its military occupation of Cambodia, but they in turn were confined to bases operating along the border with Thailand and were incapable of dislodging the Vietnamese. The Chinese, as the supporters of the Khmer Rouge (the principal resistant force) and the de facto allies of Thailand, were also the diplomatic associates of the ASEAN states in their successful fostering of international diplomatic opposition to Vietnam.

Although the Malaysian and Indonesian governments claimed to fear the longer-term threat of China and saw Vietnam as a possible buffer to China, the Vietnamese proved to be too intransigent to respond positively to initiatives from them to display some flexibility. Consequently, the Chinese were able to take advantage of the situation to deepen economic ties with all the ASEAN countries, which included the conduct of direct trade with Indonesia even in the absence of diplomatic relations. That extended their relations beyond the Indo-Chinese issues.[47] Nevertheless, residual problems remained, with local unease concerning the rising power of China, especially in the light of its historical legacy of claimed superiority. These included uncertainty about the character of the interlocking webs of loyalties of the ethnic Chinese and Beijing's claims upon them; conflicting claims to the Spratly Islands in the South China Sea; and, more broadly, worries about the extent to which the leaders in Beijing understood the concerns of their neighbours and were willing to act with restraint.

It was the ending of tripolarity and of the Cold War that brought this period of Chinese foreign policy to an end. Gorbachev's fulfilment of the essentials of Deng Xiaoping's three preconditions for normalizing relations paved the way for his visit to Beijing in May 1989. Instead of that turning out to be a triumph for Deng, it contributed to the greatest crisis of his rule. The subsequent killings in Beijing on 4 June ended the honeymoon with the West and changed China's international relations, especially as this bloody event was followed only months later by the relatively bloodless ending of communist rule in Eastern Europe and the end of the Cold War itself.

Notes

1 In a book written by Chinese scholars who had carried out research training in the United States, the editors described their country as 'a regional power with global strategic significance and political influence'. See Yufan Hao and Guocang Huan (eds), *The Chinese View of the World* (New York: Pantheon, 1989), p.xxix.

2 Steven Levine, 'China in Asia: The PRC as a Regional Power' in Harry Harding (ed.), *China's Foreign Policy in the 1980s* (New Haven: Yale University Press, 1984), p.107.

3 Samuel S. Kim, 'China's International Organizational Behaviour' in Thomas W. Robinson and David Shambaugh (eds), *Chinese Foreign Policy: Theory and Practice* (Oxford: Clarendon Press, 1994), p.417.

4 Jonathan D. Spence, *The Search for Modern China* (London: Hutchinson, 1990), pp.162–64.

5 Michael H. Hunt, 'Chinese Foreign Relations in Historical Perspective' in Harry Harding, *China's Foreign Relations in the 1980s* (*op.cit.*), p.10.

6 Edgar Snow, *Red Star Over China* (London: Pelican Books, revised and enlarged edn, 1972), pp.128–29.

7 Wang Gungwu, 'Pre-Modern History: Some Trends in Writing the History of the Song (10th–13th Centuries)' in Michael B. Yahuda (ed.), *New Directions in the Social Sciences and Humanities in China* (London: Macmillan, 1987), pp.1–27.

8 John Gittings, *Survey of the Sino-Soviet Dispute* (London: Oxford University Press, 1968), pp.166–67.

9 For this and the previous quotation, see William C. Kirby, 'Traditions of Centrality, Authority and Management in Modern China's Foreign Relations' in Thomas

W. Robinson and David Shambaugh (eds), *Chinese Foreign Policy: Theory and Practice* (Oxford: Clarendon Press, 1994), p.17.

10 Harry Harding, 'China's Co-operative Behaviour' in Robinson and Shambaugh (eds), *Chinese Foreign Policy (op.cit.)*, pp.384–92.

11 See the discussions by Carol Lee Hamrin, 'Elite Politics and Foreign Relations' in Robinson and Shambaugh (eds), *Chinese Foreign Policy (op.cit.)*, pp.70–112; and Kenneth Lieberthal, 'Domestic Politics and Foreign Policy' in Harding, *China's Foreign Relations in the 1980s (op.cit.)*, pp.43–70.

12 Wang Jisi, 'International Relations Theory and the Study of Chinese Foreign Policy: A Chinese Perspective' in Robinson and Shambaugh (eds), *Chinese Foreign Policy (op.cit.)*, p.493.

13 This paragraph has drawn on Wang Jisi, *International Relations Theory … (op.cit.)*, pp.481–505; Steven I. Levine, 'Perception and Ideology in Chinese Foreign Policy' in Robinson and Shambaugh (eds), *Chinese Foreign Policy (op.cit.)*, pp.30–46; and Lucian Pye, *The Mandarin and the Cadre: China's Political Cultures* (Ann Arbor: Center for Chinese Studies, University of Michigan, 1988).

14 Chi-Kin Lo, *China's Policy Towards Territorial Disputes: The Case of the South China Sea Islands* (London: Routledge, 1989), pp.27–28.

15 Michael B. Yahuda, *China's Role in World Affairs* (London: Croom Helm, 1978), pp.47–48.

16 These were: (1) mutual respect for each other's territorial integrity and sovereignty; (2) non-aggression; (3) non-interference in each other's internal affairs; (4) equality and mutual benefit; (5) peaceful coexistence. It will be seen that these stress statism and that their vague terms apply best to relations between governments from divergent political systems. Not surprisingly, they have tended to be downplayed during the more revolutionary phases of Chinese foreign policy and to be highlighted during the more moderate ones. They have been revived during the 1990s as a way of deflecting the more intrusive of the post-Cold War international norms, but it is doubtful how applicable they might be in the more interdependent world within which the PRC is seeking to integrate itself.

17 Michael Leifer, *Dictionary of the Modern Politics of South-East Asia* (London: Routledge, 1995), p.211.

18 For a detailed account, see Stephen Fitzgerald, *China and the Overseas Chinese* (Cambridge: Cambridge University Press, 1972).

19 Jay Taylor, *China and Southeast Asia: Peking's Relations with Revolutionary Movements* (New York: Praeger, 2nd edn, 1976), ch.5, pp.251–372.

20 Steven M. Goldstein, 'Sino-Soviet Relations' in Robinson and Shambaugh (eds), *Chinese Foreign Policy (op.cit.)*, particularly pp.237–44.

21 Allen S. Whiting, 'The Sino-Soviet Split', *The Cambridge History of China*, vol.14 (Cambridge: Cambridge University Press, 1991), p.493.

22 *Ibid.*, p.499.

23 This theme is developed in Goldstein, 'Sino-Soviet Relations' *(op.cit.)*. For a hard-hitting account of Mao's approach and the problems it raised for China, see Edward Friedman, 'Anti-Imperialism in Chinese Foreign Policy' in Samuel S. Kim (ed.), *China and the World: Chinese Foreign Relations in the Post-Cold War Era* (Boulder: Westview Press, 1994), pp.60–74.

24 Whiting, 'The Sino-Soviet Split' *(op.cit.)*, p.502.

25 This is the argument of Melvin Gurtov, *China and Southeast Asia – The Politics of Survival* (Lexington: Heath Lexington Books, 1971).

26 For accounts, see Neville Maxwell, *India's China War* (London: Pelican, 1970); Alastair Lamb, *The China–India Border* (London: Oxford University Press, 1964); and Allen S. Whiting, *The Chinese Calculus of Deterrence* (Michigan: University of Michigan Press, 1975).

27 Cited in Michael Leifer, *Indonesia's Foreign Policy* (London: George Allen and Unwin, 1983), p.69.

28 Yahuda, *China's Role in World Affairs* (*op.cit.*), pp.149–54.

29 Barry Naughton, 'The Third Front Defence: Industrialization in the Chinese Interior', *The China Quarterly* 115 (September 1988), pp.351–86.

30 Whiting, *The Chinese Calculus of Deterrence* (*op.cit.*), pp.170–95. Interestingly, Hanoi made this charge after the 1979 war with China: See Ministry of Foreign Affairs, Socialist Republic of Vietnam, *The Truth About Vietnam–China Relations Over the Last Thirty Years* (Hanoi: Foreign Languages Press, 1979), p.35.

31 For further detail and analysis on the above two paragraphs, see Thomas W. Robinson, 'China Confronts the Soviet Union: Warfare and Diplomacy on China's Inner Asian Frontiers', *The Cambridge History of China*, vol.15 (Cambridge: Cambridge University Press, 1991), pp.218–301.

32 This paragraph draws on Jonathan D. Pollack, 'The Opening to America', *The Cambridge History of China*, vol.15 (*op.cit.*), pp.423–25.

33 For an account of reactions in Southeast Asia, see Taylor, *China and Southeast Asia* (*op.cit.*), pp.337–55.

34 *Ibid.*, p.422.

35 Yahuda, *China's Role in World Affairs* (*op.cit.*), p.262.

36 For further details, see relevant *Southeast Asia Year Books* (Singapore: Institute of Southeast Asian Studies, 1974, 1975 and 1976); and *Asia Year Books* (Hong Kong: Far Eastern Economic Review, 1974, 1975 and 1976).

37 For an extended analysis, see Nayan Chanda, *Brother Enemy: The War After the War* (New York: Harcourt Brace Jovanovich, 1986); and Robert S. Ross, *The Indo-China Tangle: China's Vietnam Policy, 1975–1979* (New York: Columbia University Press, 1988).

38 For Chinese and Vietnamese claims and counter-claims about the alleged perfidy of the other, see Ministry of Foreign Affairs, *The Truth About Vietnam–China Relations …* (*op.cit.*); and *On the Vietnamese Foreign Ministry's White Book Concerning Vietnam–China Relations* (Beijing: Foreign Language Press, 1979).

39 For details of the negotiations and of Sino-American relations at this time, see Pollack, 'The Opening to America' (*op.cit.*), pp.435–56.

40 For an account of the gradual improvement in relations in the early 1980s, see Gerald Segal, *Sino-Soviet Relations after Mao* (London: International Institute for Strategic Studies, Adelphi Papers no.202, 1985).

41 Wang Jisi, 'A Chinese Perspective' (*op.cit.*), p.486.

42 Paul H.B. Godwin, 'Force and Diplomacy: Chinese Security Policy in the Post-Cold War Era' in Kim (ed.), *China and the World* (*op.cit.*), p.172.

43 Harry Harding, *A Fragile Relationship: The United States and China Since 1972* (Washington, DC: The Brookings Institution, 1992), ch.5 'Reconciliation', pp.138–72.

44 For an extended treatment, see Allen S. Whiting, *China Eyes Japan* (Berkeley: University of California Press, 1989).

45 For a detailed analysis of many of the relevant aspects, see *The China Quarterly* 136 ('Special Issue: Greater China', December 1993).

46 *Ibid.* See also Kevin Rafferty, *City on the Rocks* (London: Viking, 1989). On the negotiations, see Robert Cottrell, *The End of Hong Kong* (London: John Murray, 1993).

47 For accounts of the economic relations, see John Wong, *The Political Economy of Southeast Asia* (London: Macmillan, 1984); and Chia Siow-Yue and Cheng Bifan (eds), *ASEAN–China Economic Relations: Trends and Patterns* (Singapore: Institute of Southeast Asian Studies, 1987).

7 Japan and the Asia-Pacific

From the early twentieth century, Japan has been central to any conception of the Asia-Pacific as a region. In the build-up to and during the Pacific War this found expression primarily in the abortive attempt to impose an economic empire by force.[1] After 1945 Japan emerged as the most dynamic economic centre of the region within a strategic and economic order established by the United States.

Japan is more than a regional power. Its economy is of global significance and geopolitically it is located at the junction of American, Russian and Chinese interests. For its part, Japan has been uncertain as to whether to regard itself as primarily a highly developed country that is part of the Western world, as in the Trilateral Commission interacting with Europe and North America, or as still very much an Asian power that is wary of Westernization and able in its own way to provide leadership to its Asian neighbours. In practice, however, Japan has played a relatively quiescent role in global affairs even where its own security interests may be seen to have been directly involved. This is largely a consequence of responsibility for its security having been assumed by the United States ever since its defeat in 1945. The relative quiescence has also been underpinned by domestic support for the principles of the 1947 'peace constitution' and by the pattern of domestic politics that emerged after the end of the American occupation in 1952. Only with the end of the Cold War did that pattern of Japanese domestic politics begin to change, and in this new period Japan developed an international ambition that was expressed in a demand for a permanent seat on the Security Council of the United Nations, which was significantly qualified by a continued refusal to assume attendant military responsibilities.

Throughout the period of the Cold War, the United States in effect guaranteed the security of Japan and maintained an international free trade order that allowed Japan to pursue its own narrow commercial interests. Japan resisted all American attempts to persuade it to participate in collective security schemes and avoided involvement in international strategic affairs. Indeed, during the 1950s and 1960s Japan essentially followed the US lead in foreign affairs (while refusing to 'share responsibilities') and it was only in reaction to the 1971 'Nixon shocks', in which he failed to inform them of his opening to China and of his abrupt withdrawal of the US dollar from the gold standard, that the Japanese began to develop a somewhat independent course. Even then the fundamental neomercantilist approach did not greatly change, as Japanese foreign policy continued to be primarily reactive while seeking to avoid becoming embroiled in international conflicts.

The impact upon Japan of having most of its security responsibilities undertaken by the United States has been complex and many sided. Emerging out of the period of the US occupation that ended in 1952, the security arrangement that became central to American strategy in the Cold War era was first used by Prime Minister Yoshida Shigeru as a means by which Japan 'gave exclusive priority to pursuing economic recovery and maintaining political stability ... [while deferring] indefinitely the task of preparing the Japanese people themselves for a return to the harsh realities of international politics'.[2] This set a course that became institutionalized. The neomercantilist policies initially adopted in the 1950s had profound effects upon the structure of domestic politics that in turn reinforced the character of those policies in dealing with the outside world.

The Yoshida approach in effect sought to reach an accommodation between those Japanese nationalists who found it demeaning for Japan to be confined to the status of dependency in security matters and those who adhered to the ethos of the 1947 'peace constitution' which pledged Japan to foreswear war and the use or threat of force as an instrument of policy. Yoshida himself in later life came to regret the course that he had set. In 1963, nearly ten years after leaving office, he wrote:

> For an independent Japan, which is among the first rank countries in economics, technology, and learning, to continue to be dependent on another country is a deformity (katawa) of the state. ... I myself cannot escape responsibility for the use of the constitution as a pretext (tatemae) for this way of conducting national policy.[3]

But the die was cast so that, even thirty years later, Japanese security was still dependent upon the United States without obliging Japan to reciprocate or to contribute to regional security.

Since the end of the Cold War the relationship between Japan and the United States has remained at the core of the security architecture of the Asia-Pacific, but it has been subject to new stresses and challenges. The demise of the Soviet threat and the greater salience of economic and domestic issues in American foreign policy has given a new edge to long-standing problems in the relations with Japan. The huge trade surpluses that Japan has enjoyed with the United States have become much more contentious as economic disputes have ceased to be counterbalanced by the cooperative dimension of the security problems of confronting the Soviet Union. A more nationalistically assertive Japan has resented American pressure to change its economic practices and to be more supportive of American leadership in world affairs, even on issues fundamental to Japan, such as the Gulf War of 1991 and the North Korean nuclear problem since 1993. Within Japan, however, these issues and the Gulf in particular were seen less as problems that involved the country's national interests directly and more as matters that concerned relations with the United States.[4]

Japan's foreign relations have also been constrained by the legacy of the history of its aggression in the Asia-Pacific before 1945, with which it has yet to come to terms satisfactorily – at least in the eyes of many of the victims of that aggression, especially in East Asia. Even those Japanese who adhere most strongly to the ethos of the 'peace constitution' have tended to see their country as a victim of the Pacific War rather than as its vicious perpetrator. They dwell in particular on the horrors of the atomic bombs dropped on Hiroshima and Nagasaki. In this respect they converge with more right-wing Japanese nationalists who play down the significance of Japanese aggression and wartime atrocities, often to the annoyance of neighbouring countries and to the embarrassment of Japanese prime ministers who have to demand the resignation of such people from the cabinet.

Japan's neighbours have also professed concern about the possible re-emergence of Japanese militarism. Not only do they point to a failure to come to terms with its aggressive past, but they also note the speed with which Japan could transform itself into a country that could project overwhelming military power throughout the region. Due to its advanced technological capacities and its high levels of military spending, Japan in 1990, it was claimed, possessed a military capability which 'must be rated first class in global, as well as regional, terms'.[5] Although certain inadequacies such as shortages of reserve forces and logistical weaknesses currently limit the exercise of Japanese power, it is believed in the region that these and other problems could be overcome very quickly indeed if the Japanese 'mood' were to change suddenly.

The possibility of such a transformation cannot be excluded because of the country's insularity and sense of vulnerability. Before the forceful advent of the West in the mid-nineteenth century, Japanese history involved only limited interactions with others. The people of its four principal islands are remarkably homogeneous. Despite having emerged as a great trading and industrial country in the last 140 years, Japan has retained a relative parochialism. But that has been coupled with a sense of vulnerability, not only due to the possible threats of militarily superior powers, but also because of its lack of natural resources and its dependence upon external supplies. Despite having been perhaps the prime beneficiaries of international order since the end of the Second World War, Japanese customarily think of the international environment as potentially threatening and prone to sudden upheavals. Their task has been to detect trends and accommodate themselves to them. Many see Japan's enhanced economic and political role within the region allied to its continuing neomercantilism and assertive nationalism as leading inexorably to a resurgence of militarism – especially if this were allied to a sharp change in the international environment that was adverse to Japan.[6]

Japanese perspectives, not surprisingly perhaps, do not encompass what to them would appear to be at best a far-fetched notion that they might resume the militarist path of old. In delineating 'four Japanese scenarios for the future', the nearest the political scientist Takashi Inoguchi came to identifying what he called a Pax Nipponica was an economically dominant Japan that could act as a balancer among more continental powers – rather like Britain in the nineteenth century. But even this role is predicated on what he regarded as the unlikely neutralization of nuclear weapons.[7] His own view about Japan's international role was more circumspect. Writing in 1993 he observed: 'At present, Japan's interests derive largely from its "search for an honourable place in the world community", from its apprehension of being isolated and from its genuine desire to make positive contributions to international security.' But too much should not be expected as 'Japan's historical legacy, its weakly articulated vision of its international role and its feeble leadership will prevent it from taking up some responsibilities with vigour. These, however, are constraints that Japan will have to live with for the foreseeable future.'[8] There is therefore an abiding enigmatic quality to Japan's role in Asia as its history, economic significance and immediate military potential point to leadership capacities that are dormant, like a volcano that could nevertheless erupt if the pressures upon it were to suddenly change.

The domestic sources of foreign policy

The combination of highly activist neomercantilist economic policies and the generally cautious and reactive approach to the outside world that characterizes much of Japan's foreign policy may be said to be anchored in the structure of its government and politics. But, at the same time, that also draws upon deeply set ideas about Japan's identity and the legacy of Japanese history. The Japanese system of government has been characterized by continual rule by conservative parties (predominantly the Liberal Democratic Party (LDP) since its formation in 1955) in a triumvirate with the business community and above all the semi-autonomous bureaucratic ministries. The LDP has been notoriously factionalized; and the business community has been divided into four main groups. Nevertheless, especially in the 1950s and 1960s, a consensus prevailed on the necessities of reconstruction and high economic growth. This was achieved under the highly favourable external conditions provided by American hegemony, the general growth of the international economy and ready access to the American domestic market on a non-reciprocal basis.

The principal ministries involved in foreign relations included the Ministry of Foreign Affairs (MFA), the Ministry of International Trade and Industry (MITI), the Ministry of Finance (MoF) and the Ministry of Fisheries and Food (MAFF). Their interests often conflicted: MITI was primarily concerned with the promotion of Japanese economic interests based on its domestic industrial constituency; MoF was concerned with limiting budgetary expenditure; MAFF was concerned with defending farming and fishing interests and it benefited from an electoral system that was skewed in favour of farmers; and the MFA, bereft of an obvious domestic constituency, was in a relatively weak position as it sought to reconcile the domestic, not to say parochial, thrust of the external dimensions of Japan's interests with the demands made upon Japan, primarily by the United States.[9]

This resulted in a decision-making process that was singularly effective in blocking most initiatives and that was simultaneously and paradoxically extremely well suited to adapting to changing circumstances. Various Japanese scholars have commented adversely on the powerful relationships that bind vested interests, bureaucrats and politicians in ways that dilute initiative: 'Reform efforts evaporate like drops of water on a hot griddle.' Moreover their alliance is said to have 'closed Japan tight to the rest of the world'.[10] This system, however, has also proved remarkably capable in monitoring trends and, when necessary, adapting to changes. This was true, for example, of the two oil crises in the 1970s, which left Japanese industry even more competitive as it became even more efficient in its use of energy and, later, of the re-evaluation of the Yen in 1985 which accelerated the distribution of production capacity, especially to Southeast Asia. But it is a system that gives rise to neomercantile practices rather than the provision of leadership or easy contribution to international public goods.[11]

Despite being the products of factional manoeuvrings that owe little to debates about public policy and still less to foreign-affairs issues, Japanese prime ministers have been able to practice personal diplomacy and at times to provide leadership in foreign affairs. Japanese commentators have tended to credit each of their post-war prime ministers with a distinctive personal approach that at times shaped policy in crucial ways.[12] While acknowledging the centrality of prime ministers in the Japanese foreign-policy process, outside observers tend to draw attention to the constraints that limit their capacity to exercise leadership.[13]

The effectiveness of these constraints must be understood against the backdrop of modern Japanese history and within the context of the conflicting systems of ideas that have shaped Japanese thinking about their role since 1945. The former inculcated the sense that, as an outsider and a late developer, Japan had to assess the international conditions set by the great powers and respond to them so as to best advantage Japan. The latter set up a tension between the pattern of ideas associated with the so-called peace constitution, by which the Japanese were pledged to renounce war forever, and the ideas associated with the security alliance with the United States. Japanese leaders were forever seeking to balance the two. Above all, the 'lesson' of the last 150 years since this insular and self-absorbed country was forcibly opened up to the Western world has been that Japanese must be ever vigilant about the vulnerability of their country. As a state that became uniquely dependent upon trade, it has been concerned about securing supplies; and as an island chain of global geopolitical significance, Japan has been concerned about the shifting balance of forces between the great powers. As Kenneth Pyle has observed:

> since the Meiji Restoration, Japanese leaders have had a keen sensitivity to the forces controlling the international environment; they tried to operate in accord with these forces and use them to their own advantage. A shrewd

politician grasped the 'trend of the times', adapted Japanese policy to these trends, and benefited from them.[14]

Historical forces, the character of the domestic political system and the strength of the appeal of the peace constitution within Japan combined to intensify this reactive quality of Japanese foreign policy. The policy has not been without its successes and arguably it has served Japan well. The country has prospered and become an economic superpower without becoming embroiled in the many wars and armed conflicts that have taken place in the Asia-Pacific region. However, Japan's reactive neomercantilism and the parochial character of its intractable decision-making processes has meant that external pressure alone has made it respond to the demands of international society about rules of trade. But as Japanese nationalistic pride has grown so has resentment at the pressure exerted by outsiders.

Yet it is the very growth of Japan's economic significance that has impacted adversely upon its partners and caused them to demand changes in Japanese practices. This is nowhere more evident than in the economic relations with its security benefactor and most important partner, the United States. Problems in the imbalance of trade which began in the 1970s have troubled the relationship, and intensified as the Cold War came to an end. As American pressure increased, the Japanese reaction continued to be one of reluctant adjustment. This has elicited a strong nationalist reaction, typified by the famous 1989 book co-authored by the chairman of Sony, entitled *The Japan That Can Say 'No': The New U.S.–Japan Relations Card.*[15] As is evident from the title, this is essentially a negative response rather than an alternative assertion of positive leadership.

Beginning in 1993/94, however, the Japanese political system responded to domestic and external changes that in large measure flowed from the ending of the Cold War, thereby commencing what many regard as a prolonged process of transformation. The Japanese Socialist Party could no longer sustain its cherished ideological positions and the Liberal Democratic Party finally split, spurred in part by voter dissatisfaction with its long-running corruption scandals. This resulted in 1994 in the first non-Liberal Democratic government for nearly forty years. It remains to be seen whether the projected electoral reforms will be carried out and much would then depend on whether that would set in tow a ripple effect that would contribute to systemic change. The Japanese economic miracle has been buttressed domestically by a conservative coalition of protected agriculture, organized business and a national bureaucracy imbued with economic nationalism. Externally it has flourished under the American security guarantee and an international economic order shaped, however imperfectly, by the United States. Japan is currently in a process of transition whose outcome may determine whether, under the new conditions in the post-Cold War period, critical aspects of this nexus will change in any fundamental way. The only other source for profound change would be a major 'shock' from the outside that would once again remind the Japanese of their country's vulnerabilities and that would cause them to reorientate their society as they have done before in modern history.

Japan's re-emergence under American hegemony, 1945–70

There is considerable merit to the view that, following the largely American occupation, Japan has since 1952 focused on its own economic development and trade, little troubled by considerations of security and foreign policy. This was a period of exceptional American power in international affairs and the Japanese benefited both from the security guarantee and the favourable external economic conditions provided by the United States. But such a view would be incomplete as it would overlook Japanese success in quite deliberately forging a foreign policy based on neomercantilism that enabled it to resist American demands that it play a greater role in regional security, especially on a collective basis. Thus Japan was able to conduct trade with the People's Republic of China, despite the American embargo, and to establish relations with the Soviet Union. At the same time, the Japanese were able to take advantage of American initiatives on their behalf to re-establish economic ties with Southeast Asia. Consequently, by the end of this period Japan not only emerged as a major economic power second in size only to the United States, but also began to exercise significant independent influence within the Asia-Pacific region.

The occupation was notable in its early years for the changes that it brought about in the constitution, local government, the judiciary, law, labour relations, land tenure and education. The principal objectives were to extirpate the influence of militarism and to advance democratization of Japanese society. From the point of view of foreign policy the most important change was the famous chapter 9 in the constitution of 1947. In its original form it would have unambiguously pledged Japan to foreswear the development of its own armed forces, but the final version qualified this somewhat by allowing for an interpretation that pegged that to the aim of an 'international peace based on justice and order'. That left open the prospect of preparing for defence against aggression as a legitimate option in an imperfect world.[16] The amendments were introduced to assuage the Japanese side, but by 1948 the American approach changed as the advent of the Cold War caused them to regard Japan as an ally to be cultivated rather than a defeated enemy to be punished. This led to a harsher treatment of the left and of trade unions and to a more favourable attitude towards the business and conservative elements. Washington was also tiring of paying the bill for keeping Japan afloat, and it was anxious for its economic recovery to take place. In this new atmosphere the old conglomerates, the former Zaibatsu, resumed operations. By 1949 the many thousands who had been purged because of their past links with the war government were beginning to be re-admitted to civil and political life. And in July 1950, a month after the outbreak of the Korean War, permission was granted for the creation of a National Police Reserve, a paramilitary force 75,000 strong, in readiness to take over domestic security from the Americans.

The change in the American attitude accelerated the process of moving towards a peace settlement and bringing the occupation to an end. The Japanese left was embittered by the American change of course and it was also divided. But its increasingly anti-American posture paradoxically centred on the quintessentially

American document, the famous Article 9 on peace. In his negotiations with John Foster Dulles, who had come in 1950 to try to draw Japan into America's Cold War coalition, Prime Minster Yoshida was able to draw upon the opposition of the left as one of his key arguments against Japan being called upon to take an activist role. After protracted negotiations Yoshida made minimal concessions (for example, he agreed to increase the number of the police reserves, who were to be renamed the National Security Force, from 75,000 to 110,000, instead of the 350,000 demanded by Dulles) and secured an approach that was to prevail for the next four decades and beyond:

1 The principal national goal was Japan's economic rehabilitation, and to this end economic and political cooperation with the United States was essential.
2 Japan was to remain lightly armed and free of entanglement in international strategic issues so as, *inter alia*, to minimize internal divisions – what Yoshida called 'a 38th Parallel' in the hearts of the Japanese people.
3 Bases would be provided for the American armed forces in order to gain a long term guarantee for the security of Japan.[17]

The approach was predicated on the conviction that the imperatives of the Cold War determined that the Americans would deploy significant forces in Japan and that they would suffice to deter the Soviet Union. Japan would be insulated from the hard choices of international politics and security while pursuing economic goals amid conditions of political stability. Indeed, by 1995 the domestic situation had settled into an almost fixed pattern, as the sets of political parties essentially polarized into a socialist party that became a permanent opposition and the Liberal Democrats, who became the party of government. Meanwhile, the myth took root of a Japan that, as a country that had been uniquely scarred by the atomic bomb and especially endowed by its peace constitution, was especially committed to peace.

The negotiations with Dulles, however, also exacted a price for Japan's opting out of collective security responsibilities. The security treaty that was signed on the same day as the San Francisco Peace Treaty (8 September 1951) was unequal also in terms of security obligations, and it preserved many of the prerogatives enjoyed by the United States during the occupation. Although, together with the British, the Japanese had been successful in barring both Chinas from attending the Peace Treaty (if the PRC were not to be allowed to attend by the United States, then the ROC should not attend either), Yoshida had no alternative but to recognize Chiang Kai-shek's ROC as the legitimate China.

There was, however, a substantive body of opinion in business circles that demanded economic access to the PRC, seen as necessary for Japan's recovery. Being alert to the needs of the Japanese economy the Americans facilitated the utilization of Japanese reparations as a way of gaining access to the resources and markets of the Southeast Asian countries.[18] This set a pattern of unbalanced trading relations as Japan exchanged raw materials for value-added manufactures. However, notwithstanding these arrangements, an unofficial trade agreement was signed in Beijing on 1 June 1952 by Japanese businessmen. In September Japan joined the newly established CHINCOM, the allied committee formed to limit trade with the PRC. The Japanese drew a balance between the conflicting pressures between the US and the ROC on the one side and the PRC on the other. In July 1953 the House of Representatives of the Japanese Diet unanimously passed a resolution calling for the development of trade with the PRC as the first step towards improving relations between the two countries. Indeed, between 1952 and 1958 four unofficial trade agreements were signed. Although notionally trade and politics were separate, even in Japanese eyes the two were closely related.

Despite a hitch in relations in 1958 after the more right-wing and former member of the wartime cabinet Kishi Nobusake visited Taiwan, trade relations gradually resumed, and in 1962 they were formalized into two types of transaction, 'Memorandum Trade' and 'Friendly Trade'. Since Japan was precluded from normalizing relations with the PRC because of its American-sponsored recognition of the ROC, all sides understood that the Memorandum Trade offices in the respective capitals served the purposes of unofficial missions. MITI bureaucrats served in Beijing and Foreign Ministry officials served in Tokyo. Although relations were fraught with problems relating to PRC suspicions of Japanese ties with Washington and especially Taipei and to the consequences of political turmoil in the PRC itself, Japan remained China's most important capitalist trading partner and, as Sino-Soviet circumstances changed in 1968, there were signs of a movement in Japan towards recognition of the PRC.[19]

Japan's relations with the Soviet Union during this period also followed a line independent of the United States. Yoshida was replaced as prime minister in 1954 by the more nationalistic Hayatoma Ichero. He tried to take advantage of the more relaxed international environment to pursue a peace treaty with the Soviet Union. In the event, that fell through because of the territorial dispute over the four groups of islands immediately to the north of Japan. In Japan there was an underlying sense of betrayal at the Soviet occupation of the islands that in the Japanese view were falsely claimed as part of the Kuriles group and that in any case had been acquired at the end of the war by a Soviet violation of their non-aggression pact, which Japan had done nothing to provoke. But the two states were able to agree to normalize relations in 1956 and this paved the way for Japan's admission into the United Nations. A possibility for a compromise over the islands was floated for a while but it came to nothing, in part because of pressure from an alarmed Dulles and the confusions of domestic Japanese politics.[20] After this brief opening, Japanese relations with the Soviet Union reverted to their previous levels of animosity as the Soviet Union was unable to loosen Japan's ties with the United States and the Japanese were unable to make progress on their claims to the northern islands or in gaining access to their traditional fishing grounds in the Sea of Okhotsk. There was little, therefore, to change their legacy of historical rivalry and suspicion. This reinforced the hostility that was embedded in their opposing alignments in the Cold War.

Japan's relations with the United States were not greatly affected by these divergences from core American policies. Throughout the 1950s and 1960s, Japan enjoyed privileged access to American domestic markets without being required to reciprocate. In the 1950s and 1960s Japan was seen by the United States as the linchpin of the 'free world' in Asia. It was strategically located and it was a resounding success as a democracy and as a capitalist economy. The only 'hiccup' in the relationship during this period occurred when Prime Minister Kishi sought to renew the security treaty with the United States on a more equitable basis in 1960. It aroused the fury of the left and led to riots that caused American President Eisenhower to cancel his planned visit for the signing ceremony. But the rioting was aimed principally at Kishi himself and his handling of the episode, for it died down almost as quickly as it erupted and it was not followed by further anti-American demonstrations. If anything the episode served to consolidate the Yoshida approach by impressing on the Americans the dangers of exerting pressure on Japan to adopt a more active strategic role.[21]

The United States instead encouraged Japan to join the several international economic organizations that shaped the international economic order. These included the OECD, the General Agreement on Tariff and Trade (GATT), and the International Monetary Fund (IMF). Japan was also a founder member of the Asia Development Bank (ADB). Moreover, Japan had benefited economically from the Korean War during its early stage of recovery and, in the late 1960s, as it had become an economy of the first rank, it also benefited from the Vietnam War.

Typically, there was no question of Japan participating in the war, but American use of bases in Okinawa aroused both nationalist and pacifist sentiments within Japan. Prime Minister Sato in 1967 had raised the question of the reversion of Okinawa to Japanese sovereignty during a summit with President Johnson, but without success. But in a meeting with President Nixon in 1969 it was finally agreed that sovereignty would revert in 1972.[22] By this stage, however, the configurations of power had begun to change significantly, especially in Asia, and that was to bring a significant adjustment of Japanese policies towards the region.

An independent foreign policy, 1971–89

During this period Japan fashioned a number of foreign relations initiatives that collectively suggested a more active and independent foreign policy, despite still sheltering under the American security umbrella and despite the central role that was still accorded to relations with the United States. These initiatives may be seen as a response to a relative decline in American hegemonic power, as expressed in the Nixon Doctrine and in the removal of the American dollar from the gold standard. But they also reflected responses to the two oil crises of the 1970s and to the emergence of tripolarity in the Asia-Pacific. But more than just response was involved in Southeast Asia, where Japan began to take a more active role with a view to contributing to regional order. This was also the period when the imbalance in Japanese–American trade relations began to inject a note of discord into the proceedings. Meanwhile Sino-Japanese relations began to move out from under the American shadow to acquire a character and dynamic of their own.

Although the Nixon Doctrine as it emerged from his press conference in Guam in 1969 had alerted the Japanese to the American intention to scale down their military commitments in Asia, his decisions in 1971 to open relations with China and to take the US dollar off the gold standard came as shocks. What was particularly galling was the failure to consult or inform them significantly in advance. The cavalier way in which fundamental Japanese interests had apparently been overlooked was more than a blow to self-esteem. Japan of course hastened to normalize its own relations with Beijing. But Beijing's bargaining position was stronger and recognition was delayed until Prime Minister Sato, to whom Beijing objected as being sympathetic to Taiwan, was replaced by Tanaka Kakuei. The threat of damage to the international economic order that was implicit in the withdrawal of the US dollar from the gold standard was soon confirmed for Japan by the 1973 oil crisis. Japan quickly responded to the threat of the Arab oil embargo by abandoning the American pro-Israeli stance in favour of a pro-Arab position.

Forced in effect to adopt a more independently conceived foreign policy, Japan under the rubric of 'omni-directional' foreign relations fashioned a series of policies designed to protect its interests. These called for the insurance of having access to as many markets and sources of supply as possible, so as to minimize vulnerability in the event of closure of any one source. But in the Asia-Pacific it was also necessary to develop means of treating with China and of contributing to order in Southeast Asia in the wake of the American withdrawal.

The relationship with China was highly complex in view of their emotionally charged history and the mixed feelings over superiority and inferiority stemming from Japan's cultural indebtedness and its greater economic modernity. The difficulties were further compounded by the suggested complementarities of their economies amid major differences in their political systems and by concerns about their potential rivalry as the major regional powers. The first step to be taken in the new international environment was to complete the process of normalizing relations. The key issue was that of Taiwan. Japan's basic policy since 1952 had been to try to maintain relations with both Chinas. This accorded with history and with Japan's economic interests. Moreover, there was important support for Taiwan in sections of Japanese business and within the LDP. A clever formula was found, by which Japan established formal diplomatic relations with Beijing and maintained an ostensibly unofficial mission in Taipei. Normalization was followed up by agreements on fisheries, air carriers and so on. An important territorial dispute emerged over sovereign claims to a group of rocky islands (Senkaku in Japanese and Diaoyutai in Chinese) which would determine the division of the continental shelf and rights to possible oil and other reserves. Typically, the issue was left to be resolved by future generations. From a Japanese perspective, relations with China were troubled by a Chinese tendency to seek to exploit differences between Japanese domestic factions and interests. The Japanese were also irritated by what was regarded as politically inspired, rather than genuinely felt, Chinese sensitivity to periodic attempts by nationalist Japanese members of cabinet to play down the significance of Japanese aggression during the Pacific War. Nevertheless, trade rapidly grew between the two sides, enhancing Japan's position as China's most important trading partner. But this also gave rise to friction, in part because the Chinese side felt entitled to favourable treatment on account of past wrongs from the war, for which they had not claimed reparations, and in part because of the favourable balance enjoyed by Japan. But the greatest concern of Japan was to avoid being drawn into Beijing's anti-Soviet coalition.[23]

Japan's first and perhaps most ambitious foreign-policy initiative emerged with regard to Southeast Asia. Known as the Fukuda Doctrine after the prime minister who enunciated it in Manila on 18 August 1977, the policy was designed to signify a political commitment from Japan to contribute to stabilizing Southeast Asia. The initiative was stimulated by the confluence of a number of developments, notably the American disengagement from the sub-region following its debacle in Vietnam in 1975; the emergence of three communist states in Indo-China; and the resurgence of ASEAN as a more self-conscious political entity, as signified by its first summit in Bali in 1976 and the concomitant treaties designed to set the principles for the conduct of relations in Southeast Asia. Fukuda in fact attended the second ASEAN summit held in Kuala Lumpur in August 1977. Specific Japanese concerns arose from the growing significance of the sub-region for the Japanese economy and from the perceived need to improve the poor image of Japan as shown in the 1974 demonstrations in Thailand and Indonesia which, despite their local causes, took an anti-Japanese dimension. More broadly, Japan has a direct interest in the stability of the sub-region and, in the absence of American leadership, the Japanese prime minister, supported by more domestic parochial interests and encouraged by approaches from within ASEAN, felt emboldened to take the initiative.

The doctrine was phrased in typically Japanese diplomatic language. Its first principle emphasized Japan's commitment to peace and to the rejection of military power as a basis on which it would contribute to peace and prosperity elsewhere. The second committed Japan to develop trust and mutual confidence to include social and cultural areas as well as the political and economic. Finally, and to the point, Japan was declared to be an equal partner with ASEAN, pledged with others to strengthen its solidarity and resilience and aimed at 'fostering a relationship with the nations of Indochina' so as to contribute to peace and prosperity 'throughout Southeast Asia'.[24] In other words, Japan sought to bring about an accommodation between Vietnam and the ASEAN countries.

Considerable diplomatic effort was directed towards implementing the new policy: exchange visits were arranged with Vietnamese and ASEAN leaders; Washington was cajoled to recognize Vietnam; and Japan tried to use its economic instruments to promote its goal of bridging the gap between Vietnam and ASEAN and of weaning Vietnam away from the Soviet Union. But the larger strategic and political momentum was moving in the opposite direction. A polarization was beginning to form between the Soviet Union and Vietnam on the one side and the United States and China on the other, with ASEAN increasingly being drawn towards the latter. Although the die was cast by the Vietnamese invasion of Cambodia in December 1978, it was not until the Soviet invasion of Afghanistan a year later that the Japanese government finally gave up on its attempts to draw Vietnam away from dependence on the Soviet Union.[25] But Japanese prime ministers continued to cultivate ASEAN. Indeed, one of the effects of the Fukuda Doctrine was to begin the process of what became the annual Post-Ministerial Conferences (PMCs), which began in 1977 and also included Australia and New Zealand. Japan had become a regular political and security dialogue partner of ASEAN, as well as a dominant economic influence in the region.

In view of the thrust of its diplomacy in Southeast Asia, it was perhaps ironic that the conclusion of the peace and friendship treaty with China in August 1978 contributed to the polarization of international politics in East Asia and to the tightening of ties between the Soviet Union and Vietnam. Perhaps it illustrated Japan's inexperience (in contrast to the PRC) in conducting a coordinated international political and strategic set of policies. But the treaty with China may also be seen as indicative of Japanese difficulties in dealing with both the Soviet Union and China.

Following the changes in the international environment in the early 1970s, the Soviet Union attempted to engage Japan with a mixture of enticement and implied threats. Seeking to play on a section of Japanese business that was interested in contributing to the development of Siberia and gaining access to resources there, Moscow held out the promise of participation in oil projects. Moscow also hinted that it might reopen discussion of the disputed islands with the objective of signing a peace treaty. Meanwhile, it had not abandoned its long-standing aim of loosening Japanese ties with the United States. But it also had a more immediate aim of heading off Chinese attempts to secure their own peace treaty with Japan that would include a clause committing the two to oppose 'hegemony', which Moscow, with good reason, thought was directed against the Soviet Union. In the event, the Soviet Union overplayed its hand. The project for oil development was shifted further west in Siberia and the terms offered to the Japanese became confused. It also became clear that no concessions were to be offered on the disputed islands. The Soviet Union then proposed that in lieu of a peace treaty the two sides could sign a treaty of good neighbourliness. When the Japanese balked, the Soviet side published their draft in order to bring pressure to bear on Japan. Not surprisingly, the attempt backfired and Japan signed a treaty with the PRC.

Although this involved a face-saving compromise that placed the 'anti-hegemony' clause in the preamble and, for good measure, added that the treaty was not directed at any third party, the die was effectively cast. Whether or not this was immediately appreciated in Japan, it was effectively cast into an anti-Soviet coalition including the PRC and the United States.

But strains soon developed in relations with China. Japanese firms had eagerly responded to the overblown plans announced by the temporary leader Hua Guofeng in early 1978, and by the following year had got their fingers badly burnt as the Chinese defaulted on various projects. The Japanese business community was appalled by the lack of an appropriate investment infrastructure in China, the absence of appropriate laws and dispute settlement procedures, and by the complexities of bureaucratic procedures. The Chinese side, however, suspected darker motives at work on the Japanese side. The result was that, despite the enormous increase in trade and the regular payments of large amounts of official development aid (ODA), Japanese firms throughout the 1980s did not directly invest in China in a big way. Although trade continued to expand rapidly between the two sides, by the late 1980s Hong Kong had replaced Japan as the PRC's leading trader. China's leaders professed to see evidence of the re-emergence of militarism in Japan in revisions of school textbooks to gloss over Japanese aggression and atrocities in the Pacific War and in the statements and actions of leading politicians to the same effect. Moreover, China's leaders seemed to find that fierce public denunciations could bring about retractions in Japan. In 1985 Chinese students demonstrated against the 'second (economic) invasion' by Japan. They complained about allegedly unfair Japanese trade practices and compared Japan unfavourably with other developed countries for holding back on the transfer of technology. The Japanese for their part resented what they regarded as Chinese interference in their domestic affairs. Such complaints resonated with the deeper problems at issue between the two sides.[26]

Meanwhile, in 1979–80 Prime Minister Ohira Masayoshi commissioned a number of high-powered studies to debate and formulate a new national agenda for Japan as it approached the twenty-first century. By common agreement, Japan was seen to have gone beyond the process of 'catching-up' and, as one of the world's most powerful economies and leader in many aspects of advanced technology, it was felt that it should no longer follow the established practices of its foreign relations. The result was the emergence of a new slogan of 'comprehensive security', which ostensibly stressed the multidimensional quality of security. As noted by a Japanese scholar, 'concealed in this idea is the hope that Japan's contributions to international betterment such as foreign aid, debt rescheduling, and contributions to international agencies will be considered supportive of American policy'.[27] By the time of the accession of Prime Minister Nakasone (1982–87), the emphasis had become one of both responding to a more assertive nationalist mood and demonstrating Japan's value as a partner of the United States through economic liberalization and upgrading the defence capabilities of the Self Defence Forces. The latter was aimed at 'overcoming the previously strong image of Japan as an economic spoiler and military free-rider and at creating an image of Japan as an economic and military supporter'.[28] But it did not involve the assumption of a conventional security role. This attempt to gain American approval while simultaneously responding to the more assertive nationalist mood could and did backfire. American complaints at allegedly unfair Japanese trading practices did not abate. Indeed, in 1989 they led to the so-called

Structural Impediments Initiative that involved each side suggesting to the other that it change fundamental aspects of its domestic system, which in turn only served to accentuate the nationalistic distaste for the other that existed in both countries.

Interestingly, one of the more successful attempts to tackle the enormous and deep-seated trade imbalance between the US and Japan, which was to transform Japan's relations with the ASEAN countries in particular, was the so-called Plaza Agreement of 1985 that resulted in a significant revaluation of the Japanese Yen. In order to remain competitive Japan exported considerable manufacturing capacity to the so-called four Asian tigers and to the increasingly stable and investment-friendly ASEAN countries. This resulted in a complex economic triangle involving Japan, the East Asian countries and the United States, with the latter serving as the principal market.[29] As a result Japan modified its trade deficit with America, but at the cost of increasing its deficit with the other economies of Pacific Asia.

However, far from improving Japanese relations with the United States, the effects of these economic changes were to intensify the problems. The Japanese economy prospered as the growth in intra-Asian trade exceeded that of Asian trade with the United States, and it heightened in America a sense that the country was in relative decline. In the late 1980s considerable publicity was given to purchases by Japanese companies not only of American companies but also of American icons, such as Times Square. By the end of the 1980s the 'Japanese way' was being touted in the United States as superior to that of America. For example, the provocatively titled book, *Japan as No. 1*, by the respected Harvard scholar Ezra Vogel, which was published in 1979, became a bestseller. Meanwhile there were signs for those who were able to read them that something was amiss with the new stage of the 'Japanese miracle'. For instance, property prices had rocketed beyond reason, as at one point the real-estate value of metropolitan Tokyo was judged to be greater than that of the entire USA.

Japan's independent foreign policy during this twenty-year period was still predicated on the American security guarantee, which was in turn anchored in the Cold War order. Japan had become an independent contributor to stability in ASEAN, but it had no means of pursuing the agenda of the Fukuda Doctrine in the teeth of the determination of China and the United States to isolate Vietnam. Within certain strategic limits set by its security dependency on the United States, Japan had fashioned an independent relationship with China (and Taiwan), and its poor relations with the Soviet Union were the product of bilateral factors as well as the antagonism inherent in its alliance with the United States. More generally, Japan's neomercantilist policies had been modified rather than transformed, and that was evident in the Asia-Pacific as well as in the wider world.

Notes

1 F.C. Jones, *Japan's New Order in East Asia* (London: Oxford University Press, 1954).
2 Kenneth B. Pyle, *The Japanese Question: Power and Purpose in a New Era* (Washington, DC: AEI, 1992), p.26.

3 Cited in *ibid.*, pp.27–28.

4 There are two contrasting arguments about Japan's diplomacy in this regard: the first is impressed with its shortcomings and failures and the second with its successes in achieving its relatively limited goals. For good examples of the two arguments, with the critical one first, see Michael Blaker, 'Evaluating Japan's Diplomatic Performance' and John Creighton Campbell, 'Japan and the United States: Games That Work', both in Gerald L. Curtis (ed.), *Japan's Foreign Policy after the Cold war: Coping With Change* (New York: M.E. Sharpe, 1993), pp.1–42 and 43–61, respectively.

5 Reinhard Drifte, *Japan's Foreign Policy* (London: Routledge, for the Royal Institute of International Affairs, 1990), p.35.

6 See scenarios two and three in Richard P. Cronin, *Japan, the United States, and Prospects for the Asia-Pacific Century: Three Scenarios for the Future* (Singapore: Institute of Southeast Asian Studies, 1992), pp.111–18.

7 Takashi Inoguchi, *Japan's International Relations* (London: Pinter, 1991), pp.166–67, 172–73.

8 Takashi Inoguchi, *Japan's Foreign Policy in an Era of Global Change* (London: Pinter, 1993), pp.153 and 146, respectively.

9 For a clear account, see Sueo Sudo, *The Fukuda Doctrine and ASEAN* (Singapore: Institute of Southeast Asian Studies, 1992), pp.13–17. For an example of this in practice, see pp.136–46.

10 Respectively, Takashi Inoguchi and Nakatani Iwao, cited in *ibid.*, p.108.

11 For an extensive analysis of Japan's 'immobilism' in key areas of domestic politics and foreign policy, see J.A.A. Stockwin *et al.*, *Dynamic and Immobilist Politics in Japan* (London: Macmillan Press, 1988).

12 See, for example, Sueo Sudo, *The Fukuda Doctrine and ASEAN: New Dimensions in Japanese Foreign Policy* (Singapore: Institute of Southeast Asian Studies, 1992), p.14.

13 See Pyle, *The Japanese Question* (*op. cit.*), pp.107–11; and Reinhard Drifte, *Japan's Foreign Policy* (*op. cit.*), pp.17–19. See also the discussion of Donald C. Hellmann, 'The Imperatives for Reciprocity and Symmetry in U.S.–Japanese Economic and Defense Relations' in John H. Makin and Donald C. Hellmann (eds), *Sharing World Leadership? A New Era for America and Japan* (Washington, DC: AEI, 1989), pp.237–66.

14 Pyle, *The Japanese Question* (*op. cit.*), p.110.

15 By Akio Morita and Shintaro Ishihara (New York: Simon and Schuster, 1991).

16 For elaboration see J.A.A. Stockwin, *Japan: Divided Politics in a Growth Economy* (London: Weidenfeld and Nicholson, 2nd edn, 1982), pp.203–5 and, more broadly, ch.10, pp.196–218.

17 Pyle, *The Japanese Question* (*op. cit.*), p.25.

18 For details see Lawrence Olson, *Japan in Postwar Asia* (New York: Praeger, 1970).

19 Wolf Mendl, *Issues in Japan's China Policy* (London: Macmillan, 1978), ch.1, pp.1–31.

20 On the latter see Donald C. Hellman, *Japanese Foreign Policy: The Peace Agreement with the Soviet Union* (Berkeley and Los Angeles: University of California Press, 1969).

21 For accounts of their relations in this period, see William J. Barnds (ed.), *Japan and the United States: Challenges and Opportunities* (New York: New York University Press, 1979); and Franklin B. Weinstein (ed.), *US–Japan Relations and the Security of East Asia: The Next Decade* (Boulder: Westview Press, 1978).

22 For details see Akio Watanabe, *The Okinawa Problem: A Chapter in Japan–US Relations* (Melbourne: Melbourne University Press, 1970).

23 For an account from a Japanese perspective of this period in the relationship, see Wolf Mendl, *Issues in Japan's China Policy* (*op. cit.*).

24 This and the preceding paragraph draw on Sueo Sudo, *The Fukuda Doctrine and ASEAN* (*op. cit.*).

25 *Ibid.*, p.204.

26 For accounts of the problematic relationship (as viewed primarily through Chinese perspectives), see Allen S. Whiting, *China Eyes Japan* (Berkeley and

Los Angeles: University of California Press, 1989); and Laura Newby, *Sino-Japanese Relations: China's Perspective* (London: Routledge, for the Royal Institute of International Affairs, 1988). For an account of the problems of the economic relations in the early 1980s, see Chae-Jin Lee, *China and Japan: New Economic Diplomacy* (Stanford: Hoover Institution Press, Stanford University, 1984).

27 Inoguchi, *Japan's International Relations* (*op. cit.*), p.26.
28 Inoguchi, *Japan's Foreign Policy in an Era of Global Change* (*op. cit.*), pp.37–38.
29 Mitchell Bernard and John Ravenhill, 'Beyond Product Cycles and Flying Geese: Regionalization, Hierarchy, and the Industrialization of East Asia', *World Politics* 47, 2 (January 1995), pp.171–209.

Section II

The post-Cold War period

Part I

The era of American pre-eminence

8   From unipolarity to multipolarity, 1991–2010

The new structure of international relations and the Asia-Pacific

The sudden and totally unexpected disintegration of the Soviet Union brought to an abrupt end a bipolar system that had spanned the world for the previous four decades. It was one characterized not only by a strategic conflict between the two superpowers and the balance of nuclear power, but also by a clash between two distinct ideological, political and economic systems. At a stroke the old world order disappeared to be replaced by uncertainty as to how best to understand the new era of international politics. With the removal of the worldwide divisions of the Cold War system and with the recognition that Soviet style socialist economics were not a viable alternative to the market-based international economy all the barriers to the worldwide spread of capitalism disappeared. This left the United States as the sole superpower to enjoy what was called its 'unipolar moment'.[1] The spread of globalization and the attendant rapid economic changes were to see the centre of gravity of the international political economy shift decisively from the Atlantic to the Pacific. The main beneficiary of globalization was China despite, or as its rulers claim, because of the continued rule of the Communist Party. China rose from being primarily a regional great power into becoming a global actor. Not only did it become the world's leading manufacturer, but it also became a major economic player in the Middle East, Africa and South America. China's rise, however, has also been accompanied by the rise of others, such as India and Brazil, and a resurgent Russia, while Japan remains an important player. Although the United States still remains the only truly global power, with an economy accounting for nearly 25 per cent of the world's GNP (IMF 2009) and by far the most powerful military forces, outnumbering the next sixteen countries (SIPRI 2009), its relative power has been reduced by the 'rise of the rest'.[2] Therefore the structure of international politics after the first decade of the twenty-first century is best captured by the concept of multipolarity, despite continuing American pre-eminence.

In the two decades that have passed since the end of the Cold War it has become clear that the geopolitical boundaries of the Asia-Pacific region have changed, partly due to the effects of globalization and the intensification of transnational issues and partly because of political developments attendant upon the repositioning of the great powers and the more important role played by middle and lesser powers. The break-up of the Soviet Union occasioned the emergence of independent states in Central Asia and, due to the strategic, political interests of China and Russia, the significance of Central Asia became a new factor in the region. Russia itself, as the successor in many respects to the Soviet Union, at first almost ceased to be a major player, but as it has since re-established a degree of domestic political order and coherence, it has once again sought to become a significant player. The rise of India has introduced this major power into the region as a player of growing economic and strategic influence, beyond its traditional confinement to South Asia. But Afghanistan and Pakistan are still excluded from the region notwithstanding the pervasiveness of the American-led war on terror, or India's ongoing deep-rooted conflict with Pakistan centring on Kashmir and China's 'all weather friendship' with that country. One indication of the difference between the claims of India and the other two to membership of the Asia-Pacific region is that India is a member of most of the region's institutions, while Pakistan and Afghanistan are not.

The United States remained as the sole superpower, but despite its apparent dominance, the United States was unable to reshape the world in accordance with its vision of free markets and democratization. For example, the American attempt to persuade China to improve its practice of human rights by using trade as a lever failed miserably in 1994 after a year of trying.[3] Similarly, the American-led attempts to address the problems of civil wars and the breakdown of order within states through humanitarian intervention, as displayed in the Balkans, did not prove successful in Somalia. Following the declaration of the war on terror after 9/11 in 2001, the US launched a war against the Taliban in Afghanistan and then another in Iraq, which had yet to show signs of imminent conclusion at the time of writing in July 2010. These two hugely costly wars have constrained the US strategically and contributed to the nation's indebtedness. The United States has also failed to prevent the spread of nuclear weapons first to India and Pakistan, then to North Korea and possibly Iran. When combined with the impact of the gravest financial crisis since the Great Depression of the 1930s the perception grew in much of the world, including at home, that the United States was in relative decline.

The turning point was '9/11', less because of the impact of the terrorist act itself (huge though that was) than because of the reaction of the Bush administration in launching two long wars and pursuing economic policies that culminated in the great financial crisis of 2008. By the end of the first decade of the twenty-first century the United States may still have remained the world's sole superpower, but it's so-called hegemony was being successfully challenged by the combined effect of the rise of the independent power of China and, to a lesser extent, India, Brazil and a resurgent Russia. Even though little could be done on a global scale without American leadership, America could no longer act unilaterally. It had to act multilaterally, or perhaps more accurately, in partnership with others. These poles, or other centres of power or global significance, which also included the European Union and Japan, differed markedly in their characteristics and capabilities and were by no means in alignment together to balance American power. Rather they were separate constellations of power, some seen as rising – notably China, India and Brazil – while others were perceived by comparison as stagnating if not actually declining – Japan and the EU – and Russia was seeking to restore lost Soviet power. However, there was no question of these great powers combining to balance against American power, yet such was their respective weight in world affairs that collectively they ended up constraining the US from being able to act successfully on its own. These powers both cooperated and competed with each other and each still found its relationship with the United States to be more important than any other relationship. Yet the United States and its Western partners, who hitherto had dominated the international economy, found that they could not properly address the problems, which arose from the American-created financial crisis of 2008, in the previous manner through their Group of 7 or 8. The previously formed Group of 20 dramatically came into its own as this much larger gathering (which included the rising powers) met in Pittsburgh and London in 2009 to agree on measures to manage the crisis. The United States found that it could not necessarily get its own way. The same was true of the Copenhagen Meeting in December 2009 to deal with climate change.[4]

It was globalization and the adoption of appropriate economic and trade policies that enabled China and India to rise. In this sense globalization was principally an economic phenomenon, but globalization also facilitated the revolution in communications associated with computers and other forms of telecommunications. On the downside, however, globalization also facilitated the growth and expansion of transnational terrorism, crime, communicable diseases, illegal migration and money laundering, and it intensified the impact on the international community of the dangers posed by failed states. These so-called non-traditional security concerns threatened the wellbeing of national societies and called for more cooperative means of dealing with them even as traditional security worries were still evident in parts of the world, notably in Asia. Although the new non-traditional security problems were global in scope, they could only be addressed through the actions of states.

Globalization, therefore, was paradoxical in its effects upon states: On the one hand, the process penalized economically those states that preferred to close their doors to the international economy or who refused to adapt their commercial laws and practices to those which prevailed in the new globalized world, such as North Korea and Myanmar (Burma). Therefore it was argued that the process of globalization eroded the capacity of states to determine their own socio-economic preferences.[5] On the other hand, however, many aspects of globalization, especially in the non-traditional security areas, required the presence of strong domestic state institutions if these new issue areas were to be properly addressed. Effective state institutions were required even in the economic sphere if markets were to be properly regulated and laws duly enforced. The paradox was even greater with regard to the truly global problem of climate change, where all were agreed that common action was needed, but where in practice state interests in the end predominated, as was evident at the Copenhagen conference of December 2009.

The end of bipolarity also opened the way to the further development of regionalism and regional institutions. In Europe this entailed both the deepening and the widening of the European Union and in East Asia it led to the formulation of new concepts of regionalism and the proliferation of regional institutions and meetings. These largely grew out of the extension of the scope of ASEAN (Association of South East Asian Nations), which was the only regional body to have been formed exclusively by Asian states during the Cold War period. Its institutional practice, known as the 'ASEAN Way', put the emphasis on informality, consensus, non-interference and voluntarism, meaning the unenforceability of resolutions. In that sense it was more limited than the main regional institutions of Africa or America, let alone of Europe. Perhaps it was precisely its relatively loose character that enabled the new institutions it inspired such as APEC (the Asia-Pacific-Economic-Cooperation forum) founded in 1989 and the ARF (ASEAN Regional Forum) founded in 1994 (to advance cooperative security) to include China within their ranks and help incorporate the giant country within the patterns of regional diplomacy.

Another product of the end of the Cold War was that states found that their room for manoeuvre both at home and abroad had increased, as they were no longer subject to the discipline of what might be called the axis of conflict imposed upon them by the conflict between the two superpowers. That had an impact on how people thought about the nature of governance at home and about the external roles of their countries. Great and medium powers especially found that they had to reconfigure their identities anew. This was true of such diverse powers as China, India and Japan. In China this occasioned the replacement of socialism by nationalism as the main instrument for appealing to the people. India, bereft of Soviet support, threw off its semi-socialistic economic system for a more market-led approach. In the case of Japan the end of the Cold War brought about an end to the so-called San Francisco system. These developments were related to their repositioning of themselves in international affairs. More generally, because the regional security alliances, the so-called hub and spoke system centring on the US, no longer had an external enemy, they had to be re-examined and reformulated to meet new and unprecedented circumstances.

The looseness of the international system in comparison to the more rigid bipolar character of the Cold War system allowed for greater latitude for domestic politics to shape the foreign policies of states. That in turn contributed to the looseness and uncertainties of the post-Cold War era. The economic dimensions of international politics acquired greater salience in Asia in part because of the growing significance of economic globalization and in part because of the importance of national economic performance to the popularity of governments and the legitimacy of their political systems.

Despite its relative decline, the US remained the key provider of public goods in terms of trade and security. This applied especially to East Asia, where its military superiority has been the main guarantor against the outbreak of inter-state wars in what is still a region seeking to overcome the threat of war; and where its navy guarantees the sea lanes for the trade on which the region depends and where access to its domestic market is still important for continuing regional high economic growth rates.[6]

The end of the Cold War impacted upon the Asia-Pacific very differently from Europe. The fall of the Berlin Wall in 1989, followed shortly afterwards by the dissolution of the Soviet Union in 1991, marked the end of communist rule in Europe and indeed the whole system of communism. The division of Europe was no more and the way was open for the expansion of NATO and the widening of the European Union to embrace virtually all the European states up to the bor-ders of Russia. The end of the Cold War in Europe led to a fundamental and systemic transformation as democracy and the market replaced communist rule and the command economy throughout the half of Europe formerly dominated by the Soviet Union.

In marked contrast to the situation in Europe, the end of communist rule in the Asia-Pacific did not simultaneously accompany the end of bipolarity. China, Vietnam and North Korea continued to be ruled by communist parties. Perhaps this was because of the strong nationalist roots of these parties and, unlike the Mongolian People's Republic (the only other country in Asia ruled by a communist party), none was a satellite of the Soviet Union. They survived the effective demise of communism as an ideology and as an alternative to capitalist economics. As a result a residual flavour, if not the substance, of Cold War poli-tics remained in the region. Thus, notwithstanding China's adoption of a more market-orientated economy and its growing integration into the capitalist international economy, Sino-American relations were still heavily shaped by the differences between their respective political systems. Particularly in view of the end of Communist Party rule in Eastern Europe later that year, 1989 brought that Sino-American difference into sharp focus, as the Tiananmen massacre of 4 June was remembered in the US as signifying all that was wrong with a regime that was willing to shoot peaceful demonstrators. Whereas China's communist leaders remembered it as an occasion in which they saved the country from chaos, even as the Americans allegedly sought to change their system by an insidious process of 'peaceful evolution'. In their view the systemic collapse of communism in Europe was caused in part by the application of that policy by the US. Even the ostensibly friendly policy towards China, known as 'engagement', that was adopted by the Clinton administration later in the 1990s included the objective of seeking to encourage the eventual development of pluralistic democratic politics in China.[7]

In East Asia, the immediate political changes brought about by the end of the Cold War were essentially power-related consequences of the dissolution of the Soviet Union. The purpose of America's military alliances in the region was no longer as clear cut. The strategic rationale that had brought China and the United States together in opposition to the Soviet Union was no more. China itself was freed from the threat (albeit a declining one) of attack from the north and enjoyed new strategic latitude. Those conflicts in Asia whose prosecution depended entirely upon the Soviet Union – Afghanistan and Cambodia – were settled as Soviet support came to an end. But other local conflicts stemming from the Cold War, notably those of Korea and Taiwan, remained in place although their conduct and significance were altered by the structural changes in the international system.

Interestingly, most of the changes involving the expansion of the scope of the market and of democracy in the region took place well before the end of the Cold War. Thus for China the key turning point for the embrace of the market was 1979 rather than 1989, while Vietnam, which, like China, retained Communist Party rule, declared its own economic reform programme in 1986. What has been called the 'Third Wave of democratization' by which authoritarian regimes gave way to more democratic rule in the Philippines, Taiwan, Thailand and South Korea took place before the collapse of communism in Europe. Although each of these countries had its own distinctive story to tell about its process of democratization, they all shared some factors in common, including their having undergone rapid economic growth, urbanization and increased opening to the outside world, including a dependence on the American market and its provision of security.[8]

In the last decade of the twentieth century American superiority extended well beyond the military sphere and the advanced technology on which it rested. American pre-eminence also stemmed from its economic strength, in which its GNP alone accounted for over 25 per cent of the world's total. The United States was the major market for all the important economic centres such as Europe and East Asia, it attracted the most foreign direct investment (FDI) and its currency was the most important one for all international transactions. It was the leading centre for international finance and it dominated the world's key international economic organizations, including the IMF and the World Bank. In short, it was the economy of the United States that drove the other economies forward. In the terms of Susan Strange, the United States dominated the four structures of power: military, financial, trade and knowledge.[9] American pre-eminence also drew strength from what Joseph Nye has called its soft power, that is to say from its capacity to influence others and shape their agendas as the result of the spread of its culture through the mass media, and the appeal of its political and economic systems.[10]

By the beginning of the second decade of the twenty-first century the significance of American power had weakened in many respects. The two long wars in Iraq and Afghanistan had taken their toll on the US military and had substantially increased American indebtedness. Combined with the impact of the financial crisis of 2008, the United States was seen both at home and abroad to be facing several years of struggle to recover from its recession and the two wars. Yet America remained as the only provider of the economic, trade and security public goods in the Asia-Pacific. In effect the US continued to underwrite the

basis on which the East Asian states, notably China, were able to pursue economic development and rapid growth as their primary goal. In addition America
provided a principal market for East Asian exports, protected the global lines of
communication and transport and remained the cornerstone of the international
institutions, which under-girded the international economy. To be sure the
United States was no longer able to do so alone, but even in a more multilateral
context, American leadership and capabilities were vital if the new challenges to
the international system were to be met.

Bereft of the clear axis of conflict provided by the confrontation between the
two camps, the United States found that it lacked a unifying theme to guide its
overall strategy towards the different parts of the world together, or to provide
coherence for the foreign policy of the world's pre-eminent power.[11] Theorists of
political international economy had long argued that a system dominated by a
hegemon was one that would enjoy stability.[12] In practice, however, neither the
administrations of Clinton nor of Bush 43 (the younger) provided that kind
of hegemonic stability. The former encouraged globalization and the expansion
of democracy and the market, but it did not do so consistently. It provided
uncertain leadership in the development of the doctrine of humanitarian
intervention and it did not provide a coherent strategic doctrine that sought to
explain where, when and for what purposes the administration would use the
overwhelming power at its disposal.[13]

The administration of Bush the younger began with the intention of developing
a coherent new strategic approach that took account of the changes since the end
of the Cold War and, in the process, alienated several allies by its dismissal of the
significance of those international institutions and agreements that he saw as
constraints upon American freedom of action.[14] But the terrible terrorist attacks
of 11 September 2001 transformed the American approach as Bush declared a
'war on terror', with the result that the pursuit of terrorism and the related war
on Iraq overtook the strategic concerns identified before 9/11 and left America in
a reactive rather than a proactive position in the Asia-Pacific. Thus American
hegemony has not led to what President Bush 41(the elder) identified at one point
as a 'new world order'. Even though Bush 43 significantly modified his unilateralist and militarist approach in his second term (2004–8) he was still regarded
in low esteem in much of the world, damaging American prestige. It was only
in Asia that Bush's policies were held in relatively high regard as he had engaged
China, encouraged the rise of India, supported Japan and other allies and
partners.[15]

The Obama administration chose from the outset to accept the new limits
within which the United States could act in world affairs and it embraced
a multilateralist approach and sought partnerships with others, notably China,
as a means of tackling the new problems of finance and climate change, as well as
the more established ones of non-proliferation and the various transnational
problems affecting the security of states. Obama also reached out to adversaries
in the hope of resolving problems through a diplomacy based on a mixture
of carrots and sticks, rather than by demonstrations of military superiority.

Obama's soaring rhetoric set long-term goals of nuclear disarmament, of reconciliation with the world of Islam and new deals with Africa and Asia. Obama began his presidency with much acclaim as hopes were raised by his persona and the conduct of his electoral campaign. Yet such has been the broadness of his goals that it became difficult to discern the key strategic priorities of his administration.[16] He has yet to be rewarded with any substantive success in the international sphere, but it is perhaps too early to assess his approach after only a year and a half in office.

Following this broad overview of the immediate post-Cold War period, this chapter will be divided in to two sub-sections, divided roughly by the impact of the Al Qaeda terrorist attacks on the US on 11September 2001. The first will explore in greater detail the ramifications for the region of the changes brought about by the end of the bipolar system that characterized the Cold War. It will then consider the significance of the regional institutions that mushroomed in the region since 1989, including China's induction and active participation in them, as well as the enhanced role of lesser and medium powers. The American reinvigoration of its alliances will be evaluated alongside development of its crises with North Korea and in cross-Strait relations with China and Taiwan. Attention will be given to the debate over 'Asian values' that gripped the region in the mid-1990s until the onset of the financial crisis in 1997/1998. It will assess the political impact of the financial crisis on the region, noting the dissatisfaction with the role played by the US. Finally, it will argue that by the turn of the century the region was developing a multilayered and multitextured approach to security as it came to terms with the rise of China.

The second part will analyse developments in the first decade of the twenty-first century, focusing on the implications of the consequences of 9/11 for the region, notably for the role of the United States. It will survey the continuing problems posed by the North Korean and Taiwan crises and the different attempts to address them. The enhanced position of China and the rise of Indian influence will be examined in the context of great-power relations, including the relative decline of Japan. Developments of regional institutions and the difficulties in moving towards regional integration will be examined. The chapter will conclude by evaluating the extent to which America may be have said to have declined and the extent to which China's growing military strength has changed the distribution of power in the region.

I – 1991–2000: The repositioning of the major powers

Perhaps the most important structural change that followed the end of the Cold War system of bipolarity was the repositioning of the great powers. At first many thought that Japan would be the main beneficiary of the new era. Japan was thought to be replacing the United States with seemingly unlimited funds and an apparently superior economic model.[17] In the words of an American Senator, 'The Cold War is over and Japan has won.'[18] But the 'victory' was short lived as the Japanese economic miracle burst in 1992 casting Japan into prolonged relative decline. However, it was not until 1995 that the true dimensions of American pre-eminence were fully recognized in the region. China's rulers, for example, claimed in 1992 that the world was multipolar and it was not until 1995 that they recognized that the United States was still in their terms the 'hegemon'. The Chinese then described the international system as made of 'one superpower and several major powers'.[19]

The significance of American predominance was shown throughout the 1990s when it used its power to help preserve regional order. Thus the United States alone took the lead in identifying and then dealing with the North Korean threat to develop nuclear weapons in the 1993 crisis that ended in the 'Framework Agreement' of 1994, by which the North was to be compensated for giving up its quest for nuclear weapons by the provision of economic aid, energy supply and the building of nuclear reactors that could not be used for military purposes. The US then took the lead in updating the alliance with Japan by reaching agreement on 'New Guidelines' in 1996/97. They were framed in response to what was regarded as insufficiently robust participation by Japan in the first Gulf War of 1990 and again in the Korean nuclear crisis of 1993–94 (despite the significance to Japan of both events).

The contribution of the New Guidelines to regional order that went beyond their purely bilateral security concerns was evident from the fact that Japan's agreement to sign up to them was invigorated by its response to the Chinese attempt to intimidate Taiwan by displays of military force in 1995–96. Chinese belligerence was stopped by the arrival on the scene of two US carrier-led battle groups, one of which had been based in Japan.[20]

The display of overwhelming force in the region was a powerful demonstration to all the states of the region of the American ability and determination to uphold regional order and stability. The United States also updated its alliances with Australia, the Philippines and others.

The spread of economic globalization, which led to huge changes by facilitating the economic rise of Asia and especially that of China was due in no small part to American leadership. The Clinton administration actively promoted globalization and in so doing it provided the public goods from which all the countries in the region benefitted, except for North Korea and Burma, which deliberately kept their doors closed to the international economy. Although intra-regional trade grew significantly in the 1990s, it was the openness of the American domestic market as the consumer of last resort that was the most important, alongside those of the EU and Japan. The forging of an agreement between China and the US was the key to China's eventual entry into the World Trade Organization (WTO) in 2001. However, the limits of American economic power became evident when its attempts to tie the countries of the Asia-Pacific into a legally binding free-trade agreement in 1993 and 1994 through APEC foundered in 1995, when, on encouragement by Japan, it was decided that member states would carry out the agreement on a voluntary basis only.[21] As against that the United States successfully persuaded Japan to put a halt to the Malaysian idea of an East Asian Group or Caucus on the grounds that it discriminated against America. But in the next decade the United States did not place obstacles to the emergence of the ASEAN Plus Three, which at that stage did not appear to be deliberately aimed at diminishing American influence. However, American prestige suffered as a result of the Asian Financial Crisis of 1997, when the United States seemed more concerned with protecting foreign investors than its Asian partners, notwithstanding the fact some 200 million people were thrust back into poverty as a result. That led to a questioning of the so-called Washington consensus favoured by the IMF and by mainstream American economists.[22] Thus by the beginning of the new millennium America remained predominant, even though it could not impose its will on Asian states against their interests.

However, the scale of American predominance became evident from the failure of attempts to develop a coalition of major powers to offset it. Russia in particular, in the 1990s and through to the early years of the twenty-first century, sought to balance against American power by forming partnerships with China and with India, and it even aimed at establishing a strategic triangle involving the three powers.[23] Little came of these attempts as each of the three regarded its relationship with the United States as more important to its strategic and economic wellbeing than anything the other two had to offer – especially as their interests diverged in many respects. On becoming president in 2000 Putin visited Beijing in July after first hosting President Clinton in Moscow in June. Ostensibly Putin and President Jiang Zemin joined together in common opposition to American plans to develop ballistic missile defence systems (BMD), but a careful examination of the respective texts of their agreement showed apparently slight, but telling, differences with regard to Theatre Missile Defence (TMD). In the Russian version the two merely 'protested' whereas in the Chinese version they 'opposed'. The Russians were less concerned about TMD than their Chinese partners, who feared it would be used to protect Taiwan, despite American statements that such a system in Northeast Asia would be targeted at North Korea. The Chinese also feared that BMD might degrade their own nuclear deterrent. The significance of the difference became clear when Bush 43 announced his intention to withdraw from the Anti-Ballistic Missile (ABM) Treaty in late 2001. The Chinese government officially regarded the impending move as 'destabilising', but when Bush actually made the official announcement on 13 December Putin said that, although it was a mistake, Russian security was not endangered.[24] In other words, the Russians and Chinese openly diverged in their reaction to a matter of great strategic significance to China.[25]

Nevertheless the rapprochement between Russia and China was historically significant as it not only overcame the Maoist legacy of hostility, but it helped establish a more peaceful and equitable relationship than had existed for the previous two centuries. The breakthrough between Gorbachev and Deng Xiaoping of May 1989 was soon superseded by subsequent events. China's leaders had been initially alarmed by the collapse of the USSR and the emergence of Yeltsin as the leader of Russia. But the two sides soon recognized their mutual interest in drawing down the forces deployed near their common border and in cultivating their common interests. Setting aside all ideological and systemic differences the two began to settle their border disputes. Within three years the two had reached a number of agreements, which culminated in 1994 when they claimed to have established a 'cooperative partnership', upgraded two years later to a 'strategic' one, as they were bound together by common opposition to American 'hegemony'. But as we have seen, despite their rhetoric, the partnership was limited and each had more at stake in cultivating working relations with the US than with the other. The Sino-Russian relationship illustrates a significant characteristic of the relationships between the great powers, namely their peculiar combination of cooperation and competition that precluded the establishment of alliances. As we shall see, Russia and China worked together to establish a regional organization in Central Asia, but they sought different things from it. Seeking to re-establish a dominant position in the region, Russia aimed at building on the Soviet legacy of military deployments in two or three of the six new republics and at continuing to route the region's energy pipelines through Russian territory. China, however, became in effect the guarantor of the independence and territorial integrity of the new states against possible Russian claims on what it chose to regard as its 'near abroad', while seeking to prevent them from offering support or bases to disaffected minorities in bordering Xinjiang. China's main approach to the region was to promote market-based economic exchanges and particularly to gain access to the region's resources, notably energy. To that end agreement was reached about building oil and gas pipelines to China.[26]

The divergence of interests between China and Russia is best understood in terms of competition rather than rivalry. In many respects they shared a common antipathy to what they regarded as American hegemony or unipolarity. They shared a distrust of Western-led 'humanitarian intervention' in the Balkans and elsewhere, which was reflected in their voting in the UN Security Council, even though each made its own calculations with respect to the use of the veto. Indeed one of the ways in which they sought to constrain the US from using its overwhelming military power to intervene in third parties was to insist upon the need to gain prior permission from the UN Security Council. Similarly they both disliked the way in which democracy spread to the former Soviet satellites and states of the Soviet Union – seeing the process as not only inspired by the West, but as actively and stealthily promoted by the United States. As the 1990s unfolded it became clear that the balance between China and Russia had changed decisively in favour of the former. In contrast to the chaos that was Russia, China had an effective government that was presiding over a successful and rapidly growing economy. The situation of the 1950s and 1960s had been turned by almost 180 degrees. It was Russia now that began to consider China as a possible model for its own development, while at the same time fearing China's economic penetration. As one scholar put it, their new 'axis' was no more than one of 'convenience'. In practice the two did not attempt to coordinate their approaches to current international issues, even when these overlapped. Thus the Russians and the Chinese often pursued parallel policies in the UN and elsewhere with regard to Iraq, Iran, North Korea and so on, without actually consulting closely to advance their common diplomatic positions.

Relations between the other regional great powers in the 1990s were even less cordial. India and Japan had few dealings with each other. India was not a major trading country and in fact its trade with Japan did not even reach 1 per cent of either Japanese imports or exports and it did not reach even 10 per cent of Indian trade.[27] Japan was one of the countries that objected strongly to India's nuclear tests of May 1998 and maintained sanctions against India until 2000. It was not until the beginning of the twenty-first century that India began to play a more active role in the broader Asia-Pacific region and it did so primarily due to its new-found relations with the United States.[28] Although both India and China sought to improve relations after the end of the Cold War, with exchanges of high-level visits, trade remained negligible and they remained wary of each other throughout the 1990s. Chinese leaders and scholars tended to regard India with a degree of disdain, while the shock of defeat by China in 1962 still reverberated in Indian circles. The Indian nuclear tests of 1998 followed quickly by similar tests in Pakistan further divided the two Asian giants. The joint condemnation of the tests by the presidents of China and the United States did little to improve relations, but ironically the crisis provided the opportunity for the United States to start cultivating its relations with India. The statement by the Indian Minister of Defence that the detonations had been prompted by concern about China damaged relations, but only temporarily. By the turn of the century both China and India took steps to mend the relationship even though mutual distrust was still evident.[29]

Sino-Japanese relations deteriorated in the 1990s despite their growing economic ties. This gave rise to the saying that their 'economics were hot and the politics cold'.[30] More overt nationalist sentiments in both countries, especially in China, brought to the fore disagreements about the degree to which Japan had atoned for its history of aggression against China. Japan in turn was challenged by the rise of China. Japan's invigorated alliance with the United States was seen in China as opening the way to Japan playing an active military role in the region and beyond, raising doubts about whether the alliance did serve China's fundamental interest by vitiating the need for Japan to develop as an independent military power. Maritime territorial disputes became more acute and each eyed with suspicion moves by the other to enhance its security. Yet even as their rivalry intensified by the end of the twentieth century, both sets of leaders recognized the mutual advantages of their economic cooperation.[31]

Another major structural change brought about by the end of the bipolar system was the dissipation of the central strategic balance to which regional and sub-regional conflicts had previously been attached. It was the unravelling of these linkages that brought the Third Indo-China War to an end and made possible a peaceful settlement for Cambodia under UN auspices. Consequently, in the 1990s conflicts tended to remain local or regional in their significance unless they involved any of the great powers or they raised issues that the international community could not ignore. Thus conflicts between Southeast Asian states no longer troubled the external powers.[32] Whereas the North Korean issue involved the United States and the regional great powers primarily because of the prospect of the acquisition of nuclear weapons by North Korea. It was this that gave a new international dimension to the Korean conflict. The Chinese, who had hoped that their diplomatic recognition of the South in 1992 would be accompanied by American and Japanese recognition of the North, came up against an American refusal because of doubts about the North's nuclear programme. In fact the North began to accelerate its work to develop nuclear weapons at the end of the Cold War because it had lost the support of its two main protectors, the Soviet Union and China. As a weak underdeveloped state it sought a deterrent against the United States.[33] The other major legacy from the Cold War that continued to be a source of conflict of major international scope was the Taiwan issue, which pitted the United States as the protector of Taiwan against China, which claimed the island as part of its territory.

In sum, the first decade in the post-Cold War period approximated to the Chinese characterization of 'one superpower and several major powers'. As the major powers repositioned themselves, there was no question of their developing some kind of united front to balance against the superior power of the United States. First, their respective relations with the United States were more important to their strategic and developmental interests than relations with each other. Second, the major powers may have had some interests in common, but they also had divergent ones too. Consequently, they both cooperated and competed with each other. As the United States retained its primacy there was no question of creating some kind of concert of powers akin to the European example at the Congress of Vienna after the defeat of Napoleon. Third, although the possibility of military conflict could not be ruled out, especially with regard to North Korea and Taiwan, the probability of open warfare between the major powers was low, notwithstanding the continued significance of traditional security concerns. The United States was able to intervene to diffuse the Taiwan crisis in 1996 and to use its good offices to persuade Pakistan to withdraw its forces from Kargil in 1999, before conflict could break out with India, which had mobilized up to a million troops.[34] Finally, the United States as the leader of the international system expended much effort in trying to integrate a rising China into the norms and institutions of international society and of the region.

The search for new identities

The end of the Cold War not only involved the repositioning of the great powers, but it also led them to search for new identities. Freed from the rigidities of the Cold War, major powers found themselves in circumstances where their domestic politics as well as their foreign relations could not continue as before. The disintegration of the Soviet Union not only changed the basis of security and diplomatic arrangements in the Asia-Pacific, but also effectively brought to an end the idea that its socialist economic model was a viable alternative to capitalism. The ramifications of this were felt in China and India, where there were still adherents to socialism among the elites as well as powerful bureaucracies with vested interests in continuing to administer a centrally run economy. Japan too felt the impact, as its political system was very much the product of Cold War arrangements worked out with the United States in the early 1950s. The 'San Francisco System' could no longer be run as before. Japan's new uncertainties were not just the product of the end of the Cold War, but were in many respects caused by the depression and economic stagnation that followed the bursting of its financial bubble in 1992.

In China, where the shock of the collapse of the Soviet Union was deeply felt among China's rulers, the initial response was to batten down the hatches and revert to a more a centralized approach to running the economy and it was only once Deng Xiaoping managed to overcome the majority of his comrades in 1992 that the country was truly launched on the course of rapid economic growth, economic reform and opening up to the international economy. These developments also undermined socialism as an ideology that could command popular support. That resulted in Communist Party-led campaigns to promote nationalism as a basis for uniting the people under the circumstances of ensuring political stability and rapid economic growth. The nationalism or 'patriotism' that was encouraged emphasized strongly the image of a China that was victim of predatory incursions and aggression by Western powers in the nineteenth and early twentieth centuries, culminating in the brutal aggression of the Japanese who supposedly were defeated by the Chinese people under the leadership of the Communist Party. The effect of the message was to encourage the educated young in particular to be vigilant against alleged slights by foreign countries and especially Japan as China sought to re-establish the greatness it had enjoyed before the advent of the West. But China's new nationalism did not mask elite differences over the course of the reforms and hence as to what kind of identity China should move towards.[35]

Japan spent most of the 1990s constrained by a political system that seemed incapable of carrying out the bold reforms needed to resuscitate an economy apparently mired in deflation. The interlocking of the main economic and financial institutions with those of the ruling Liberal Democratic Party and the main government ministries, which underlay previous success, proved to be difficult to unravel, especially as reform required those vested interests to make the change themselves. Nor did it seem that there was popular pressure for fundamental change. An amendment of the voting system in 1993–94 did not of itself bring about the hoped for two-party system, although it did lead to a short-lived coalition government that for the first time did not include the LDP.[36] The failure to provide coherent leadership able to carry out necessary reforms meant that Japan was unable to develop a more prominent political role or indeed to provide effective economic leadership when the Asian economic crisis struck in the summer of 1997. The United States prevented the acceptance of Japan's proposal to set up an Asian Monetary Fund. Japan's domestic system was deadlocked and most people felt too comfortable to risk the ruptures that reform would entail, even though there was general agreement that reforms were needed. There was not much popular pressure for fundamental change among the elite; the virtual demise of the socialist party led to a shift in the conservative direction by the political mainstream. The 'San Francisco System' as epitomized by the Yoshida doctrine, under one-party democracy, had seemingly come to an end, but it was not clear what would replace it. With the disappearance of its adversary, the Soviet Union, against whom the alliance with the United States was first forged, Japan had to find a new role for itself in the world. Debates ensued between those who wanted a more 'normal' Japan free of the constraints of the 'peace constitution' and those who valued the distinctiveness of the constitution, which allowed Japan to be uniquely a 'peace country' with variants in between, but all were agreed on the desirability of seeking permanent membership of the UN Security Council.[37]

It was in 1991 that India changed course and came to abandon its variant of socialist economics and set aside its attachment to 'Non Alignment'. The turnaround was occasioned by the run on its reserves as a result of the spike in oil prices caused by the first Gulf War. However, the new course of encouraging capitalist enterprise, foreign direct investment and opening up to trade and the international economy, was clearly related to the broader changes following the end of the Cold War and the demise of the Soviet Union – India's only major ally. The new market-orientated economic policies have led to rapid growth rates and the transformation of India's standing in the world. However, as a democracy, India's rise has been caught up at home with difficulties in overcoming entrenched interests and accommodating to new social changes arising from rapid economic development. Having abandoned the moralistic but outdated Nehruvian stance of non-alignment, Indian elites have struggled to find a new balance between idealistic principles and realpoilitik. The country's rise has brought about a major reorientation of relations with the United States, while the old troubles of relations with Kashmir, Pakistan, terrorism and Afghanistan continue to affect India's attempt to reach out beyond the confines of South Asia.[38]

In each of these major powers the new course that was adopted was not universally welcomed. Continual debates took place about the new policies and underlying those debates were arguments about the identities of these countries and the directions their foreign policies should follow.

The development of regional institutions

The looser structure of international relations that emerged after the end of the Cold War provided opportunities and incentives for a renewed emphasis on regionalism in the Asia-Pacific. With the removal of the bipolar straightjacket, the different states of the region began to see an advantage in developing regional institutions, in part to uphold their interests in relation to other regions, notably Europe, and in part to avoid or to minimize potential conflicts within the region now that the constraints of bipolarity had been removed. Since relations between the major powers were still characterized by distrust and incipient rivalry, new space opened up for lesser states to take the initiative in this regard.[39]

ASEAN, whose international prestige had grown as a result of its diplomatic role in the Third Indo-China War, was seen as providing a model for linking the very disparate states of the Asia-Pacific region in a common association. It was also inconceivable that any pan-regional grouping could exclude ASEAN. An association of only the developed countries of the region, for example, would have been divisive and counterproductive. The centrality of ASEAN to any attempt to build regional institutions was strengthened by the clashes of interest between the major powers. The enhanced role of the lesser powers, however, was necessarily subject to the limitation of their own role being acceptable to the major powers.

In a context in which the great powers China, Japan, the United States and, less directly, India, Russia and Australia (as a middle power) were actively engaged in the region, the lesser powers stood to gain from establishing regular patterns of interaction on a regional basis. The expectation was that China, which had all along preferred to deal with the lesser powers separately, as its bargaining strength was greater, would nevertheless see an advantage in a regional association, as a means of demonstrating its peaceful and cooperative intent while ensuring that the rules and norms of conduct were agreeable to it and thus reducing its costs of ensuring that its interests were respected.[40]

Japan had long been interested in finding a regional format to integrate better into the region and to be accepted as a legitimate major player despite the legacy of the Second World War. Despite the so-called lost decade of the 1990s, Japan continued to be the leading trader and investor in most of the Southeast Asian countries and it played the major role in helping them financially to recover from the Asian Financial Crisis of 1997.[41] China, however, as the rising great power, had a new-found interest in integrating itself into the region, partly for economic reasons and partly to counter lingering fears about its possible threat to its neighbours. China also hoped to use its regional links to help to balance or constrain the overwhelming power of the United States. The United States, as in effect the regional hegemon, was at first antagonistic to the prospect of a regional multilateral security institution lest it weaken the American security treaty ties with key states in the region. But it welcomed possible economic regional institutions, seeing them as a means of gaining acceptance for the principles of free trade long advocated by Washington. Since both China and the US were founding members of the ARF in 1994 it appeared that the US had softened its objections to the security dimension of regionalism, seeing it as a means of inducting China into a network that would constrain it from challenging the American security position in the Asia-Pacific.

As will be argued below, the new regional institutions have influenced great-power behaviour. The United States found that it had to give way in its attempt to impose a rule-binding agenda on the principal economic association of the region. China soon began to drop its suspicion of multilateralism and indeed become an enthusiastic promoter of certain kinds of regional institutions, even as it found its freedom of manoeuvre constrained in its pursuit of territorial claims in the South China Sea.[42]

A large number of regional institutions were created and developed in the 1990s. They were all marked in one way or another by the experience of the Association of Southeast Asian Nations (ASEAN) since its establishment in 1967 – the only Asian regional organization that endured through the remainder of the Cold War. Unlike the European Union, which is often upheld as the model of what a regional organization should be like, ASEAN never aspired to economic and political union. Nor was it a rule-making body subjecting its members to the discipline of adhering to its laws and regulations. It was in fact designed to sustain the independence and sovereignty of member states and to encourage regional and national resilience. It operated by consensus and informality. Practising non-intervention, it facilitated the avoidance rather than the resolution of conflicts.

Ironically, ASEAN itself cannot be said to have prospered in the 1990s. The benefits from the period of prosperity were largely dissipated by the financial crisis of 1997–98, and yet that was the time of the final expansion of ASEAN to include all ten states of Southeast Asia. The Indo-Chinese states were not only poorer than the original members, but their political systems and administrative capacities differed considerably as well. The incorporation of Myanmar, which was done in part to mitigate growing Chinese influence over the country, posed new problems on account of the brutal nature of the regime. Such prospects as existed for ASEAN to develop into a kind of security community were dissipated under these circumstances. Not only did member states vary widely in terms of size, population, culture, language and political systems, but they also had differ-ent security interests. Their emphasis on non-intervention has not helped in managing the rise of transnational economic activity in the region, nor have their bilateral defence arrangements led to a wider web of linkages. Meanwhile, the attempt at community building was strained by controversies between the more democratic and the more authoritarian states over the merits of 'flexible engage-ment' (a form of interventionism) and the difficulties in managing the enlarged grouping. It was argued in the 1990s that ASEAN 'now is in serious need to reinvent itself'.[43]

Curiously, the regional institutions that seemed to do well, or relatively so, were those that addressed security rather than economic concerns. Arguably, international economic institutions even of the regional variety require clear rules-based criteria for action if they are to be effective.[44] If performance is to be entirely voluntary there will be few governments that will impose rules that are bound to hurt one or another domestic sector or interest on a non-reciprocal basis. Whereas security of the more intangible cooperative kind, involving con-fidence and security-building measures, is more easily entertained, especially if it is seen to reduce tensions.

APEC, the Asia-Pacific Economic Cooperation forum, was formed in 1989 as the Cold War was coming to an end. It built on ideas and non-governmental institutions which had been developed over the previous two decades and it was also set up as a response to what was seen as the establishment of a 'fortress Europe' and as a means of keeping America 'in', while keeping the EU 'out'. Hence the oddity of the exclusion of the EU from the main regional economic institution and its inclusion in the security grouping. If the EU is effective in any aspect of its external relations it is in the economic rather than the security realms. The aim of APEC was to focus on capacity building and coordinating the handling of trade through establishing common customs procedures and so on. Starting with twelve members (the then six members of ASEAN and the six developed economies of Australia, Canada, Japan, New Zealand, South Korea and the US) it soon expanded to reach its current membership of twenty-one. That increased its geographical scope and its economic size, but the enlarged membership and the great diversity of the economies magnified the problems of organizational effectiveness.

Meetings were held annually at rotating host countries whose governments took responsibility for setting the agenda and the organization of the meeting. This arrangement militated against institutional effectiveness and continuity as each hosting government felt the need to make its own mark on the forum. In 1993, when the US hosted APEC in Seattle, President Clinton expanded the objective of the institution to include the establishment of free trade among the developed economies by 2010 and the others by 2020. He also instituted the practice of holding informal summit meetings. The attempt to make the free-trade agreement legally binding on member states ran into difficulties as members, including China and Japan, let it be known that they proposed to carry out the agreement on a voluntary basis only. This was confirmed at the meeting in Osaka in 1995. That indicated that APEC members were unwilling to move towards a kind of rule-making and law-enforcing economic community. This was corroborated by the subsequent failure to carry out an ostensibly easier programme of 'Early Voluntary Sector Liberalization', adopted in 1997. Not surprisingly, APEC was of little use in addressing the Asian Financial Crisis of 1997–98.

The problems lay in the structure and processes of APEC (cynically described as 'A Perfect Excuse to Chat') itself. Additionally, the goals of free trade are better achieved through a universal body such as the WTO with its means of demanding compliance with its rules. Although APEC may have helped on the margins in terms of its functional work groups, the principal benefits APEC has brought to its members lie less in the economic than in the political sphere. It has helped to build confidence among member states and its series of informal summits have enabled leaders to meet to address significant bilateral matters that might otherwise have been left to fester. More than once Chinese and American leaders have found the occasions very useful indeed.

The main forms of regional economic arrangements in fact owed little to formal institutions and more to the business economic logic of patterns of investment, trade and the development of chains of production. Such inter-state institutional arrangements that were made did not involve APEC at all. The ASEAN Plus Three (the ten ASEAN states plus China, Japan and South Korea), which began in 1997, and the China–ASEAN Free Trade Agreement of 2000, combined with other arrangements between ASEAN and other states emerged out of the ASEAN series of meetings with dialogue partners.

The main security institution established in the 1990s was the ASEAN Regional Forum (ARF). It is perhaps easier to say what the ARF is not than what it actually is. It is not an institution for collective defence, nor is it a concert for the management of regional security.[45] Unlike APEC, the ARF, which was formed in 1994, was not the product of a long series of institutional precursors. Unlike Europe, Asia did not have multilateral integrated organizations such as NATO and the EU on which to draw. Nor did Asian countries share a common perception of threat, either during or after the Cold War. Rather, their security concerns tended to be directed towards each other. Their requirement, therefore, was for a security dialogue that would contribute to building confidence and encouraging cooperation as a means of addressing conflicts or potential conflicts. Prompted by Japan and concerned about a possible withdrawal of American forces from the region, ASEAN leaders agreed in 1993 with their Post-Ministerial Conference (PMC) dialogue partners, the US, Japan, Australia, New Zealand, South Korea and the EU, to create a security dialogue institution. ASEAN members in particular wanted China to participate as well, so that this rising great power in the region should not feel that it was the target of the new institution and also in order to encourage it to participate in the consultative processes that had proved effective within ASEAN in reducing tension and avoiding conflict between members. Although the Chinese at this point preferred to deal with their neighbours on an individual basis rather than as a group, they did not want to be left out or to excite suspicion by preventing the creation of the institution. Besides which, the Chinese saw potential in the institution for constraining the United States. The United States, for its part, recognized that its own security alliances were not at risk and saw the new organization as playing a part in integrating China into the region in a peaceable way. Given the divergent attitudes and implicit rivalries between the major powers, it was not surprising that the initiative for establishing and leading the association was left to ASEAN.

The initial stated purpose of the forum as agreed at the inaugural meeting in Bangkok in July 1994 was for ASEAN and its dialogue partners to work with other regional states to 'foster the habit of constructive dialogue and consultation on political and security issues of common interest and concern' in order to make 'significant efforts towards confidence building and security cooperation in the Asia-Pacific region'. Foreign ministers attended the meeting and the intention was that the ARF should remain in the charge of foreign ministries of member states. Defence ministers were not invited and it was not until 2001 that the first regional meeting of the latter took place, interestingly under the auspices of the London-based International Institute of Strategic Studies, rather than of an organization based in the region. At the second meeting in Brunei in August 1995 a concept paper was agreed that looked for an evolutionary pattern of development in three stages, 'the promotion of confidence building, development of preventive diplomacy and elaboration of approaches to conflicts'. The formulation of the last stage had been chosen at the insistence of China in preference to the more robust concept of conflict resolution. By the end of the century the ARF had made considerable progress in various spheres, but it was unable to move to the second stage. Nevertheless, the broader concept of cooperative security was perhaps applicable to a region which was no longer divided by clear-cut enmities and was characterized by relationships that were neither those of allies nor of adversaries.

The ARF established processes for meetings of senior officials and for Intercessional Support Group meetings that enhanced transparency in defence matters through encouraging dialogue on security perceptions, the regular publication of defence white papers, attendance of observers at major military exercises of member states, exchanging officer training at each other's military academies, participation in the UN conventional arms register and so on. China has gradually been persuaded of the value of cooperative security. In 1995 China gave way and allowed ASEAN as a group to discuss with it the sensitive issue of the Spratly Islands. A year later its foreign minister, Qian Qichen, openly acknowledged the contribution of the ARF. The Chinese began to see multilateral security cooperation as a means of checking American 'hegemony' and its alliances in the region. The absence of specific binding obligations and the consensual approach appealed to Chinese leaders who saw themselves as representatives of a rising power that could use the approach as a means to have their growing influence and power accepted within the region without causing antagonism. The corollary from the perspective of the lesser powers resident in the region was that the rising China would be more aware of their views and perspectives and would be less likely to pursue its interests aggressively.[46] Beyond the China question, the ARF has contributed to the promotion of confidence among member states in that it has cultivated a habit of dialogue on security matters of both the traditional and the transnational kinds that would have been inconceivable before the 1990s.

The ARF could not have been expected to be the venue for determining the outcomes of conflicts where competing great-power interests are deeply embedded, as in the case of Taiwan, Korea or Kashmir. The challenge for the ARF, however, was to move beyond stage one of confidence building to stage two of preventive diplomacy. The concept has been defined operationally, but the barriers against implementing it have been formidable given the profound differences of interest and security perceptions within a region that also includes most of the world's great powers. The cooperative security promoted by the ARF ultimately depends upon the reassurance given to many of the smaller states by the security of the more traditional kind provided by the United States through its series of bilateral alliances in East Asia.

The Shanghai Cooperation Organization (SCO) was formally established in June 2001 from what was called the Shanghai Five, which itself was formed in 1996 (i.e., after China's accession to the ARF). Its origins are instructive about the evolution of Asian regional institutions and of how China came to accept multilateralism as a tool of its diplomacy.

The first early steps were the development of confidence-building measures (CBMs) taken in the course of border negotiations with the Soviet Union and with its successor states on the borders of China, namely, Russia, Kazakhstan,

Kyrgyzstan and Tajikistan. Beginning with unilateral moves that were reciprocated by the other side, Beijing and Moscow first withdrew troops from their
border, then reduced vigorous patrolling, until they had built sufficient mutual
confidence to coordinate further measures through meetings of military personnel
at local and regional levels as accompanied by negotiations in their respective
capitals over their disputed borders. Following the collapse of the Soviet Union
these negotiations were continued, but on a multilateral basis in Moscow with
representatives of the three new Central Asian republics taking part. That was a
product of necessity because Moscow, as the capital of the former Soviet Union,
had all the necessary documentation and Central Asian negotiating teams
had been diplomats of the former Soviet Union. The incremental steps taken to
reach agreements provided China's leaders with sufficient confidence in the value
of conducting diplomacy on a multilateral basis. They recognized that, far from
combining against China, the four former member states of the Soviet Union
could work with China together in accommodating their core interests.[47]

Russia and China were to a certain extent competing for influence. Russia was
keen to assert itself in the former Soviet republics, often describing them as its
'near abroad'. Andrei Kozyrev, the then Russian Foreign Minister, claimed in
1994 that Central Asia was part of the Russian sphere of influence. Relations with
China, therefore, helped the Central Asian states consolidate their sovereignty
and territorial integrity. They were able to resist Russian demands that ethnic
Russians in the new republics be given dual citizenship. However, nearly all
joined the Russian sponsored 'Collective Security Organization' (CSTO), which
promoted the real integration of the militaries of member states. By 1996 the
experience of working together led to the creation of the Shanghai Five, who
signed the 'Agreement on Confidence Building in the Military Field along the
Border Areas', soon followed by the 1997 'Agreement on Reducing Each Other's
Military Forces along the Border Regions'.

In 2001 the group took on the more formal name of the Shanghai Cooperation
Organization as it expanded to include Uzbekistan (Turkmenistan refused to
join). The SCO took on the commitment to oppose jointly the 'three evils' of
terrorism, separatism and religious extremism. From time to time member states
carried out joint military exercises and an anti-terrorist centre was established in
Bishkek, Kyrgyzstan. The main Russian interest was in retaining the region as a
sphere of special political and military influence and in utilizing the Soviet legacy
of systems of energy and transport routes that linked the region to the outside
world through Russia. China's interest lay in ensuring that the Central Asian
states would not harbour disaffected minorities from neighbouring Xinjiang and
in gaining access to the region's rich resources, especially of energy. Although
China basically had to start from scratch, it opened the door to economic interactions that in the next decade would eventually exceed the trade volume of
Russia.[48]

As with ASEAN, the SCO was riven with differences between member states
and the rhetoric of achievement was rarely matched on the ground. Leaving aside
the disparities between the great powers of Russia and China and the Central

Asian republics, the latter differ in size, in resource endowments; there are also disagreements about borders and there is a degree of distrust between them. Nevertheless the SCO proved useful for the new republics in helping to consolidate independence and raise their international profiles. They were able to attract investment from EU countries and US oil multinationals and to expand trade with EU countries in particular. Indeed the republics benefitted from the economic competition between Russia and the West. The organization was useful to Russia and China in reducing terrorist threats emanating from Afghanistan and it helped China in limiting the links between disaffected minorities in Xinjiang and their ethnic brethren in Central Asia. Throughout the 1990s Russia was able to maintain its economic influence in the region despite the new and growing economic inroads made by China. But although the Russians retained some military forces and bases in the region, notably in Tajikistan, they were unable to transform common membership in the Collective Security Treaty Organization (CSTO) into providing the SCO with a military dimension. Such military exercises that did take place were carried out exclusively on a bilateral basis.[49]

North Korea

As already argued, the end of the bipolar structure itself dissipated the central strategic balance to which regional and sub-regional conflicts had previously been attached. Consequently, in the 1990s conflicts tended to remain local or regional in their significance unless they involved any of the great powers or they raised issues that the international community could not ignore. Thus it was the prospect of the acquisition of nuclear weapons by North Korea that gave a new international dimension to the Korean conflict, especially in view of its unprincipled policies of proliferation that risked weapons of mass destruction ending up in the possession of other 'rogue' states or terrorist groups. By virtue of the involvement of the United States, Japan, China and Russia, the Korean conflict could not be considered as one of only local significance. At the same time the looser structure of the international system was indicated by the capacity of the North to act independently of its only and vital patron, China, and by the way in which the South pursued policies towards the North, which were not coordinated with its superior ally, the United States.

The Korean issue began in the early 1990s as a local issue between the two Korean states as they reached a number of agreements. These were reached in response to the end of the Cold War and the disintegration of the Soviet Union, but once it was realized that the transformation in the international environment did not require either to change track, they reverted to their previous state of mutual distrust and acrimony. A turning point for the North was when the Chinese recognized the South in 1992, adding to the sense of betrayal and isolation instigated by the earlier recognition of the South by Gorbachev in 1990. What seemed to sour what might otherwise have been a more promising development between the two Koreas was the huge economic disparity between them (intensified by the ending of Russian and Chinese subsidies to the North) and the incapacity of the North Korean regime to carry out economic reforms (perhaps along Chinese lines) that might have enabled the economy to recover. With a failing economy and famine stalking the land, the regime found succour through the secret development of a nuclear programme which gave it what it saw as a deterrent against the US and a bargaining counter to use to extract economic supplies from those it deemed its enemies. It also developed a range of missiles and material for the production of weapons of mass destruction, which were exported to what the US regarded as rogue states in exchange for much-needed foreign currency.[50]

It was the development of a nuclear weapons programme and the suspected proliferation of WMD by North Korea that led to two major confrontations with the United States. The first, which almost led to a US attack on the North, was resolved in 1994 by a 'Framework Agreement'. This was essentially a grand bargain by which North Korea would abandon its quest for nuclear power, which it claimed was for peaceful purposes, in return for economic aid, supplies of heavy oil and the building of two light water nuclear reactors. The latter could not be used to make nuclear weapons. The supply of oil would continue until the two reactors had been built and made operational. Ostensibly that agreement would meet North Korea's acute economic shortages and energy needs. At that time the country was undergoing a severe famine. The aid to the North drew on broad international support to be managed through the establishment of a Korean Peninsular Energy Development Organization (KEDO).

However, at issue for the North was not just economics. Rather it was the survival of the regime. Until the end of the Cold War its two giant neighbours, China and the Soviet Union, had propped up the North and the North had skilfully exploited the differences between them to its own ends. With the end of their support the North found itself in dire straits. In fact China's leaders had tried in vain to persuade their difficult ally to follow the Chinese economic path of reform and openness. The provision of economic support was a necessary, but insufficient means for regime survival.[51] The regime saw itself under threat from America and its allies, without being certain of the backing from its remaining ally, China. The North had sufficient artillery massed near the DMZ that could devastate the Southern capital Seoul and the 20 million people living in the greater metropolitan area, who accounted for a quarter of the total population of the South. But the Northern army would then be rapidly annihilated by a combination of American and South Korean forces. The Chinese who had recognized the South in 1992 had hoped to elicit corresponding recognition of the North by the US and Japan, but that did not materialize. The North therefore sought recognition and a peace treaty with the US that would lead to a more amicable relationship between the two and that would lead to a new order in Northeast Asia. In any event the Northern regime looked upon the acquisition of nuclear weaponry as the ultimate guarantor of its survival.

Meanwhile, the South began to see its interests as different and not always in correspondence with those of its main ally and supporter, the United States.

204 The post-Cold War period

There were intimations of this under its first democratically elected president, Kim Young Sam. As a conservative who came to office with the blessing of the former military rulers he did not openly depart from American policy, but he nevertheless reached independent agreements with the North on the denuclearization of the peninsula and on holding a series of bilateral talks. However, it was under President Kim Dae Jong that the divergence with the US became more apparent. In pursuing what was called a 'sunshine policy' Kim Dae Jong sought to engage the North through economic palliatives and social interactions. He even held a summit meeting with the North Korean leader Kim Jong-Il in the summer of 2000. It later emerged that this was made possible by a covert bribe of the leadership in the North. The sunshine policy found an echo with President Clinton, who in the dying weeks of his presidency sought some kind of accommodation with the North. Secretary of State Madeleine Albright visited Pyongyang and a senior North Korean reciprocated with a visit to Washington. But the Clinton presidency came to an end before the matter could be carried forward and, as we shall see, the incoming Bush administration had an altogether different approach.

Taiwan[52]

Taiwan remained the one issue which had the potential to lead to armed conflict between America and China. As noted in the last section on the Cold War, Taiwan had long ceased to be central to their Cold War confrontation and the management of Taiwan in Sino-American relations was ostensibly framed by their three communiqués of 1971, 1979 and 1982, coupled on the American side by the Taiwan Relations Act of 1979. What changed in the 1990s were the greater emphasis on nationalism in China and, more importantly, the transformation of Taiwan into a fully fledged democracy. In the 1980s Taiwan was still subject to a KMT dictatorship that claimed the right to rule China in the name of the Republic of China. In other words, it did not dispute Beijing's claim that Taiwan was a part of China. The difference was over who was entitled to rule the Chinese people. Moreover the formulation in the 1972 Shanghai Communiqué that America did not challenge the claim that Chinese on both sides of the Taiwan Strait agreed there was but one China still applied. However, the democratization of the island gave legitimate political voice to a significant proportion of the population who did not accept that they were Chinese in the sense of wanting unification with the Mainland. The rise of a party whose charter called for outright independence challenged a fundamental tenet of the new nationalism of the PRC, which claimed that China's unity was incomplete without the inclusion of Taiwan. Further, as seen from Beijing, continued American military support for the island could only be driven by an unstated desire to keep China disunited, thereby preventing its rise to the greatness it deserved. As seen from the United States, the democratization of Taiwan intensified the American commitment to its defence, even as its military strategic importance may have declined as a result of the transformative effects of the technological revolution in military affairs.

The stage was set for a confrontation with the leadership of President Lee Teng-hui, who had assumed the leadership of the KMT as the protégé of the late Chiang Ching-kuo in 1988. Once he had consolidated his leadership, Lee, who was Taiwan born and who had been to Japanese and American universities, sought to reflect and indeed to give leadership to Taiwanese feelings of their own separate identity from China and of the desire to retain their own state rather than be integrated into the Chinese mainland. His position soon undermined the attempt in 1992–93 to establish a basis for establishing agreements to regulate the burgeoning economic and social links that were fuelling unofficial cross-Strait relations. Taiwan rapidly became one of the largest investors in China and China became a leading market for Taiwanese goods. But the Chinese side determined that it needed to upgrade its military capabilities in order to deter and, if necessary, forcibly prevent Taiwan from formally separating itself from China. Indeed it was also thought that the military might at some point have to impose unification.

Matters came to a head in 1995 when the United States government went back on its word to Beijing and responded to pressure from Congress to allow Lee Teng-hui to visit the country in June, where, contrary to previous undertakings, he delivered a highly political speech. In Beijing's view Lee's provocations would not have been possible without the backing of Washington. It responded the following month with military exercises opposite Taiwan that simulated an invasion, and by firing six missiles only eighty-five miles to the north and south of Taiwan. A few months later in March of 1996 the Chinese repeated the exercise so as to intimidate the people in advance of the presidential elections (the first ever). Contrary to their expectations Lee Teng-hui won easily. But more to the point from a strategic perspective the United States sent two carrier-led battleships to the area. That brought the Chinese displays of force to an end.

The crisis had the effect of alerting both the Chinese and American presidents to the dangerous potential for armed conflict over Taiwan, and they both took steps to improve relations, culminating in an exchange of presidential state visits in 1997 and 1998. President Clinton made a point of emphasizing the significance of the new stage in Sino-American relations, by describing it as building towards a strategic partnership. The crisis had another and perhaps more ominous result in persuading the Chinese military that it had to build capabilities that would deter or deny American forces access to the area around Taiwan.

The stakes rose for all sides, especially after the Taiwanese elected the leader of the Democratic Progressive Party (DPP) to be president in 2000. The charter of the DPP called for independence, but Chen at first was at pains to disclaim any such aim. A distrustful Beijing followed the response of Washington, which in turn tried to discourage Chen from provoking Beijing. In a sense Washington became hostage to the domestic politics in Taipei and Beijing. Chen's policies were driven very much by domestic Taiwanese concerns and Beijing's reactions to his moves were shaped to an extent by political developments among the elite, which were largely hidden from the outside world. While none of the parties sought military confrontations, the fear in Washington especially was that the potential for warfare was ever present. The fact that the main driver of change in cross-Strait relations was the domestic politics on each side is illustrative of the way in which the strategic relations of the great powers in the new international system can be held hostage by parochial domestic politics.

Asian values

The significance of the debate over 'Asian values' in the mid-1990s is that it was a response to the agenda of enlarging the scope of free markets and democracy that was set out by President Clinton's first national security adviser, Anthony Lake, in 1993. Attempting to sketch out a new vision and sense of purpose for the United States in the new era after the end of the Cold War, and drawing on the popular academic mantra of the time that democracies do not go to war with each other, Lake called for a concerted effort by Americans to expand the scope of democracy and free markets, which, once adopted, in addition to their intrinsic merits, were thought to lead ineluctably to democratization.[53] This doctrine prompted the United States for the first time to challenge some of its allies and friends in Asia whose political systems fell short of what Americans took to be the proper standards of democracy. Erstwhile friends of the United States in East Asia, notably the leaders of Malaysia and Singapore, took great exception to suddenly becoming the objects of criticism and to being subject to pressure to reform their political systems.

The nature of the rejection of Lake's vision went beyond the standard nationalistic criticism of decrying Western interference and alleged attempts by the West to reassert control, to questioning the underlying validity of Lake's proposition. The Malaysian Prime Minister, Dr Mahathir Mohammed, and the Singaporean Prime Minister, Lee Kuan Yew, asserted that the mainsprings of their 'economic miracle' (as the World Bank called it) were what they called 'Asian values' as opposed to those prevailing in the West, which they depicted as undermining social cohesion. They argued that it was precisely the values of thrift, hard work and dedication to education, family centeredness and respect for authority that enabled them to become more economically dynamic than the West. Furthermore, they argued that it was their recognition of the importance of the community as a whole, as opposed to the Western over-insistence on the rights of individuals, that stopped their societies from becoming suffused with the social ills of the West, where economic disparities and drug abuse, alongside the prevalence of single-parent families, were said to be growing.[54]

Although much of this may be seen as self-serving behaviour by strong, determined (not to say autocratic) leaders, the Asian values debate raised real and profound problems. Given that the different UN declarations, including the charter itself, which member states had signed, attested to there being universal values, it still left open the question as to how communal and individual rights were to be balanced, and above all who was to judge and to act upon alleged infringements, especially if to do so would be to contravene the doctrine of sovereignty. The difference between the 'capitalist regulatory state' and the 'capitalist developmental state' had long been one of the roots of discord between the United States and Japan. At issue in Malaysia and Singapore was also the question of how to accommodate ethnically and socially diverse societies, in the case of the one, and a society whose ethnic composition and economic role made it unusually vulnerable to its more powerful neighbours, in the case of the other. Matters were not helped when the American vice-president, Al Gore, representing his government at an APEC meeting in Kuala Lumpur, publicly sided with Dr Mahathir's erstwhile deputy, Anwar Ibrahim, who had been deposed, amongst other reasons, for advocating political reform and implying criticism of the prime minister.[55]

The Asian financial crisis, which began on 2 July 1997, when the Thai government could no longer defend the Baht against the US dollar, soon spread to neighbouring countries and affected the whole of East Asia. As Francois Godement put it, 'the basic cause for the crash must be identified as the confrontation between global market forces and local institutions which have not adapted well enough to new realities.'[56] The crisis wreaked havoc throughout the sub-region and most of the affected countries had to go cap-in-hand to the IMF. It exposed the weakness of the claims made about an Asian economic miracle and it weakened several of the resident governments, undermining altogether that of Indonesia. It also undermined faith in the so-called Washington consensus of free markets, including free capital flows and floating currency values, as the United States and the American-based international financial institutions were more concerned to ensure the restitution of foreign investors and speculators than to protect the interests of the affected countries, who suddenly found 200 million people (about a quarter of the population of these countries) thrust back into poverty. Fortunately the region's economy was able to recover relatively quickly.

After the financial crisis hit East Asia in 1997/1998, the question of Asian values lost most of its political significance and became largely a matter for academic debate. Few would accept the proposition that there was a distinct set of Asian values as such. Even East Asia, let alone Asia as a whole, is too diverse to allow for that. But the values in Asia do shape attitudes towards government and the practice of politics, even as these change with the impact of rapid economic development and the enormous social changes to which that gives rise. There is therefore an unavoidable tension between the impact of globalization and the pressures for adherence to universal norms and values on the one side and the influence on states of past values and customs amid the necessity of maintaining an often-fragile social and political order on the other. Given the dominance of the United States in the immediate post-Cold War era, it has become the main source of pressure for the adoption of what America sees as universal values and practices. At the same time, it has become the main object for opprobrium by those who resist those pressures or who seek to promote alternative visions. The so-called debate on Asian values may have been superseded, but the issues it raised will continue to reverberate, especially as a rising authoritarian power, China, is beginning to challenge American 'soft power'. The apparent success of China's Communist Party-led state capitalism has reignited the debate.

Except that this time it is some Westerners who argue that the so-called Beijing consensus is superior to the allegedly defunct Washington consensus.[57]

II – 2001–11: The new significance of China

The first decade of the twenty-first century in the region was initially marked by the American focus on the 'global war against terror', leading to the US being constrained by overstretching its military in the wars in Afghanistan and Iraq, culminating in it being dragged down by a financial crisis and an economic downturn largely of its own making in 2008–9. Second, the decade was marked by the astonishing rise of China, which building on its rapid economic growth rates and its growing exports became a major player not only in the region, but also in the world as a whole. These two developments led the incoming Obama administration in 2009 to seek China out as a necessary partner for addressing global and regional problems. With China emerging largely unscathed from the global economic downturn and with America seemingly bogged down politically as well as economically, a new Chinese diplomatic assertiveness became evident.

Despite its perceived relative decline the US has continued to provide the public goods to the region even as its regional priorities and its ability to act upon them became less clear. Thus the Bush administration encouraged the rise of India as a counterweight to China and took the lead in having its status as a nuclear power accepted by the international community. The Obama administration, however, initially put more emphasis on seeking a partnership with China, even as it praised Indian economic achievements as the world's largest democracy. Japan, America's most important ally in Asia, posed problems for the US as for most of the decade its LDP government was circumscribed in its attempt to assist the US in Iraq and Afghanistan until the advent in 2009 of the DPJ (Democratic Party of Japan) raised broader problems about the nature of the alliance itself. Meanwhile Sino-Japanese relations improved from 2006 onwards and the new DPJ government in Japan went out of its way to deepen relations with China. Nevertheless tensions remained and were ignited in September 2010 by clashes over Islands in the East China Sea.

China's rapid economic growth helped fuel its drive to modernize its armed forces so that in the first decade of the twenty-first century they had gone beyond seeking to deter an American military intervention near Taiwan to beginning the acquisition of a blue-water navy that was capable of making its power felt in the East and South China Seas.[58] In March 2010 it was further claimed that China was building a navy for 'deep sea defence'. There was no sign, however, of China developing a new vision for regional or global order, as its leaders continued to focus on its many domestic problems and to seek resources to feed its huge economic growth machine. Its Asian neighbours, however, benefitted greatly from the growth of the Chinese economy. Yet most distrusted China and its growing influence over them. India sought to strengthen its defences against what it saw as a resurgent giant neighbour that raised the stakes in their border dispute and that was active in establishing a presence in the Indian Ocean and in cultivating relations with India's neighbours at India's expense. Southeast Asians also strengthened their military forces in the light of China's growing military capacities in the South China Sea and looked to others, notably the United States as a counterbalance.[59]

The North Korean issue became more complicated, especially since the testing of nuclear devices in 2006 and 2009. A diplomatic mechanism, the Six Party Talks (6PT), was established in 2003 to negotiate denuclearization and agreements were reached in 2005 and 2007 about the denuclearization of the North, but North Korea has not carried them out, as China continued to prop up the regime economically. The United States has reassured its South Korean and Japanese allies of their protection through America's extended deterrence. Meanwhile China has continued to play a key role as the facilitator of the 6PT. As noted earlier, American and Chinese interests in the denuclearization of the North both converge and diverge. But they agree that only a diplomatic solution is acceptable as the all-round damage that a military conflict would cause is unacceptable to either side. The Chinese refusal to condemn the North for the sinking of a South Korean naval vessel in March 2010 and their simultaneous enhancement of economic links with the North made more visible the different priorities of China and the US. If China was concerned above all with the stability of the North the US was concerned primarily with the North's proliferation proclivities and its provocative behaviour.[60]

Taiwan remained a key issue in Sino-American relations, especially during the Chen Shui-bian presidency of 2000–2008. Although the US was the ultimate protector of Taiwan, the Bush administration more than once took the step of publicly admonishing its government from 'unilaterally seeking to change the status quo'. But the advent of the KMT Ma Ying-jeou presidency in March 2008 and the many steps taken to improve cross-Strait relations, reduced tension and promised the establishment of a modus vivendi acceptable to both sides. However, the fundamentals of the situation did not change. Beijing's goal of unification did not command significant Taiwanese support and Beijing's military build-up opposite the island continued apace. The American commitment to enable Taiwan to defend itself still applied, as did the American policy of supporting only a peaceful resolution of the problem acceptable to both sides. The American decision in early 2010 to sell $6.5 billion worth of weapons to the island evoked a particularly angry response from a China that demanded American acceptance of what were called its 'core interests' now that Chinese power had reached the point where it sought to be treated as America's equal. The Taiwan question perhaps even more than the Korean one still has the potential to draw America and China into an armed conflict that neither side wants.[61]

The key to regional stability and security seemed to turn on Chinese-American relations. The question of how the United States could accommodate China's surge to ever greater power status has been made difficult by more pressing Chinese demands for acceptance of its 'core interests' in sovereignty claims over Taiwan, and maritime Exclusive Economic Zones (EEZs) stretching from its immediate coast to cover most of the South China Sea. The acceptance of these demands would transform the distribution of power in the region as a whole and it would undermine the American position as the stabilizing power in East Asia. It could throw into jeopardy more than a century of American strategic policy in the Western Pacific to prevent the emergence of a major power capable of dominating the region. At the same time China and America had become interdependent economically, both in terms of trade and in finance. China's mercantilist economic strategy depended on America to continue to provide the public goods in the Asia-Pacific and the United States required cooperation from China if it were to address a whole range of issues from the nuclear questions involving North Korea and Iran to more global problems of climate change and other transnational problems. China and America differed greatly in terms of their history, their modern experience, their societies and their political systems to the extent that it was difficult to build trust between them. The two powers tended to carry out hedging strategies against the possibility that the other might carry out policies damaging to its major security interests. But gnawing at the American position was that most Asian countries, including all its allies, had come to depend on the Chinese economy even as they still looked to the United States as their security guarantor. But given the growing interdependence between China and the United States, doubts necessarily arose about American willingness or ability to come to the aid of allies threatened by China.

The uncertainty in Sino-American relations, combined with the rise of India, the importance of South Korea and Japan and the significance of ASEAN, which included the newly awakening Indonesia, led to a complex pattern of regional security. It was both multitiered and multilayered. It was multitiered because the United States, though weakened, was still the provider of public goods. It was the ultimate guarantor of the safety of the seas, on which the trade of all the East Asian countries depended. Although the volume of its trade with countries of the region may no longer have exceeded that of China, it was still the main market for the chains of production that characterized regional economic relations. China was becoming the hub for the regional economies, but for many it was also a dangerous competitor for foreign investments and domestic foreign markets. It had also become Asia's greatest military power. Unlike the United States, China had maritime territorial disputes in the region and its growing influence, in Southeast Asia especially, was viewed with degrees of trepidation.[62]

Despite its decline, Japan, which at the time of writing (summer 2010) was about to be displaced by China as the country with a GDP second only to the United States, was nevertheless a major power in its own right. It was in effect an economic and political competitor with China in Southeast Asia and China's leaders were conscious of the Japanese capacity to become once again a significant military power and even possibly a nuclear one. India, which had become both a partner and a competitor of China, began gradually to establish a presence in Southeast Asia, where it was welcomed by Singapore.

Security was also multilayered as the regional institutions, especially of Southeast Asia, encouraged the development of patterns of cooperative security. Indeed it was precisely by embracing the norms of cooperative security and working with the regional institutions that China was welcomed as a partner by the resident states of Southeast Asia, who nevertheless kept a wary eye on the giant in their midst, conscious of the destabilizing role it had played in the Maoist era and of its claims to superiority before the advent of the Europeans. There is a wide gap between China's interpretations of history and those of many of its neighbours. The contemporary Chinese account is of a benevolent and peaceful unitary state that never sought to expand or to intimidate its smaller neighbours. Vietnamese, Koreans and others remember the history differently. Conscious of the apprehensions of their Southeast Asian neighbours in particular (despite these rarely being voiced in public) China's leaders have been keen to emphasize their peaceful intent and to stress the significance of their so-called win-win economic exchanges. They have sought to cultivate soft power in the region through encouraging students to attend schools and universities in China, through tourism, social and educational exchanges and even military-to-military relations. Thus the concern of the Southeast Asians to avoid confrontations with China and the Chinese interest in promoting good relations has provided another layer to regional security.[63] However, in 2009 and 2010 China became more assertive in asserting its sovereignty over disputed maritime territories, to the discomfort of its neighbours, which elicited a tough response from the US at a meeting of ASEAN Regional Forum in July 2010. Much to the annoyance of the Chinese, the Americans insisted that continued access to the international waters of the South China Sea was a major interest of the US and they favoured a militarized solution to the territorial dispute in the sea as opposed to the series of bilateral settlements favoured by the Chinese side.

The growing salience of non-traditional security issues tended to work in favour of raising China's profile in the region as few could be addressed without the participation of this Asian giant, which shared land and maritime borders with most of the East Asian countries. Further, China's cooperative security approach was well suited to addressing these new security matters. These tended to be of a transnational character that affected the domestic security of states, rather than classic inter-state military conflict. They ranged from terrorism conducted by non-state actors unconstrained by territorial bounds to international crime involving narcotics, the smuggling of people, to money laundering, pandemics, climate change and even natural disasters. Such problems could not be addressed by one state alone, however powerful. Nor could they be managed by international organizations, although they had a role to play. Above all they called for cooperation of a new kind between states. Dealing with terrorists, international criminal gangs and so on required the different agencies of state governments, corporations and NGOs to work together. In the case of terrorists and criminals, intelligence agencies and domestic police forces now had to learn how to share information and work together. Similarly, money laundering, pandemics and so on went well beyond the provenance of foreign and defence ministries. Even when the military are brought in to help deal with natural disasters, their role is far from the conventional one, as demonstrated by their actions in the aftermath of the terrible tsunami of 2004.

The Significance of 9/11

From a regional perspective 9/11 was important as it changed the whole American approach to the Asia-Pacific (as well as to the rest of the world). President Bush made what he called the global war against terror and those states that harboured terrorists the main priority of his foreign policy and posed the question of whether others were for or against the US. The governments of the major powers and of the states of the region all pledged to help the US. Jiang Zemin, who hosted the annual meeting of APEC barely a month later, turned over the agenda to Bush, who immediately focused on opposition to terror. China signed up to the new cause, which also resonated with its position in the SCO. It agreed to share intelligence and to work with the US to stop money laundering and to limit proliferation of WMD, which now took on a new urgency to prevent them falling into the hands of terrorists. Having no territory or population to defend, it was felt that terrorists could not be deterred like state governments and it was therefore all the more important to strengthen the measures against proliferation. China duly took measures to rein in companies which the Americans had accused of proliferating in the past. Although the US resisted Chinese persuasion to regard all Muslims who resisted Chinese rule in Xinjiang as terrorists, the US government did so condemn one of the Uighur organizations. At a stroke China had been transformed from a strategic competitor of the US to one whose relationship was described as 'cooperative and constructive'. Bush usually added the word 'candid', which was usually avoided in Chinese publications.[64]

The other great powers in their different ways all helped the US in the war to dislodge the Taliban government and Al Qaeda from Afghanistan that was launched barely a month after 9/11. Japan rapidly passed legislation to allow its Self Defence Forces (SDF) to provide armed logistic support. This was the first time that Japan had despatched its armed forces to participate in armed conflict, and it involved naval vessels going through the waters of East and Southeast Asia to the Indian Ocean. As an example of the transformed strategic realities of needing to be onside with the Americans, the Chinese maintained a discrete silence on a development that would have disturbed them greatly under different conditions. India and Pakistan pledged to help the US side, which then faced the problem of balancing its relations with the two, particularly as the Bush administration had decided to recognize India as a great power that need not always be tied with its protagonist, Pakistan. Yet in 2002 the two nearly came to war over a Pakistani incursion into an area close to Kashmir and the US helped to diffuse the crisis as the Chinese behind the scenes both reassured Pakistan about its security and encouraged moderation. Russia with Chinese support allowed the US to establish bases in Central Asia for its war against Afghanistan even though neither was enthusiastic about the unprecedented American military presence in a region important to the security of both.

In Southeast Asia the single-minded American pursuit of its anti-terrorist agenda, especially in the Philippines, did not evoke opposition in the countries of Southeast Asia, especially as Indonesia, with its own home-grown Jemaah Islamiya terrorist group, was hit by at least four major bombing incidents between 2000 and 2009. Improved intelligence operations by local security forces aided by the US and Australia were instrumental in greatly weakening the terrorist groups despite their ties to Al Qaeda. Resident states, however, were troubled by what they regarded as the American neglect, during the Bush administration, of other issues of immediate concern to countries still recovering from the Asian financial crisis of the late 1990s. Their security interests dovetailed with their need to develop their economies and although the Japanese and American commercial presence in the region still exceeded that of the Chinese, the latter were seen as the more active. The sense of American neglect intensified as the Bush administration became preoccupied with its wars in Afghanistan and Iraq in particular and as its attention was drawn to Northeast Asia. The fact that the two wars were depicted as wars against Islam eroded the regard with which the US had been held in Indonesia and Malaysia, where Muslims were in the majority.[65]

The generally favourable response to the American war against the Taliban and Al Qaeda in Afghanistan was dissipated with the launch of the war against Saddam Hussein in Iraq in 2003. Russia and China had made no secret of their unhappiness in the UN Security Council at what they regarded as the American rush to war and they drew quiet satisfaction from the divisions that occurred between the United States and some of its main NATO allies in Europe. Japan and South Korea, however, offered symbolic military support. But American prestige suffered as it got bogged down in its two long and costly wars and as its military became overstretched. By the end of the first decade of the twenty-first century it became clear that the main regional beneficiary was China. Most states in the region were keen to hedge against the uncertainties posed by China's rise and were less confident in the reliability of the United States as the guarantor of security and stability against the potentially disturbing consequences of China's growing weight and its more powerful and opaque military force. Apart from the question of the extent of the degradation of American military power in the wake of its still ongoing wars in Iraq and Afghanistan, concern was arising as to how America and the Obama administration in particular would seek to balance its need to cultivate a partnership with China to deal with the high priorities of both regional and global issues and simultaneously to prepare for the risk that China's rise might turn sour for America's allies and friends in the region.

Towards regional integration in Southeast Asia?

The first decade of the twenty-first century witnessed a vigorous economic recovery by the countries of Southeast Asia from the Asian financial crisis of 1997–98 and a reinvigoration of attempts to move towards a tighter form of regionalism within the framework of ASEAN. However, the continual emphasis in practice upon the ASEAN Way, that is the procedure for reaching agreements based on non-interference, consultation and consensus, militated against the movement towards a rules-based organization. Hence the notable achievement of agreeing upon a charter for ASEAN on its fortieth anniversary in 2007 was diminished somewhat by the evident gap between the aspirations to establish a rules-based organization committed to democracy, the rule of law, human rights and good governance and the ability to put these into practice. Although the Secretariat was given new powers to monitor and to compel adherence to agreements, it was not given the means to discharge its new responsibilities, as it only had sixty officers to oversee ten highly diverse countries with a total population of nearly 600 million.[66]

Nevertheless ASEAN had recorded significant successes. First it has managed the avoidance of military conflict among member states, despite rivalries, inter-ethnic tensions that criss-cross national boundaries, and border disputes. Second, it has continued to be a successful diplomatic community in that its collective international presence exceeds by far the sum of its different parts. Third, it has been variously the convenor, facilitator and regional architect in arranging for many regional groupings involving the great powers. Given the strategic distrust between them they have been content to assign ASEAN a leadership role in regional associations, notably the ASEAN Regional Forum, (ARF, 1994) the ASEAN Plus Three (APT, 1997) and the East Asian Summit (EAS or ASEAN Plus Six, 2005). Fourth, ASEAN has facilitated the establishment of groups to address pressing functional issues, including the Mekong Regional Council established in 2005 by Cambodia, Laos, Thailand and Vietnam to promote sustainable development of water and related resources in the Mekong Basin, a grouping which has strengthened their leverage in negotiating with China about its dam building higher up the river.[67] Other examples include the Malacca Straits Council of 1969 between Indonesia, Malaysia and Singapore, supplemented by subsequent agreements such as in 2004 and 2010 to promote safety and to tackle pollution in the Straits; and the ASEAN Defence Ministers Meeting, first set up in 2006, which is designed in particular to address together non-traditional security problems.

With regard to economic integration, much progress has been registered, but with the exception of Singapore most of the countries have similar economic profiles and consequently rely mainly upon external markets for the marketing of their produce. Although intra-ASEAN trade has continued to grow rapidly since the 1990s, it still accounts for just under 25 per cent of the Association's total trade (unlike say the EU, the value of whose internal trade is over 60 per cent of total trade). Nevertheless, one of the declared aims of ASEAN is to establish an economic community as one of the three pillars (the other two being political/security and socio-economic) for the inauguration of an ASEAN Community in 2015. Arguably, the opening of free-trade and economic-partnership agreements with most of its key trading partners in the first decade of the twenty-first century contributes to the development of the ASEAN economic community. But set against that are the many bilateral FTAs and so on, that have been established bilaterally between member states and external economies, which have resulted in a variety of often contradictory economic arrangements that militate against reaching genuine economic integration in the near future.[68]

Given the diversity of the membership, the disparity in levels of economic development and the differences of their political systems, it is not surprising that the ASEAN countries have found integration difficult. None of the ten members can take the sustainability of their political systems for granted and all ten are highly protective of their sovereignty, which may explain why in practice most states still adhere to the norm of non-interference and have yet to accede to following a rules-based organization, despite their declared obligation to do so. Thus despite tariff reductions, and collective FTAs with China, India and others, the rhetoric about economic integration has tended to outshine real achievement.

New patterns of security

In formal or institutional terms, two forms of security were evident in East Asia at the end of the first decade of the twenty-first century. The first was the long-standing American-led pattern of bilateral alliances, often referred to as a 'spokes and hub' system because America alone is at the 'hub', with strategic responsibilities for the region as a whole, while its separate allies focus on their parochial interests. This system of legally bound obligations to mutual defence as set out in formal treaties provides the framework for the deployment of American forces in the western Pacific and it is augmented by various agreements with several of the ASEAN states to provide logistic support for American forces traversing the South China Sea. The second pattern is based on the ASEAN-derived approach of cooperative security, and is involved with the building of trust on a multilateral basis with the goal of mitigating existing disputes and eventually finding means of resolving them. Cooperative security is the declared agenda of the ASEAN Regional Forum and, although it has not moved much beyond the stage of confidence building towards preventative diplomacy, let alone to 'approaches to resolving conflicts', that initial stage has continually been expanded into new forms of confidence building. Both patterns were re-invigorated in the latter part of the 1990s; the first through American initiatives in refining its alliances to meet more current needs, and the second through Chinese activism in regional multilateral institutions. In the first decade of the twenty-first century they came to be seen as hedging strategies as China, the rising power, sought to bolster its relations with neighbouring states as insurance against possible American containment and the US deepened military relations with allies and partners to deter and to insure against the prospect of a China that could become unduly militarily assertive.[69]

The two patterns were long seen by the ASEAN countries in particular as not only compatible, but as re-inforcing each other. By the 1990s the ASEAN states, including Indonesia, had recognized that China had to be integrated into their sub-region and that this was best done by a policy of what was called 'constructive engagement', and by encouraging the active participation of other great powers and the US especially so as to provide a peaceable balance of power.[70] Once the Chinese at the turn of the century stopped criticizing the American alliance system as outdated and reflective of Cold War attitudes, the compatibility of the two patterns was finally confirmed, easing China's pressure on its Southeast Asian neighbours. Indeed, once the Chinese began to accommodate themselves to American superior power in Asia instead of seeking vainly to establish coalitions against it, the way was open to deepening China's engagement with its ASEAN

216 The post-Cold War period

neighbours who had less reason to suspect China of seeking to establish an exclusive sphere of interest in their sub-region.

Cooperative security has been enhanced by a series of new agreements that are supposedly economic in nature, but which carry significant political overtones. These include the ASEAN Plus Three (APT) association of the ten ASEAN states plus China, Japan and South Korea that developed initiatives ostensibly designed to stabilize and mitigate future monetary crises through currency-swap arrangements, as agreed in Chiang Mai, Thailand, in 2001. It is very doubtful whether they would really help in an emergency, as they lack the specific mechanisms to monitor or to interfere in the domestic financial arrangements of member states. Their significance lay in the political signal of demonstrating a determination to extend the areas of cooperation of the East Asian states to the exclusion of others, notably the US.[71]

Arguably, the cooperative security arrangements served the function of upholding the sovereignty and independence of states whose political systems were fragile and which faced domestic security threats of separatism, ethnic and religious strife. Cooperative security, of course, was designed precisely for relations between states that were neither allies nor foes. This consultative and cooperative approach enables such states to strengthen the basis of their coexistence and to deepen mutual trust. In that sense it is well suited to relations between the ASEAN states as well as to integrating China within the region in a way that does not challenge the other great powers. The United States has also benefited from the new Chinese approach, as it could be comfortable in the knowledge that its security dispositions in East Asia were no longer being systematically challenged by China's leaders at a time when their country was seen to be on the rise in the region.

As argued earlier, a more informal pattern of security has emerged between the great powers of the region as they manoeuvre for advantage. Given the scale and likely duration of American strategic pre-eminence, their manoeuvring or jostling for position should not be considered an exercise in the balance of power, as that is usually understood. In addition, the United States has little to fear of their combining together or establishing some kind of multipolar arrangement to contain or limit the exercise of American power.[72] Not only is the gap between America and the rest of them combined too great in terms of military power and related technologies, but such was the significance of the American economy at the turn of the century that each of the other great powers needed the United States more than it needed any of the others. Or, put differently, ensuring access to the American market and to American investment was so critical to their continued economic development that they could not afford to risk losing either, especially as none of the other powers can substitute for what America provides.

Japan and China, as the most important great powers in the region, share this pattern of overt cooperation and subtle rivalry. Notwithstanding their booming economic relations and their deepening economic interdependence, there has been no corresponding improvement of relations in other spheres, as followers of the liberal persuasion would have expected. Despite the rhetoric of cooperation and the attempts to institutionalize relations, the leaders on both sides are continually called upon to calm situations of hostility that have tended to erupt in the relationship.[73] Meanwhile, a rivalry is evident in their relations with ASEAN countries, as each one's initiative to emphasize the special quality of their particular economic and political relationship with ASEAN and its different members is soon followed by a similar response by the other. In sum, great-power relations in the region are characterized by both cooperation and competition, ensuring that the growing economic integration of the region is not accompanied by corresponding moves to establish a political community.

However, the greatest change in the security relationships of the Asia-Pacific since the turn of the new century was the rapid emergence of China, not only as the key economy that was changing the pattern of economic relationships as it became the main driver of economic change, but also as a confident player in regional diplomacy backed by a formidable and growing modern military arsenal that is seen by many in the region as the newly emerging force with which they must all come to terms. China's trade with America's allies in the region began to exceed the value of their trade with the United States even before the 2008/2009 financial crisis. Even though the significance of this was more apparent than real because a considerable portion of this trade was simply part of a supply chain whose destination was ultimately the American market, the trend was important. The growth of the economies of American allies and partners in East Asia was being tied more closely to the fortunes of the Chinese economy. If the Chinese leaders were to succeed in increasing domestic consumption as a proportion of the GDP the country's economic importance to its neighbours would grow at the expense of the American market. In the wake of the 2008 financial crisis it has become clear that the disjunction between the growing economic dependence on China by America's regional allies and their dependence on the United States for security will raise new problems for America and its allies.

As China has become a global economic actor so its security interests have correspondingly grown. China has become a major importer of metal and especially energy resources and it has economic assets to protect in the Middle East, Africa and even Latin America. The Chinese government has become concerned about the security of its lines of communication because of their vulnerability to superior American naval power. It has invested in overland routes to the Bay of Bengal via Myanmar and to the Arabian Sea via Pakistan. It has also invested in port facilities in Sri Lanka and elsewhere in the Indian Ocean, and in the process has awakened the suspicion of India. The growth of the Chinese navy, which is strengthening its blue-water capabilities, has alerted neighbours in the South China Sea with whom China has disputes about the sovereignty of islands and the adjacent maritime resources. Some of these, notably Vietnam and Malaysia, have responded by acquiring advanced weapons to protect their interests.

China's professions about the peaceful nature of its rise and the relative opacity surrounding its military modernization and strategy, combined with its growing military reach and its more assertive posture following its perceived success of running its economy amid the global economic recession, have deepened the geopolitical uncertainties.[74] Most of the resident states have sought to strengthen their

218 *The post-Cold War period*

economic ties with China, while simultaneously seeking to deepen the American commitment to the region. In that sense the Southeast Asian governments welcomed the readiness of the Obama administration to sign the Treaty of Amity and Cooperation (TAC), which was seen as necessary if the US were to become a member of a future Asian Community. Australia has made a point of strengthening its military ties with its US ally even as it deepens its economic dependency on the Chinese market for its mineral resources. The US has held annual military exercises in the Bay of Bengal, but the joint one held in 2007 with Australia, Japan and Singapore as well as India drew a démarche from China, which sought information from all five. Not surprisingly, the Chinese were told that it was not directed at them, but both the exercise and the Chinese response indicated the degree of manoeuvring and strategic distrust between the regional powers.

If the nature of the Sino-American relationship is the ultimate key to regional order, the significance of how the other major powers relate to the two should not be overlooked. As will be examined in greater detail in the chapter on the United States, the hitherto close alliances with Japan and South Korea have become more problematic as each searches for a new identity and seeks to balance the alliance with good working relations with China. The role of India and the inconsistency of American approaches to it by the Bush and Obama administrations are illustrative of the uncertainties of great-power relations. Perhaps the key to future developments will be whether America can continue to be relied upon to provide the public goods for this vast region. Unlike the regional great powers, the United States has no territorial disputes in the region and it has been more broadly committed to free trade and to keeping its market open. Were it to decline, as anticipated by some in the region, it is difficult to see who could provide alternative leadership. Important as the United States continues to be, it has ceased to be the unipolar power. The Asia-Pacific now confronts the uncertainties of multipolarity. The United States still provides the main public goods for the region, as elsewhere, but the immediate future will be shaped by how a more chastened United States meets the challenge of a newly assertive China.

Notes

1 Charles Krauthammer, 'The Unipolar Moment', *Foreign Affairs* 70, 1 (1990–91) pp.23–33.
2 A phrase drawn from Fareed Zakeria, *The Post American World* (New York: Norton, 2009) p.1.
3 For details see, Nancy Bernkopf Tucker, 'The Clinton Years: The Problem of Coherence' in Oksenberg *et al.* (eds) *Making China Policy: Lessons from the Bush and Clinton Administrations* (Lanham, MD: Rowman and Littlefield, 2001) pp.45–76.
4 See for example, *The Economist*, 'Climate change after Copenhagen', December 30, 2009.
5 Susan Strange, *State and Markets: An Introduction to Political Economy* (London: Pinter, 1994). For a more recent analysis see, Ava Winterbourne, 'The Erosion of State Sovereignty'. Available online: www.associatedcontent.com/article/2359682/the_erosion_of_state_sovereignty_.html?cat-37. Accessed 16 May 2010.
6 Robert G. Sutter, *The United States in Asia* (Lanham, MD: Rowman and Littlefield, 2008).

7 For Chinese views, see David S. Shambaugh, *The Chinese Communist Party: Atrophy and Adaptation* (Berkeley: University of California Press for the Woodrow Center Press, Washington DC, 2008). For an American view, see Tucker (*op. cit.*) and for a critique of the assumptions underlying the policies of engagement, see James Mann, *The Chinese Fantasy: How our Leaders Explain Away Chinese Repression* (New York: Viking, The Penguin Group, 2007).

8 Alvin Tofler, *The Third Wave* (New York: William Morrow, 1980; Hong-Mao Tien (ed.), *Taiwan's Electoral Politics and Democratic Transition: Riding the Third Wave* (New York: M.E. Sharpe, 1995); and Catherine E. Delapino, *Anchoring Third Wave Democracies: Prospects and Problems for US Policy* (Washington DC: Georgetown University Press, 1998).

9 Strange, *State and Markets* (*op. cit.*)

10 Joseph Nye, *Soft Power: The Means to Success in World Politics* (New York: Public Affairs, 2004). See also his *Bound to Lead: The Changing Nature of American Power* (New York: Basic books, 1990).

11 For example, two of America's most distinguished practitioners and writers on international politics were moved to write on why America *still* needed a foreign policy, even though they differed as to what that should be. See Henry Kissinger, *Does America Still Need a Foreign Policy?* (New York: Simon and Schuster, 2002); and Joseph Nye Jr, *Why the World's Only Superpower Can't go it Alone* (Oxford: Oxford University Press, 2002).

12 See the classic texts of Robert Gilpin, *The Political Economy of International Relations* (Princeton: Princeton University Press, 1987); and *Global Political Economy: Understanding the International Economic Order* (Princeton: Princeton University Press, 2001).

13 For balanced, but critical, overviews, see William G. Hyland, *Clinton's World Remaking American Foreign Policy* (Westport, CT: Praeger, 1999); and John Drumbell, *Clinton's Foreign Policy Between the Bushes* (London: Routledge, 2009).

14 Alexander Moens, *The Foreign Policy of George W. Bush, Values, Strategy and Loyalty* (Farnham, Surrey, UK: Ashgate, 2004).

15 Sutter, *The US in Asia* (*op.cit.*).

16 Henry Nau, Obama's 'Foreign Policy: The Swing Away from Bush, How far to go?' *Policy Review* 60 (April–May, 2010).

17 See the account of Japanese views in Edward J. Lincoln, *Japan's New Global Role* (Washington, DC: Brookings, 1993) pp.212–14.

18 Senator Tsongas cited by Maureen Dowd, 'The 1992 Campaign Memo: Voters Want Candidates to Take a Reality Check.' *The New York Times*, 17 February 1992.

19 See, Tang Shiping and Zhang Yunling, 'China's Regional Strategy' in David Shambaugh (ed.), *Power Shift: China and Asia's New Dynamics* (Berkeley: University of California Press, 2005).

20 Michael D. Swaine, Tousheng Zhang and Danielle F.S. Cohen (eds), *Managing Sino-American Crises: Case Studies and Analysis'* (Washington, DC: Carnegie Endowment for International Peace, 2006), especially chapters 7 and 8, which present American and Chinese views respectively, pp.251–326.

21 John Ravenhill, *APEC and the Construction of Pacific Rim Regionalism* (Cambridge: Cambridge University Press, 2001).

22 Francois Godement, *The Downsizing of Asia* (London and New York: Routledge, 1999).

23 Yeggeny M. Primakov, *A World Challenged: Fighting Terrorism in the Twenty-First Century* (Washington, DC: Brookings, 2004), chapter 5, 'Centers of Power: One or Many?' pp.94–101.

24 For the Chinese reaction see, *Arms Control Today*, November 2001, available online: http://armscontrol.org/act/2001.11chinanov01.asp; and for Putin's response see, *Russia Weekly*, No.184, December 2001, available online: www.cdi.org/Russia/184–1cfm. Both were accessed on 24 January 2010.

25 For an analysis of Sino-Russian relations see, Bobo Lo, *Axis of Convenience: Moscow, Beijing and the New Geopolitics* (Washington, DC: Brookings, 2008).

26 Martha Brill Olcott, 'Central Asia: Carving an Independent Identity among Peripheral Powers' in David Shambaugh and Michael Yahuda (eds), *International Relations of Asia* (Lanham, MD: Rowman & Littlefield, 2008) pp.234–57.
27 Rajesh Mehta, 'Indo-Japanese Trade: Recent Trends' RIS Discussion Paper (Research and Information System for the Non-Aligned and Other Developing Countries, India Habitat Centre, New Delhi, No. 12/2001).
28 Sumit Ganguly, 'The Rise of India in Asia' in Shambaugh and Yahuda (eds) *International Relations of Asia* (*op.cit.*) pp.150–69.
29 For an excellent study, see Jonathan Holslag, *China and India: Prospects for Peace* (New York: Columbia University Press, 2010).
30 Michael Yahuda, 'The Limits of Economic Interdependence: Sino-Japanese Relations' in Alastair Iain Johnston and Robert S. Ross (eds), *New Directions in the Study of China's Foreign Policy* (Stanford: Stanford University Press, 2006) pp.162–85.
31 Mike M. Mochizuki, 'China-Japan Relations: Downward Spiral or a New Equilibrium' in Shambaugh (ed.), *Power Shift: China and Asia's New Dynamics* (*op. cit.*), pp.135–50.
32 For accounts of territorial and other disputes in Southeast Asia after the end of the Cold War, see Donald E. Weatherbee, with others, *International Relations in Southeast Asia: the Struggle for Autonomy* (Lanham, MD: Rowman & Littlefield, 2005).
33 See Mike Chinnoy, *Meltdown: The Inside Story of the North Korean Nuclear Crisis* (New York: St. Martin's Press, 2008) chapter 1, 'Without You there is no US' pp.1–20.
34 Rand: 'The Significance of the Kargil Crisis', available online: www.rand.org/pubs/monograph_reports/MR1450 ch2.pdf. Accessed 21 March 2010.
35 Joseph Fewsmith, *China Since Tiananmen: The Politics of Transition* (Cambridge: Cambridge University Press, 2001).
36 J.A.A. Stockwin, *Governing Japan: Divided Politics in a Major Economy* (Oxford: Blackwell Publishers, 1999).
37 Richard J. Samuels, *Securing Japan: Tokyo's Grand Strategy and the Future of East Asia* (Ithaca: Cornell University Press, 2008). See also Michael J. Green, 'Japan in Asia' in Shambaugh and Yahuda (eds), *International Relations in Asia* (*op. cit.*), pp.170–91.
38 Edward Luce, *In Spite of the Gods, The Rise of Modern India* (New York: Random House, 2007) and Stephen Philip Cohen, *Emerging Power, India* (Washington, DC: Brookings, 2001).
39 Louise Fawcett and Andrew Hurrell (eds), *Regionalism in World Politics: Regional Organization and International Order* (Oxford: Oxford University Press, 1996); Edward D. Mansfield and Helen V. Milner (eds), *The Political Economy of Regionalism* (New York: Columbia University Press, 1997); and Andrew Gamble and Anthony Payne (eds), *Regionalism and World Order* (Basingstoke: Palgrave Macmillan, 1996).
40 Weatherbee, *International Relations in Southeast Asia* (*op. cit.*), pp.148–49.
41 Cao Yunhua, 'U.S.-ASEAN, Japan-ASEAN Relations and their Impacts on China' in Saw Swee-Hock, Sheng Lijun and Chin Kin Wah (eds), *ASEAN China Relations Realities and Prospects* (Singapore: ISEAS, 2005), especially pp.117–21.
42 For an excellent account of China's embrace of multilateralism, see Bates Gill, *Rising Star: China's New Security Diplomacy* (Washington, DC: Brookings, 2007).
43 Amitav Acharya, *Constructing a Security Community in Southeast Asia* (London: Routledge, 2001) p.208.
44 Much of this and the following three paragraphs draw on Ravenhill, *APEC … (op. cit.)*. For a more optimistic view, see Ellen Frost, *Asia's New Regionalism* (Boulder, CO: Lynne Reinner Publishers, 2008).
45 For accounts of the ARF, see Michael Leifer, *The ASEAN Regional Forum* (London: International Institute of Strategic Studies, Adelphi Papers No, 302, 1996) and Desmond Ball and Amitav Acharya (eds), *The Next Stage: Preventive Diplomacy and Security Competition in the Asia-Pacific Region* (Canberra: Strategic and Defence Centre, Australian National University, 1999).

46 For an account of China's adaptation to ARF norms in Southeast Asia, see Rosemary Foot, 'China in the ASEAN Regional Forum: Organizational Processes and Domestic Modes of Thought' *Asian Survey* XXXVIII, 5 (May 1998) pp.425–40.

47 Michael Yahuda, 'China's Multilateralism and Regional Order' and Jianwei Wang, 'China and SCO: towards a new type of interstate relations' in GuoGuang Wu and Helen Landsdowne (eds), *China Turns to Multilateralism: Foreign policy and regional security* (London: Routledge, 2008), pp.75–89 and 104–26 respectively.

48 Bates Gill and Matthew Orensman, *China's Journey to the West* (Washington, DC: Center for Strategic and International Studies, 2006).

49 See Olcott, 'Central Asia … ' (*op. cit.*).

50 For a broad overview, see Don Oberdorfer, *The Two Koreas* (Boston: Addison Wesley, 1997). For an account of the first nuclear crisis, see Leon V. Segal, *Disarming Strangers: Nuclear Diplomacy with North Korea* (Princeton: Princeton University Press, 1999). See also Mike Chinnoy, *Meltdown: The Inside Story of the North Korean Nuclear Crisis* (New York: St. Martin's Press, 2008) ch. 1 pp.1–20.

51 Scott Snyder, *China's Rise and the Two Koreas: Politics, Economics, Security* (Boulder, CO and London: Lynne Riener Publishers, 2009) especially, ch. 7, pp.163–82.

52 The following analysis draws on Alan D. Romberg, *Rein in at the Brink of the Precipice: American Policy Towards Taiwan and US-PRC Relations* (Washington, DC: Henry L. Stimson Center, 2003); Richard Bush, *Untying the Knot: Making Peace in the Taiwan Strait* (Washington, DC: Brookings, 2005); and Alan M. Wachman, *Why Taiwan?* (Stanford: Stanford University Press, 2007).

53 Lake's speech of 21 September 1993, available online: www.mtholyoke.edu/acad/intre/lakedoc.html. Accessed 5 June 1997.

54 The former Singaporean senior foreign ministry official and dean of the Lee Kwan Yew School of Management, NUS, has long taken the intellectual lead on this issue. See, for example, his 'An Asian Perspective on Human Rights and Freedom of the Press' in Peter Van Ness (ed.), *Debating Human Rights* (London: Routledge, 1999) pp.80–97.

55 Jurgen Haacke, *ASEAN's Diplomatic and Security Culture* (London: RoutledgeCurzon, 2003) pp.187–88.

56 Godement, *The Downsizing of Asia* (*op. cit.*), p.29.

57 There is an extensive literature on this. See notably, in order of publication, Joshua Cooper Ramo, *The Beijing Consensus* (London: The Foreign Policy Center, 2004); Martin Jacques, *When China Rules the World: The End of the Western World and the Birth of a New World Order* (London: Penguin, Allen Lane, 2009); Stephan Halper, *The Beijing Consensus: How China's Authoritarian Model will Dominate the Twenty-First Century* (New York: Basic Books, 2010); and Ian Bremmer, *The End of the Free Market: Who Wins the War Between States and Corporations?* (USA: Penguin Group, 2010).

58 See the detailed publications in three volumes by the US Naval Institute Press (Anapolis, MD): Andrew S. Erickson *et al.* (eds), *China's Nuclear Submarine Force* (2007); Gabriel B. Collins, *et al.* (eds), *China's Energy Strategy* (2008); and Andrew S. Erickson *et al.* (eds) *China Goes to Sea* (2009).

59 IISS, *Strategic Survey 2009* (London: Routledge, 2009) pp.338–51.

60 Snyder, *China's Rise and the Two Koreas* (*op. cit.*), pp.149–58.

61 Alan D. Romberg, 'PRC-Taiwan-United States' in *China Leadership Monitor 32* (Hoover Institution, Stanford University, Spring 2010).

62 For an American view, see Ashley J. Tellis, 'Preserving Hegemony: The Strategic Tasks Facing the United States,' in Ashley J. Tallis *et al.* (eds), *Strategic Asia 2008–2009: Challenges and Choices* (Seattle: The National Bureau of Asian Research, 2008), pp.3–37.

63 Ernest Bower, 'China's Activities in Southeast Asia and Implications for US Interests.' Testimony before the US-China and Economic Review Commission, 4 February 2010.

64 For China's response to 9/11, see Gill, *Rising Star*, (*op. cit.*), pp.127–31.
65 Evelyn Goh, 'A Study of U.S. policy towards Southeast Asia' in Tellis (ed.), *Strategic Asia* (*op.cit.*) pp.261–95.
66 Donald Emmerson (ed.), *Hard Choices: Security, Democracy and Regionalism in Southeast Asia* (Stanford: Stanford University Press, 2008).
67 Milton Osborne, 'The Mekong River Under Threat', *The Asia-Pacific Journal: Japan Focus*, 17 April 2010. Available online: file:///SE%20Asia/The%20Mekong%20 20under%20threat%20M%20Osborne.html.
68 The formation of the different groupings, their different aspirations and the economic data are all drawn from the official website of the ASEAN Secretariat.
69 Evelyn Goh, 'Great Powers and Hierarchical Order in Southeast Asia: Analyzing Regional Security Strategies', *International Security*, 32, 3 (Winter 2007/8), pp.113–57.
70 On constructive engagement by ASEAN members, see the chapters by Michael Leifer, Yuen Foong Khong and Amitav Acharya on the engagement of China by Indonesia, Singapore and Malaysia, respectively, in Alastair Iain Johnston and Robert S. Ross (eds), *Engaging China* (London: 1999) pp.87–108, 109–28 and 129–51, respectively. On the balance of power, see Ralph Emmers, *Cooperative Security and the Balance of Power in ASEAN and the ARF* (London: Routledge, 2004).
71 Michael Vatikiotis and Murray Hiebert, 'How China is Building an Empire', *Far Eastern Economic Review*, 20 November 2003.
72 For an elaboration see Joseph S. Nye Jr, *The Paradox of American Power* (Oxford: Oxford University Press, 2002) especially ch. 1, pp.1–40.
73 'The Optimists Have the Lead, for Now' in Satu Limaye (ed.), *Asia's China Debate* (Honolulu: Asia Pacific Center for Security Studies Publications, December, 2003) pp.11.1–11.8. The depth of hostility from younger Chinese nationalists is explored in Peter Hays Gries, *China's New Nationalism: Pride, Politics and Diplomacy* (Berkeley: University of California Press, 2004); and for an argument that the leaders exhibit a more pragmatic form of nationalism, see Suisheng Zhao, *Nation State by Construction: Dynamics of Chinese Nationalism* (Stanford: Stanford University Press, 2004).
74 Michael D. Swaine, 'Perceptions of an Assertive China', *China Leadership Monitor*, 32 (Spring 2010). Available online: http://hoover.org/publications/china-leadership-monitor. Accessed 3 July 2010.

9 The United States

From the end of the Cold War to the war on terrorism and beyond

In the two decades or so since the end of the Cold War, the United States' role in Asia has changed from that of the unipolar superpower, which promoted the spread of globalization and the virtues of democracy, to the leader of the global war against terrorism and finally to the chastened superpower, bogged down in two wars in Iraq and Afghanistan and tied down by an economic recession second in depth only to the depression of the 1930s. With the rise of other powers, notably China, but also India and a resurgent Russia, and with more difficult relations with allies, including Japan and South Korea, the United States is looking ahead to a difficult second decade of the twenty-first century, where it is still expected to provide leadership despite the emergence of a more multipolar world.

American policies in the region, as always, were shaped in large part by its global concerns. Deprived of the disciplines imposed by the bipolar system that helped to order priorities and determine which conflicts in different parts of the world required what kind of response from the American side, American interests became more difficult to define and they were more openly contested. At the same time, the demands of foreign and strategic policy could no longer be expected to prevail over domestic economic and political interests. The domestic dimensions of foreign policy became commensurably more important. This became true for the other states in the Asia-Pacific with whom the United States had to deal, notably China, Japan, Russia and India. The world had become more uncertain and complex. As the sole surviving superpower, America had no peer competitor in the military realm. But it did not enjoy similar superiority in the international economy. Indeed, until well into the 1990s there was a widespread view that America was in economic decline relative to Japan, the EU and, increasingly, a rapidly rising China.[1] Additionally, as the prospect of war between the great powers receded, local wars, wars within states and problems that failed states posed to international security became more salient. The nature of security itself changed to include the transnational variety that threatened the civil order within established states. These trends were accompanied by the impact of the information age and the speed of globalization, allowing for greater roles to be played by non-state actors.[2]

Despite these new uncertainties, America was at first imbued with a sense of major triumph, as its system of democracy and the market (or capitalism) had prevailed over the Soviet alternative so comprehensively that no alternative seemed viable.[3] However, the American tendency to agitate for the extension of democracy and the market to other countries was initially tempered, first by the Bush administration's slowness in readjusting to the unexpected post-Cold War condition, and second, by a caution induced by a sense of America's relative economic decline. Nevertheless, as the first Gulf War showed, it was left to America to form an international coalition and provide the bulk of the military capabilities to dislodge Saddam Hussein's troops from Kuwait. America still sought and was expected to provide leadership in world affairs. However, it was far from clear how the United States was to take the lead in establishing what President Bush called, momentarily, a 'new world order', when the character of the new era seemed confused and elusive. However, in the aftermath of China's Tiananmen disaster Bush was concerned not to allow relations with Beijing to fall away, resulting in an isolated regime that might turn inwards again. In that sense he sought to maintain key power relations in the Asia-Pacific unchanged.[4]

By the time President Clinton took over the helm in January 1993, it was becoming clear that it was Japan and not the United States that was in relative economic decline. Although the new administration paid much attention to the promotion of democratic values, it also took the lead in advancing American commercial interests as spurred by the revolution in information technology and globalization in which Americans had a lead. Not surprisingly, it found difficulties in establishing a balance between the two. But the main concern of the Clinton administration was less with foreign affairs and more on 'remedying domestic, mostly economic problems'.[5]

The new external environment raised new issues, as Western democracies were no longer prepared to overlook terrible crimes against humanity, now that the Cold War constraints and the fear of nuclear war had been removed. Sovereignty was no longer regarded as a shield behind which domestic rulers could massacre citizens or violate the rights of minorities with impunity. That gave rise to forms of humanitarian intervention with the concomitant need to cooperate with like-minded allies and to work through international institutions. By the time of Clinton's second term in office, America was seen as the major proponent of globalization and of expanding interdependencies beyond the economic to the social and cultural spheres. In the case of the Asia-Pacific, this bore fruit especially in the agreements that enabled China to enter the World Trade Organization (WTO). Yet the relative neglect of strategic–political developments in the Asia-Pacific was addressed in part by consolidating the alliance with Japan and by the summitry with China. But little attempt was made to balance relations between the two. Meanwhile Clinton managed the first nuclear crisis with North Korea with a degree of success.[6]

However, during this latter period a second theme emerged as a critique of the Clintonian approach that put emphasis on a more strategic and geopolitical calculus. The object was to ensure that American pre-eminence should endure and that the American national interest should not be compromised, as in the Clinton presidency, by following '"illusory" norms of international behaviour'.[7] The Bush administration assumed office in 2001 full of confidence in the overwhelming superiority of what it saw as American values and of the capabilities of its armed forces. It was determined to pursue a new strategic approach unrestrained by multilateral institutions. But it was soon overtaken by the impact of 9/11, the sudden recognition of the vulnerability of the American public to terrible attack from unconventional sources and the subsequent focus on the 'global war on terror', which reduced all other American foreign-policy interests to a lesser priority. Indeed, it raised the question of whether the US had a coherent strategy towards the Asia-Pacific region other than the pursuit of terrorists in Southeast Asia and what seemed to be essentially a reactive one designed to avoid any outbreak of conflict lest that detract from the focus on the greater Middle East (i.e., the war on Iraq and the continuing military conflict in Afghanistan).

By its second term the Bush administration began to take note of the enormous toll which the two wars took on American resources and on its standing in the world. The wars were very costly not only in dollar terms (estimates vary between $1 trillion and $4 trillion depending on how much of the collateral costs to veterans and lost-opportunity costs are taken into account, but also in lives, resources and the more intangible dimensions of lost prestige, and disenchantment with the two wars at home. The two wars were not paid for by increased taxation and the costs contributed to American indebtedness.[8] They also strained relations with allies who contributed to the war efforts despite their unpopularity among their domestic constituents. However, in Asia Bush succeeded in cultivating relations with China while opening up new strategic relations with India. The principal problem with Bush's legacy in Asia was North Korea, where a divided administration failed in the end to prevent it from acquiring nuclear weapons.

The Obama administration successfully addressed one of the failings of Bush by raising American prestige and it sought to change the American agenda towards addressing more global problems such as climate change and the immediate international financial crisis. To this end it embraced multilateral approaches and in Asia much emphasis was initially placed on a partnership with China and on cultivating the region, which supposedly had been neglected by the previous administration. But as the complexities of working with China became evident and as Obama became more preoccupied with domestic issues, it became less clear how the Obama administration intended to balance the different American interests and obligations in the region. Nevertheless in response to China's greater assertiveness the United States made new moves in the summer of 2010 to show its commitment to the region and to the peaceable settlement of conflicting maritime territorial claims.

Analysis and discussion of American policies in the region will follow both thematic and chronological sub-divisions, as these tend to coincide with changes in approaches by successive American administrations.

The adjustment to the end of the Cold War in East Asia, 1989–94

It took some time before American policy fully adjusted to the end of the Cold War in East Asia. Although policy was less than consistent in terms of the conduct of each of the presidential administrations, as well as between them, the fundamental structures on which American policies were based did not change. That is to say, first, America retained its strategic preponderance that continued to provide security for the region as a whole; and second, it kept its domestic market relatively open, so that the US continued to play a key role in facilitating the success of the export-led growth strategies of the East Asian economies. These two structural pillars enabled the US to continue to uphold its long-standing national interests in the region, identified nearly 100 years ago. These consisted of: (1) ensuring that no regional power could successfully challenge the US position; and (2) promoting market access to American business.[9]

The end of East Asian involvement in the international strategic concerns that had characterized the bipolar era meant that the regional and indeed the individual concerns of East Asian states became more salient in the development of regional order. Relations between the East Asian great powers, on the one side, and their smaller neighbours, on the other, were no longer structured around the Cold War axis of conflict, of which America had been the key driver. While the East Asian great powers were primarily focused on their region, America, as the only global power, addressed the region with domestic and global concerns in mind. These different perspectives were to pose new challenges to the US as it persisted in its attempts to provide leadership in this region, as elsewhere. Thus, although the US maintained its series of bilateral alliances in the region, the character of the alliances necessarily began to change, as they were no longer buttressed by the need to confront a common foe. The divergences of interests between the United States and its various allies became more evident with the passage of time. New challenges presented themselves to the US as it sought to make its global and regional interests more congruent, while at the same time trying to ensure that the alliances met the interests of its partners. It also became difficult for the US to balance relations between its key ally, Japan, and its potential partner, China.[10]

At first, especially as America seemed to be leading the world community as a whole in forcibly ending the Iraqi annexation of Kuwait, President Bush enthused about the emergence of 'a new world order' based on a 'a new partnership of nations ... whose goals are to increase democracy, increase prosperity, increase the peace, and reduce arms'. The phrase 'new world order' soon assumed an ironic twist in the chaotic aftermath of the Gulf War, but the rhetoric concerning the spreading of democracy and the free market found new expression in the Clinton administration as its national security adviser, Anthony Lake, advanced the doctrine of 'enlargement' as a core concept for a foreign policy that would assist the spread of these Western practices. It seemed to some as if the end of the Cold War was akin to the end of a major international war that facilitated the establishment by the victors of a new international order, as at the conclusion of the two world wars earlier that century.[11]

Although the West and the United States may be said to have won the Cold War, it would be more accurate to suggest that the Soviet Union and communism lost it. To be sure, the United States had not been inactive and it had played a critical role in facilitating settlements of long-standing regional conflicts that had been integral to the Cold War in the late 1980s and the early 1990s, particularly in ending the Soviet occupation of Afghanistan in 1989 and facilitating the settlement of the Cambodian conflict in 1991. Yet it soon became apparent that uncertainty and self-questioning rather than the exultation in victory more accurately conveyed the American mood.

These problems of reorientation were exacerbated in the Asia-Pacific by the general perception of America as being in relative economic decline, especially in contrast to Japan's seemingly inexorable rise as an economic power.[12] It was not until about 1995 that America's pre-eminence was finally recognized and even then this was not fully accepted in the region, as the Chinese continued to claim until the turn of the twenty-first century that a multipolar world was in the process of emerging. Further, Asia had not been transformed in the way that Europe had by the end of the Cold War; the communist regimes of North Korea, Vietnam and above all China survived the ending of the Cold War and they regarded the American rhetoric about the new world order and the enlargement of the scope of democracy as aimed at undermining their political systems. This was especially true of China in the years immediately following the Tiananmen massacre of 4 June 1989. Additionally, the new American rhetoric also aroused hostile reactions from previously friendly regimes, such as Singapore and Malaysia, which had become more nationalistically assertive as a result of the exceptional performances of their economies.

In response to calls from Congress, the Pentagon published in the spring of 1990 a major review of the strategic future in the Asia-Pacific. Although it still regarded the Soviet Union as a military threat, the review stressed that in the future America's role would be as the 'regional balancer, honest broker, and ultimate security guarantor'. It added that if the Soviet threat were to decline substantially, the American military presence would continue to check the 'expansionist regional aspirations' of 'second tier' states. That may be seen as a reference to China, whose strategic significance as a partner against the Soviet Union had come to an end and whose appeal to the US as a reforming communist state had been eclipsed by the Tiananmen disaster. The review also noted that the American forces in the Pacific were needed for responding rapidly to crises elsewhere, for example in the Middle East. Accordingly, the review stated that about 10,000 out of a deployment of about 110,000 troops would be withdrawn within a five-year period and it implied that if the strategic environment continued to improve in the region more substantial withdrawals would take place.[13] In 1992 another strategic review foreshadowed plans to reduce US deployments in East Asia still further, but in February 1995 Assistant Secretary of Defense for International Security Joseph S. Nye sought to reassure Asian governments in a new official East Asian Review that cutbacks resulting from the end of the Cold War had finished and 'no further changes in war fighting capability [were] currently planned'. In particular the Review paid renewed attention to Japan and prepared the ground for updating the alliance in the form of new guidelines that were agreed in 1996 and outlined in 1997.[14]

American allies and friends in the region, however, were not fully reassured about the commitment to retain sufficient military force deployed in the Asia-Pacific. They recognized that irresistible pressures for further withdrawals could arise from within the US. Moreover, they were concerned about the extent to which the United States would 'check' possible expansionism in the region. The United States had already indicated to the Philippines in the 1980s that their treaty did not extend to the latter's territorial claims in the South China Sea, where the littoral Southeast Asian states fear China's creeping assertiveness. Moreover, the United States decided to withdraw altogether from its bases in the Philippines when the agreement over them expired in 1991. This was occasioned partly by the enormous damage inflicted by the volcanic eruption of Mt Pinatubo on Clark Airfield, but it was also spurred by the long, bitter negotiations with the Filipino government, which, under pressure from nationalists, demanded payments and conditions that the US was not prepared to meet in the new era. Singapore hastened to provide the use of certain limited facilities, but it could not provide an effective replacement to the huge air and naval bases that the US had given up in the Philippines. Yet despite repeated official American pledges to retain the current force level of deployments in the region, many friendly governments feared that, perhaps within ten years, American domestic pressures would lead to their recall. Interestingly, Thailand, America's long-term ally in the region, turned down an American request to establish offshore supply depots to be used in the event of emergencies in the region and in the Gulf. The Thais explained that this might be opposed on nationalistic grounds and, besides, it might give offence to the Chinese. As for the security role of American forces, it was recognized that this might forestall the emergence of a regional hegemon and a possible great-power rivalry between China and Japan, but it was openly doubted whether American force would be used in regional conflicts beyond Korea and possibly Taiwan.[15]

Secretary of State Baker did not favour the new multilateralism in East Asia, fearing that it might dilute the significance of America's bilateral alliances. The Clinton administration, however, embraced the concept of multilateralism, as a complement to, rather than as a diminution of, its series of bilateral alliances. Recognizing the concern to find a means of drawing China into more regular patterns of cooperation and security discourse in the region, the United States provided encouragement at the Post-Ministerial Meeting of ASEAN in Manila in July 1992 for the development of a new multilateral organization. This eventually bore fruit with the establishment of the ASEAN Regional Forum (ARF) that held its inaugural meeting in Singapore in July 1993. Although essentially a consultative body, the ARF, which includes the major states of the Asia-Pacific and most of the East Asian states, was seen as an important body for incorporating

China within multilateral approaches in the hope that it would develop as a 'good citizen of international society' as it inevitably grew in power.

On the occasion of his first visit to South Korea and Japan in the summer of 1993 President Clinton articulated a vision of an Asia-Pacific community that would buttress the region's economic significance. Seeing the Asia-Pacific Economic Cooperation forum (APEC) as the only available inter-governmental institution, President Clinton took the opportunity of its scheduled ministerial meeting in Seattle in November 1993 to enhance its significance by convening a summit meeting of member states. Clinton depicted an emerging Asia-Pacific community that, uniting on free-trade issues, would develop ever closer ties. The occasion also provided an opportunity for him to meet for the first time the president of China, Deng Xiaoping's designated successor Jiang Zemin, so as to improve the rather acrimonious atmosphere between the two great states of the region. But the difficulties of sustaining the purpose underlining the vision of community soon surfaced, as in succeeding months the United States found itself in dispute with many of the states of East Asia about trade and human-rights matters. As for APEC itself, it was not at all clear that this essentially consultative organization could bear the more proactive demands that the American government sought to make of it. Nevertheless, at the next meeting in November 1994 in Bogor, Indonesia, it was agreed to set a deadline for the development of free trade among member states for the year 2010 for the industrialized economies and 2020 for the developing economies. However, APEC had yet to develop an effective secretariat capable of transforming the broader purposes into specific blueprints for action.[16] Japan in particular resisted attempts to make comprehensive free trade compulsory and, as the host of the next APEC meeting in Osaka, it effectively brought the American design to an end by declaring that adherence to the free-trade goals would be entirely a voluntary matter. Since few governments would deliberately pay the political costs of confronting powerful domestic interests unless there was no alternative, the free-trade deadlines lost much of their significance.[17]

Relations with China

The conduct of relations with China raised a variety of major problems that involved balancing conflicting goals and differences between the legislative and executive branches of government. There was the constant difficulty of gauging its current significance as a power as opposed to that of its potential power; especially as its sustained high economic growth rates and economic impact within the region brought it more sharply into focus as the rising power in the Asia-Pacific, and perhaps in the larger world. In addition, its many domestic problems raised the question as to whether the regime would be able to survive. The revulsion in the US to the Tiananmen killings of 4 June 1989, coupled with the collapse of communism elsewhere and the long-term social implications of China's economic reforms, persuaded some within the United States that China's communist system could not endure, and that it was America's duty to assist in its passing.

Two approaches emerged. One called for encouraging gradual change through a process of constructive engagement, which, would continue a dialogue with China's leaders to prevent a new isolation of the country and to encourage the more reform-minded leaders. Economic interactions would be continued so as to encourage entrepreneurs and the rise of a new middle class, which it was thought would gradually push the country towards democracy. The other approach called for the maintenance of sanctions and the exercise of political and economic pressure to uphold human rights and to carry out political reform.[18]

President Bush favoured the first approach and Congress espoused the second. Under pressure from Congress, where human-rights groups had begun to lobby against China in the late 1980s, President Bush imposed sanctions against the Chinese government in the immediate aftermath of Tiananmen. These involved ending meetings between leaders, cutting off military ties and the sale of military-related technology, and suspending official financial assistance. Almost immediately, Bush countered his own sanctions by secretly sending a senior official to Beijing and repeating the exercise a few months later. Alarmed by what he regarded as the spiralling downwards of Sino-American relations, Bush took various measures to limit the damage amid strong Congressional criticism. Eventually, there were responses from the Chinese side. But the domestic conflict within the United States soon centred on making the granting of MFN (Most Favoured Nation – that is, the terms of trade offered to any other state) conditional on improving human rights. Congress voted against a renewal of China's MFN status that was due in 1990, but not with a sufficient majority to override Bush's presidential veto. The next step in improving relations demonstrated the significance of presidential preferences, when Bush made a point of meeting the Chinese foreign minister in Washington in November, after his abstention in the UN Security Council had allowed the passage of a resolution to enable the use of force against Iraq.[19]

Sino-American relations nevertheless remained in a fragile condition. There was continued opposition in the US to China's repressive political system and the constant violations of human rights. The Bush and Clinton administrations constantly chafed at what they saw as Chinese violations of norms and rules against the proliferation of weapons of mass destruction and the export of missiles. The Chinese government was also placed under constant pressure for not observing proper trade practices, acting illegally, not protecting copyright and so on. The Chinese side suspected the United States of harbouring a design to undermine the regime and also of seeking to obstruct China's rise to the great-power status that they claimed its history and size merited. Hence China's leaders tended to react angrily to what was regarded as interference in internal affairs and to unequal treatment. The difficulties were compounded by differences over trading questions. American statistics showed what was then regarded as a huge trade deficit as their trade grew, reaching in 1993 US$23 billion (n.b. by 2009 it had grown tenfold) and in 1994 US$30 billion (second only to Japan). The Chinese figures showed a different story of almost balanced trade. While the Bush administration sought to open up the Chinese market, Congressional critics sought to withhold the renewal of MFN. A practice developed by which Congress would vote against renewal only to be vetoed by the president, who was confident that there would not be a majority to override him.[20]

With the advent of President Clinton in January 1993 there was a conjunction of a Democratic president and a Democratic majority in both houses of Congress, allowing a different approach to be tried based on executive action. But this owed more to meeting the needs of Clinton's domestic agenda than to a carefully crafted policy on dealing with China. The president set the specific criteria for improving China's observance of human rights if MFN were to be renewed. Meanwhile, despite the growth of trade between them, Sino-American relations worsened as the Americans not only condemned the Chinese on human-rights issues, but they also accused them of nuclear proliferation, violating commitments to uphold the Missile Technology Control Regime and exporting weapons of mass destruction. Indeed, at one point a Chinese ship, the *Yinhe*, was tracked to the Gulf on the charge that it was carrying ingredients for chemical weapons to Iran, only to be found in the end to be carrying no such cargo.[21] But in May 1994, when the deadline was due on the MFN issue, it was Clinton who backed down, even though he acknowledged that the Chinese side had not met his conditions. Business pressure was intense, as was the proposition that many American jobs might be lost, but Clinton was also swayed by the importance of not alienating the Chinese government at a time when its cooperation was sought in handling the North Korean nuclear crisis of 1993–94. Moreover, America's allies in Asia were anxious about the destabilizing consequences of a breakdown in Sino-American relations. In the event, Clinton's volte-face did not give rise to great problems with Congress.[22]

Yet Sino-American relations did not greatly improve, as the American side was still concerned about China's failings as a trade partner and by its failure to meet the minimum conditions for accession to the GATT. The Chinese side resented the American demands and continued to suspect that the Americans had a hidden agenda of trying to weaken the Chinese communist system and to block its emergence as a great power. Negotiations between the two tended to be characterized by public acrimony, with agreements being made only at the very last minute. The two sides also differed over Taiwan, which the administration was obliged by the Taiwan Relations Act to protect. But over and beyond the particularities at stake, the conduct of America's relations with China was bedevilled by the incompatibilities of their respective political cultures and by the suspicion that China's emergence as an independent great power would necessarily challenge deep-seated American interests. These problems were compounded by the inconsistencies of President Clinton himself and the lack of cohesive decision-making on foreign affairs in general that characterized the Clinton administration.[23] Moreover, it seemed as if every issue that Washington regarded as a matter of international principles or norms found the US and the PRC on opposite sides. There was also a lack of coherence in the Clinton administration's avowed policy of constructive engagement with China. A careful analysis of Clinton's policy towards China argued that it was possible to discern at least three different approaches towards engagement: 'principles engagement' sought to further a human-rights agenda; 'security engagement' favoured military-to-military exchanges; and 'commercial engagement' asserted the applicability to China of the administration's broader preoccupation with growth and development at home and abroad.[24] If many within the foreign-policy elite in Washington saw the handling of relations with China as evidence of the Clinton administration's maladroitness, the view in Beijing was altogether different. By 1995 many of the foreign-policy elite in Beijing concluded that a determined effort to contain China's rise to greatness could be detected as a consistent strand running through the apparently disconnected agencies of the different branches of government and the media in the United States.

Relations with Japan

Many of the American problems with Japan acquired greater salience as the exigencies of the Cold War disappeared. Trade issues in particular loomed larger, especially in the American perspective. As the American trade deficit with Japan continued to grow, from US$46.2 billion in 1985 to US$49.1 billion in 1989 and then to US$64 billion in 1993, the American government became dissatisfied with the previous approaches that had demanded the removal of trade barriers and negotiating voluntary quotas on Japanese exports. Congress in particular reacted to public-opinion surveys showing in 1989 that more Americans felt that Japanese economic power was a greater threat to the United States than Soviet military power. Two approaches were debated and in time the United States tried each in turn. The first called for opening the Japanese home markets to construct a 'level playing field' and the second demanded a results-orientated policy of managed trade that targeted particular trade balances or market shares of nominated sectors.

President Bush opted for the first. In launching the Strategic Impediments Initiative in 1989–90, the Bush administration initiated what has been called 'the most intrusive and sweeping effort by one sovereign country to alter the economic policies and business practices of another'.[25] The Japanese soon responded by arguing that the problems stemmed in part from American structural deficiencies. In the end a two-way agreement was reached, but not before nationalist sentiments were further inflamed on both sides. However, American fears of the alleged dangers of Japanese investment in their country (which, interestingly, never exceeded that of Britain) abated as the Japanese depression that began in 1992 caused much of that investment to be withdrawn. President Clinton's administration tried the managed-trade approach. But the effect of these trade disputes was to make it more difficult to reach agreements and understandings on other issues.

The security partnership was weakened by difficulties in establishing co-development and co-production of advanced weapon systems and by continued disagreements over the free-rider issue. The problem in demanding ever-greater financial contributions from Japan for American force deployments was that it might heighten resentment in both countries at the image of American soldiers as hired mercenaries. The tardiness with which Japan agreed to contribute to the initial Western effort in imposing sanctions against Iraq in the summer of 1990 was somewhat mitigated by the alacrity with which the Kaifu government announced its US$13 billion contribution to Operation Desert Storm. But even this was qualified and it evoked American criticism about Japan's unwillingness to share the human and political risks of providing a military contribution.[26]

Although still close, Japanese and American security perspectives in the Asia-Pacific coincided less in the post-Cold War era. The question of Japan's territorial dispute with Russia over the four northern islands was no longer seen by the United States as linked with the former strategic objective of containing the Soviet Union. For its part, Japan did not share the high regard that America gave to the domestic regeneration of Russia and it did not invest capital there on a commensurate scale. Regarding the key question of China, Japan was less concerned by political repression in that country and it was more worried about the adverse consequences of isolating its giant neighbour; hence the Japanese were keen to incorporate it into the region's economic system. Japanese interests were best served by an American approach to China that was not conflict ridden, but at the same time by one that did not invite close collaboration either. A new and complex triangular relationship was emerging between Washington, Beijing and Tokyo, with Washington at the apex. Beijing relied upon Washington to prevent Japan from emerging once again as an independent military power, and Tokyo depended on Washington to provide it strategic protection and to treat China as neither an adversary nor as a close ally. Washington was tasked with maintaining a balanced relationship with both, while facilitating the economic rise of the one and the budding independence of the other.[27] However, the immediate problem for Washington was how to encourage Japan to overcome the problems experienced during the Gulf War and to play a more active military role in support of American forces in the region, without arousing the worst fears of the Chinese and the Koreans about what they saw as a revival of Japanese militarism.

Relations with Korea

American policy towards the two Koreas continued to be shaped by global as well as regional concerns. It was the prospect of the acquisition of nuclear weapons by the North and the implications that would have for further nuclear proliferation in Northeast Asia and in the Third World that gave a global dimension to what would otherwise have been a regional question of how to unravel this last vestige of the Cold War in the region. This gave rise to tortuous and inconsistent diplomacy by the United States, and by the Clinton administration especially, and at one point it seemed as if open warfare might break out.

By 1991 the Americans had confirmed their suspicions about the nuclear facilities being developed by the North and demanded that it submit to inspections by the International Atomic Energy Agency. It eventually agreed, but only after President Bush had removed all remaining nuclear warheads from the South at the insistence of the South. President Bush was then subject to criticism in Washington for having given away his main bargaining chip for nothing. In the event, IAEA inspections took place in 1992 and evidence was found that some nuclear facilities had been used for purposes other than those originally claimed. Having been all but abandoned by its Cold War backers, the Soviet Union and China, the North felt vulnerable and exposed to the unconstrained power of the US. Accordingly, it claimed the right to develop a nuclear deterrent for the purposes of defence. The North then refused to allow mutual inspections, as previously agreed with the South. The North appeared to seek a resolution through a bilateral arrangement with the US that would lead to a peace agreement and the exclusion of both China and the South. The Clinton administration sought to involve China and was unprepared to leave out its ally, South Korea. The problem was that it seemed as if the issue could not be settled peacefully, leaving armed conflict as the only alternative. But after the visit to Pyongyang in May 1994 by former-President Carter it appeared that new progress was possible. Even the death of Kim Il-sung in July did not bring the new negotiating process to a halt.[28]

A complex agreement was eventually reached on 13 August 1994, by which Pyongyang agreed in effect to give up over a five-year period its suspected capability to develop nuclear weapons in return for an American commitment to satisfy its more immediate energy needs with oil supplies to the value of US$5 billion and to arrange for the provision of two new light water reactors and other high-tech products. The United States also undertook to normalize diplomatic relations and reduce barriers to trade and investment. Although it was appreciated that the agreement could unravel during the complex process of its enactment, the agreement was hailed as a breakthrough and it had the effect of diffusing the immediate crisis.[29]

The Clinton administration was criticized at home for giving in to blackmail and for reaching an agreement that could not hold. But the constraints under which Washington had negotiated the agreement were severe. The option of armed conflict was ruled out because of the vulnerability of the South and metropolitan Seoul's 20 million people to the thousands of pieces of artillery along the DMZ. The application of sanctions would have required the blessing of the UN and the active participation of the Chinese. This was unlikely in view of Chinese fears of the possible collapse of the North – a fear that was shared by the South, which, in view of the experience of West Germany's unification with the East, lacked the means to pay the immense costs of a sudden chaotic unification that would have followed. On the positive side, the South was keen to supply the two reactors as part of its general agenda of establishing economic influence over the North with a view to developing a gradual process of reunification. China's immediate interest was in preserving the status quo, which would allow the North to remain a buffer and give time for a gradual evolution towards economic reform there. Such a development would enhance Chinese influence over the peninsula as a whole. The Chinese therefore used such influence as they possessed in Pyongyang to encourage a negotiated settlement; and the Americans were fulsome in their praise for China's behind-the-scenes diplomacy that facilitated the 1994 agreement. Japan also praised the Framework Agreement. Like the others, it felt that any alternative would have been worse. At the time there was an expectation by some in Washington that the Northern regime would not survive much longer. Its failing economy was in such deep crisis that it could not survive without massive foreign aid, and the totalitarian character of the regime was so severe that it seemed incapable of following the Chinese example of economic reform. Meanwhile, by the application of pressure and by leaving the Chinese little alternative but to use such influence as they possessed in Pyongyang, the United States was able to show that the North had not 'got away with it' and this showed that there was no easy option for other 'mavericks' to acquire nuclear weapons.

The Clinton presidency: engagement and globalization, 1994–2000

In late September 1993 the administration tried to set out a framework and set of guidelines for US foreign policy, to meet growing criticism that it lacked focus. In a speech on 20 September, Secretary of State Warren Christopher rejected isolationism and called for a renewal of internationalism, arguing that the end of the Cold War had left the US with the responsibility and a 'unique capacity' to provide leadership. The following day the national security adviser, Anthony Lake, set out the purpose underlying that leadership as the 'engagement and enlargement' of the American core values of democracy and market economics. He committed the administration to giving the highest priority to strengthening the ties with the major market democracies and to preventing the ability of 'backlash states' in particular to threaten the 'circle of democracy'. Among the backlash states of Iran, Iraq, North Korea and Burma, he initially included China. Even though he later backtracked from that, Lake nevertheless raised disquiet in Beijing. As noted in the previous chapter, it was this speech that was to spark off the counter-claim of the alleged superiority of Asian values by the friendly Southeast Asian governments of Malaysia and Singapore.[30]

Ironically, only earlier that summer, in response to a sense of deteriorating relations with China that involved trade and proliferation issues, the Clinton administration had developed a policy which Assistant Secretary of State Winston Lord called 'enhanced engagement'. This was meant to address the various and growing discrete problems with China through more intensive and frequent high-level meetings between the two sides. It was then linked to Clinton's call for an informal summit meeting of the leaders of APEC due to be held later that year in Seattle, which would provide an opportunity for the first meeting between Presidents Jiang and Clinton.

It was in May 1994 that the Clinton administration finally accepted that it could not compel China to pursue a human-rights policy to American liking on pain of withholding from it access to the American market on normal trading terms, known as Most Favoured Nation treatment (MFN). Like other US presidents who had come to office determined to apply a tougher approach to China (such as Reagan over Taiwan), Clinton, who had indicated in the 1992 campaign for the presidency that he would be determined to hold the Chinese government to greater account over its human-rights record arising out of Tiananmen, had to change course in the face of Chinese realities. Except, in this case, the pressure did not just arise from an obdurate China, but from domestic sources too, notably the American business community and indeed from the administration's Department of Commerce, both of whom were exercised about the significance of the fast-growing Chinese market. Within the Pentagon there was also an interest in restoring military-to-military exchanges with the Chinese. Thus the commerce secretary and the secretary of defense paid visits to Beijing later that September and October respectively, where they were well received.

The vague term 'engagement' came to mean in practice a focus on establishing regular meetings by the top leaders and their respective ministers and on developing an interdependent relationship with China that would encourage not only a wide range of economic exchanges, but also exchanges in the military sphere and other dimensions of government as well as in areas beyond the government, such as social, cultural and educational interchanges. The policy could accommodate both tougher and softer approaches that varied from the insistence upon holding China to account to the extent of imposing select sanctions for violations of agreed trade practices, infringements of intellectual property rights and for allowing the proliferation of WMD, to allowing a greater range of compromises in the interest of avoiding confrontations. Underlying both approaches was the view that the policy of 'engaging' China would lead in the long run to changes in that country that would make it more market-orientated and more liberal politically. Meanwhile, policies of engagement held out the promise that Americans would benefit from China's rapid economic growth and that they could 'guide the newly emerging power into channels of international activity compatible with American interests'.[31] Engagement was used as an alternative to policies that called for isolating or containing China as an authoritarian state that oppressed its own people and that was a threat to American interests and, indeed, to American friends and allies. Constructive engagement was also designed to demonstrate to China's leaders that, whatever their differences on specific questions, the United States genuinely looked forward to working with a stronger and more prosperous China that was better integrated into the international community.

Inherent in the policy of engagement was the tendency to give China the benefit of the doubt in the short term in the hope of significant changes in the longer term. The policy of engagement required continual judgments as to which transgressions by the Chinese could be overlooked or treated softly and on which it was necessary to take a firm stand. In other words, whatever the theory, in practice the policy of engagement always entailed the potential for disagreement. Those who emphasized the benefits of commercial engagement were less exercised by the possibility that exports of high technology might be used by the Chinese military against US interests than those who were more focused on the security aspects of engagement. The more immediate problem was that the policy encountered a roster of different responses from various groups that were influential in Congress. Human-rights groups continued to demand that China be treated more severely for its government's continuing suppression of dissent, ethnic minorities, independent religious groups, trade unionists and so on. Christian fundamentalists were highly critical of China's policies on the one-child family and especially on abortion. Others saw China as a growing military threat to American interests in Asia and as a proliferator of WMD. Against a background of generally unfavourable reporting on China by television, radio and the newspapers, there was a significant gap between the executive and the legislative branches of government on China policy.[32]

In February 1995 the United States released the East Asian Security Review (also known as the Nye initiative), which for the first time sought to sketch out American strategy for this part of the world in the post-Cold War period. It once again emphasized America's long-term commitment to the security of the region and underlined the importance of the alliance with Japan as being the vital structure for the American-directed security system in the region. Indeed it presented the alliance as an indispensable part of America's capacity to play its role as a global power. This was seen as non-controversial within the US and it also provided a rationale for re-energizing America's other alliances in the region, including those with Australia and even the Philippines.[33]

As part of the process of normalizing relations with Beijing, Washington followed a delicate policy of helping Taiwan to defend itself, while calling for a peaceful negotiated settlement between the two sides. Originally, US policy was based on the premise that the governments on both sides of the Taiwan Strait agreed there was but one China of which they were a part, but disagreed as to who was the legitimate government of the country. Taiwan at that point was still ruled by a dictatorial party (the KMT) that had come from the mainland in the late 1940s and had suppressed the local residents. As Taiwan democratized in the 1990s those circumstances changed. Much to the chagrin of Beijing, the KMT under the leadership of the local-born Lee Teng-hui began to stress the separate character of Taiwan as a democracy whose legitimacy was derived from the people of Taiwan. Beijing began to build a military capability to enable it to invade or at least attack the island as a deterrent against it becoming formally independent. At the same time, Beijing strongly suspected that the United States (or powerful groups within it) was tacitly encouraging separatist elements within Taiwan so as to prevent unification, keep China divided and block its emergence to its rightful place as a major power. For its part, the Clinton administration did not pay much attention to the issue in its early years. China had lost its strategic significance and its government was still treated with considerable reserve. Indeed, in keeping with some European allies, Washington had marginally upgraded the character of its representation on the island without regard to Beijing's views.[34]

In a context in which Deng Xiaoping had become incapacitated by advanced age, Jiang Zemin sought to stamp his authority on this major issue of the identity and unity of China by putting forward in January 1995 what were called his eight points for bringing about peaceful unification. Lee Teng-hui answered these in April, and it was then announced in May that a meeting between the (unofficial) representatives of the two sides would take place in Beijing in July. It was at this point that Clinton gave in to bipartisan pressure in Congress to allow Lee Teng-hui to make a private visit to his alma mater, Cornell University, in June to receive an honorary doctorate. Only a little earlier, Secretary of State Warren Christopher had assured his Chinese counterpart, Qian Qichen, that the visit would not take place. Contrary to what he had led his hosts to expect, Lee then delivered a highly political speech. Ever suspicious of Lee's possible separatist agenda, especially as Washington supposedly encouraged it, Beijing decided that it had to show that it was serious about its preparedness to use force to stop Taiwan from separating from the mainland. In July, amid a campaign of vilification of Lee, Beijing launched several missile salvos into the Taiwan Strait, some eighty-five miles north and south of Taipei, and it also conducted threatening military exercises on its side of the Strait.

Washington was alarmed by the deterioration of relations with China and attempted to show that the policy of engagement was still on course. The Chinese were given assurances that there would be no recurrence of visits such as that by Lee Teng-hui, although carefully circumscribed transit visits would still be allowed. A summit meeting was hastily arranged between Clinton and Jiang on the occasion of the latter's visit to the UN in October. But to no avail, as in November Beijing resumed its aggressive military exercises on its side of the Strait as part of its coercive diplomacy against supposed Taiwanese separatists. Indeed, it garnered some success from the election results for the Legislative Assembly in Taiwan that December when Lee's ruling party, the KMT, lost seats to the pro-unification New Party. As Washington was still trying to re-engage China, Beijing pressed what it saw as its advantage against an America that was supposedly loath to risk war casualties by threatening more military exercises and missile launches in the build-up to the first presidential elections in Taiwan that were due on 21 March. This time, however, Washington had no option but to respond, but it did so with care by announcing well in advance that two carrier battle groups would be deployed in the area (but not in the Strait itself) and letting both Beijing and Taipei know that the objective was 'precautionary'. Lee Teng-hui duly won the presidential election handsomely and the crisis quietly came to an end.[35]

The crisis proved to be something of a turning point for the Clinton administration's policy towards China. The management of the crisis was judged a success: 'A minimal show of force in the region ... work[ed] to reduce tensions, show American resolve, facilitate democracy on Taiwan, and leave room for making further improvements in U.S.–China relations.'[36] The crisis also alerted the administration to the need to pay more attention to China. But Congress and the wider public were more struck by what was seen as Beijing's bullying amid its egregious violation of its commitments on proliferation and intellectual property rights (IPR), as well as its deliberate suppression of human rights. A similar outcome resulted from the administration's seemingly irresolute handling of a case in which China allowed the shipment to Pakistan of 'ring magnets' used for the extraction of enriched uranium from uranium gas. A compromise was reached by which the US did not impose sanctions and the Chinese stated that they would not cooperate with unsafeguarded nuclear programmes. In Congress and the media it was claimed that the administration had once again caved in to business interests. But the administration saw it as a successful example of engagement in practice, whereby intensive negotiations led to a better understanding of each other's positions that then allowed for a settlement that saved face for both sides. Another example was provided by a deal over IPR that was achieved in June 1996 after protracted negations and posturing by both sides.[37]

However, Sino-American relations did not exist in isolation. In April 1996 President Clinton visited Japan, where he signed with Prime Minister Hashimoto a Joint Declaration on Security – 'Alliance for the 21st Century' – that called for a review of the 1978 guidelines about Japan's contribution to security in the Asia-Pacific. This had been a long time coming, as a result of the dissatisfaction on both sides about Japan's role in the 1991 Gulf War. The idea was to enable Japanese forces to contribute more effectively in support of US forces in the event of their being engaged in conflict in the region, especially in the case of Korea. Apparently, no thought had been given to the Taiwan issue in the course of the protracted negotiations. But Chinese military actions over Taiwan had alarmed the Japanese public and eased passage of the agreement through the Diet.[38] The Chinese reacted with hostility, claiming that the agreement was aimed at a containment of China and that it threatened China's sovereignty over Taiwan. Once again it demonstrated the difficulty in pursuing an integrated international strategic policy in the post-Cold War period. In particular, the problem was aggravated by a failure to think in terms of managing the triangular relations with Tokyo and Beijing.

The re-election of President Clinton in 1996 did little to narrow the gap between the administration's policies of engaging China and the domestic critics. Moreover, Clinton personally attracted partisan hatred to an unusual level and matters were not helped by his having to contend with a Republican-controlled Congress. His re-election was accompanied by scandals in which China-related figures were exposed as having illegally donated funds to the coffers of the Democratic Party. However, Sino-American relations began to improve substantively at the official level due in large part to the more determined effort by the Clinton administration to focus on engaging the country. Jiang Zemin paid a state visit to the US in October 1997. By this time China had signed the two UN conventions on human rights and had recovered Hong Kong without any of the upheavals or challenges to the Hong Kong way of life that had been much anticipated in the media. Jiang's visit was high in ceremonial symbolism, and the Chinese side appeared to regard it as a greater success than did the Americans. The Chinese appeared to think that the US had moved the greater distance in improving the relationship and that it recognized the success of China's reforms and that a rising China would be a force for the good. In the course of the visit it was agreed to 'build toward a constructive strategic partnership'.

Meanwhile, Congress for the most part sought to highlight the misdeeds and shortcomings of the PRC regime and the failure of the president to press harder for changes in China's behaviour.[39]

By this time the Asian financial crisis had struck. Washington, which was presiding over an expansive economy that was the leader in the information revolution, a prime beneficiary of globalization and the locomotive of the world economy, took a narrowly conceived orthodox economic approach. It insisted on the International Monetary Fund taking the lead in imposing austerity on the hard-hit economies. Washington ensured that the Japanese proposal of establishing an Asian monetary fund was turned down. The result was that for some East Asian countries the crisis led to massive downturns in their economies, the impoverishment of a nascent middle class and fundamental restructuring. Indonesia was particularly hard hit, leading to the fall of the government and almost to the break-up of the country as the result of religious and ethnic violence and separatist revolts. Consequently, it effectively lost its role as the bedrock of ASEAN, weakening the significance of the association still further. The Clinton administration, however, saw the issue through the prism of democratization and globalization, and took little heed of the geopolitical implications.[40] The financial crisis, however, contributed to the deterioration of the standing of the so-called Washington Consensus that called for deregulation, privatization, free markets and democracy as the cure-all for economic wellbeing regardless of the circumstances of the countries involved. The effects of Washington's handling of the Asian financial crisis were deleterious to American longer-term interests.

In 1998 Clinton reciprocated Jiang's visit by making a grand tour of China. Unlike such visits by previous presidents, he did not stop over in any other country and the duration of his nine-day visit was also without precedent. The visit was rich in symbolism, not least in terms of suggesting a new level of closeness in Sino-American relations by re-emphasizing the move towards establishing a 'constructive strategic partnership'. This was boosted by the two presidents jointly condemning India's tests of nuclear weapons and by the lavish praise given to China by senior American officials for not devaluing its currency during the Asian crisis, while at the same time blaming Japan for not doing more. Clinton also made a statement on Taiwan in which he went further than any previous president had done in public by expressing opposition to Taiwan joining any international organization where sovereignty was a requirement for membership, in addition to opposing the two standard possibilities of an independent Taiwan and a One China, One Taiwan (collectively known as the 'three noes'). Hitherto Clinton had confined his opposition to Taiwan's effort to join the UN. Both the statement about a strategic partnership and the three noes proved highly controversial back home. Congress meanwhile reeled under reports of China's illicit acquisition of American missile and nuclear weapons technology through spying activities and because of a presumed laxity in administering safeguards, in part allegedly as a consequence of donations to electoral funds by figures related to Chinese firms. In other words, there was insufficient domestic backing for the new spirit of partnership. The persecution by the Chinese authorities of the newly formed China Democracy Party was regarded in the US as demonstrating complete disregard for Clinton's message on human rights and as a bad mark against his policies. Moreover, there was disquiet in Japan, especially at having been 'passed by'. Typically, the Clinton administration had given little thought to the longer-term issues of managing the triangular relationship between Washington, Tokyo and Beijing. At times it seemed even to favour Beijing over Tokyo.[41] The joint condemnation by Clinton and Jiang of India's nuclear tests emphasized what was seen as the undue significance given to the new partnership with Beijing.

The adverse reaction at home to Clinton's visit presented the administration with the task of showing that the cultivation of special relations with Beijing was worthwhile. Much effort was then devoted in Washington to encouraging China to present finally a policy package that would make possible the country's entry to the World Trade Organization, which would accelerate the reform process in China and facilitate its deeper integration into the rules-based international economy. Such a development would be seen as a vindication of the policy of engagement; it would serve American commercial interests and take Sino-American relations to a new level. It was symptomatic of the difficulties the Clinton administration had in conducting relations with China that the issue was addressed against the backdrop of growing Chinese nationalist anger with the US, arising out of its air attacks against the former Yugoslavia, which began in late March 1999. This was seen as an example of what a hegemonic America might one day seek to inflict on China. The fact that this was done without the sanction of the UN Security Council in the name of humanitarian intervention intensified Chinese concerns. However, it was characteristic of Washington at that time to think of China as a regional rather than a global power, despite the rhetoric to the contrary. American actions in the Balkans were undertaken with hardly any thought given to their impact on China.

Apparently, Premier Zhu Rongji was able to visit Washington in April 1999 with a WTO package only after Jiang Zemin prevailed over considerable opposition among the leaders in Beijing. However, Clinton at first turned down Zhu's package of proposals, even though it met most of the American requirements, because he feared Congress would not accept it. The administration nevertheless published Zhu's proposals on the internet. Zhu returned to China having 'lost face' and he was subjected to criticism over the concessions made in his package. Less than a month later American planes bombed the Chinese embassy in Belgrade. Washington claimed the bombing was an accident, while most Chinese in and out of government claimed it was deliberate. The incident sparked off huge demonstrations in China, which to the dismay of many Americans were led by elite students who had access to Western sources of information, showing that those most exposed to Western influence could still be capable of articulating strong nationalistic and anti-Western sentiments. The incident was a major watershed for many Chinese, ending their illusions about American benevolence towards their country. Nevertheless China's leaders decided in the end that the main target for their patriotic ire would continue to be Japan.[42]

Meanwhile, further problems emerged in Sino-American relations as Congress released the lengthy Cox Report, detailing extensive alleged Chinese thefts of American military technological secrets. At the same time, Beijing's persecution of high-profile dissidents even before Clinton left China in 1998 demonstrated to many in Washington that Clinton's public endorsements of human rights had made no headway. Finally, Lee Teng-hui roiled the waters of cross-Strait relations on 9 July with his very public assertion that relations with the Chinese mainland constituted a 'a state-to-state relationship, or at least a special state-to-state relationship'. In Taipei it was claimed that Lee's statement had in part been prompted by Clinton's apparent leaning to the side of Beijing, as suggested by his three noes. In response to Beijing's suspicions that Washington may have had a hand in the matter, the Clinton administration expended considerable effort to reassure Beijing that it had played no part in this; and that it remained firmly attached to its 'One China policy'. At the APEC summit in September in Auckland, New Zealand, Clinton let Jiang know of his frustration with Lee Teng-hui and then pressed him on reviving the WTO agenda. Eventually, in November 1999, the breakthrough was made in Beijing and an agreement was reached.[43]

The significance of the dangers inherent in the acquisition of nuclear weapons by new powers was recognized in the course of the Indo-Pakistani armed conflict over Kargil, lest it should lead to escalation to the nuclear level. The Pakistani side had occupied territory on the Indian side of the Line Of Control and was eventually dislodged with difficulty by the massed Indian forces, but only after the Americans had mediated a diplomatic resolution. In addition to accentuating American concerns about the dangers of proliferation the crisis also alerted the United States to the importance of safeguarding the nuclear weapons of the two sides, especially that of Pakistan, to which the United States extended expert advice.

Clinton's last year as president was characterized by frenetic foreign policy activity as he sought to make his mark in history. He overcame considerable domestic opposition to steer successfully through Congress the necessary legislation in support of China's entry into the WTO, and notably in granting China Permanent Normal Trading Relations (PNTR was by this time preferred to the easily misunderstood Most Favoured Nation terminology). But in the end Beijing's harsh approach to the presidential elections in Taiwan in March 2000 and its blank refusal to respond in other than negative terms to any of the conciliatory signals offered by the victor, Chen Shui-bian, all had a negative impact on American views of China. Certainly Chen Shui-bian was the leader of the opposition party that had previously espoused independence and was therefore highly suspect in the eyes of Beijing. But, by the same token, having won in the teeth of Beijing's threats, he could hardly have been expected to knuckle down to Beijing's terms, and it behoved China's leaders to explore his tentative suggestion regarding 'One China', rather than dismiss it as 'lacking sincerity'. From an American perspective it was an 'opportunity missed'.[44] The popular American view of China was not improved by the spectacle of Beijing using all its dictatorial powers to suppress the Falun Gong movement. Denounced as a dangerous cult by Jiang Zemin, it was seen by most observers as just one of many Buddhist sects that had begun to flourish in China to fill the spiritual vacuum left by the decay of communist ideology. Few Americans saw China as a constructive partner, let alone a budding strategic one. Seventy-seven per cent of Americans polled in 2000 saw China as an adversary or a rival, with only 12 per cent regarding it as a friend or strategic partner.[45]

Clinton's last minute attempt to settle the North Korean issue through engagement and personal diplomacy also proved to be unsuccessful in the end. The euphoria of the summit meeting between the leaders of North and South Korea in June 2000 soon died, largely because of the refusal of the North to discuss possible tension-reducing measures with the South. The 'sunshine policy' of South Korean President Kim Dae Jong garnered little positive response from the North. It was in this context that the Clinton administration sought to develop its own policy of engaging the North. That weakened the sunshine policy as the North sought to bypass the South and deal with the US directly. The last three months of Clinton's presidency saw the second in command of the North's military being received in the Oval Office in the White House and the secretary of state, Madeleine Albright, being regaled with a propaganda extravaganza in praise of the North Korean leader in Pyongyang. Clinton himself would have gone too, had an agreement to end the North's missile programmes been reached before his leaving office in January 2001.[46]

However, the Clinton presidency's main legacy in the Asia-Pacific rested less on what might be called the standard political and security agenda and more on the newer agenda of globalization. Even so, the Clinton administration revitalized America's alliances with Japan, South Korea and Australia – the cornerstones for the American provision of security for the region as a whole. However, the more enduring legacy may turn out to be the promotion of globalization. That included encouraging structural economic reforms and supporting the new multilateral institution building in the region. It also addressed some of the non-traditional security threats, such as transnational crime and environmental challenges. Considerable effort was devoted to integrating China into international institutions involving proliferation and trade (such as the WTO). The administration also promoted democratization and human rights. It was committed as well to peacekeeping and peace enforcement. As we have seen, its efforts were not always crowned with success and its policies were often inconsistent. But, despite a fractious and often hostile Congress and an American public that was even less interested in the outside world than in the Cold War years, the Clinton administration persevered with its broad globalist agenda. Although it was not clearly spelt out and its implementation was often patchy and inconsistent, globalization and engagement can nevertheless be seen as underpinning much of the approach to Asia by the Clinton administration. This may have shaped much of the Clinton approach to China, which tried to balance engagement with an encouragement, often on pain of sanctions, to observe international norms on proliferation and to join relevant conventions and institutions, and to do likewise with regard to trade and economics. In that sense it contrasted sharply with the more realist approach of the incoming Bush administration, especially before 9/11.

The Bush presidency, the first term: from traditional strategy to the war on terrorism, 2001–4

The Bush administration came to office with a totally different approach, which was shaped largely by a group labelled variously as the 'neo-cons' or 'the Vulcans', who viewed the world in terms of a conflict between good and evil and sought an altogether more robust foreign policy in support of what they saw as the strategic interests of the United States and its allies. The influence of the 'neo-cons' was most evident in the first term of the Bush presidency and while it did not disappear entirely in his second term there was a significant change of tone and a greater appreciation of the virtue of diplomacy. Hence it is more than usually convenient to divide the analysis into two sections in accordance with his two terms.

In a number of highly publicized moves, President Bush made it clear that his main interest was in promoting what he saw as America's national interest, regardless of whether that coincided with existing international institutional practice. He was soon regarded with concern in Europe as a unilateralist who was causing a significant transatlantic rift. Unlike his predecessor, Bush had few troubles with Congress. But his administration was deeply divided between a Department of State that favoured on the whole a more diplomatic approach to foreign affairs and a Department of Defense that favoured a tough, assertive approach based on American manifest pre-eminence.

With regard to the Asia-Pacific, policy initially focused on cultivating relations with key allies, notably Japan, rather than emphasizing the engagement of China. As America's key strategic partner in the region, the administration refrained from hectoring its Japanese ally on the need to restructure the economy to overcome the long stagnation, as had been the tendency of the Clinton administration, and focused instead on encouraging Japan to play a more active security role in cooperation with the US. Wittingly or not, this emboldened the more nationalist side of the ongoing debate in Japan about its role in world affairs. However, relations with South Korea got off to a bad start because Bush was very much opposed to his predecessor's policy of engaging the North. For good measure he let it be publicly known how much he 'loathed' the North Korean leader for allowing his people to starve while he sought to acquire WMD.[47] Kim Dae Jong, the president of the South, suffered a setback when he was unable to elicit support for his sunshine policy during a visit to the White House. In many respects this set the tone for relations with the South. Washington appeared to be insensitive to a growing sentiment in favour of engaging the North, which in turn resulted in a certain resentment of the United States that played a part in the election of Kim's successor, Roh Moo Hyun.[48] That may be seen to have been illustrative of many of the problems the Bush administration began to encounter with long-standing allies, who were no longer as tightly bound by common perceptions of threat that existed during the Cold War.

At the outset Bush took a more sympathetic attitude towards Taiwan than his predecessor. He offered to sell the island a wider array of weaponry than had the

Clinton administration and in March 2001 the president went so far as to appear to break with the policy of 'strategic ambiguity' to declare that he would do 'whatever it takes' to defend Taiwan. Relations with China, however, did not deteriorate. This was partly because Bush did not repeat his campaign rhetoric of regarding China as a 'strategic competitor' and partly because China was coming to terms with American pre-eminence and it recognized that it could ill afford a major dispute with a robust America.

The administration's strategic overview prior to 9/11 was provided in the Quadrennial Defense Review.[49]According to the document, American forces would be restructured to meet the changes since the end of the Cold War by shifting from a 'threat-based' to a 'capabilities-based' planning. It further stated that America would preserve its global dominance and that it would be prepared to take a more proactive approach by being prepared to engage in pre-emptive war, while still being ready to defeat attacks and punish aggression. The main security challenge was identified as the rise of new major powers and, in parti-cular, there was the 'possibility' that 'a military competitor with a formidable resource base will emerge in the [Northeast Asian] region'. This was a clear reference to China, as Russia was treated as a potential partner.

In the event, the harsher approach to China did not materialize. In April the Bush administration confronted its first crisis, as a reconnaissance plane (an EP-3) had to make a forced landing on the Chinese island of Hainan after colliding with a Chinese jet plane that was buzzing it off the Chinese coast. The Chinese pilot was killed and became an instant hero, as a new tide of nationalism engulfed the country. The American plane and its crew were detained. After nearly two weeks of a diplomatic standoff, the American side issued a muted apology and the crew was released. The negotiations were conducted by the State Department, and it was a prelude to a less confrontational approach by the administration towards China than might have been expected given earlier statements. For one thing, Bush was scheduled to go to Shanghai in October for the annual APEC meeting, and neither the American nor the Chinese side wanted further trouble at this point.[50] As with the Taiwan crisis of 1996, so with this EP-3 crisis, the result was to persuade the Americans to pay more attention to Beijing and its concerns.

The impact of 9/11

The terrible attacks of 11 September 2001 changed America and its foreign policy almost overnight. Henceforth, in the words of its president, America was at war, and the question was whether others were for or against the US. It was a war of a different kind – a war against something identified as international terrorism and those states that harboured such terrorism – and it called for a readiness to engage in pre-emptive attack lest terrorists should strike, perhaps even with WMD. Deterrence was not feasible against groups with no fixed terri-tory, no fixed assets and no settled population for whom they were responsible. Concerns about the dangers of proliferation took on new dimensions, as the fear was not only that 'rogue states' might acquire terrible weapons, but also that they might fall into the hands of terrorists willing to use them against large concentrations of civilians in the US and other Western countries. Clearly, much of the previous foreign-policy thinking and strategic planning that had been developed in the previous few months had been superseded. Homeland security took on a new meaning and a new urgency. Intelligence and intelligence coordination with other countries acquired greater significance. It became necessary to cooperate with others on tightening financial controls, not only to prevent money laundering and possible disruption to the international financial order, but also to stop the flow of funds to terrorist organizations. Problems with failed states now went beyond concern about the spillover effects of disorder, famine, refugees and criminality, to include concern about their being havens for terrorists. Henceforth, the administration would seek partners according to the mission and would not allow adherence to a coalition or an alliance to determine the mission. Moreover, the war on terror would soon lead to a war against the Taliban regime of Afghanistan that harboured Al Qaeda and, more controversially, in 2003, to a war against the Saddam Hussein regime of Iraq.[51]

The administration changed course in its attitude to the major powers in Asia, namely Russia and India as well as China and Japan. Obviously, there was less change with regard to Japan, to whom as a long-standing ally the administration had already decided to pay more attention. But even with regard to Japan the approach shifted from cultivating it as a possible ally against a rising China to seeing it as a particularly close friend in a web of partnerships with other great powers. Instead of seeing the great powers as potential rivals in balance-of-power terms, the Bush administration sought to cultivate them as partners working in concert against the common threat of terrorism. Given the scale of American pre-eminence, the United States had little to fear of their combining against it under the framework of multipolarity, even though the leaders of the great powers during the later 1990s had from time to time claimed to favour this. In practice none of the great powers could afford to so alienate the United States as to risk America taking countermeasures against it. At the same time, the US recognized after 9/11 that it too needed their support and that it would be counter-productive for the United States to try to play the major powers off against each other. That in turn had the effect of reducing the significance of the attention paid by Washington to the points of difference and conflicts of interest that still remained with each of the powers.

Significantly, the major powers of Asia immediately recognized the scale of the change. Jiang Zemin acted with unprecedented speed for a Chinese communist leader in ensuring that his supportive telephone call to Bush reached him in Washington on that very day. Japan, of course, did so too. The Japanese Diet very quickly passed legislation demanded by Prime Minister Koizumi to enable the Self Defence Forces (SDF) to provide armed logistic support for the looming American campaign against the Taliban regime in Afghanistan. This was the first time since 1945 that Japan had dispatched its armed forces to participate in an armed conflict, and it involved naval vessels going through the waters of East and Southeast Asia. Later, in early 2004, Koizumi went even further in prevailing upon the Diet to allow a contingent of up to 1,000 soldiers from the SDF to be sent to Iraq to contribute to establishing order there. That would be the first time since the Pacific War that Japanese soldiers were sent to what was in effect a combat zone, where they might be attacked and forced to fire back. Moreover, they were not doing so under UN auspices![52]

Jiang Zemin used the occasion of the APEC meeting that was held in Shanghai barely one month after 9/11 to establish what was to become a new partnership with the US. Jiang set aside the prepared agenda to allow Bush to take it over with the issue of terrorism. From a US perspective it was important to have the support of China, the long-term ally of Pakistan and a major power in the region. China had its own fears of Islamic terrorism in Central Asia and it promised to provide intelligence and to support efforts to establish better controls over international finance in Hong Kong as well as its own banking system. The US, however, resisted Jiang's transparent attempts to tar all his adversaries (notably religious groups and 'separatists', such as Tibetans and Taiwanese) with the brush of terrorism. However, Bush agreed to characterize Sino-American relations as 'cooperative and constructive' and he also added the word 'candid', which was rarely cited in Chinese publications.[53] The following year the Chinese side met one of the prime American concerns about proliferation by introducing a legislative package that would enable the authorities finally to control the relevant exports from Chinese sources. The Americans reciprocated by recognizing a Muslim organization operating in Xinjiang as a terrorist one. That gave considerable legitimacy to China's suppression of alleged separatists in Xinjiang, which was universally condemned by human-rights groups in the West. The American designation of the organization as terrorist also helped to assure the Chinese that the US did not contest Chinese territorial bounds in Central Asia and that its forces deployed in the region would not be used in support of Muslim groups demanding more freedom from Beijing.

The Bush administration also developed new senses of partnership with India and Russia. Not only was India recognized as one of the great powers of the region, but its standing as a democracy enhanced its image in Washington, especially as its economy was becoming more open and market-orientated. The difficulty, of course, was being able to maintain good relations with the government of General Musharraf in Pakistan at the same time. The latter was vital to the American-led war and the attempt to establish a new order in Afghanistan. The assistance of Pakistan was also crucial in the struggle to subdue the remnants of the Taliban and Al Qaeda located in the borderlands between the two countries, where they enjoyed support from local tribes and elements of the Pakistani armed forces and intelligence organization (the ISI). Kashmir continued to be the key stumbling block between India and Pakistan. It had also become one of the core issues for Islamic extremists, who carried out terrorist acts in Kashmir and even in the Indian heartland. A summit meeting between the Indian and Pakistani leaders took place in July 2001, but it did not meet the expectations of either side and relations deteriorated to the point in 2002 that the two countries came close to war over Kashmir and the Bush administration played an important role in diffusing the crisis. China also played a role behind the scenes, both in giving reassurance to a Pakistan that was conscious of its vulnerabilities and in encouraging moderation. It was very much in America's interest to promote better relations between India and Pakistan and, indeed, the Bush administration was instrumental in encouraging the new phase, which was characterized by a summit meeting between the leaders of India and Pakistan in January 2004 that has led to further negotiations at lower levels.[54]

The relationship with Russia was complex and covered many issues and regions, but it touched on the Asia-Pacific only at the margins. The Bush administration cultivated Russia as an important partner in the war on terror, especially in Central Asia, where Russian influence over former members of the Soviet Union was still strong. American forces were able to operate bases in the region with Russian agreement. Russia had been committed to fighting Islamic extremism and terror long before 9/11, and it had no difficulty in supporting American efforts, gaining in return a significant reduction in American protests against excessive Russian use of force in Chechnya. Russia's agreement to engage in a major reduction of nuclear missiles in effect set aside its objections to the American withdrawal from the ABM treaty. That brought to an end Russia's common stand with China against the American intention to develop national and theatre systems of missile defence, which significantly strengthened the American hand in East Asia. For example, the Chinese found that they could no longer sustain their outright opposition to the Americans on ballistic missile defence and they had no alternative except to think in terms of negotiating with the US at some point, so as to try to ensure that Chinese interests would be taken into account.[55]

The single-minded emphasis on the war on terrorism won support in much of the rest of the region, but concern was raised about American lack of sensitivity to the local and regional context of terrorism in Southeast Asia. Malaysia and Indonesia, with majority Muslim populations, had long been concerned about the impact of more fundamentalist influences from the Middle East on their more tolerant and moderate forms of Islam. They had histories of inter-ethnic strife and of religious violence and they were mindful of the adverse influence on their Muslim population of American attacks on Muslim countries and of American support for Israel. The Philippines, as a predominantly Christian country, welcomed a degree of American military support and training against one Islamic group identified as terrorist with links to Al Qaeda, but the long-standing insurgency in Mindanao owed little to external support by fundamentalists, and there was concern from opposition parties that the government was using the 'war on terrorism' for its own local purposes.[56] Singapore, however, was more consistent in its support for Bush, especially as its security forces had uncovered a plot by an Indonesian-based Muslim group with links to Al Qaeda to try to establish an Islamic Republic to include Indonesia and Malaysia.[57] However, the dreadful bombings in Bali and the Marriott Hotel in Indonesia, in October 2002 and March 2003 respectively, finally brought home to the resident governments that they too faced a serious problem.

However, most of the governments of Southeast Asia were primarily concerned about their economic prospects, especially as they now faced a new economic challenge from China, barely after having recovered from the crash of 1997/ 1998. Continued economic growth was seen as vital in the difficult task of consolidating or even establishing order (for example in the case of Indonesia). Although they all looked to the US in one form or another as a kind of hedge against China, and although at this point they all still relied much more on the American than the Chinese market, they were nevertheless disappointed with the continuing exclusive focus on terrorism by the US government. Bush's address to the APEC Meeting in November 2003 said hardly anything about how America might respond to the transformative economic impact on the region of the rise of China. The contrast with China's new Premier Wen Jiabao, who touched on all the broad issues and offered reassurance and new forms of co-operation, could not have been more marked. Thus, although they recognized that terrorism did constitute a major threat, which required them to coordinate more effectively within ASEAN and also to work more closely with the US, they had other important needs that were not being addressed by the Bush administration.[58]

South Korea, like Japan, also contributed its forces to the war against Afghanistan. But the rancour over Bush's summary rejection of Clinton's policy of engaging the North, coupled with his refusal to endorse Kim Dae Jong's sunshine policy, which was already highly controversial in South Korean politics, created new divisions between the South and its huge ally. That had the effect of further weakening Kim's standing in Korean politics, where the scandals associated with his sons and the revelation that the North Korean leader had been given US$500 million to attend the June summit of 2000 severely damaged his sunshine policy, especially as it was deemed by most South Koreans to be one-sided, as the South poured hundreds of millions of dollars into the North without eliciting cooperative responses. At the same time, Bush's approach heightened dissatisfaction with America among the young, who had no memories of the Korean War and who associated American policy with support for the former discredited dictators. In particular, it sharpened objections by locals to the conditions of the status of American forces stationed in Korea, in the wake of an incident in June 2002 in which an American armoured vehicle had crushed to death two Korean girls. American–South Korean relations were hardly helped by the fact that the incoming President Roh Moo Hyun won his election by exploiting the mood of hostility to the US. In a context in which the value of South Korean trade with China had begun to exceed its trade with the US and in which the Korean economy was becoming more closely linked with China, it seemed that the South was no longer as dependent on the United States. It was developing more freedom of diplomatic manoeuvre than had previously been the case, both in engaging the North and in exploring new relations with other regional powers, notably China. Nevertheless, when pressed, President Roh also persuaded his parliament to allow South Korean troops to participate in the effort to bring order to Iraq after the 2003 war.[59]

The two regional hot spots

Like President Clinton before him, President Bush had to contend with the eruption of crises in the Korean peninsula and across the Taiwan Strait. Neither had come to office with the intention of addressing either of these long-standing problems. Products of the Cold War, the Korea and Taiwan problems involved highly complex combustible mixes of remnants of civil war confrontations, systemic differences between democracies and tyrannies, regional rivalries, and differences of interest between the great powers, with the heavy commitment of the United States.

The greatest problem that confronted the Bush administration in the Asia-Pacific was how to deal with the nuclear programme of North Korea – a country Bush had listed in his State of the Union address of January 2002 along with Iraq and Iran as belonging to the 'axis of evil'. The administration came to office dissatisfied with the policy of engagement of the previous administration, which was seen as not having produced the necessary commitment from the North to end its medium to long-range missile programme and its missile sales. Many within the administration also disliked the Framework Agreement of 1994, on the grounds that it was based on giving in to blackmail and that in any case it was not working. But the administration was deeply divided on what alternative policy it might pursue. On the one side were those (mainly in the Department of Defense) who argued that there was no point in negotiating, as the North would never give up its nuclear card – its only 'deterrence' and guarantor of survival – and that sooner or later the US would have to press for a change of regime that would probably require the use of force, but would certainly require the application of sustained pressure on the North. In Vice President Cheney's famous words, 'We don't negotiate with evil. We defeat it.' Against that it was argued that the risks of warfare were too high. In addition to the artillery threat to the 20 million people who lived in Greater Seoul, the problems in dealing with the aftermath of a Northern collapse would be unacceptably high and the potential for a chaotic and disastrous outcome in Northeast Asia as a whole was very real. Hence the only path immediately open was that of negotiation. In any event, the American military commitments in Iraq and to a lesser extent in Afghanistan ruled out the option of carrying out any major military attacks on the North, at least for the time being.[60]

Bush froze discussions with the North until a review of relations reported in June 2001. On the basis of the review, Bush said that he would negotiate without preconditions, but that the agenda would focus on the North's implementation of the 1994 Framework Agreement, on verifiable constraints of missile development, on a ban on the export of missiles and on reducing the North's threatening conventional military posture. The North rejected this as a demand for its unilateral disarmament, and insisted that it was necessary for American forces to be withdrawn from the South before it would discuss such matters. Meanwhile, talks should address the compensation due to the North for delays in completing the two light water reactors scheduled for 2003, in accordance with the

1994 agreement. A standoff ensued, which was not breached during Bush's visit to South Korea in February 2002, despite his belated endorsement of Kim Dae Jong's sunshine policy, for the American president added that he could not trust a leader who starved his own people and again accused the North of being evil.

However, the North had reason to open talks with the US in order to try to diffuse the threat the regime perceived it was under, especially because of the new American doctrine of pre-emption. It also needed to keep its door open if it was to receive the additional economic aid that it continually required. Preliminary contact was made between the two foreign ministers at the ninth ARF meeting in July, and in October 2002 the American Assistant Secretary of State for East Asian and Pacific Affairs, James Kelly, visited Pyongyang, where apparently he received confirmation (later denied) of American intelligence that the North was developing a uranium enrichment programme. Seeing that as evidence of the North's duplicity over the Framework Agreement, the US promptly suspended the supply of heavy fuel oil and the work on the light water nuclear reactors. The North then withdrew from the Non-Proliferation Treaty, discharged the international inspectors and announced that it would begin work to extract plutonium from the 8,000 fuel rods that had been sealed by the inspectors. Thereafter it claimed that it had to develop a deterrent against an American attack and argued that it would only freeze and then abandon its nuclear programme if the US would first guarantee it against attack, provide it with aid, end sanctions and normalize relations.

Talks only became possible in the end after the Chinese had brought pressure to bear on the North, allowing them to broker talks between the North and the US in Beijing in April 2003. At this point the US refused to accept that threats arising out of the North's nuclear and missile programmes were exclusively an American concern and insisted that all the regional states under immediate threat should participate in the talks. A meeting duly took place in Beijing in August 2003 under the chairmanship of China that included South Korea, Japan and Russia, as well as North Korea and Japan. The parties simply stated their positions and agreed to meet again. By this stage, concerned about the problem of proliferation of WMD technology and missiles by the North, the Bush administration established the Proliferation Security Initiative to allow the inspection of ships suspected of carrying illicit cargo from North Korea. Although such inspections could only take place within the territorial waters of states and not on the high seas the PSI increased the pressure on the North.

A second set of meetings took place in Beijing in February 2004. In principle, an agreement was possible if the North would agree to stop its nuclear programme, and allow for the complete, verifiable and irreversible dismantling of the programme in return for acceptable security guarantees from the US and its neighbours and the provision of sufficient economic 'compensation' or aid. That would lead to the normalization of relations with the North, including the removal of sanctions and the development of economic relations. However, the depth of distrust between the two sides suggested that there could be no early resolution.[61]

Both the strengths and weaknesses of America's pre-eminence in the Asia-Pacific were demonstrated by the impasse over Korea at the end of Bush's first term. It was principally up to the United States to determine an outcome to the Korean problem, even though its regional neighbours would be the first to feel its effects. But, as already noted, American superior military force could not be used, except in response to a Northern attack, otherwise the 15 million people of the greater Seoul area would be at the mercy of the Northern thousands of pieces of artillery deployed within range. Since the Bush administration did not want to negotiate bilaterally with the North, the only alternatives, whether regime change in the North or the pursuit of a peaceful settlement through negotiations, would only be possible with the assistance of China. China's interests on the Korean peninsula did not fully coincide with those of the US. The impact on the South would be grave, as it would undermine the hopes of building on the policy of engagement to reach a lasting accommodation. From an American perspective the nuclearization of the North not only raised the prospect of turmoil in this dangerous part of the world, where divergent interests of the great powers intersected, but also raised global issues related to the war on terror. In addition to the possible use of WMD by the North against American bases and other facilities within range, the North could be the provider of WMD to other rogue states or even terrorist organizations. But the North was principally concerned with the US, which alone threatens the survival of its regime. The United States, however, found it useful to bring its allies and partners collectively to confront the North. Thus, despite its overwhelming power and its position as the hegemon of the global system, the US has found itself severely constrained.

Taiwan surfaced as a potential crisis in the autumn of 2003 in the build-up to the presidential elections due on 20 March 2004. The incumbent president, Chen Shui-bian, declared his intention to change the constitution by a referendum. Few disputed that the present constitution was unsatisfactory, particularly in its failure to specify clear checks and balances between the executive and legislative branches of government, which had led to a deadlock between the two for much of the Chen presidency. But what roiled Beijing was the choice of the instrument of a referendum, as it was seen as a move towards basing the claim to sovereignty on the people of Taiwan alone. The existing constitution was promulgated on the Chinese mainland in 1947 by the then-ruling Kuomintang (KMT) before it evacuated to Taiwan, and it is based on the principle of one China, of which Taiwan is a part. Beijing saw the proposed referendum as an underhand attempt to establish a base in preparation for formal independence.

Washington understood that Taiwan was the one issue on which the leaders in Beijing believed they could not compromise, without risking their hold on office. While Beijing might be willing to leave a negotiated settlement until circumstances might be propitious, it was unwilling to tolerate developments that would block eventual unity and it was thought to regard any formal separation of the island as an independent state as a cause for war.

As noted earlier, Beijing did not react with immediate animosity to the early policy of the Bush administration to be more protective towards Taiwan and to supply it with more advanced weaponry. There was an implicit acceptance by both Washington and Beijing of a status quo across the Taiwan Strait, by which Beijing would not attack and Taiwan would not become formally independent. However, when the president of Taiwan breached this understanding, Beijing looked to Washington in the first instance to keep him in check. Despite being sympathetic towards Taiwan, President Bush, on receiving Premier Wen Jiabao in December 2003, publicly chided Chen for 'indicat[ing] that he may be willing to make decisions unilaterally to change the status quo, which we oppose'.

Chen then backtracked somewhat and declared that the referendum on 20 March would be confined to registering the need to defend against Beijing's nearly 500 missiles targeted at the island, and a second one would be about the desirability of peaceful negotiations. The apparent compromise satisfied neither Beijing nor Washington, as it still left open the prospect of a victorious Chen retuning to a referendum on the constitution at a later date, as he had indicated that he might. But the nub of the problem had now shifted to Washington, in the sense that Taipei relied on Washington to deter Beijing and Beijing turned to Washington to restrain Taipei. One difficulty for Washington stemmed from not allowing its broader policy towards China to be held hostage to Taiwan, while simultaneously seeking to restrain a democracy without undermining it through excessive intervention or even creating adverse reactions. Another difficulty arose from divisions within the Bush administration, as well as historically between Executives that had many reasons to maintain good relations with Beijing and successive Congresses that were critical of Beijing and inclined to favour Taiwan, especially once it had democratized. Once again, the limitations of American power were evident. America's predominance may be said to have enhanced its stake in cross-Strait relations, and arguably recent developments had brought it nearer to the unwanted role of being an arbiter. But the constraints on American action meant that it could do little more than react to the unpredictable initiatives by Taipei and Beijing, which in turn were driven by domestic imperatives.[62]

Bush's second term: the reassertion of diplomacy, 2005–8

Although the Bush administration became bogged down in the wars in Iraq and Afghanistan to the loss of massive resources and American prestige throughout the world, its standing in the Asia-Pacific had not been affected so badly. From 2005 onwards, multilateralism was no longer disparaged and the doctrine of pre-emption was quietly dropped. Diplomacy returned as a key instrument of foreign policy. It was as if the hubris of 2002 and 2003 were replaced by nemesis in 2005. Personnel changes also played a part in encouraging this less confrontational approach: Several of the key neo-cons departed; and the appointment of Condoleezza Rice to replace Colin Powell as Secretary of State, who unlike the former was trusted by President Bush as a close confidante, ensured that consideration of diplomatic options received a more sympathetic hearing.[63]

Bush's second term was marked in the Asia-Pacific by a great deal of continuity with his first. Good relations were maintained with allies and relations with China remained cordial and if anything the relationship thickened. At the same time Bush developed a 'strategic partnership' with India and succeeded in persuading the US Congress and the Nuclear Suppliers Group to reach agreements allowing India to import peaceful nuclear materials. The Chinese side was not best pleased, but took care not to allow the deal to spoil its relations with the US.

North Korea

A new readiness to negotiate with the North became apparent in 2005. Yet divisions in Washington persisted in part because of the lingering effects of the neo-cons and in part because of continuing turf wars between bureaucracies, which remained a barrier against developing direct talks with the North. In effect the Bush administration became dependent on China to continue to convene the Six Party Talks (6PT) for the conduct of the formal negotiations, even though, as we have seen, American and Chinese interests on the Korean peninsula over-lapped in some ways and diverged in others. The Bush administration, however, continued to send mixed signals, with Bush and Rice disparaging Kim Jong-Il and his regime on the one side, and expressing a readiness to resume the 6PT on the other. In the end it took a personal initiative by the US chief negotiator Christopher Hill to enable diplomacy to restart.[64] On 19 September 2005 a Declaration was issued laying out the principles agreed between the US, North Korea and the other four parties on resolving the nuclear issue. However, mixed signals on the US side continued as a harder-line statement was issued from Washington. Meanwhile, operating without much reference to the State Depart-ment, the US Treasury announced that it had targeted a small bank in Macau for money laundering and corrupt activities on behalf of North Korea. The resulting sanctioning of the bank had the effect of stopping all other banks from dealing with the North and of causing the impounding of US$25 million belonging to the North. With tensions mounting the North Koreans first tested missiles including the long-range Taepodong in July 2006, which led the UNSC to issue a sanctions resolution against the North. But on 9 October, the North carried out a nuclear test and, presumably to satisfy its Chinese ally, it then declared that it was still committed to the denuclearization of the Korean peninsula. Yet another UN Sanctions resolution was passed, but like the first, the resolution was neither mandatory, nor did it provide a basis for the use of force.

The Americans had tried to use the Chinese to bring pressure to bear on the North and indeed the Chinese Premier Wen Jiabao had called for 'restraint'. The Chinese were outraged by the nuclear test and denounced the North's behaviour as 'brazen' – a term usually reserved for imperialists and other enemies. Concerned about possible reactions in South Korea and Japan, the US government immedi-ately reassured both allies of the continued viability of its extended deterrence in order to obviate moves by either to acquire its own nuclear deterrent. The Chinese side soon cooled its anger with the North and began to press the US to show flex-ibility to enable all sides to return to the 6PT.[65] The North insisted, however, that first the sanctions on the Macau bank be lifted and that the US$25 million be returned to Pyongyang. This led to bilateral negotiations with the US which the Bush administration had long resisted and an agreement in Berlin that supposedly would lead to a deal designed to end the North's nuclear programme. That in turn led to complex negotiations in Beijing resulting in an agreement to curtail the nuclear programme by stages linked to the provision of fuel oil. It amounted to Bush accepting a 'freeze' by the North and an agreement similar to Clinton's Framework Agreement, which he had dismissed on becoming president in 2001. US officials claimed that the new agreement went further as it committed the North to dismantling its nuclear facilities; that the phasing of the fuel supplies meant that the bulk would be delivered at the end, once the North had carried out its part of the bargain; and finally that the agreement involved all members of the 6PT. However, the deal was denounced by the supporters of Bush's previous tough stand and others were quick to point out that for all the tough talk of the previous five years the North now had a nuclear device, with enough plutonium to make up to ten bombs.[66]

The North did shut down its nuclear reactor at Yongbyon, even blowing up the water cooler tower. In October the State Department removed the North from its list of state sponsors of terrorism. But the process of implementing agreements about verification and the phasing of aid proved to be difficult and the North Korean refusal in December 2008 to accept a Chinese-drafted agreement led to an American refusal to supply the fuel that would have followed the agreement, and that in turn led to the North restarting its nuclear programme.[67] Arguably, Bush's diplomatic approach to the North may have been more successful had it not been delayed by his initial hard line of the previous four to five years, and even in the ensuing years to the end of his presidency Bush's new approach was still plagued by divisions within his ranks. There is no doubt that the mixed signals from the Bush administration accentuated the paranoia in Pyongyang about the American threat to the survival of the regime. As against that, it can also be argued that a regime which was either unwilling or incapable of carrying out economic reform along the lines of China or Vietnam would most likely have continued to develop a nuclear weapons programme as the ultimate deterrent against foreign adversaries. In any event, American options were limited as the vulnerability of the 20 million people in Greater Seoul to North Korean artillery made a military attack to enforce a change of regime out of the question.

Relations with allies

The way the Bush administration dealt with the North had a deleterious effect on relations with both the South Korean and Japanese allies, but not to the extent of putting the alliance in jeopardy, as may be seen from the fact that both sets of governments contributed to the wars in Iraq and Afghanistan despite popular opposition.

During the first phase of the administration's approach (2001–4) Kim Dae Jong and his successor Roh Moo-Hyun felt ignored. Bush had little time for their 'sunshine' polices of engaging the North and took no account of the divergence between his view of the North as a member of the 'axis of evil' and the majority view in the South, which regarded the North as 'errant cousins', or at any rate as members of the same family. Indeed Roh's election to the presidency was due in no small part to a climate of anti-Americanism, especially among younger voters who had no experience of the 1950–53 war and who tended to regard the invocations of the 'threat from the North' by the military dictators and conservatives prior to Kim Dae Jong's election in 1998 as little more than thinly disguised excuses to shore up their rule. Previous American governments were regarded as complicit in that exercise. The divergence between the US and its Southern ally created difficulties for the alliance. Some members of Roh's cabinet openly contemplated moving closer to China, whose economy was becoming more important to the South than that of the US.

Fortunately for the alliance, the Chinese at that point alienated Korean nationalist sentiments in 2004 by issuing a government-sponsored study claiming that the ancient kingdom of Koguryo which spanned the territory of Korea and northeastern China had been a part of China, thereby denying the Korean claim that the kingdom was one of the founders of the Korean state. Concerns about possible Chinese goals of subordinating its Korean neighbour also emerged from a new rivalry between China and South Korea for economic influence over the North.[68] But relations between the Bush and Roh administrations were not easy: Roh feared American belligerence against the North and persuaded Washington, despite misgivings by both sets of military, to agree in due course to transfer Operations Command of their joint forces to the South. At one point Roh sought to develop a more independent role for South Korea as a 'balancer' among the great powers and he even contemplated having the American nuclear umbrella withdrawn.[69] Perhaps it was also fortunate from the American perspective that the behaviour of the North towards its benefactors to the South was always negative. The missile tests of the summer of 2006 began to change attitudes in the South. The election of the more conservative Lee Myung Bak in December 2007 was a turning point in North–South relations. Lee did not share his predecessor's views of the benefits of the engagement with the North and began to cut back on economic assistance. The North in turn denounced him in shrill terms. The new atmosphere provided the basis for improving the strategic relations between the US and its South Korean ally. But although relations between Bush and his South Korean ally may have ended on a happier note, the relationship also demonstrated that it was contingent on domestic developments within the South and the Southern response to behaviour by the North and by China.

American relations with Japan were also affected by differences over Korea, but unlike the Clinton presidency, the Bush administration seemed to manage to engage China without disturbing the Japanese ally.[70] Notwithstanding the close personal relations between President Bush and Prime Minister Koizumi, the latter visited Pyongyang twice in September 2002 and again in May 2004 after extensive secret negotiations, which were not disclosed to Bush, although he was informed shortly before the visit. Koizumi and the subsequent Prime Ministers Abe, Fukuda and Aso complained about what they regarded as the failure to be

fully consulted by the Bush administration on its dealings with the North. Fukuda
in particular felt marginalized by Bush's removal of the North from the list of
states sponsoring terrorism as that overlooked the significance of the Japanese
abductees. The Japanese government also complained about being left in the
dark by Christopher Hill's conduct of negotiations with the North and with China
in the lead-up to 6PT meetings. At times the Bush administration was irritated by
the priority given by the Japanese to the question of the abductees, when from an
American perspective major national security issues were at stake, including the
prospect of the proliferation of WMD by the North ending up in the hands of
terrorist organizations.[71] A further problem for the US arose out of the differences between Japan and South Korea over the latter's dealings with the North.
Japanese took more seriously the missile threat from the North, especially after
one of its missiles overflew the main island of Japan to land only several hundred
miles away in the Pacific Ocean. The two also had difficulties in agreeing upon
an historical evaluation of the Japanese annexation of Korea (1910–45) and the
disputed sovereignty of islands off the Korean coast.[72]

The differences between the South and Japan and between the US and each
of them respectively loosened their alliances with the US without undermining
them. Neither had a viable alternative to the alliance as a means of hedging
against China, whom they distrusted all the more due to its rapidly growing
military might, and to its failure to deal more robustly with a desperate and belligerent North Korea. As noted earlier, successive governments in the South and
in Japan responded positively to American requests to assist in the wars in Iraq
and Afghanistan. An additional sign of the strength of the alliance was the
agreement of Japanese and American Ministers of Defence at the Security
Consultative Committee in October 2005 that *inter alia* they both sought a
peaceful resolution to the Taiwan problem – an agreement that was much criticized by Beijing. Moreover, after complex negotiations over a five-year period
the US and Japan agreed on 11 July 2006 on a plan to relocate some of the US
marines from Okinawa to the island of Guam and to remove the base from urban
Futenma to a less populated site in the island.

China

During the last four years of Bush's presidency it became clear that the United
States was coming to terms with the rapidity of China's rise as an economic and
political global player, which transcended the regional limitations of its growing
military power – even though aspects of that growth troubled Washington. Since
China's embrace of economic reform in the late 1970s the United States had
played an active role in encouraging it to become a member of the international
system and the time had come, in the words of Deputy Secretary of State Robert
Zoellick in September 2005, 'to urge China to become a responsible stakeholder
in that system', so the two great powers could tackle the wide-ranging global
problems that lay ahead and reduce their mutual distrust.[73] This was a theme
that was to be central to President Obama's initial approaches to China. But the

Chinese reacted cautiously to the 'stakeholder' idea, as many saw it as an invitation to follow American leadership (or hegemony) in world affairs. It was one thing for China's leaders to embrace the concept of being a 'responsible power', which they could define as they wished, but it was quite another to accept an American concept as to how responsibility could be defined.

On the whole American relations with China deepened in many respects during these four years. The US continued to rely on China's governorship of the 6PT to drive forward the negotiations over North Korea's nuclear programme and it expressed appreciation for the Chinese role in reaching the agreements of 2005 and 2007, even though they did not lead to success as the North refused to allow proper inspection and verification of the ending of the programme. Bush prevailed in the end over the hardliners in his administration, who did not accept Chinese claims about the limits of their influence over the North and about their inability to bring greater pressure upon their North Korean ally.[74]

The deeper and wider relationship was evident from the new high-level institutionalized dialogues begun by the two sides in this period. In 2005 Zoellick launched a senior-level dialogue on strategic issues and the following year Secretary of the Treasury Henry Paulson initiated the US-China Strategic Economic Dialogue. Both met twice a year with the participation of high-level officials. The latter became the vehicle for the expression of American complaints about what they regarded as unfair practices that led to American job losses. In particular they continually cited the undervalued Chinese currency – even though the Chinese allowed a slow appreciation from 2005–8 that amounted to about 20 per cent. Other regular complaints included Chinese failure to implement laws on intellectual property rights and insufficient attention being paid to the safety of food, toys and so on. Various exchanges between the military also took place, including visits by leading military officers, port visits by naval ships and even a joint naval exercise for sea rescue, but the US side remained dissatisfied by the inadequacies of Chinese military transparency and by the sense that the Chinese side did not allow American visitors the same level of access to military facilities and knowhow as was given to Chinese visitors. Washington was particularly concerned by the Chinese anti-satellite test of February 2007 involving the destruction by a missile of a worn-out satellite. No warning or information was given about the test, which had profound implications for American satellite-based communications. In fact the Foreign Ministry denied all knowledge for two weeks following the test, raising further questions about civilian control of the military.

The Taiwan issue was less divisive than in the past, even though the Americans brought pressure to bear on their EU allies in 2005 not to lift the embargo on sales of arms to Taiwan, and Beijing's adoption that year of a law against cession was deemed 'unhelpful' by the State Department. Bush's decision to seek Congressional approval for the sale of arms to Taiwan evoked only pro forma objections from Beijing. The key issue from Beijing's point of view was that Bush regarded the Taiwan President Chen Shui-bian as a troublemaker and it was felt that Bush could be relied upon to thwart his attempts to promote the island's independence. Beijing in turn tacitly accepted Bush's insistence that Beijing would not use force to try and settle the issue. The election of the KMT candidate, Ma Ying-jeou, to the presidency in March 2008 had the effect of removing Taiwan as a contentious issue in Bush's last year in office.

However, strategic rivalry was evident between China and America, as indicated by Bush's readiness to spend considerable domestic political capital in consolidating the 'strategic partnership' with India that he announced in the course of his visit there in March 2006. In his last year in office Bush overcame considerable opposition in Washington to ensure the passage of a bill allowing India access to civil nuclear materials despite its long-standing unwillingness to sign the Non-Proliferation Treaty. He also promoted official international acceptance of this through the Nuclear Suppliers Group, which took place despite discreet lobbying against it by China. Bush's cultivation of a strategic relationship with India was regarded in Beijing as an attempt to balance against China. Nevertheless that did not undermine the cordiality of China's official relations with Washington, demonstrating that Beijing did not wish to weaken a relationship that was regarded as serving its core interests of facilitating economic growth, maintaining good relations with neighbours and therefore helping to sustain continued rule by the Communist Party. But as Bush came to the end of his presidency, the scale of the American financial crisis became clear, especially if coupled with the cost of the ongoing two long wars in Iraq and Afghanistan, the cost of which in Iraq alone was calculated in March 2008 at $3 trillion and rising at $12 billion a month – $16 billion if Afghanistan were included.[75] No wonder that many in Beijing concluded that this time the United States had really begun the process of relative decline. Overall it was not a good legacy to pass on to President Obama, despite Bush's relative success in this region.

The Obama presidency

President Obama brought to his office enormous worldwide personal popularity that stood in stark contrast to the low standing of his predecessor. Because of his early years in Indonesia and his later home in Hawaii Obama described himself as America's 'first Pacific president'. He saw himself as a 'game changer', who would demand of all countries that they accept in equal measure their rights and responsibilities in the international system. He put less stress on the promotion of democracy than Bush and his chief of staff, Emanuel Rahm, has described Obama as less of an idealist and 'probably more realpolitik, like Bush 41'.[76] The National Security Strategy published under his name in May 2010 called for collective action to serve the 'common interest' of combating violent extremism; non-proliferation; balanced and sustainable economic growth; meeting the challenges of climate change, armed conflict and pandemic disease. It called for engagement with friends and allies, but declared that 'we are working to build deeper and more effective partnerships with other key centers of influence including China, India and Russia' and others including Brazil, South Africa and Indonesia.'[77]

In his first year in office Obama sought out China in particular as a partner for the United States in addressing the crucial global challenges of the financial crisis, non-proliferation and climate change. Unlike previous presidents, he was determined to start relations with China on a good footing. His Secretary of State, Hilary Clinton, explained on her first visit to Asia in February 2009 why human rights would not figure large in her dealings with China's leaders: 'our pressing on these issues can't interfere with the global economic crisis, the global climate change crisis and the security crisis.'[78]

Obama's own visit to China in November 2009 sought to underscore what he saw as the new partnership with China, described by some in Washington as the G-2. Presidents Hu and Obama issued a lengthy Joint Statement listing many areas where they would cooperate. But that proved to be the highpoint of the Sino-American partnership. Not only was their cooperation not much in evidence at the much-vaunted international climate change conference in Copenhagen, but also a relatively junior Chinese official berated President Obama at one point.[79]

In fact the Chinese had indicated throughout the year that, while they were pleased to be described by American leaders as global partners, they were not interested in signing up to such a partnership – still less on American terms. Earlier in the year China's leading bank official had called for a new reserve currency to be based on the IMF Special Drawing Rights and the Chinese Premier Wen Jiabao publicly called on the US to safeguard Chinese reserves and investments in the US dollar. Meanwhile the Chinese had re-pegged their currency to the dollar and refused American requests to revalue or to take other steps to reduce the enormous American trade deficit with China. American companies were increasingly complaining that they were being discriminated against in the Chinese domestic market. The Chinese in effect focused on their own national interest and Hu Jintao demanded of Obama that he respect Chinese 'core interests', defined as Taiwan, Tibet and Xinjiang, to which was added the Chinese claims in the South China Sea. In fact in March 2009 Chinese vessels had harassed an American naval ship in the South China Sea for operating in China's Exclusive Economic Zone (EEZ), which the Americans claimed was legally in international waters, whereas the Chinese self-serving interpretation of international law denied this.[80]

Relations took a downturn in early 2010 as the Chinese responded unusually sharply to the White House's announcement to Congress of its intention to sell US$6.5 billion's worth of defensive weapons to Taiwan and the announcement that Obama would meet the Dalai Lama in March, having put off such a meeting in October 2009 out of deference to Chinese sensibilities. The Chinese also took exception to Hilary Clinton's support of the position Google took to withdraw from China on account of censorship. As an article in the *China Daily* put it, 'in 2009 the Sino-American relationship was too good to be true'. Articles appeared in the Chinese press quoting senior military officers and the public at large calling for taking a hard line against the US. In the United States and in Japan and Southeast Asia the view was that China had become unusually assertive.[81]

It seemed at one point that mutual expectations had moderated and on the sidelines of the G-20 meeting in Canada in June Hu Jintao accepted Obama's invitation to a formal state visit later in the year. In one respect their relationship had benefitted greatly from the election of the KMT leader Ma Ying-jeou to the presidency in March 2008. From Beijing's perspective Taiwanese independence had been taken off the table as both sides of the Taiwan Strait were able to reach many agreements on expanding economic, social, cultural and educational exchanges, culminating in the landmark Economic Cooperation Framework Agreement (ECFA) of 29 June 2010, designed to lower tariffs on their two-way trade of $150 billion and improve market access in services. Although the core of the problem continued to exist, both sides were prepared to leave it to be addressed sometime in the distant future.[82]

Relations with Japan under the newly elected Democratic Party of Japan headed by Premier Yukio Hatoyama proved to be difficult. Having been elected with a huge majority the DPJ eclipsed the LDP, which had ruled almost uninterruptedly for more than fifty years, the party leaders had little or no experience in government and did not enjoy the familiarity with Washington of the LDP. Although Hatoyama claimed that the alliance with the US was central to Japanese foreign policy he demanded that it should be based on equality, in accordance with his election pledges. But it was not clear what this entailed. He also sought closer relations with China and the establishment of an ill-defined Asian community to be based on what he called 'yuai' (fraternity), which was also unclear. Meanwhile, much to the chagrin of Washington, he sought to renegotiate the 2006 agreement about the relocation of the US Marine base in Futenma, Okinawa – again to satisfy an electoral pledge to the people of Okinawa, who were aroused by the prospect. The issue roiled relations for the best part of a year until he accepted the core of the original agreement in June and promptly resigned. The new Prime Minister Naoto Kan proved to be made of sterner mettle and established a more amicable relationship with the Obama administration. Nevertheless, in the previous year the relatively harsh treatment of a democratic ally that was said to be the cornerstone of America's strategic presence in the region and beyond was contrasted unfavourably with what was seen as Obama's courtship of China.[83] What helped to bring the relationship back to an even keel was the behaviour of China and North Korea.

North Korea had greeted the advent of the Obama administration with missile tests in April, in contravention of a UNSC resolution, and then announced its withdrawal from the 6PT in response to the international condemnation. It then conducted its second nuclear test on 25 May, which led to the imposition of further sanctions by the UNSC in June. The North responded with the launching of another round of missiles in July. Despite having co-signed the UNSC resolution on sanctioning the North, the Chinese Prime Minister Wen Jiabao visited Pyongyang in October and signed several economic agreements, which at least violated the spirit, if not the letter, of the sanctions resolution, with the effect of reducing such impact as they may have had on the government in Pyongyang. The Obama administration, having vowed to make no concessions to Pyongyang

in order to bring it back to the 6PT and face up to its commitments on denuclearization of 2005 and 2007, had become in effect dependent on China to coax
the North back to the 6PT. Not surprisingly, no progress had been registered by
the time of writing in July 2010.

The sinking of a South Korean ship, the *Cheonan*, by a North Korean torpedo
on 26 March 2010 near the disputed Northern Limit Line in the West Sea, as
confirmed by an international inspection team, created trouble for the North and
for China. The North denied any responsibility and the Chinese, having delayed
by a month sending their condolences for the deaths of forty-six sailors, continuously called for restraint and the maintenance of stability, but refused either
to examine the report of the inspection team or to condemn the North. Consequently China alienated both the South Korean and Japanese governments and
created difficulties for Sino-American relations. By demonstrating that it placed
its own narrowly conceived national interest in sustaining the regime in the North
above regard for what was seen by America and its Asian allies as the North's
reckless behaviour regarding the testing and proliferation of WMD, made even
worse by its provocative sinking of a South Korean ship and the ratcheting up
of tension in Northeast Asia, the Chinese had shown that they could not be
relied upon as partners in establishing a rules-based regional order. At the next
G-20 meeting, held in Canada in June 2010, Obama took the opportunity to firm
up the alliance with South Korea, describing it as the lynchpin of regional
security, and to agree with Lee, his Korean counterpart, that the US–Korean
FTA negotiations almost completed by Bush two years earlier would now be
completed by the next G-20 meeting in November 2010. Few other developments could have demonstrated that Obama's commitment to Asia was for real
and that he was prepared to spend political capital in overcoming opposition
from within his own Democratic Party to achieve it.[84]

The one country in which Bush was held in higher regard than Obama was
India. New Delhi was taken aback by Obama's failure to even mention India by
name in his first major speech on Asia in Tokyo in November 2009, prior to his
going to China. Grave offence was taken at the passage in the Sino-American
Joint Statement of 17 November 2009 signed by Obama and Hu in which the
two pledged to 'work together to promote peace, stability and development in
that region'. Not only was it demeaning to India, but it indicated that the US was
going to work with China, India's rival and Pakistan's 'all weather ally', to shape
the political order of India and its neighbours. The fact that the White House
hastily assured New Delhi that this was a mistake and that the US government
had no such intentions only rubbed salt into the wound as it indicated that India
was so far from the consciousness of Obama and his foreign-affairs advisers that
the offending passage went unnoticed in the first place. Since then Obama has
made amends of sorts by hosting the Indian Prime Minister Momohan Singh
on his first state visit and banquet at the White House and by heaping praise
on India as a cherished global partner with which America shares interests
and (unlike China) common values. In early 2010 Obama also completed
Bush's move to allow India access to American civil nuclear technology.

US–Indian relations continued to thicken in many ways, including not only commerce but military relations as well, and both sides have benefited from the successful and politically active Indian community resident in the US. Nevertheless Obama has yet to gain the level of trust in India that was enjoyed by his predecessor.[85]

The Obama administration was anxious to show that unlike its predecessor it would demonstrate American commitment to participate in the regional associations centred on Southeast Asia. To that end it overcame the doubts of military planners in Washington and early on signed up, in March 2009, to ASEAN's Treaty of Amity and Concord, which bound signatories to certain norms of behaviour in the region and was a condition of their being considered for membership of the East Asian Summit. In doing so it followed what all the other great powers had done up to six years earlier. Obama attended the APEC annual meeting in Singapore in November 2009 and became the first American president to hold a separate meeting with the ten members of ASEAN. But his commitment to the region was somewhat tarnished by his postponement of a scheduled visit to Indonesia three times for pressing domestic reasons. He is held in high regard in Indonesia because he attended school there as a youngster. Although the Indonesian president expressed complete understanding of the postponements, Obama indicated by them that this was not among his highest priorities.[86]

It is perhaps too early to pass judgement on Obama's foreign policy and on his approaches to Asia. But it is only fair to point out the difficulties of his legacies of the hugely burdensome wars in Iraq and Afghanistan and of the continuing economic crisis. Moreover, long-term developments in Asia that long antedated Obama's presidency were weakening the resources that America could bring to bear in Asia, especially as compared with China. Thus China's trade and economic relations with Asian countries, and especially key American/Asian allies such as South Korea, Japan and Australia, as well as most of the Southeast Asian countries, exceeded those with the United States and the gap was growing. In many instances China was becoming attractive to Asian students at the expense of the United States. A paradox was developing in which the economic wellbeing of most Asian states was becoming dependent on China, whom they did not fully trust, while their security depended on US military power, whose long-term commitment to the region was doubted to a certain extent and whose willingness to confront China on their behalf could not be taken for granted. Nevertheless the US has demonstrated that it will continue its military missions as usual, despite a new Chinese assertiveness, which is attempting to impose limits upon them in China's EEZ and in adjacent seas. Indeed in response to Chinese assertiveness in the South China Sea and to the pressure exerted by Southeast Asian diplomats in Washington, Secretary of State Hilary Clinton raised the American commitment to the region at an ARF meeting in Hanoi in July 2010. She declared that 'the US has a national interest' in resolving claims in the South China Sea, adding that the US favoured 'a collaborative diplomatic process for all claimants' and that 'we oppose the use or threat of force by any claimant'.

The Chinese foreign minister responded by repeating Beijing's long-standing position that the dispute should not be 'internationalized'.[87]

Notes

1 There was a considerable 'declinist' literature in the late 1980s and early 1990s that argued that America had passed its peak. The most influential book was Paul Kennedy, *The Rise and Fall of the Great Powers: Economic Change and Military Power 1500–2000* (New York: Random House, 1987). The influence of the declinist literature persisted well into the 1990s. For example, a highly praised textbook on China's foreign relations (Samuel S. Kim (ed.), *China and the World* (Boulder: Westview Press, 3rd edn, 1994)) included a chapter on Sino-American relations that stated almost as a matter of course that, while still significant a player in East Asian security, the US 'is by now only one of many players, having lost its once dominant position' (p.84).
2 Joseph Nye Jr., *The Paradox of American Power* (Oxford: Oxford University Press, 2002), especially chs. 2–3, pp.41–110.
3 Francis Fukuyama, *The End of History and the Last Man* (London: Penguin, 1993).
4 Robert S. Ross argues that, by restoring important aspects of the relationship with China, Bush helped minimize the slide into a more conflict-ridden relationship, which would have damaged both American interests and threatened the stability of the region. 'In retrospect,' he suggests, 'the president's policy appears even more appropriate than it did at the time.' See his 'The Bush Administration: The Origins of Engagement' in Michel C. Oksenberg, Ramon H. Myers and David Shambaugh (eds), *Making China Policy: Lessons from the Bush and Clinton Administrations* (Lanham, MD: Rowman and Littlefield, 2001), p.1.
5 Nancy Bernkopf Tucker, 'The Clinton Years: The Problem of Coherence' in Oksenberg *et al.* (eds), *Making China Policy* (*op. cit.*), p.46.
6 No less a person than Colin Powell, the then Secretary of State, told President Bush that the Clintonites had managed to 'cap Yongbyon [the nuclear reactor] … nothing came out of there for years. And they got a moratorium on missile shooting. So don't say it was all bad.' Interview by the esteemed Japanese journalist Yoichi Funabashi on 31 March 2006. See his *The Peninsula Question: A Chronicle of the Second Korean Nuclear Crisis* (Washington DC: Brookings, 2007), p.153.
7 Condoleezza Rice, 'Promoting the National Interest', *Foreign Affairs* 79, 1 (January–February 2000), p.48.
8 Linda J. Bilmes and Joseph E. Siglitz, 'The Iraq War Will cost US $3 trillion, and Much More', *The Washington Post*, 9 March 2008. They claimed that theirs was a conservative estimate, which excludes the costs to the US economy as a whole, which if taken into account would raise the cost to $4 trillion (nearly half the national debt at that time). For a development of this argument, see Roger Buckley, *The United States and the Asia Pacific Since 1945* (Cambridge: Cambridge University Press, 2002).
9 See the chapter by Michel Oksenberg, 'China and the Japanese–American Alliance' in Gerald L. Curtis (ed.), *The United States, Japan and Asia* (New York: W.W. Norton & Co., 1994), pp.96–121.
10 Seiichiro Takagi, 'The Asia-Pacific Nations: Searching for Leverage', in Oksenberg et al. (eds), *Making China Policy* (op. cit.) pp.259–260.
11 Madeleine Albright, 'The Testing of American Foreign Policy', *Foreign Affairs* 77, 6 (November/December 1998), pp.50–51, in which the then Secretary of State compared her situation to that of Dean Acheson, who as Secretary of State was responsible for overseeing the creation of the new order after the end of the Second World War.
12 This is the unstated theme of the distinguished Japanese scholar Takashi Inoguchi in his book *Japan's International Relations* (London: Pinter Publishers, 1991). See especially

ch. 6, 'Shaping and Sharing Pacific Dynamism', pp.127–40. Published two years later, his book *Japan's Foreign Policy in an Era of Global Change* (London: Pinter, 1993) conveys an altogether more sombre and uncertain tone.

13 US Department of Defense, 'A Strategic Framework for the Asian Pacific Rim: Looking Towards the 21st Century' (Washington, DC, April 1990).

14 *International Herald Tribune*, 28 February 1995. The document itself, 'East Asia Strategy Review', can be accessed online at www.defenselinkmil/news/Feb1995/b022795_bt092–95.html.

15 For an extensive discussion of American security dilemmas in the late 1980s and early 1990s, see William Tow, *Encountering the Dominant Player: U.S. Extended Deterrence Strategy in the Asia-Pacific* (New York: Columbia University Press, 1991); and the articles on America and Asia by Robert A. Scalapino, Bernard K. Gordon and Stephen W. Bosworth in the *Foreign Affairs* series, 'America and the World', in 1989/1990, 1990/1991 and 1991/1992 respectively (69, 1; 70, 1; and 71, 1).

16 John McBeth and V.G. Kulkarni, 'APEC: Charting the Future', *Far Eastern Economic Review* (24 November 1994), pp.14–15.

17 John Ravenhill, *APEC and the Construction of Pacific Rim Regionalism* (Cambridge: Cambridge University Press, 2001), pp.157–65.

18 The different arguments are detailed in James Shinn (ed.), *Weaving the Net: Conditional Engagement with China* (New York: Council on Foreign Affairs, 1996).

19 For detailed accounts of the China policies of the Bush and Clinton administrations, see relevant chapters in Patrick E. Tyler, *A Great Wall: Six Presidents and China* (New York: Public Affairs, 1999); and James Mann, *About Face: A History of America's Curious Relationship with China, From Nixon to Clinton* (New York: Alfred A. Kopf, 1999). For an excellent insider's account, see Robert L. Suettinger, *Beyond Tiananmen: The Politics of U.S.–China Relations, 1989–2000* (Washington, DC: The Brookings Institution, 2003).

20 For accounts of Sino-American relations during the Bush administration, see Harry Harding, *A Fragile Relationship: The United States and China Since 1972* (Washington, DC: The Brookings Institution, 1992), ch.8, 'Deadlock', pp.247–96; Ross, 'The Bush Administration' (*op. cit.*), pp.21–44; and Robert S. Ross, 'National Security, Human Rights, and Domestic Politics: the Bush Administration and China' in Kenneth A. Oye *et al.* (eds), *Eagle in the New World: American Grand Strategy in the Post Cold War Era* (New York: HarperCollins, 1992).

21 Nayan Chanda, 'Drifting Apart', *Far Eastern Economic Review* (26 August 1993), pp.10–11.

22 For a more detailed account of this and the Clinton period, see Tucker, 'The Clinton Years' (*op. cit.*), pp.45–76.

23 Harry Harding, 'Asia Policy to the Brink', *Foreign Policy* 96 (Fall 1994), pp.57–74. See also William G. Hyland, *Clinton's World: Remaking American Foreign Policy* (Westport, CT: Praeger, 1999).

24 Tucker, 'The Clinton Years' (*op. cit.*), pp.46–47.

25 Mike M. Mochizuki, 'To Change or to Contain: Dilemmas of American Policy Towards Japan' in Oye *et al.* (eds), *Eagle in a New World* (*op. cit.*), p.344.

26 See *ibid.*, pp.348–53.

27 See Oksenberg, 'China and the Japanese–American Alliance' (*op. cit.*).

28 For detailed accounts, see Don Oberdorfer, *The Two Koreas* (Boston: Addison Wesley, 1997); and Leon Segal, *Disarming Strangers: Nuclear Diplomacy with North Korea* (Princeton: Princeton University Press, 1998).

29 For a contemporary view, see Nigel Holloway and Shim Jae Hoon, 'North Korea: The Price of Peace', *Far Eastern Economic Review* (25 August 1994), pp.14–15. For more considered accounts, see Oberdorfer and Segal, cited in note 28.

30 For the text of Lake's speech, see W. Anthony Lake, 'From Containment to Enlargement' (21 September 1993, School for Advanced International Studies,

Johns Hopkins University, Washington, DC), online at www.mtholyoke.edu/acad/
intre/lakedoc.html.

31 For the source of the quotation see, Robert G. Sutter, 'Domestic Politics and the
U.S.–China–Taiwan Triangle' in Robert S. Ross (ed.), *After the Cold War: Domestic
Factors and U.S.–China Relations* (New York: M.E. Sharpe, 1998), p.77.
32 For an incisive critique of the concept and policies of engagement with China, see
James Mann, *The China Fantasy: How our Leaders Explain Away Chinese Repression*
(New York: Viking, The Penguin Group USA, 2007).
33 See Yoichi Funabashi, *Alliance Adrift* (New York: Council on Foreign Affairs, 1999),
ch.12, 'The Nye Initiative', pp.248–79.
34 Richard Bush, 'Taiwan Policy Making Since Tiananmen' in Oksenberg *et al.* (eds),
Making China Policy (*op. cit.*), pp.185–87.
35 Suettinger, *Beyond Tiananmen* (*op. cit.*), ch.6, 'Crisis Over Taiwan', pp.200–63. See also
Mann, *About Face* (*op. cit.*), ch.17, pp.315–38.
36 Suettinger, *Beyond Tiananmen* (*op. cit.*), p.262.
37 Mann, *About Face* (*op. cit.*), pp.344–45.
38 Suettinger, *Beyond Tiananmen* (*op. cit.*), p.262.
39 Tucker, 'The Clinton Years' (*op. cit.*), pp.58–60.
40 Francois Godement, *The Downsizing of Asia* (London: Routledge, 1999), ch.6,
'Challenging Asian Politics', pp.151–78.
41 Tucker, 'The Clinton Years' (*op. cit.*), pp.61–63. For the impact on Japan, see
Reinhard Drifte, *Japan's Security Relations with China* (London: RoutledgeCurzon, 2003),
p.164.
42 Suettinger, *Beyond Tiananmen* (*op. cit.*), pp.363–77.
43 Tucker, 'The Clinton Years' (*op. cit.*), pp.67–70.
44 Suettinger, *Tiananmen* (*op. cit.*), p.405.
45 *Ibid.*, p.399.
46 See the account in International Institute of Strategic Studies, *Strategic Survey 2000/
2001* (London: Oxford University Press, 2001), pp.191–99.
47 Bob Woodward, *Bush at War* (New York: Simon and Schuster, 2002), p.340.
48 John Larkin, 'New Leader New Crisis', *Far Eastern Economic Review* (9 January 2003),
pp.12–16.
49 For analysis, which also compares this with the review that was published after 9/11,
see Harry Harding, 'Asia in American Grand Strategy: The Quadrennial Defense
Review and the National Security Strategy' in Robert M. Hathaway and Wilson Lee
(eds), *George W. Bush and Asia: A Midterm Assessment* (Washington, DC: Woodrow Wilson
International Center for Scholars, 2003), pp.43–56.
50 For an account of the approaches of the Bush administration to China and East Asia
before 9/11, see Kenneth Lieberthal, 'The United States and Asia in 2001', *Asian
Survey* XLII, 1 (January–February 2002), pp.2–7.
51 For a considered, if at the end critical, analysis of the Bush transformation of
American foreign policy, see Ivo H. Daalder and James M. Lindsay, *America
Unbound: The Bush Revolution in Foreign Policy* (Washington, DC: The Brookings
Institution, 2003).
52 Sebastian Moffett *et al.*, 'Japan: Marching On To A New Role' *Far Eastern Economic
Review* (15 January 2004), pp.18–21.
53 Lieberthal, 'The United States and Asia in 2001' (*op. cit.*), pp.1–13.
54 For a brief background, see International Institute of Strategic Studies, *Strategic Survey
2002/2003* (London: Oxford University Press, 2003), 'The Delicate Strategic Balance
in South Asia', pp.205–19. See also Jay Solomon, 'South Asia: Trade Trumps War'
Far Eastern Economic Review (15 January 2004), pp.14–17.
55 On the Russian perspective, see Gilbert Roznan, 'Russian Foreign Policy in Northeast
Asia' in Samuel S. Kim (ed.), *The International Relations of Northeast Asia* (Lanham, MD:
Rowman and Littlefield, 2004), pp.201–24.

56 For a detailed study of the war on terrorism in Southeast Asia, see Rommel C. Banlaoi, *War on Terrorism in Southeast Asia* (Quezon City: Strategic and Integrative Studies Center, 2003).

57 Barry Desker, 'The Jemaah Islamiya Phenomenon in Singapore', *Contemporary Southeast Asia* 25, 3 (December 2003), pp.489–507.

58 For an account of how China turned that to its advantage, see Michael Vatikiotis and Murray Hiebert, 'How China is Building an Empire', *Far Eastern Economic Review* (20 November 2003), pp.30–33.

59 For an analysis of the complex relations involving South Korea and China and the US see, Scott Snyder, *China's Rise and the Two Koreas* (Boulder: Lynne Reiner, 2009), especially ch. 7, 'The China–South Korea-Security Triangle', pp.163–82. For background on South Korea, see Chung-in Mooon and Taehwan Kim, 'South Korea's International Relations: Challenges to Developmental Realism?' in Kim (ed.), *International Relations of Northeast Asia* (*op. cit.*), pp.251–79.

60 For an account of the divisions within the Bush administration, see Jim Mann, *Rise of the Vulcans Inside the Bush War Cabinet* (New York: Viking Press, 2004).

61 International Institute of Strategic Studies, *Strategic Survey 2002/2003* (*op. cit.*), pp.194–205.

62 On this point see Jonathan D. Pollack (ed.), *Strategic Surprise* (Newport, RI: Naval War College Press, 2004). The previous paragraphs on Taiwan drew on Alan D. Romberg, *Rein in at the Brink: American Policy Towards Taiwan* (Washington, DC: Henry L. Stimson: 2003; and Richard C. Bush III, *Untying the Knot: Seeking Peace in the Taiwan Strait* (Washington, DC: Brookings, 2005).

63 Alexander Moens, *The Foreign Policy of George W. Bush: Values, Strategy and Loyalty* (Farnham, Surrey, UK: Ashgate, 2004).

64 Chinnoy (*op. cit.*), pp.233–40.

65 For an analysis of Chinese interests regarding the North see Snyder, *China's Rise and the Two Koreas* (*op. cit.*) pp.142–49.

66 They were a loosely defined group associated with the twenty-five signatories of the 'Statement of Principles,' Project for the New American Century, 3 June 1997 (www.newamericancentury.org/statementofprinciples.htm). They were prominently represented in Bush's security establishment.

67 No less a person than Colin Powell, the then Secretary of State, told President Bush that the Clintonites had managed to 'cap Yongbyon [the nuclear reactor] … nothing came out of there for years. And they got a moratorium on missile shooting. So don't say it was all bad.' Interview by the esteemed Japanese journalist Yoichi Funabashi on 31 March 2006. See his *The Peninsula Question: A Chronicle of the Second Korean Nuclear Crisis* (Washington DC: Brookings, 2007), p.153.

68 Snyder (*op. cit.*) pp.94–102.

69 See, Snyder (*op. cit.*) pp.186–93 and Chinnoy, *Meltdown* (*op. cit.*) p.262.

70 For an account of relations during the eight years of the Bush presidency see, T. J. Pempel, 'Japan: Divided Government, Diminished Resources.' In Tellis *et al.* (eds), *Strategic Asia 2008–09* (*op. cit.*) pp.106–33.

71 Michael Green and Nicholas Szechenyi, 'U.S. – Japan: Waiting for elections', *Comparative Connections*, A Quarterly E-Journal on East Asian Bilateral Relations (Haiwaii: Center for Strategic and International Studies. Available online: http://csis.org/files/media/csis/pubs/ vol. 10, no. 2. July 2008.

72 Funabashi, *The Peninsula Question* (*op. cit.*), 'Collapse of the Japan-U.S.-Consensus' pp.425–31.

73 Robert B. Zoellick, 'Whither China: From Membership to Responsibility', Remarks to National Committee on U.S.-China Relations, September 21, 2005. Available online: www.state.gov/s/d/rem/53682.

74 For a representative view of the hardliners see, John Bolton, *Surrender is not an Option: Defending America at the United Nations and Abroad* (New York: Threshold Editions,

Simon & Schuster, 2008) 'Epilogue: The Munchkins Win on North Korea', pp.310–13.
75 See note 8.
76 Cited by Peter Baker, 'Obama Puts His Own Mark on Foreign Policy Issues', *New York Times*, 13 April 2010.
77 'National Security Strategy' 30 May 2010. Available on line: www.WhiteHouse.gov
78 Editorial, *The Washington Post*, 24 February 2009.
79 Mark Lynas, 'How do I know China wrecked the Copenhagen deal? I was in the room', the *Guardian* 22 December 2009. Available online: www.guardian.co.uk/enviroment/2009/dec/22/copenhagen-change-mark-lynas. Accessed 20 January 2010.
80 Dane Lawrence, 'China Flash of Maritime Muscle May Mean Power Push in Asia Seas', Bloomberg, 24 March 2009.
81 Michael Swaine, 'Perceptions of an Assertive China.' *China Leadership Monitor*, 2010 No. 3, 11 May 2010, Hoover Institution, Stanford University.
82 Jonathan Adams, 'China, Taiwan forge strongest ties yet with sweeping trade deal' *Christian Science Monitor* (www.CSMonitor.com), 29 June 2010.
83 This paragraph draws on accounts in *Comparative Connections* (*op. cit.*) for the years of 2009–10.
84 Chris Nelson, 'Trade Policy Lives! G-20 "Saves" KORUS', *The Nelson Report* 28 June 2010.
85 Summit Ganguly, 'America's Other Strategic Dialogue: U.S.-India rapprochement has stalled under President Obama, *The Wall Street Journal*, 30 May 2010.
86 For a Southeast Asian view of the region's importance to the US, see Eul-Soo Pang, 'A Strategic Re-Engagement and the US.' *Asia Pacific Bulletin* 59, 29 April 2010 (Washington, DC: The East-West Center).
87 AP. 'US wades into South China Sea Disputes', 25 July 2010.

10 China

China's ascent to global economic power and political influence

In the twenty years since the end of the Cold War, China has gone on to recover from its relative isolation following the Tiananmen massacre of 1989 to become by the end of the first decade of the twenty-first century a major global economic and political power courted by the world's only superpower as its most important partner in tackling global problems. At the same time China's booming economy has placed it at the centre of the economies of the Asia-Pacific region, and its deft diplomacy has turned China into a proactive player that is shaping the new regionalism in East Asia and a participant in developing a new global order. The modernization of its armed forces has begun to transform China's military strategic significance from essentially a continental power to one with a burgeoning oceangoing naval capability, which is beginning to challenge the maritime distribution of power in the region. Yet despite China's new assertiveness, at the time of writing in mid-2010, China is enjoying better relations simultaneously with the United States, all the regional great powers and all its neighbours than at any other time in modern history. There have been times when it has had better relations with one or more of these countries, but not with all of them at the same time.

China's rapid rise is a product of its phenomenal economic growth. In 2009 it replaced Germany as the world's leading exporter and it has begun to play an increasingly important role in the economies of Africa, the Middle East, the Caribbean and South America. It has become a key figure in the G-20 meetings (regarded since 2008 as more important than the G-8) and its voting weight in the IMF has increased. China's importance in the UN system has grown and it has become a serious contributor to UN PKO. Many global problems cannot be properly addressed without China's participation. These include addressing global economic imbalances, preventing the proliferation of WMD, tackling climate change issues, countering international terrorism, preventing health pandemics and so on.

Yet at the same time China's leaders project uncertainty and even a degree of anxiety in the major pronouncements of the Communist Party or the Government. Their main focus is domestic, where China confronts a host of structural problems, which they say can only be addressed through developing the economy continuously at a high rate of growth. Only that combined with the cultivation of patriotism will, they believe, ensure the social stability necessary to retain the Communist Party's monopoly of power. The character of its politics combined with the immensity of China's domestic problems gave rise to the concept of China as a 'fragile superpower'.[1]

It is only in the ten years since the beginning of the twenty-first century that China has suddenly emerged as a global power. Perhaps it is not surprising that the Chinese are uncertain as to what kind of global power they have become, or even if they are really a global power.[2] Although China's leaders may appreciate being regarded by the Obama administration as an equal, China is not a global power like the United States. Even with the current depressed state of the US economy its GNP is three to four times greater than that of China. China cannot project military power far beyond its borders. It has only recently begun to feel its way as a maritime power and it will remain principally a continental power for the immediate future. Nor is China a centre of technological innovation comparable to Japan or Europe, let alone to the United States. Perhaps more significantly, despite much talk of the 'Chinese model' or the 'Beijing Consensus', neither the Chinese government, nor its many academics and commentators on international affairs, present their country as a model. China cannot build on its political values of nationalism and Communist Party rule to project a universal message, which can appeal to others in the way that America can point to the abiding appeal of democracy and free markets. 'State capitalism' or 'authoritarian capitalism' is not unique to China and it has been tried with considerable degrees of success by then-developing countries, such as Japan and South Korea. The Chinese government tends to project an image of the country in a number of ways, not all of them consistent. China is said to be a great power (*da guo*) whose voice must be heard on every important issue. At the same time China is also said to be a developing country. Although its aggregate GNP is poised to rank second in the world by the end of 2010, its per capita GNP, according to the IMF, ranks ninety-seven in the world – just below Namibia. As one Chinese scholar told me in September 2009, 'China has many faces.'

A beneficiary of the end of the cold war

From a strategic longer-term perspective China has benefitted greatly from the end of the Cold War. The disintegration of the Soviet Union brought to an end the lingering threat from the north and for the first time in more than 150 years the Chinese land mass was free of the prospect of incursion by more powerful countries. At a stroke China acquired a new strategic latitude that enabled it to devote more attention to modern economic development in the south and the east and open up to the largely maritime regional economies of East Asia and beyond. Once the fear of invasion from the north was removed it became possible for its military to focus more on modernization to meet the new forms of warfare as demonstrated by the American demolition of the Iraqi army in short shrift in 1990. Henceforth China was able to concentrate primarily upon economic development without the fear of invasion or of major wars close to home.

The new geographic dispensation facilitated the transformation from Maoist politics of divisive class struggle to Dengist politics of national unity. The KMT and the people in Taiwan were no longer regarded as class enemies to be liberated, nor were the Chinese overseas, especially in Southeast Asia, regarded as suspect any more. Rather the people on Taiwan were now regarded as compatriots to be wooed so as to encourage them to unite with the Motherland and the Chinese overseas were now to be regarded as fellow 'descendents of the Yellow Emperor' to be cultivated so as to promote the regeneration of the homeland. Likewise the return of Hong Kong could now be negotiated and Hong Kong businessmen be encouraged to transfer their manufacturing and business knowhow to the Mainland. These adjacent ethnic Chinese communities provided the main source of investment and momentum for economic growth, which transformed the Chinese economy in the first place, and which continue to provide more investment than any single country.[3]

China's expansion from being mainly a regional power to a global one has been a product of its continuing double-digit annual economic growth and the astonishing expansion of its international trade, especially in the first decade of the twenty-first century. The value of its trade leapt from $474 billion in 2000 to $2.207 trillion in 2009, when it replaced Germany as the world's leading exporter. China also became a major participant in the trade and development of Africa and Latin America, where the value of its trade with each grew from around $10 billion in 2000 to $107 billion in Africa in 2007 and $140 billion in Latin America.[4] During the same period China's foreign exchange reserves grew exponentially from $165 billion in 2000 to over $2.4 trillion in 2010. By the end of the first decade of the twenty-first century China had become the world's largest importer of coal, iron ore, copper, manganese and many other raw materials and, according the International Energy Agency, China has passed the US to become the world's leading energy consumer, despite Chinese denials.[5] It was economic growth at home that led to the extraordinary expansion of China's international economic relations and its dependency on the imports of raw materials, especially energy that in turn led to the extension of China's national interests beyond its immediate territorial bounds. Although sovereignty and territorial integrity still rank high, the national interest has expanded to include the need to ensure access to resources in foreign lands and the defence of trade routes. China's pursuit of these interests is tempered by its need for a stable international environment in the region and the wider world. China therefore has its own reasons for participating in attempts to deal with global problems such as piracy, proliferation, finance, climate change and so on. The question is whether the way China's leaders conceive of their national interests in this regard can enable them to act in coordination with other key international actors. In the view of the Obama administration China's active cooperation is essential if these problems are to be addressed with any degree of success.

China has been a principal beneficiary of the intensification of the spread of economic globalization since the end of the Cold War. Perhaps paradoxically, China has also experienced the development of what has been called

a 'new nationalism' in the same period.[6] This arose in part because of the intensive campaign of 'Patriotic Education' launched by the Communist Party and its
head, Jiang Zemin, in the mid-1990s and in part by the adoption of nationalism
by the young, who are ever sensitive to alleged slights by foreign countries and to
possible compromises of China's 'rightful claims' by China's leaders. A campaign
designed to uphold the legitimacy of China's rulers after the decline of the appeal
of socialistic ideology has turned out to be a very mixed blessing.[7]

China's main foreign-policy goals, however, remain firmly rooted in its
domestic concerns. As one of its leading foreign-policy managers, State Councilor
Dai Bingguo, put it recently, 'China's number one core interest is to maintain its
fundamental system and state security; next is state sovereignty and territorial
integrity; and third is the continued stable development of the economy and
society.'[8] The focus on maintaining Communist Party rule and the attainment of
nationalist goals, economic development and social stability, is an indicator that
however confident China's leaders may appear in the eyes of the world, they do
not take their success at home for granted. It also is a reminder that China's rise,
though rapid, has been incremental. There has been no grand plan or strategy
aimed at increasing China's role in world affairs. The rise has been the product of
economic development and of the military modernization that economic growth
made possible. Therefore the growth of China's weight in world affairs is best
examined in chronological stages.

Recovery from the Tiananmen disaster, 1989–93

The Chinese authorities recovered from the Tiananmen disaster and the subsequent unexpected collapse of the communist regimes in Eastern Europe and the
demise of the motherland of communism, the Soviet Union, by focusing on economic development at home and by cultivating ties with Asian neighbours as they
waited for the tide of Western ostracism to retreat. They did so over a two to
three year period, and not without heated debate at home. The initial reaction of
the majority of the communist leaders was to draw down the shutters against
what was depicted as a Western campaign to undermine the communist system
by a process of what was called 'peaceful evolution'. That was traced way back to
the avowedly anti-communist US Secretary of State of the 1950s, John Foster
Dulles. The Western emphasis on human rights was seen very much as part of
that campaign. It may be recalled that China's leaders (unlike their Soviet counterparts) had been spared such criticism during the 1960s and 1970s, when the
most egregious violations of human rights took place. Only towards the end of the
1980s did Western human-rights organizations begin to target China. The initial
reaction of China's leaders was to see the raising of human-rights issues as unwar-
ranted interference in China's domestic affairs. After Tiananmen the human-rights
question was seen as part of alleged attempts by Westerners to undermine communist rule. The more conservative, or leftist, leaders, who were now in the
majority, held Deng Xiaoping personally responsible for the Tiananmen disaster,
for having pressed the reforms too fast and for having chosen unreliable

successors in the persons of Hu Yaobang and Zhao Ziyang.[9] As Deng lost some of his political standing the conservative/leftist leaders sought to slow down the reforms and reduce the opening to the outside. Matters were only settled in the early spring of 1992 when Deng Xiaoping made a 'southern tour', in which he made a series of speeches that had the effect of swinging the country away from leftist conservatism and towards rapid economic growth and deeper integration with the international (capitalist) economy.[10]

Deng, who had ostensibly stepped down from all his formal posts in 1989, after Tiananmen, used his informal position as core leader to ram home the message that the real danger to Communist Party rule would be a failure to deliver on the economy. It was simply unacceptable to return to Soviet-style economics (even of a reformed kind) and blame the disorders of Tiananmen on 'bourgeois liberalization' as a product of the reform process and the opening to the West. One of the major reasons for the collapse of the Soviet Union, he and his supporters argued, was the failure of its economy to respond to the needs of its people. The 88-year-old Deng argued that the principal danger to China came not from economic reformers, but from the leftists and their ideological conservatism.

Thereafter, Deng's agenda of economic reform and opening was not seriously challenged again. With careful management by his successors, that agenda provided the avenue through which China was to emerge into a position of respect and leadership in the region a decade later. There was, however, a third item on his agenda: the insistence on 'stability' as provided by the Communist Party's retention of the monopoly of power. This effectively put an end to any further serious consideration being given to political as opposed to economic reform. Arguably, the preservation of party power was the core of his legacy and Jiang Zemin linked support for the party and its leaders to the upholding of patriotism. The legitimacy of party rule became based on the provision of economic growth and patriotism. Monopolistic rule by the Communist Party ostensibly provided the platform on which the country could focus on economic goals, and it also prevented the many new sources of social conflict that were being generated by the rapid pace of economic and social changes from overwhelming public order. But at the same time the refusal to engage in serious political reform obstructed the emergence of a civil society with a plurality of groups and organizations that would facilitate tackling many of the new problems arising from economic disparities, corruption and so on, and would also help in holding officials to account. The division between the Communist Party conservatives and reformers continued to haunt the elite in the years to come. But the consensus was against significant political reform, especially as Chinese politics became more bureaucratized.[11]

The Tiananmen massacre, however, gave China's rulers the opportunity to take greater note of the significant roles their neighbours could play in China's foreign relations. As China became an international pariah and the object of sanctions by the United States, the European Union and the Group of Seven (as it then was), it was noticeable that China's Asian neighbours refrained from joining the chorus of condemnation. Not only were they wary of Western-led 'interference' in the internal affairs of Third World countries, but also they were especially concerned about the consequences of isolating China. They did not wish to see China once again withdraw into itself, with its leaders fearful and suspicious of the outside world and its people shut off from the world. Having seen the benefits to their own security and wellbeing of a more outwardly engaged China in the 1980s, they had much to fear from a return to the containment of the 1950s and 1960s. Additionally, whatever the views of Western countries about the benefits of the possible collapse of China's communist regime, China's neighbours knew that the possible breakdown of the Chinese state and the attendant chaos and misery would bring those living within reach of China nothing but trouble and economic hardship. This has long been the view in Japan, and it became evident after Tiananmen that most of China's Asian neighbours took the same view as they sought to develop relations with the giant country rather than join the Western countries in imposing sanctions. In time this became the view of most Western governments.

Furthermore, China had become a key player in the resolution of the Cambodian conflict, and it was this that prompted President Suharto of Indonesia to recognize China in 1990 (having long refused to do so because of China's alleged involvement in the failed 1965 coup). Singapore soon followed suit. Japan also made it clear in the G-7 that it was reluctant to impose sanctions in the first place, and it was instrumental in lifting the embargo on loans soon after. For their part China's leaders, perhaps for the first time, recognized the contribution that the region could make to China's diplomacy and economy. Foreign Minister Qian Qichen began to reach out to neighbouring countries on the ostensible grounds of 'China's traditional friendship' and pushed for establishing official relations with ASEAN, and on 19 July 1991 he attended a session of the ASEAN Ministerial Meeting.[12]

China's leaders proved adept at using their country's standing as a great power to break through the isolation imposed by sanctions. In 1990 the British Prime Minister, John Major, had to go to Beijing and meet with Premier Li Peng (who had declared martial law prior to the massacre in Tiananmen Square), in order to reach an agreement on Hong Kong's new airport that was deemed essential for the future of the territory prior to its return to Chinese sovereignty in 1997.[13] In November 1990, in return for not vetoing a UN resolution authorizing an attack on Iraq for annexing Kuwait by force, China's Foreign Minister, Qian Qichen, was invited to the White House to meet President Bush, who in any event was only too pleased to find a strategic rationale for improving relations.[14] South Korea also sought to reach across to China in the hope of breaking the impasse imposed by the legacy of the Cold War and of bringing more pressure to bear on North Korea to be more accommodating to the South. Unofficial economic relations were established, building on the informal economic links established in the late 1980s between ethnic Koreans in China's northeast and South Korea. A breakthrough was reached in 1992, when China recognized South Korea and indicated that it would not try to block its entry into the United Nations, thus forcing the hand of the North, who had no other supporter.[15]

China was not going to allow supposed ideological affinities to stand in the way of the pursuit of its national interests. That also signalled to the rest of the region that China did not see itself as the leader of the remnant communist world and that it had no intention of establishing a fraternal entity of communist states in the region.

Most of the East Asian countries were seeking to draw China into the pattern of multilateral relations of the region so as to socialize the country into accepting a pattern of relations that had helped the diverse countries to avoid conflict, respect each other's interests and contribute to shoring up their respective state-hoods. ASEAN in particular was keen to establish what was called a pattern of 'constructive engagement', so as to inculcate in its leaders something of the 'ASEAN Way'. Despite the fact that (or perhaps because) China had passed a law in 1992 defining its sovereign territory as all of its maritime claims, including the Spratly Islands (claimed in whole or in part by five others, including Taiwan), ASEAN was keen to develop consultative relations with the giant country.[16] Efforts in that regard were begun between the two sides in 1993, and in July that year the Chinese foreign minister joined with those of ASEAN, its seven dialogue partners, its three who enjoyed observer status and Russia in agreeing to inaugurate the ASEAN Regional Forum as a vehicle for addressing regional security issues.[17] Earlier, in August 1991, China had been admitted into APEC alongside Hong Kong (which technically was still under British authority) and Taiwan (under the name of Chinese Taipei). This was indicative of Beijing's readiness to present a soft and responsible image abroad, despite the hardness of domestic politics in the aftermath of Tiananmen.

Within two to three years of the Tiananmen disaster China had established good working relations with nearly all its neighbours. As seen from China, these relations were valuable in themselves for stabilizing the immediate external environment at a time of internal political vulnerability, and they were also useful as a counter to what was seen as the American-led campaign to contain and punish the Chinese regime. China's neighbours, in turn, were keen to engage their giant neighbour in constructive relations, given the uncertainties of the years immediately following the end of the Cold War. In effect these developments were the fruit of China's greater strategic latitude in the wake of the collapse of the Soviet Union and the disappearance of its latent threat to Chinese security. These developments also proved to be the genesis of a concerted regional policy by China, showing China's diplomatic skill and adaptability. They also proved to be the building blocks for China's re-emergence as a rapidly growing economy, which was tied into the East Asian region and the wider international economy.

From enmity to 'partnership': relations with the US during the Clinton administration, 1992–2000

Notwithstanding the gains the Chinese had achieved in relations with their neighbours, the relationship with the United States was the principal issue in

China's foreign policy. From a geopolitical perspective the United States was by far the dominant player in China's region and, now that the Soviet Union had dissolved, it was evident that China could not develop what was in effect an export-led economic strategy in the teeth of American opposition. Yet it was difficult to cultivate cooperative relations with a country that seemed bent on challenging China's political system. Additionally, many in China's elite were convinced that the United States was opposed to the rise of China because it threatened to reduce or even displace American power and influence in the region. This view was reinforced by the perceptions that, despite its absolute strength, the US was in relative decline as a superpower and that it was being restrained by the emergence of a more multipolar world. It was generally thought at the time and subsequently that the American interest in preventing Beijing from unifying Taiwan was to keep China divided and hence limit its capacity to emerge as a truly great power.[18] Most Chinese entertained ambivalent attitudes towards America: the United States was admired as providing the yardstick against which to measure China's progress and relative power, but it was also feared for allegedly blocking China's rise and for seeking to impose its own political values on China. As far as the military were concerned, their ability to bring credible coercive power to bear on Taiwan to prevent it from declaring independence required the capacity to inflict sufficient damage on any American naval forces that might intervene so as to keep them at bay. Likewise, the only country that could degrade the deterrent capabilities of China's nuclear forces was the United States. Finally, it was the United States that dominated the sea lanes and key trade routes, on which the Chinese economy increasingly depended. Yet, from an economic perspective, it was essential to retain cooperative relations with the US. Not only was it China's largest single market and source of advanced technology, but it also provided the public goods in the region and more broadly in the wider world, from which China's economy benefited. This was well understood by Deng Xiaoping, who famously cautioned his successors against openly challenging the US and charged them in foreign affairs: 'Observe the development soberly, maintain our position, meet the challenge, hide our capacities, bide our time, remain free of ambitions, and never claim leadership.'[19]

Tiananmen continued to cast a long shadow over China's relations with the United States, even as a slow recovery from the nadir of 4 June 1989 took place during the administration of Bush, the elder. Although it helped that Bush himself sought to restore amicable relations, it did not alter the fact that most of China's leaders regarded the US as an ideological adversary, whose general policy in the world was inimical to the interests of China (as these were understood by China's communist leaders). They regarded the American policy of criticizing the pursuit of its Tiananmen enemies as a human-rights issue as a continuing attempt to destabilize Communist Party rule and to undermine the stability of the country. Similarly, they characterized the economic sanctions endorsed by the president in the same vein – even though these were considerably milder than what Congress had had in mind. The Chinese abstention on the UN vote on Iraq in 1990 was less an endorsement of the American position than an unwillingness to stand alone in blocking action against Iraq at the UN Security Council. In fact, the Chinese came closer to the Russian position of seeking to find a negotiated settlement. In the event, the Chinese were taken aback by the display of awesome American power and the ease with which its revolution in military affairs enabled the US to achieve a rapid victory. The Iraqi armed forces were in many ways equipped with more advanced Soviet weapons than those available to the Chinese themselves. The Gulf War revealed to China's leaders how far behind they were and how vulnerable they had become to American power. The Chinese military changed their whole concept of modern warfare as a result and they began to conduct new types of military exercise, with the US regarded by most as the expected enemy.[20]

By 1992, however, the Chinese felt surer about their domestic political recovery and, as was noted previously, Deng Xiaoping had swung the main driver of Chinese politics early that year away from a leftist preoccupation with the threat of 'peaceful evolution' from the West towards a policy of going all out for economic growth and opening to the outside. The US too had begun to shift away from the shocked reaction to Tiananmen. The agenda of Sino-American relations began to be dictated by battles over the question of tying in the annual extension of normal trade conditions (technically known as Most Favoured Nation treatment – MFN) to China's human-rights performance. Congress determined that, in the event of Beijing's failure to satisfy the US on specific matters of human rights, it would revoke MFN. President Bush was able to veto the proposed bill every year, as there was not a sufficient majority to override the veto. But it meant that every year the Chinese government found what it saw as its legitimate domestic security concerns subject to political battles in Washington, with the threat of what it saw as economic blackmail. Additionally, the US also objected to China's sales of missiles and its proliferation of weapons of mass destruction (WMD) to Pakistan and to what later were termed 'rogue states'. Another issue was the growing American concern about the infringement of intellectual property rights. From the perspective of China's rulers, most of the American concerns focused on China's internal affairs, and the human-rights question in particular related to issues that went to the heart of the preservation of the Chinese communist system itself. The final year of the Bush administration also raised afresh the problem of Taiwan. For reasons of domestic electoral politics, President Bush announced in August 1992 that he would allow the sale of 150 F-16 military aircraft to Taiwan. In China this was seen as a violation of the 17 August 1982 agreement that limited the quality of arms sales that the US could sell to Taiwan. More significantly, the sale of the F-16s, coupled with the agreement of the US to press for Taiwan's admission to the GATT and to permit Taiwanese holding senior positions in government to visit the US, persuaded China's leaders that the US had shifted its policy toward Taiwan. 'Henceforward, no arms sales would go uncontested, no visit unprotested, no hint of change in the procedures for US–Taiwan relations unchallenged.'[21]

With the advent of the Clinton administration, from a Chinese perspective things went from bad to worse. First, President Clinton endorsed the approach by

Congress of making the granting of MFN in 1994 conditional on China's performance in a number of areas, including human rights. Second, Anthony Lake, Clinton's national security adviser, declared that the broad objective for the foreign policy of the new administration was to be the 'enlargement of democracy and of free trade'.[22] That could only bring more pressure to bear on China's communist rulers. Although they might have been expected to have fewer misgivings about the enlargement of free trade, they were less pleased that free trade was presented as an instrument for promoting democracy. The Chinese reaction was to stonewall on the demands of the White House and the State Department, while seeking to cultivate American economic interests, including major corporations, business groups and even the Department of Commerce. As the Chinese government dug in its heels, pressure mounted from business interests, coupled with arguments that overall relations with China should not be held hostage to a single issue such as human rights. Meanwhile, although Beijing held fast to its general position of regarding human rights as its own domestic sovereign affairs, it quietly released two prominent dissidents from custody. Clinton gave way and formally de-linked MFN from other matters.[23]

Although China's economic relations with the United States were expanding rapidly, these too raised many problems. There was a growing American deficit in trade with China, which climbed from US\$13 billion in 1992 to US\$34 billion in 1995.[24] The American market was the single largest one for China's exports, and Chinese imports from America of advanced technology, including supercomputers and aircraft, were very important for upgrading China's technological capacities. Americans complained about problems of access to the Chinese market and China's failure to implement its own laws on safeguarding intellectual property rights. The US Congress complained about the growing trade deficit as supposedly based on unfair Chinese trading practices and the use of prison labour. Meanwhile, the administration placed restrictions on the sale of sensitive military technology to China and threatened economic sanctions because of Chinese proliferation of missiles and nuclear technology, which it sold to Pakistan and to certain countries in the Middle East. China's leaders, however, proved adept at playing off foreign competitors for the Chinese market and at utilizing the allure of their huge market to stave off foreign demands for changes in their regulatory practices, which favoured local producers. The Chinese also complained about the American restrictions on the export of high technology as a cause of the trade gap and they also tried to induce American companies to encourage their government to lift the restrictions by claiming they could look to the Europeans to supply much of the technology and equipment being denied them by the American government. They also informed American business corporations of their intention to provide better access to their European competitors to the potentialities of China's huge domestic market. These disputes might have mattered less had there been leadership on both sides of the Pacific that was attentive to the broader significance of Sino-American relations.

It took the crisis over Taiwan of 1995–96 to concentrate the attention of both sets of leaders. The Taiwan question had become even more important to Beijing in the wake of Tiananmen when so much emphasis was placed on patriotism to bolster the legitimacy of communist rule. Not only had the issue of unification acquired greater salience, but the American attitude had become more suspect, as it was thought to have a stronger motive in maintaining Taiwan's separation from the mainland so as to keep China divided. Beijing had reacted warily to the beginnings of democratization in Taiwan in the late 1980s and early 1990s, but not with undue alarm as, for example, it did not attempt to prevent Taiwan's accession to APEC, insisting only on the nomenclature of 'Chinese Taipei'. There was even a point at which Beijing's 'unofficial' representative met Taipei's equivalent in Singapore in 1993. But increasingly Lee Teng-hui, the leader of Taiwan, was seen as moving Taiwan away from China and towards independence, both in domestic and external policies. As Jiang Zemin consolidated his position as successor to Deng Xiaoping, who by this time was incapacitated by advanced age, he issued an eight-point statement on Taiwan in January 1995 that expressed concern at what were seen as growing separatist tendencies, emphasized the centrality of the 'One China Principle', called for broader economic and other exchanges and asserted that Beijing sought peaceful reunification, reserving the use of force to prevent the separation of the island from the mainland and against foreign interference. The eight points were designed ostensibly to open the way to talks and to show that he was investing his prestige and personal political capital in the exercise. But Lee Teng-hui in effect rebuffed him three months later. That rebuff and Lee's whole position in widening the distance from the mainland were made possible, in the view of Beijing, only because of the connivance of the Americans, who were seen as not living up to their commitments on the 'One China policy'.[25] The American neglect of the intensity of China's commitment to unifying Taiwan with the Mainland may also be seen as a consequence of the ending of the Cold War, after which the US no longer needed China as a strategic ally against the Soviet Union.

Objecting to a visit made in June 1995 by President Lee Teng-hui of Taiwan to his alma mater, Cornell University, where he made a highly political speech, the Chinese decided that they had to show both Clinton and Lee that matters had gone too far and that they could bring pressure to bear on both. They responded the following month by conducting military exercises opposite Taiwan that simulated an invasion, and by firing some six missiles into the sea some eighty-five miles north and south of Taiwan. Notwithstanding a working summit between presidents Clinton and Jiang in New York in October, Sino-American relations did not greatly improve and in late November – one week before parliamentary elections in Taiwan – the Chinese launched even more intensive military exercises, coupled with a propaganda barrage to ram home the message that the People's Liberation Army was capable and prepared to prevent Taiwan from moving towards independence. The PLA threats arguably (at least as seen in Beijing) influenced the results of the elections, as the pro-unification New Party gained marginally and the pro-independence Democratic Progressive Party did not make as many gains as expected. Emboldened by the effect on Taiwan and by America's less than robust response, the PLA, whose influence on decision-making on Taiwan appeared to have grown, especially at a time when the unproven Jiang Zemin was seeking to consolidate his new leadership, went even further in seeking to intimidate Taiwan in the lead-up to the first ever presidential elections due on 23 March 1996. Three missiles were launched within thirty miles of each of the island's main ports in the north and the south on 8 March. Washington responded by announcing the dispatch of two nuclear aircraft carrier-led battle groups, one to be located off the east coast of Taiwan and the other off the Philippines. Together they constituted the largest deployment of naval forces in the Pacific since the Vietnam War. The PLA, as scheduled, continued its large military exercises off the coast opposite Taiwan, but launched only one more missile. This time, however, the Taiwan electorate responded adversely to Beijing's attempted intimidation: the defiant Lee Teng-hui won with a majority larger than expected and the two candidates favouring closer ties with the PRC polled only 25 per cent between them.[26]

Beijing, of course, claimed success for its tactics, suggesting that they had also persuaded Washington to cut back its alleged support for Lee's drive towards independence. But the PLA military exercises had ended ingloriously and Lee had gained strength from them. Tellingly, Beijing has not repeated such direct attempts at intimidation. While Washington may have been made more attentive to the importance of the Taiwan issue for Beijing, it was also true that the US had been drawn into demonstrating an explicit and effective commitment to defend Taiwan with a capacity to operate off China's shores with impunity. Additionally, China's bellicosity gave credence to more people in the US and even among China's neighbours to the idea that China could be a 'threat'. This was also the year (1995) in which the Philippines found that China had secretly established installations on Mischief Reef, barely 120 miles from the Filipino coast, giving rise to accusations of creeping assertiveness by the Chinese. Being unable to afford the loss of support of neighbours, the Chinese government for the first time agreed that the question of the South China Sea could be discussed collectively with ASEAN. Even though the Chinese insisted that they would only deal with disputed claims over sovereignty on a bilateral basis, this was a significant breakthrough for ASEAN. Although Beijing agreed to treat the smaller neighbours collectively at this juncture from a position of relative diplomatic weakness, this was in the end to pay dividends. At this point, however, Beijing found once again that by making procedural concessions to its neighbours it could draw on them as a kind of balance against the US.[27]

Stemming from the new strategic review (the Nye Review) of January 1995 and independently of the Taiwan crisis, the United States and Japan had agreed to upgrade their alliance to ensure that Japan would not find itself unprepared to help its US ally as it was in the Gulf War. The agreement to do so, in the form of new guidelines that allowed Japan to provide logistic support for American forces engaged in combat, was announced by the leaders of the two sides in April. China's firing of missiles in the seas near Taiwan only a month earlier in particular, as those in the north were not too far from the most southerly of Japan's islands, created an adverse reaction in Japan that helped smooth the way for the signing of the accord with the US in 1996. The Chinese reaction was predictably critical, especially as the Japanese refused to exclude Taiwan from the area in which potential logistic support might be granted. Thus the regional consequences of China's attempt to intimidate Taiwan were largely adverse, at least in the short term.[28] As against that, Beijing's readiness to use force convinced Washington thereafter about the huge significance of Taiwan for China's leaders.

One immediate favourable consequence of the Taiwan crisis from Beijing's point of view was that it encouraged both America and China to develop regular lines of communication at the highest levels. This did not mean that their long-standing disputes over intellectual property rights, proliferation, human rights, trade and so on did not continue to affect relations. However, the fact that China duly took over Hong Kong on 1 July 1997, without the shake up of its system, as many had predicted, especially following the altercations with the last Governor, Chris Patten, over the issue of democratic representation, left a good impression on international observers and on the American government. That no doubt helped to set the stage for the holding of reciprocal state visits between Presidents Jiang and Clinton, which duly took place in October 1997 in the US and the following year in China. They took place amid the pomp and splendour favoured by the Chinese president. Clinton's visit to China in June 1998 in particular marked a highpoint in the relationship. It was the first time that an American president had gone there without taking the opportunity to stop over in any other country, and it was the longest overseas trip by Clinton during his presidency (nine days). China's leaders were highly praised for not having devalued their currency during the 1997 Asian financial crisis. This was seen as a major contribution to helping to stabilize matters. In truth the Chinese had simply followed their own economic and trading interests in not devaluing.[29] China's leader was delighted to be treated as a partner by Clinton, not only in being praised over the financial crisis while the Japanese (hitherto America's mainstay ally in Asia) were openly disparaged, but also as a fellow guardian of the world's nuclear safety when they issued a joint condemnation of the Indian nuclear tests of May 1998. Indeed, the joint Sino-American communiqué spoke of the two as 'working toward a strategic partnership' – repeating the phrase first made in their summit the previous year. Clinton also became the first president to say publicly that America did not support Taiwanese membership of international organizations for which sovereignty was a requisite for membership. This had been stated before, but what drew the ire of the Taiwanese was that Clinton said it in the PRC and that he seemed to be drawing unduly close to Beijing.[30]

This high point of Sino-American concord had hardly survived the drying of the ink of the communiqué when domestic developments in the two countries showed that there was insufficient depth of support to sustain such a lofty characterization of the relationship. China's rulers moved systematically to crush the fledgling China Democracy Party, which they regarded as an unacceptable organized challenge to Communist Party rule that had been encouraged if not instigated by Clinton's visit. This outraged human-rights groups and their supporters in Congress and embarrassed the White House. Meanwhile, reports emerged in the US of illegal Chinese contributions to the electoral funds of the Democratic Party, and Congressman Cox began a formal investigation into allegations of Chinese spying in the US. The idea of China as a strategic partner came in for much criticism.

To correct what appeared to be a downward spiral in their relations, the Clinton administration pressed the Chinese side to make a special effort to join the WTO in the interests of enhancing their relations. The newly appointed Premier Zhu Rongji was receptive to this, partly in order to provide a lift to the economy in the wake of the Asian financial crisis and, more importantly, as a measure to enhance the reform process in China. The premier visited the US in April 1999, and he brought a package deal with him including nearly all the concessions the American side had hoped for. But once again the domestic problems on each side that have continually got in the way of attempts by the two sets of leaders to consolidate good relations came into play. President Clinton was worried that Congress would block the agreement because of its failure to provide protection for labour unions and manufacturers.

Although Premier Zhu had the support of President Jiang, antipathy towards America was growing in the leadership because of the American-led NATO intervention in former Yugoslavia that lacked a UN mandate and was based on the post-Cold War view in the West that 'human rights trump state sovereignty' and involved NATO in 'out of area' action. The concern was that China itself might one day become a target in, say, Tibet or Xinjiang. Clinton's rejection of Zhu's offer and the publication of it on the internet (showing which sectors in China would be vulnerable to external competition) made Zhu 'lose face' and, even worse, exposed him to criticism back home. Public sentiment had also turned against the US. The image of the United States as a beacon of liberty and democracy had been tarnished in post-Tiananmen China. Two years earlier a highly popular book, *The China That Can Say No*, gave expression to this and it was followed up by more considered 'New Left' publications that objected to globalization as Americanization.[31] Although Clinton reversed his position before Zhu's departure, letting it be known that he would accept after all, the damage had been done and it was too late.[32]

At this sensitive juncture in the relationship, the US Air Force, which had been bombing selected targets in Serbia as part of the NATO strategy of compelling its government to stop its ethnic cleansing in Kosovo, accidentally bombed the Chinese embassy in Belgrade in May. This provided a turning point as much popular nationalist anger was turned against the American embassy in Beijing and American consulates elsewhere. Premier Li Peng and Minister of Defence Chi Haotian publicly called on people to vent their ire against 'the common enemy' (the US).[33] The event and Chinese reactions to it coincided with the intensification of Jiang Zemin's angry response to the demonstration of Falun Gong adherents outside the headquarters of the communist party in Beijing two weeks earlier, suggesting a heightened sense of vulnerability.[34] Tempers had barely cooled before Lee Teng-hui claimed in an interview, broadcast internationally, that Taiwan was already in effect independent and that therefore cross-Strait relations were in a position of being 'a state-to-state relationship, or at least a special state-to-state relationship'. Beijing reacted with strident military rhetoric and looked to Washington to bring pressure to bear on Lee, which it duly did, while still stressing its 'One China policy'.[35]

A difficult summer then ensued in China, involving divisions among intellectuals and the public at large, as well as the top leadership, on how to treat the US and how to engage the broader world. What has been called the liberal view, which sought to enhance China's great-power status through improved economic performance, reform and engagement with the international economy, prevailed in the end.[36] But it was a kind of 'liberalism with Chinese characteristics', as it entailed the suppression of all perceived organized opposition to Communist Party rule from religious groups, to democrats, trade unionists and even leftist publications.[37] By the autumn Jiang had restored his authority and, recognizing entry into the WTO as an opportunity to enhance China's standing as a great power as well as to promote the reform process at home, Jiang was receptive to a Clinton request to resume negotiations. On 15 November an agreement was reached on the terms by which America would support China's entry to the WTO. That was the major hurdle to joining, although there still remained tough negotiations with the EU before the final obstacles were cleared, so that China and Taiwan (as a customs territory) became members in early 2001.[38]

Despite China's entry to the WTO and the burgeoning economic, educational and social ties between China and the United States, relations between the two countries continued to be subject to rapid fluctuations of amity and enmity. In part this related to the differences between their political systems and to clashes of values. For example, Beijing's vicious suppression of the semi-Buddhist sect Falun Gong, which attracted a large following for many who had lost out in the reform process and for whom the sect provided succour, raised the ire of both the human-rights section of the Democratic Party and the Christian fundamentalist wing of the Republican Party in joint opposition. But as seen by Jiang Zemin, Falun Gong was a pernicious religious cult led by a dangerous man who resided in the US, whose followers had penetrated into the Communist Party and which constituted a threat to political and social order.[39] But problems also arose because of disagreements over Taiwan, especially now that it had become a democracy, and, more broadly, because of differences in the respective national interests between China and the US.

These problems reflected not only differences of interest between the two sides, but also the persistence of divergent opinions among their respective elites about their relations and the lack of solid support for consolidating the relationship within their respective societies. On the American side, Jim Mann has argued that relations were conducted by a relatively small elite without the backing (and sometimes without the knowledge) of the broader public.[40] Put differently, successive presidents have failed to explain their China policies in ways that have captured the public imagination. On the Chinese side, as we have seen, there has been a long-standing mixture of admiration and resentment of America as the world's leading power that stands at the forefront of modernity, which can be a positive force for China's own modernization, while simultaneously being the main obstacle to China's rise as a great power. The relationship with the US has been frequently enmeshed with domestic political arguments and conflicts of interest over the character and pace of reform. So that in China too, attitudes and policies towards the United States remain subject to swings and fluctuations.

China's regional multilateral diplomacy, 1995–2010

Although China had become a member of several regional multilateral organizations before this date, 1995 may be seen as an important turning point marking the time when Chinese diplomacy became more active, as opposed to being for the most part reactive to the initiatives of others. Although China had become a member of APEC in 1991 and was a founder member of the ASEAN Regional Forum in 1994, it was only in 1995 that the Chinese formally agreed that issues of the South China Sea could be discussed on a collective basis with ASEAN. This was also the year in which the Philippines discovered that the Chinese had been secretly building structures on Mischief Reef, an atoll only some 120 miles from the Filipino coast. The significance of the meeting with the ASEAN group as a whole was that China gave up its relative advantage as the regional great power of dealing with these smaller states one by one. Undoubtedly, the Chinese did so because they did not want their southeastern neighbours to line up with the US against them in view of the Taiwan crisis. But the critical point was that, as a result, the Chinese began to pay more attention to their collective views, and they have been careful since then not to repeat the Mischief Reef land-grab elsewhere in the Spratly Islands chain. Moreover the Chinese Ministry of Foreign Affairs began to use the multilateral institutions of the region to diffuse the fear of China as a threat, to consolidate friendly relations, and to strengthen China's role as a leading economic power in the region.

To be sure, China had joined a great number of international organizations and signed up to a number of important binding international agreements since the new policies began in 1978. In the 1980s these were primarily key economic organizations from whose membership China benefited greatly at minimal cost to itself. But they had the effect of bringing many of China's domestic economic practices into greater conformity with current international custom.[41] China also signed up to several arms-control agreements and treaties in the early 1990s that imposed restrictions upon its behaviour, such as the Nuclear Proliferation Treaty (1992) and the Comprehensive Test Ban Treaty (1996); more generally, with the exception of transfers to Pakistan, China's observance of norms regarding arms control and proliferation has been 'no worse than that of other major powers [since the early 1990s]'.[42] Later in the 1990s China also signed the two main UN conventions on human rights.[43] Beginning in 1990 China contributed personnel to UN Peacekeeping Operations, whose numbers began to increase markedly as the decade wore on, and by the end of 2008 had reached 2,000 for the year, bringing the total of China's contribution to UN Peacekeepers since 1990 to 12,000 – more than any of the other permanent members of the UNSC.[44]

In 2008 China sent three ships on a rotating basis to participate in the international anti-piracy patrols off the Somali coast in East Africa. It provided opportunities for its navy to gain experience in operating at considerable distances from home and it also demonstrated Chinese willingness to contribute to a new form of peacekeeping. In short, China was becoming a participant in many of the international institutions and practices, as befitted a country that sought recognition as a responsible great power.

However, China's new activism in regional institutions was of a more significant character. It constituted an attempt to shape a regional order in accordance with China's interests, and interestingly, for a country with little experience of multilateral diplomacy in institutional settings, it was an attempt to do so with due regard to the interests of the smaller countries of the region. Even more interestingly, it was an attempt to do so while simultaneously seeking accommodations with the great powers of the region, Japan, India and Russia.[45]

As ever, the question of the United States loomed large. For a good part of the 1990s the Chinese appeared to think that the world was tending towards a multipolar structure that would act as a counterbalance to the power of the United States (the sole surviving superpower). But by 1999, after heated debates within the country, the Chinese had reconciled themselves to the fact that a multipolar system was not going to emerge any time soon and that, far from sinking into relative decline, the US had actually gained in comprehensive strength compared to the rest of the world and the gap between the US and the rest of the world was growing still wider.[46]

They also found that they could not rely on the various partnerships that they had established with other big powers to help them manoeuvre against the United States. As a result China's leaders moved from trying to use regional multilateralism as a means of reducing American influence to using it as a means to strengthen the Chinese presence, not in overt competition with the United States, but rather as a growing influence alongside that of the Americans.[47]

In 1997 China's leaders had articulated what they regarded as a 'New Security Concept' based on cooperative and coordinated security.[48] This is a pattern of security appropriate for countries that are neither allies nor adversaries. Indeed, it is part of the agreed objective of the ARF itself, as spelled out in 1995, that this would be achieved in three stages, beginning with confidence-building measures (CBMs) before moving on to preventive diplomacy and concluding with conflict resolution – or as the Chinese insisted it be formulated, 'approaches to solving conflict'. However, such an ordered approach was not part of the new Chinese proposal, the details of which were left rather vague beyond the encouragement for more CBMs. Indeed, it is widely held within the ARF that one of the major reasons for the failure of the Forum to proceed from the first stage of CBMs to the second stage of preventive diplomacy is due to the Chinese dragging their feet.[49] But the Chinese initially insisted that their new concept, unlike the American military alliances, was well suited to what they said was the new post-Cold War environment, characterized by 'peace and development'. The American alliances were said to be remnants of a previous era and indicative of a Cold War mentality.

These views were put to the Southeast Asians in particular. In Northeast Asia in the mid-1990s the Chinese looked forward to the removal of American forces in South Korea. They expected that they would end up exercising predominant influence on the Korean peninsula in due course.[50] Meanwhile they encouraged negotiations between the North and the US in the expectation that these would result in the acceptance of the coexistence of both Koreas, with Chinese influence growing in both.[51]

From a Chinese perspective, the US–Japan alliance in some respects had become more troubling, because it had been reinvigorated by the New Guidelines agreed between the two in 1996–97 as they allowed the Japanese to play a more active strategic role in the region. Nevertheless, the alliance was still considered to be preferable to the alternative of a Japan that was let loose to develop independent security policies. But once the Chinese accepted that they were stuck with a unipolar United States for the immediate future, they stopped harassing the Southeast Asians on this issue, accepting that they had found ways of securing various arrangements with the US as a means of hedging against China. Indeed, the Chinese accepted that the Southeast Asians preferred to engage all the great powers, including also Japan, Russia and India, so as to maximize their manoeuvrability against each. One advantage to the Chinese was that they were less feared under such circumstances, making their growing influence in the region more acceptable.[52]

China's leaders skillfully improved their position and their reception by the Southeast Asians by focusing on the economic dimensions of regionalism. Building on the framework of the ASEAN Plus Three (APT), involving the ten ASEAN countries plus China, South Korea and Japan, the Chinese presented their booming economy, which was attracting more imports from the other twelve, as an opportunity for their economies rather than as a threat. The fear in Southeast Asia was that by attracting foreign investment away from ASEAN countries and by making substantial inroads into their key foreign markets, such as the EU and the US, China posed too strong a challenge to their wellbeing. However, subsequent studies showed that these fears were misplaced.[53] Chinese diplomacy dwelt on the positive dimensions of their economic relations. In 2001 Premier Zhu Rongji proposed that a China–ASEAN free-trade agreement be reached over a ten-year period. As far as South Korea and Japan were concerned, the Chinese side was able to point out that by 2001/2002 China (including the through-trade via Hong Kong) had become a bigger market for South Korea than the US and that the Chinese economic locomotive was providing a boost for even the sluggish Japanese economy. It mattered little at this stage, as the magnitude of Chinese investment in and total trade with most of these countries was still below that of the United States and Japan. The Chinese FTA with ASEAN (CAFTA) spurred Japan to respond with its own (bilateral) free-trade agreements (FTAs) and to develop its own institutionalized relationship with ASEAN. What mattered from a Chinese perspective was that the country had largely shed its previous image as a vaguely threatening outsider and had assumed that of an active and fast-growing partner.[54]

After negotiations that lasted more than three years, the Chinese also agreed with the ASEAN countries the Declaration on the Conduct of Parties in the South China Sea, by which the resident states undertook to resolve territorial and jurisdictional disputes by peaceful means and to refrain from inhabiting presently uninhabited islands. Although the Declaration is non-binding, China's standing would be damaged if it were to be seen to be contravening it. The two sides also agreed to develop more CBMs, and to explore further possibilities for cooperative activities, bilaterally or multilaterally. China, which was already a signatory to the Southeast Asia Nuclear Free Zone, took an additional step in demonstrating its commitment to meeting the interests of its ASEAN partners by being the first outsider formally to adhere to ASEAN's 1976 Treaty of Amity and Concord that set out a code of conduct for the region based on the sanctity of national sover-eignty.[55] Since the Chinese had formally acceded to all the norms of regional inter-state conduct that the Southeast Asians claimed determined their relations, the Chinese in turn could now claim that they had been fully accepted as part-ners. Clearly, they had less to fear of ASEAN countries adopting measures with others that would be detrimental to Chinese interests. China had gained by cooperation far more than it could have expected to from its previous policy of open hostility to the US. It was far less likely, for example, that ASEAN states would provide assistance to the US in the event of Sino-American conflict over Taiwan.

China's enhanced institutional partnership with ASEAN was particularly sig-nificant in view of the fact that China's claims to virtually the whole of the South China Sea and the island groupings located there put it in dispute with at least four ASEAN states. The growth of Chinese military power especially at sea has increased the suspicions of neighbouring states, especially as China continuously asserts that its claims are 'indisputable' and has yet to suggest how the different claims can be settled beyond suggesting that the disputes could be set aside in favour of joint development. At one point a preliminary agreement to that effect seemed to have been reached with the Philippines, but the Parliament refused to ratify it on the grounds of, first, corruption and second, that if allowed, the agreement would have recognized Chinese territorial claims, which had pre-viously been denied.[56] Elsewhere the Chinese were not shy of throwing their superior weight by barring from China those oil companies who engaged in exploring Vietnam's continental shelf (in part claimed by China). China's growing naval might has sparked an arms race in the region that is real and costly even if it is not openly acknowledged.[57]

Conscious of the existence of an influential current of thought in the US, which looked at China's rise with apprehension and a sense of impending conflict between the established and the rising power, the Chinese conducted a propa-ganda campaign against what was called the 'China threat theory'. A prominent adviser to China's leaders persuaded them in 2003 to promulgate what was called the inevitability of China's 'peaceful rise' (*heping jueqi*). However, the slogan was soon dropped as the Chinese for 'rise' had the connotation of 'upsurge', which it was thought might convey the wrong idea, and the linking of that to the word

288 The post-Cold War period

'peaceful' might send the opposite message to Taiwan, which then might no longer be deterred from seeking independence. It was then decided that Deng Xiaoping's statement that China only sought 'peaceful development' was best after all, at least for official purposes.[58] The episode also revealed how seriously China's leaders took the image of their country, which they wanted to portray as a 'responsible power'.

Meanwhile the Chinese have been actively consolidating their position in Southeast Asia. Educational exchanges have expanded, Chinese tourists now visit Southeast Asia annually in their millions. The value of China's trade with ASEAN countries grew from $41.6 billion in 2001 to $213 billion in 2009.[59] CAFTA came into effect in 2010 and it is expected to offer further opportunities for trade, while at the same time demonstrating the depth of China's commitment to regionalization. Together with Japan China has provided the lion's share of the foreign exchange to the swap arrangement of the Chiang Mai Initiative, (30 per cent each) which currently stands at $140 billion and which is designed to be the first port of call for Asian countries in need. The initiative is linked with the IMF and should not be seen as an alternative.[60] The complexity of China's involvement in Southeast Asia may be seen from the differences between the participants on the Chinese side. In addition to the Ministry of Foreign Affairs, account must be taken of the Ministry of Commerce, the State Owned Enterprises, the military, the ministries involved with rail, roads, telecommunications and so on, the various provinces, notably Yunnan and Guangxi, adjacent to Burma (Myanmar), Cambodia, Laos and Vietnam and Hainan Island. These, together with individual traders and with Chinese overseas who have links to their ancestral villages, all have their own particular interests and modes of operation.

China's close relations with the resident Chinese overseas are no longer contested, but the Chinese government has been careful to avoid overt involvement in situations where issues arise between the Chinese overseas and the resident governments and peoples. Only when they were deliberately targeted by mobs, as in Indonesia after the fall of Suharto in 1998, did the Chinese government openly express its concern. In that case the Chinese government was also mindful of the agitation by its own netizens. The ambiguity of China's relations with the Chinese overseas has not been entirely overcome and this may be the consequence of continuing ambiguity about the identity of China and what it means to be Chinese. The cultural and educational affinities with China do not necessarily pose problems, but ethnicity is another matter as successive presidents of the Chinese state make annual addresses not only to the citizens, but also to all 'the descendents of the Yellow Emperor'.[61]

Nevertheless China has not had its own way entirely. Among the various proposals for establishing an East Asian community was the call to establish an East Asian Summit (EAS). The Chinese side sought to have it confined to the APT, but it had to yield to pressure, notably from Japan and Singapore, to enlarge it to include India, Australia and New Zealand. It was an open secret that Japan and Singapore wanted the larger body so as to avoid the probable dominance of China. The EAS duly met in 2005 and has continued to meet on an annual basis, without much result.[62] Since the improvement in China's relations with Japan in 2006, the Chinese have found a new framework within which to continue to call for using the APT mechanism to bring about practical results, saying that once these are in place membership could be enlarged.

Perhaps the most notable multilateral initiative undertaken by the Chinese government was in Central Asia. The Chinese were able to build on the previous experience of the incremental process of accommodation over force reductions and border agreements, begun in the last years of the Soviet Union and completed in the early to mid-1990s with the successor states, Russia and the three Central Asian states that bordered China. They first formed an arrangement with those four countries in 1994 that was to become, seven years later, the Shanghai Cooperation Organization (SCO). Embodying elements of cooperative security, the SCO went beyond these to include a joint pledge to oppose 'the three evils' of separatism, terrorism and Islamic extremism. In this way Chinese security interests in Xinjiang were linked with an endorsement, together with Russia, of the regimes and the territorial integrity of Kazakhstan, Kyrgyzstan and Tajikistan.[63] This was a region in which Chinese influence had been minimal since the fall of the Qing Dynasty in 1911 and where Russian residual power was still very great. Indeed, the Russians have established a security mechanism of their own involving CIS states, by which they are committed to come to the defence of whoever among them has been subject to attack. That may be seen as a genuine provision for security, unlike China's more nebulous concept of cooperative security. Most of the railway networks and lines of communication are still linked up with Russia and, even as the Russian economic capabilities decayed, the greatest economic beneficiaries were the Europeans.[64]

However, over the next decade China was able to negotiate and build pipelines, invest in the extraction of oil, gas and mineral resources and build the necessary infrastructure to transport these to neighbouring Xinjiang and from there to China proper. In the process the Chinese have been overcoming great distances and difficult terrain, and competition from Western countries and Russia.[65] The Chinese attached much of their prestige to the SCO, which was named after a Chinese city, had headquarters located in China and was mainly staffed by Chinese. Several military exercises have been held under its auspices. As the most successful economy of the region, China is hoping to use its local economy there to good advantage. The SCO is China's principal point of entry into Central Asia and China is keen to build on it, despite China's relative lack of power and influence in the region. Interestingly, the Chinese were instrumental in preventing the SCO from recognizing the breakaway statelets of Abkhazia and South Ossetia in 2008 as demanded by Russia.[66]

China's successful regional policies were built to a certain extent on the favourable image created by its relatively generous approach to settling its territorial disputes on the land mass of Asia (India excepted). Far from insisting on meeting its claims in full, as might have been suggested by Beijing's nationalistic rhetoric and by the pressure of its ultra-nationalistic netizens, China's rulers settled for a good deal less. One explanation, based on a thoroughly researched study, argues that China's approach was determined by its sense of domestic vulnerabilities arising from the long-standing presence of ethnic groupings (whose absolute loyalty was far from certain) in often remote border regions, some of whom straddled both sides of the border.[67] Similar generosity or flexibility has not yet been displayed in disputed maritime regions. Several reasons may be suggested: first, as primarily a continental country, China has long historical experience of managing the geopolitics of border regions involving the management of space, time and ethnicity, none of which apply to handling disputed maritime claims. Second, the United States, perceived Beijing as its main adversary, is not directly a party to its territorial disputes, nor is the United States strategically engaged in continental Asia – at least not in areas that impinge on China's border disputes. Whereas the United States is seen as the main obstacle to Chinese attainment of what they regard as their maritime rights. Concessions may be safely made to the weak on continental Asia, but not to the strong. Third, unlike territorial disputes, where each problem may be addressed differently according to local circumstances, maritime disputes must be based on universal legal principles. For example, the Chinese cannot reasonably claim one rule for naval activities by others (e.g., the United States in its own EEZ and adjacent waters) and a different one for itself in the EEZs of its neighbours (e.g., Japan).

In 2009/2010, China's more assertive policies in conducting active naval patrols in support of its reinvigorated claims to sovereignty over the disputed islands in the South China Sea threatened to weaken if not undermine the fruits of its diplomatic engagement with Southeast Asian countries in particular. ASEAN diplomats have been making representations to Washington. The American Secretary of Defense, Robert Gates, regarded the Chinese cancellation of his proposed visit to China in early June 2010 as retaliation for the American agreement to arms worth US$6.5 billion to Taiwan as uncalled for and made his annoyance public at the annual security dialogue in Singapore on 5 June 2010. Chinese behaviour regarding North Korea's sinking of a South Korean ship and their attempts to circumscribe the joint military drills of the South Korean and American forces to deter further provocations from the North disappointed Washington, especially the Department of Defense. Sino-American interactions over these and related issues culminated in Secretary of State Hilary Clinton's declaration at an ARF meeting in Hanoi in late July 2010 that the US has a 'national interest' in the resolution of competing claims in the South China Sea, which it thought should be settled through the collaboration of all and with which the US was willing to help. For good measure she added that the US opposed the 'use or threat of force by any claimant'.[68] This went far beyond the previous American position, which was confined to simply demanding that freedom of navigation through the sea lanes of the South China Sea be kept open. The immediate Chinese reaction to Clinton's statement was to reiterate its long-standing position that the South China Sea issue should not be 'internationalized.' In other words it amounted to a rejection of the new American position.

The effects of 9/11

'9/11' became a turning point in China's relations with America as both sides found a strategic interest in cooperating together to combat terrorism, although they understood the threat somewhat differently. As seen by the Bush and Obama administrations, the terrorist groups based in the 'AfPak' region constitute a worldwide threat and in particular a threat to order in Western cities. The Chinese tend to see the threat from these groups as linked to ethnic-based separatist movements in Xinjiang and Tibet. That, after all, was presented as one of the reasons for establishing the SCO for Central Asia. Nevertheless, the US and China, in cooperation with others, shared intelligence, sought to coordinate banking procedures to deny money transfers to terrorist organizations and worked together in other respects too. 9/11 had the effect of reducing, but not eliminating, the tension that manifested itself from time to time in their relationship.

The cooperation also benefitted from the transformation of Chinese diplomacy, which had begun in the mid-1990s. As China had become more engaged with the world through its participation in the institutions of the international economy, through becoming an active member in the non-proliferation regime and other multilateral, often UN-related, functional institutions, so it acquired a growing core of professional experts in these fields. These developments also coincided with a generational change as many diplomats who had been exposed to university education in Europe and North America had been promoted to more responsible positions in the Ministry of Foreign Affairs and related bodies that dealt with foreign governments and international institutions.[69]

The Bush administration came into office determined to take a tougher line on China, which it saw as a rising peer competitor. But even before 9/11 it had modified its approach somewhat as a result of the 'EP-3 incident' off the coast of southern China in April, involving a lumbering propeller-driven intelligence-gathering American plane, which downed a Chinese jet that in buzzing it crashed into it. The American crew was detained for eleven days and the ensuing diplomatic exchanges resulted in a muted American apology that led to their release. Paradoxically, the incident increased the respect that each side had for the other. Nevertheless, the following month the Bush administration announced a substantial increase in the quantity and quality of the weapons systems it intended to sell to Taiwan for its self-defence. President Bush added for good measure a major shift in US doctrine in an interview, saying that he would do 'whatever it takes' to help Taiwan defend itself. Hitherto the US position of 'strategic ambiguity' had left open the degree of support that would be rendered to Taiwan so as to prevent that from being tested by either side.[70]

The eleventh of September 2001, however, was immediately seen as a catalyst for change by both sides. The immediacy of the Chinese response, by which President Jiang telephoned his sympathy and support to President Bush that very day, was unprecedented. Similarly, his willingness to give way on his right as host to turn over much of the agenda of the APEC meeting in Shanghai in October to meet Bush's anti-terrorist purposes was also much appreciated by the American side. The Chinese were seen as partners in the war against terrorism as they helped persuade the president of Pakistan to accede to the American demands for assistance in the war against the Taliban and Al Qaeda in Afghanistan. They also began to share intelligence. The Chinese found a wider audience beyond the members of the SCO for their claim that the opposition to their rule in Xinjiang was also terroristic and was linked with external terrorist groups. The following year the State Department declared that the East Turkistan Islamic Movement was indeed a terrorist group. The announcement coincided with the promulgation in Beijing of detailed laws prohibiting proliferation of WMD and related technology. Both may be seen as signifying the closeness that had begun to develop between the two sides.[71]

The Chinese authorities seemed to acquiesce as American forces established a significant presence in Central Asia and strengthened their ties in Southeast Asia, notably in combating terrorism in Indonesia and the Philippines. Indeed, the Chinese side went so far as to offer to rescue American pilots downed in the South China Sea. Although it may have seemed that China's strategic situation had worsened, China's leaders appeared to calculate that their interests had not been greatly damaged. The bases used by the Americans in Central Asia were not near China's borders, and in any case the Russians, who were more immediately affected, did not contest them. It was not felt in Beijing that the SCO had been rendered ineffective. Its organization was strengthened and a number of joint military exercises were conducted with adjoining countries. The Chinese also found their commitment to stability in the region, as registered in their sponsorship of the SCO, useful in persuading the Asia Development Bank to provide loans for extending railway lines and upgrading roads to link Xinjiang with Central Asia. The Chinese side was also active in promoting cross-border economic relations. As for Southeast Asia, the Chinese appeared satisfied that the increased American involvement was confined largely to the question of opposing terror and that it was not an obstacle to China's enhancement of its relations with ASEAN.[72]

The Chinese government voted for the UN resolution allowing the United States to lead an invasion of Afghanistan in 2002 to topple the Taliban government and to destroy the Al Qaeda sanctuary, but while it did not favour the subsequent invasion of Iraq the Chinese government was content to let Russia, France and others lead the opposition at the UN. The American government claimed that China helped in exchanging intelligence related to Afghanistan. But the Chinese government joined with Russia at the SCO in supporting the then Kyrgyz government demand of 3 February 2009 that the Americans close their Manas base, which was an important supply stop for the Afghan war. Kyrgyz subsequently relented. However, the episode demonstrated that China's support for the American war in Afghanistan was balanced by its concerns about the American military presence in a state on its borders. Nevertheless, the American side continued to praise Chinese support in public and in particular it welcomed Chinese investment in a huge copper mine in Afghanistan and its readiness to build the necessary infrastructure.

The Chinese approach was also affected by its policies towards Pakistan and India. The hostility between the two South Asian states tied down Indian strategy and its force deployments to a considerable extent, limiting the degree to which India could confront China. Pakistan was China's 'all-weather friend', the recipient of Chinese aid in building its nuclear weapons. Since the Pakistani military and intelligence services had cultivated Islamic terror groups within the country to help sustain resistance in that part of Kashmir ruled by India, China had not pressed Pakistan unduly on the question of its relations with terrorist groups. Pakistan, and indirectly the Americans, with the use of drones to attack terrorist holdouts in Pakistan's tribal areas, have so far ensured that terrorist groups have not been able to offer effective support to Uighurs intent on resisting Chinese rule in Xinjiang. At the same time the Chinese have so far proved adept at buying off potential threats to their economic activities in Pakistan and Afghanistan. It remains to be seen whether that will continue to be effective and whether the Chinese might see it in their interests to work more closely with the United States.[73]

Be that as it may, China was a huge strategic beneficiary of the long American wars in Iraq and Afghanistan. The American preoccupation with the wars and with terrorism was perceived to have contributed to the relative weakening of its strategic interests elsewhere, including in East Asia. Indeed, rightly or wrongly, Southeast Asians felt neglected by the US, at the same time as China's interactions with the region were deepening and widening.

India

Sino-Indian relations have been transformed since the end of the Cold War. As India carried out its own economic reforms and began to emerge as a great power whose reach and influence extended beyond South Asia, China and India began to see each other as both partners and rivals. Economic relations, which had been negligible even through the 1990s, quickly began to pick up after the turn of the century. Thus trade grew from $1.7 billion in 1998 to $37 billion in 2007 and to $51.8 billion in 2008. But as in other aspects of Sino-Indian relations the value of the trade was asymmetrical, with India experiencing a trade deficit of $20 billion and the bulk of its exports being iron ore and other raw materials and its imports being mainly manufactured goods. The Indian government has complained about the imbalance and has carried out anti-dumping measures, accusing China of unfair trade practices including the undervaluing of its currency. India has also restricted the import of Chinese labour and cited strategic reasons for disallowing the bids of Chinese telecommunication companies for certain projects.[74] Nevertheless, each side asserts that their economies are complementary and that their economic relations are bound to grow.

Underlying these trade disputes is a deep-seated strategic distrust going back to the border war of 1962. From the Indian point of view, China is trying to keep India down by its military superiority, its 'all weather' quasi-alliance with Pakistan and its cultivation of good relations with all of India's neighbours. Indians also point to China's supply of Pakistan with nuclear weapons, missiles and advanced weaponry, while opposing Indian attempts to become a permanent member of the UNSC and seeking to block an agreement in the Nuclear Suppliers Group to allow India to import civil nuclear technology.[75] Additionally, Indians assert that China is building a 'string of Pearls' around India in the Indian Ocean by using ports and other facilities on the periphery of the Ocean. For their part the Chinese have long regarded India as an inferior who seeks to exercise hegemony in South Asia, but which has used its association with the United States that was built during the latter years of the Bush administration to try and contain China. If India is concerned about Chinese cultivation of its neighbours, China has also noted India's recent reach into Southeast Asia and the burgeoning of its relations with Japan and Australia. The two Asian giants have long-standing border disputes, which have gained in intensity in the last few years because of mutual anxieties that the other is fomenting trouble in territorial disputes that have a bearing on their respective existential problems. If India complains about China's assistance to Pakistan in building infrastructure in disputed areas of Ladakh and Kashmir, China has become more suspicious of India's support for the Dalai Lama and his unofficial government in exile located on Indian territory and about India's activities in its state of Arunchal Pradesh, claimed as Chinese territory – a part of which the Chinese have called 'South Tibet' since 2008.[76]

Yet both sets of leaders recognize that the two Asian giants cannot afford another war and that they must cooperate despite their rivalry. Indeed the two share some common interests that run counter to the United States, whom each wishes to cultivate. As two major developing countries the two took roughly similar positions regarding climate change at the Copenhagen meeting of December 2009 and the same applies to their attitude towards the Doha round of trade negotiations. Both invest in and import oil and gas from Iran as they share similar energy needs. Indeed both China and India separately identify themselves as simultaneously developing countries and great powers.[77] In sum, this is a highly complex relationship combining both rivalry and partnership and while China may feel that it is currently superior in economic, diplomatic and military terms, it cannot be confident that its superiority will last as India continues to rise without the demographic problems that are beginning to trouble China and with the expectation that the democratic values and practices it shares with the United States may provided the basis for a more durable partnership.[78]

Japan

Sino-Japanese relations will be considered in greater detail in the next chapter, which is focused on Japan. The concern here will be to analyse Chinese perceptions of Japan rather than to explore the development of the relationship itself. Japan has figured large in the history of China's modernization. Its defeat of China in the war of 1895 sparked the beginning of modern Chinese nationalism, which at that time took the form of demanding that China itself carry out fundamental reform or revolution to meet the challenge of modernity or otherwise face the prospect of extinction. Hence Japan was seen as a model from which China could learn. Many of China's modernizing leading intellectuals and early revolutionaries then went to Japan. These included the future leaders Sun Yat Sen and Zhou Enlai. However, opinion turned against Japan when it tried to take advantage of the preoccupation of the West in Europe during the First World War to turn China into a virtual colony in 1915 and when it then took over the German concessions in China by the Treaty of Versailles, denying China the self-determination promised by US President Wilson. Japan then remained the enemy of Chinese nationalists, especially after its invasion of Manchuria in 1931 and of China proper in 1937.[79]

Yet from Mao's perspective the Communist Party and army, which he headed, would not have survived, let alone ended up being victorious in the Chinese Civil War (1946–49) had it not been for the Japanese invasion. On the occasion of Japanese diplomatic recognition of China in 1972 Mao famously stopped Japanese Prime Minister Tanaka from apologizing for the brutal invasion, by telling him that but for Japanese 'help' he, Mao, would not have won.[80] Despite his series of campaigns against class enemies, real and imagined, Mao never initiated a campaign against Chinese collaborators with Japan. Although the war with Japan figured prominently in films, comic books and plays during Mao's rule the key figures were rarely Japanese soldiers, despite their brutality, but rather KMT landlords, officials and capitalists, who at crucial moments would be exposed as traitors. As for Japan itself, Mao argued that the trouble was its ruling class and not its people and he had hopes that even Japan's rulers would stand up for the independence and dignity of the country and end its demeaning alliance with the United States.[81]

It was only once Deng Xiaoping took over after the death of Mao that attitudes began to change. By abandoning class struggle and emphasizing national unity Deng could no longer focus enmity on the KMT as the class enemy; on the contrary he appealed to the Taiwan 'compatriots' to unite with the mainland. At a stroke, the key legitimating victory of the Communist Party shifted away from the Civil War to the defeat of Japan. With the decline of the appeal of communist ideology, Deng based his major appeal to the Chinese people on patriotism. The first campaign was launched in 1982 and it had a strong anti-Japanese component. That is why the first museums commemorating the victory over Japan and Japanese atrocities were not built before the mid-1980s. That theme was intensified particularly after the Tiananmen disaster and the disintegration of the Soviet Union, when Jiang Zemin launched a countrywide 'patriotic education campaign' beginning in 1994 whose anti-Japanese characteristics are still evident in almost daily outpourings in films, TV series, comic books, history textbooks and so on. Not surprisingly perhaps, young nationalists, denied opportunities to express other political views, fill the internet with anti-Japanese invective.[82]

However, it is also necessary to recognize that issues concerning Japan have been the cause of debates and differences within the CCP. The best-known example concerns the former leader Hu Yaobang, who fell foul of the conservatives and was dismissed as General Secretary in 1986 and whose death in April 1989 sparked the Tiananmen demonstrations. In the early 1980s he advocated learning economic development from Japan and cultivating a partnership with it. Still later, at the turn of the century, alarmed at the downward spiral in Sino-Japanese relations caused in large part by Chinese complaints about Japanese refusal to atone sufficiently for its wartime invasion and atrocities, a few commentators argued the need for 'new thinking'. They reflected views in the Ministry of Foreign Affairs and elsewhere that their economic relations and indeed China's whole strategy of cultivating its neighbours were at risk and a more normal policy should be followed. However, only once he had purged a leading member of a faction in the CCP was Hu Jintao able to initiate a new and more balanced relationship with Japan in 2006. Since then Chinese news outlets have begun to portray a more favourable image of Japan and Chinese attitudes towards Japan have softened.[83]

This is not to argue that the past history of Japanese aggression is not an important factor in Sino-Japanese relations, but it is to suggest that its significance has been exaggerated by the course of domestic politics within China. There are of course other deep-seated problems in the relationship, including a strategic rivalry between the two, territorial disputes, Taiwan (Japan's former colony), distrust arising from their different political systems and so on. These will be explored more fully in the next chapter.

The two Koreas[84]

China's approach to the two Koreas maybe seen as congruent with its general foreign policy towards the region as a whole in that a premium was put on promoting a peaceful environment in order to serve the overriding domestic goals of stability and economic development. Thus Beijing was willing to shore up the economy of the North to prevent the collapse of the regime despite its open defiance of Chinese interests in carrying out nuclear tests and demanding recognition as a nuclear power. To the continued frustration of the Chinese, the North was either unwilling or unable to carry out economic reforms as had Vietnam and indeed China. A collapse of the North threatened instability, especially to China's adjacent northeastern provinces and beyond that to Northeast Asia as a whole, which would have endangered much of the Chinese economy, the maintenance of which was necessary for continued Communist Party rule. Additionally such a collapse risked a unification of the Korean peninsula in a context in which the US, through its alliance with the South, would reach to the Chinese border. In other words the North also served as a buffer for China.

Relations with the South were based mainly in economic exchanges that grew extraordinarily rapidly so that by 2010 the value of the South's trade with China exceeded that with the US and Japan combined.[85] The two economies had become virtually interdependent, but given the disparity in size between them there was concern in Seoul about the country's economic dependency on China. However, just as Beijing was unable to use the North's total economic dependency upon China for its survival, so it was unable to translate its economic power over the South into significant political influence, for example by weakening its alliance with America. Nevertheless, Seoul thought it prudent to indicate to the US that it would not allow bases in Korea to be used to meet a military contingency involving Taiwan.

The end of the Cold War transformed China's relations with both North and South Korea. Following the normalization of relations between the Soviet Union and the South in 1990, the North became almost totally dependent on China as it broke off all relations with Moscow in retaliation for Gorbachev's recognition of the South. Meanwhile China's burgeoning economic relationship with the South led to the establishment of diplomatic relations in 1992, much to the chagrin of the North. That also led to the entry of both Koreas into the United Nations. Chinese relations with the North suffered as a result. High-level visits between the two ceased and were not resumed until 1999. Paradoxically, this coincided with the adoption by China of a policy of observing regional norms and of cultivating closer relations with the United States. But in the case of the North the Chinese improved relations, despite the intransigence of the latter and its pursuit of brinkmanship abroad, mainly because of Chinese recognition of its paramount interest in the maintenance of stability in Northeast Asia and the attendant support of the survival of the Northern regime lest its collapse lead precisely to the damaging chaos which Beijing sought to avoid at all costs.

Meanwhile, a desperate and isolated North Korean regime had turned to the development of nuclear weapons as a means of ensuring its survival. That brought about a confrontation with the United States in 1993, which could have led to war, but which resulted in what was called a Framework Agreement in 1994, by which the North agreed to give up its nuclear adventure in return for the supply of heavy oil, until two light water reactors (i.e., nuclear reactors that could not be used for military purposes) could be built for the North, and food aid.

As that agreement broke down amid mutual recriminations between the North Korean regime and the Bush administration in 2001/2002, the North admitted in October 2002 that it had been working for some time on a nuclear programme based on enriched uranium in addition to the one based on plutonium, which had been the only one known to the world outside. That admission, which was soon withdrawn, at once heightened tensions and brought the Chinese more openly into the picture. The impasse that had developed meanwhile between North Korea and the United States over procedural as well as substantive matters was broken with the intercession of the Chinese. First they brought the two protagonists together in Beijing in April 2003. Then, at the insistence of the Americans, the Chinese widened the negotiations to include Russia, South Korea and Japan for the next stage of the negotiations, chaired by the Chinese in Beijing in October that year. The Chinese, who were the main suppliers of Pyongyang's energy needs, persuaded the North to attend and they acted as unofficial intermediaries between the North and the US in seeking to determine the terms under which the six would meet again under China's auspices in Beijing.[86]

China's interests, of course, were by no means altruistic, but there was enough of an overlap with those of the United States and of the other regional states to enable it to play its role with some effectiveness. In particular, all were agreed on the desirability of a denuclearized Korean peninsula and China's interests in stabilizing North–South relations were acceptable to the other parties, even though there was an element in the Bush administration that favoured regime change on the grounds that it did not believe that the North would ever give up its nuclear weapons or its nuclear programme. But the Bush administration was already overcommitted elsewhere, notably in Iraq and Afghanistan, to the extent that it did not want another armed conflict, especially in Korea, where the costs and uncertainties could be extraordinarily high. Hence it welcomed the intercession of the Chinese, who continued to play the role of convener and facilitator of the Six Party Talks.

The North's nuclear test of 6 October 2006 shocked and angered Beijing, raising concern that it may lead to the acquisition of nuclear weapons by the South, Japan and even possibly Taiwan. Doubtless the Chinese were assured by the immediate American response to guarantee the South and Japan that they would be defended by its extended nuclear deterrence, especially as the two showed no sign of an intention to 'go nuclear'. Meanwhile Beijing had joined the other members of the UNSC in passing a sanctions resolution that was harsher than anything it had agreed to before. Despite concerns by some in Beijing that the nuclear and missile testing by the North would weaken its influence as compared with the US, China's leaders decided to enhance their economic relations with the North in the hope of encouraging economic development, which in the Chinese view would better ensure stability in the long run.

Thus although China acceded to another UN sanctions resolution in 2009 after the second nuclear test by the North, it followed this up with an intensification of economic relations with its Northern neighbour.[87] The Obama administration, which came to office in January 2009, had no answer to the conundrum posed by the North other than to call for an unconditional resumption of the 6PT and the holding of the North accountable to its agreements of 2005 and 2007, which called for the verifiable dismantling of its military nuclear programme. To this end the Obama administration looked to China to persuade the North to return to the 6PT, without result by the time of this writing in July 2010. Nevertheless, American policy has served to enhance China's standing as providing the only key to resolving the problem even though, by its actions, Beijing clearly regards the denuclearization of the North as a lesser priority than the US. In fact Beijing was seemingly prepared to pay a heavy price for its support of the North, as shown by its failure either to join in the condemnation of the North for its sinking on 26 March 2010 of a South Korean naval vessel with the loss of forty-six lives or to accept the invitation to examine the evidence as made available by the South after an international inspection.[88] Chinese behaviour drove South Korea, Japan and the US closer together. At Chinese insistence a presidential statement by the UNSC was issued on 9 July 2010 that did not specifically blame the North for the sinking of the ship and as a result the North stated that it was prepared to return to the 6PT. China may be able to claim a success for its diplomatic stance after all, as none of the other powers is inclined to forcibly confront the North.

However, the US and the South were determined to improve their defences against further provocations from the North and to demonstrate that its sinking of the ship 'would have consequences'. They decided to hold military exercises in both the Sea of Japan and the Yellow Sea (i.e., on both sides of the Korean peninsula). The Chinese then publicly demanded that no such exercise with an aircraft carrier be held in the Yellow Sea, which was claimed as vital to the defence of China. But the US and the South insisted on going ahead in both seas, claiming them as international waters. China's new assertiveness and its support for the North had the effect of distancing both the South and Japan and, more generally, it risked a strategic confrontation with the United States over access to international waters in China's vicinity.

Taiwan

This is the one issue that could derail China's strategy of economic development and the foreign relations to which it has given rise. It is a highly emotionally charged issue that goes to the heart of how China's rulers and the young netizens have defined the country's identity and national unity. Put succinctly, the insistence by China's rulers that Taiwan should have no other future except to unite with the mainland and their determination to use force to prevent it from becoming formally independent are detrimental to their stated objectives of stressing peaceful development and openness. Taiwan exercises de facto independence and as a result of democratization in the 1990s it is increasingly asserting its own political identity. Its people have no desire to unite with a Chinese mainland that is ruled by a communist dictatorship and the time is long gone when their fate could be decided without their consent. In this regard they are protected by the United States. The protection of the United States is conditional, rather than absolute. Essentially the American position is that it looks forward to a peaceful settlement between the two sides and that until such time it does not support formal independence for Taiwan, and it also opposes the use of force by the Chinese mainland. This approach has been described as 'strategic ambiguity' and it has kept the peace in this inherently volatile place since Congress passed the Taiwan Relations Act in 1979. As we have seen, the dispatch by the US of two carrier-led battle groups in March 1996 US brought to a halt Beijing's attempt to intimidate Taiwan by displays of force and the firing of missiles.[89]

China's leaders claim that China is incomplete without Taiwan. It is seen as the final reminder of the century of shame and humiliation when bits of China's periphery were detached by aggressive foreigners, and their recovery is essential for the restitution of China's dignity and standing as a great power. Indeed it is sometimes claimed that if Taiwan were not united with the mainland, others with separatist claims in Tibet, Xinjiang and possibly elsewhere would be emboldened to break up the Chinese state.[90] Some leaders suspect that the United States stands in the way of unification precisely to keep China disunited and in an inferior position. The main focus for the modernization of China's armed forces is the task of recovering Taiwan. Military spending has increased annually by double-digit figures since 1989 except for 2010, when it was scheduled to increase by 'only' 7.5 per cent. The real figure of military spending is contested, but the US government and authoritative organizations, such as London's International Institute for Strategic Studies, put it at two to three times the Chinese figure. In any event it is now second only to the US. The Chinese military is the main domestic beneficiary of China's Taiwan policy, as it is argued that without a credible military threat there would be nothing to stop the forces promoting independence on Taiwan from succeeding. The military, therefore, has become the principal institution that consistently demands taking a tough stand on Taiwan, and it also insists on the need to prepare to overcome American naval forces that may come to the aid of Taiwan.

That has had various adverse consequences for the domestic and foreign policies that China's leaders are pledged to pursue. The readiness to use force (albeit in what the Chinese consider to be a domestic matter) creates apprehension elsewhere in the region. The targeting of the US by the Chinese military necessarily complicates relations with America. The interdependence of the Chinese and Taiwanese economies means that China would incur enormous costs if it were to resort to the use of force, and the effect on the region as a whole would be very great too. Meanwhile China pays a certain diplomatic price internationally for its single-minded focus on continually insisting that others deny Taiwan and its leaders what might be called normal courtesies.

China's leaders have shown a degree of flexibility in their approach to Taiwan. Jiang Zemin focused on the need for unification and at one point stated that China could not wait indefinitely. His successor, Hu Jintao, has shifted the formal position to one of opposing secession (a law to that effect was passed in 2005), giving the leadership more time and leeway. However, developments in cross-Strait relations depend very much on the evolution of domestic politics in both Taiwan and China. In effect Beijing is in the position of having to react to the dynamics of domestic Taiwanese politics and of having to rely upon the United States to curb what Beijing chooses to regard as unacceptable provocations. Each time a leader on Taiwan is perceived by Beijing to be making changes in Taiwanese politics that portend a movement away from unification and towards independence, China's leaders react adversely. Beijing's worst fears were realized when Chen Shui-bian of the pro-independence Democratic Progressive Party won the presidential election in 2000 and again in 2004. However, his capacity to legislate was restricted as the KMT still won the majority of seats in the legislature and his attempts to move towards greater independence through referendums eventually led to a public repudiation by President Bush in the presence of China's premier in 2003. From an American perspective, Taiwan could not be allowed through its unilateral actions to undermine American relations with China. Meanwhile Beijing could take satisfaction from the visible American refusal to allow Taiwan to change the status quo unilaterally.[91]

The election in March 2008 of the KMT's Ma Ying-jeou, with his party's greater Chinese consciousness, has led to greater economic and social ties with the mainland, which Beijing hopes will lead to economic integration and eventually to some form of political integration. This has culminated in an agreement to reduce tariffs and expand areas of economic exchanges by a Common Economic Framework Agreement signed on 29 June 2010. But so far closer ties have not changed the affiliations of the people of Taiwan.[92] The position of Beijing might be improved if it were able to offer the people of Taiwan a concept of a 'One China' that they might find attractive. But so far China's leaders have failed to do so. Meanwhile the best that China's leaders can hope for is that they can continue to claim that the balance of forces and events are moving in their favour. That may also allow them to keep the Taiwan issue low on their agenda. After all, a self-governing Taiwan has not prevented China from all the successes it has achieved since embarking on the road of economic modernization in 1978.

China's ascent as a global power in the twenty-first century

China's ascent to global significance has occurred incrementally as a by-product of its rapid economic growth, especially in the first decade of the twenty-first century. It has taken place correspondingly fast and in many ways China's leaders and International Relations scholars and commentators were caught unprepared. Chinese spokesmen have long complained that the international economic and political systems are unfair because they reflect the earlier era of Western dominance. But when China was thrust into a leadership position as the only successful economy to survive the international financial crisis of 2008 its leaders had no alternative arrangements to offer other than to demand that the US maintain the value of its currency, lest it hurt China's accumulated US dollar reserves.[93] Indeed, as a major beneficiary of the international order within which China has prospered and risen peacefully, it is perhaps not surprising that the Chinese had nothing different to offer.

The Chinese government continues to approach international issues and global concerns from its own narrowly conceived interests. As noted earlier, a leading official in foreign affairs reminded his senior American interlocutors at the July 2009 Strategic and Economic Dialogue that 'China's number one core interest is to maintain its fundamental system and state security [i.e., communist party rule and the security apparatus that sustains it]; next is state sovereignty and territorial integrity; and third is the continued stable development of the economy and society.'[94]

China's outlook on the world is still shaped by a narrowly conceived nationalism in which the so-called century of shame and humiliation looms large, alongside a sense of pride in the country's achievement as a modernizing great power. As a result there is a widespread view among officialdom as well as the public at large that the West and the US in particular is still trying to keep China down, or at least prevent its rise to the great-power status to which it is entitled.[95]

China has become a global power of increasing significance in at least three respects: (1) its economic weight; (2) its economic reach into all regions of the world; and (3) its image as the rising superpower.

(1) Even before the beginning of the twenty-first century China had begun to accumulate massive foreign currency reserves, principally in US dollars, as a result of its huge and expanding trade surpluses with the US and the EU. As already mentioned, China's recent rise to international greatness is a product of its rapid economic growth, which has made it into an engine of economic growth in East Asia and indeed the wider world.[96] Beginning in the new century the government encouraged its state-owned enterprises (SOEs) to 'go out' and to 'go global'. The new strategy was built on the industrial policy of the previous decade, which emphasized the role of the big state-owned enterprises and investment in infrastructure and construction. That had the effect of intensifying the need for importing energy, various metals and other raw materials. By 2008 China had become second only to the US as an importer of oil and it was the world's largest importer of iron, copper, manganese, bauxite and others. Indeed, as noted earlier, in 2010 the International Energy Agency announced that China had passed the US as the world's largest consumer of energy.

Within the region China's growing economic significance enabled it to persuade its economic partners to pay more attention to its 'core interests', especially regarding Taiwan. For example, Australia, America's staunchest ally in the region, shifted its position of support for the American display of military power near Taiwan in the 1995–96 crisis to declaring in 2004 that it would not necessarily support the US in the event of another Taiwan contingency. In a similar vein the Australian government decided in 2008 to terminate its involvement in the Quadrilateral Dialogue including the US, India and Japan to which China had registered formal objections. The Australian example, however, also illustrates limits to the ability of the Chinese government to use its economic weight for political purposes. Despite Australia's dependence on China for economic growth, the Australian government has taken steps to limit Chinese direct influence over key sectors of the economy and it has not weakened its commitment to the alliance with the US. Its political elites and the general public are wary of the political, economic and strategic implications of a more powerful China, even as they seek to capitalize on the opportunities presented by China's rise.[97] This is also true for most of China's neighbours and not only for those who have territorial or maritime disputes with it. But the repercussions of the sharper position on the South China Sea taken by Clinton at the ARF meeting in July remain to be seen.

(2) The Chinese need for resources brought about an astonishing outreach to most regions of the world. As noted earlier, the value of China's trade with Africa and Latin America leapfrogged from about $20 billion in 2000 to over $140 billion respectively, by 2008.[98] In the process China found new markets for its manufactures and it became a contributor to the economic growth and

wellbeing of both African and Latin American countries. In some of the latter the value of its trade began to exceed the value of trade with the US, thereby reducing their sense of dependency on their giant neighbour to the north. In some cases Chinese contracts with anti-market and anti-US regimes such as Venezuela and Ecuador may be seen as contrary to American and international market interests. But in others such as Chile, Peru and Costa Rica, enhanced economic relations with China contribute to the success of market economies and the democratic processes of their government. The commerce with China on the whole contributes to the extractive industries of Latin America and to the building of infrastructure (roads, rail, ports and so on), but the import of Chinese manufactures and increasingly higher tech products threatens local producers. Likewise the import of Chinese labour and labour practices raises new problems. It is perhaps too early to assess the impact of China in Latin America and indeed the impact of this complex engagement on China itself. But it is clearly increasing China's visibility as a global player.[99]

Much the same may be said of China's renewed engagement with Africa after a twenty to thirty year hiatus since the Maoist revolutionary days. China has become a major investor in Africa, primarily in the extractive industries, and in the process it has focused on developing infrastructure. As in Latin America, the Chinese operate in both autocracies and more pluralistic and democratic countries. As in Latin America, Chinese manufactured goods have threatened the survival of local producers. But the Chinese are also investing in local industries in many cases. The Chinese approach is not encumbered by conditions imposed by those of the EU and the major economic organizations concerning good governance, human rights, transparency and sustainability. By the same token the Chinese can deliver on contracts more quickly, without being entangled by the complicated procedures followed by Western countries. However, the Chinese are increasingly sharing the same Western concerns about sustainability and the local capacity to fulfill promises. Chinese have also found themselves having to deal with local discontent about labour practices and the importation of Chinese labour. Whatever the rhetoric of Chinese leaders about equality and South–South relations, the relationship is not equal and the cultural differences are great. The novelty, the speed by which its presence has grown and the headline size of many of its investments should not obscure the fact that China's presence in Africa is still much less that that of Western countries. In 2007, for example, the total value of Chinese investment in Africa came to about \$7.5 billion, that of the US \$13 billion and of Europe \$25 billion. Nevertheless, China has become an important player in Africa and that has contributed greatly to its new global stature.[100]

(3) China draws prestige and international significance from the widespread perception of it as a superpower. Beijing, of course, denies this, as it interprets the meaning of superpower as the exercise of dominion over others. But at the same time Beijing asserts the right for its views to be taken into account on all major international issues. In Washington it is generally held that no global issue can be properly addressed without involving China. It was in Washington that the

concept of a G-2 was first advanced in 2008 separately by Fred Bergsten, a leading economist, and by Z. Brzezinski, a former National Security Adviser and a leading strategist.[101] Although the term was disavowed by the Obama administration, Obama initially placed much hope on the idea of a partnership with China as a means for addressing regional and global problems. Beijing disavowed the idea of some kind of Sino-American duopoly, but it appreciated the sense that it was being treated as an equal by the United States. Beyond that China's standing has never been higher in the rest of the world. But as a consequence of its greater entanglement with the outside world China is finding new problems and difficulties, whether in terms of its economic and commercial practices at home and abroad or in terms of addressing competing priorities.

China has emerged as an international stakeholder, but not necessarily in the terms that Robert Zoellick originally conceived in 2005. China is best understood as an international stakeholder with its own characteristics. Although it's true to say that China generally acts internationally in accordance with its narrowly conceived national interests, it has signed up to and participated actively in many international regimes and institutions that transcend them, or extend them. For example, under the terms of the non-proliferation regime China necessarily endorses the right of the International Atomic Energy Agency to carry out intrusive inspections in countries that go beyond the pristine forms of sovereignty advocated by Beijing. Similarly, in joining the WTO the Chinese government agreed to change many of its domestic laws and practices to meet WTO criteria and to allow its commercial conduct to be subject to legal adjudication by that external body.

Nevertheless there are certain patterns to its international behaviour that reflect some of the broader principles advanced by its leaders. These include the Five Principles of Peaceful Coexistence, especially those that accept the legitimacy of diverse systems of government and that advocate non-interference. The first has been interpreted to be in favour of international democratization, meaning that all states should be treated equally regardless of their different political systems and that their governments (however autocratic) should be treated as representative of their people. In other words, international democratization is not based on the idea that all states should be democracies. Similarly, Beijing sees no need to allow acts of self-determination in a post-colonial world, as that would only lead to separatism, which runs counter to the emphasis on the inviolability of sovereignty and territorial integrity. Obviously Beijing has in mind Taiwan and Tibet. Not surprisingly, Beijing does not favour the so-called colour revolutions in which authoritarian regimes have been overthrown by popular opposition encouraged by organs of civil society, which have frequently enjoyed the support of the West. As may be seen, these are positions all congruent with China's 'core interests', but they also converge with nearly all the post-colonial governments who constitute an overwhelming majority in the United Nations. This ensures built-in majorities in the UN General Assembly for China and its policies and this also helps China project an image of leadership in the developing world even though in some respects its interests diverge from that world.

Given China's position as a permanent member of the UN Security Council, it exercises a power of veto and it has used the threat of the veto skillfully to water down draft resolutions seeking to sanction governments with whom it has vital economic or strategic links. China also claims to behave as a 'responsible great power' – an ill-defined term that at least formally denotes the view that China is already a great power. In that sense it is an acknowledgement that, beyond its declared principles and the rhetoric of 'peaceful development' or 'international harmony' and so on, China's leaders take into account very seriously power considerations including those of relative power and balances of power.

As we have already seen, these different traits are in evidence in Chinese behaviour within the Asia-Pacific region. At issue perhaps is whether China can be said to have been constrained from pursuing its national-interest agenda in the region by its commitments to various international norms. One example often cited is the Sino-ASEAN Declaration of a Code of Conduct in the South China Sea of November 2002 as a cause of Chinese forbearance in forcibly asserting its claims in the South China Sea since 1995. Others point to the same example to argue that Chinese forbearance has less to do with norms and more to do with a hard-headed cost-benefit analysis as to the damage that might accrue to China's broader interests if it were to be seen to be using force to those ends. However, regardless of the precise motives, the longer the Chinese exercise forbearance the more difficult and more costly it would be for them to resort to the use of force. In that sense China has become a better international citizen. This will be put to the test now that Beijing has elevated its claims in the South China Sea to those of its 'core national interest' and it has increased its naval deployments accordingly, especially as we have seen the Americans have responded more robustly.

China's national identity

China has been free of threats of invasion or attack since the dissolution of the Soviet Union in 1991 and it has enjoyed a strategic latitude in dealing with its periphery, and indeed the world beyond, that it had not experienced for the previous 200 years or more. Therefore it is the way in which China's rulers think about themselves and their external relations which have become more important in shaping the country's attitude to the outside world and in shaping its emergence as a global power. Put differently, Chinese approaches to world order will be fashioned by the values underpinning order at home in much the same way that has been true of other global powers. For example, the Soviet Union promoted the spread of Soviet-style communism and the United States encourages the spread of democracy and free trade – values which underpin the international organizations it helped establish after the end of the Second World War.

In China's case the situation is more complex as it has risen in the last two or three decades within an international system based on norms and rules established by Western powers, notably the United States. In many respects China has had to follow them and indeed there is a considerable body of literature by

Western scholars which argues that China has been 'socialized' by them.[102] Others, however, argue that China is still very much in the process of adjusting to the modern world, as manifested by the stresses and strains of its domestic reforms and by the uncertainties attendant upon its relations with neighbouring countries and the United States.[103] Still others note that Chinese are unsettled about how to classify their country as a developing country or a major power and as to whether they are still caught up in the sense of victimhood arising from the 'century of shame and humiliation' or whether they have reached the point of taking pride in their achievement and their historical greatness.[104]

The question of China's identity and what it means to be Chinese is highly complex and debatable. It has given rise to a huge literature that is too varied to allow for a brief summary here.[105] In evaluating these different views and arguments it is important to give due consideration to the first of the 'core national interests' as defined by China's leaders, namely maintaining the rule of the Communist Party. It was insisted upon by Deng Xiaoping in resisting political reform in the 1980s, culminating in his crushing of the demonstrators on 4 June 1989, and it has been repeated by his successors, who have considerably strengthened the forces maintaining internal security. The Party has proved itself to be remarkably adaptive in maintaining its leading role, from the conductor of class struggle in the Maoist period, when Confucius and the imperial past was denigrated, to the leader of capitalist reforms and the upholder of Confucius and the inheritor of the imperial legacy in the period of modernization. Despite these tremendous changes the CCP has retained its Leninist system of organization and practices.[106]

The CCP and its Leninist organization structures China's international conduct in some very important ways. It puts the country at variance with the liberal norms that underpin much of the institutions and practices which underpin current international society. Although the Chinese government may find ways to adapt to the demands of free trade, legality, human rights and so on, there is nonetheless resistance to them at a fundamental level. This also affects the level and depth of international cooperation which it is possible to develop with China. It is not difficult to point to many examples of Chinese cooperative behaviour, but at issue is the character or quality of that cooperation. If it can be seen to result from the realist calculations or simply from the emergence of parallel interests in mutually beneficial outcomes at minimal cost, the resulting cooperation is unlikely to be robust and enduring. One explanation of what constitutes the more enduring kind claims that 'co-operation occurs when actors adjust their behaviour to the actual or anticipated preferences of others, through a policy of co-ordination. Policy co-ordination in turn implies that the policies of each state have been adjusted to reduce their negative consequences for other states.'[107] A similar point is made differently in the observation that 'inter-governmental co-operation takes place when the policies actually followed by one government are regarded by its partners as facilitating the realization of their own objectives, as the result of a process of policy coordination.'[108]

The Leninist system of the CCP requires secrecy and its regulatory character allows no disclosure of information to others, let alone allowing their participation. While the internal politics of China's neighbours are open to the extent that outsiders can easily identify the key players and interests, the arguments and the strengths and weaknesses of all sides, the same does not hold true for China. The disparity necessarily breeds uncertainty and distrust.

Finally, the character of Chinese nationalism, which has been encouraged by the CCP and promoted by the multimedia outlets of its propaganda organization, is one that still propagates a sense of Chinese victimhood derived from the 'hundred years of humiliation' that officially ended more than sixty years ago in 1949. That has become central to the historical claim to legitimacy of the CCP. Perhaps that is why the return of Hong Kong in 1997 and Macau two years later were portrayed to Chinese at home as a major achievement in the process towards completing China's unification. Interestingly, little was made of China's obligation under the agreement of 1984 with Britain, to maintain Hong Kong's separate system as confirmed by the Basic Law, and to move towards the election of the leader and the legislature by universal franchise. However, Beijing has applied united-front tactics to ensure that it is in effective control of Hong Kong and its future development. The CCP has further reinterpreted history to place itself as the upholder of China's historical greatness. Confucius is not only back in favour, but 'Confucian Institutes' have recently been established throughout the world to spread knowledge of Chinese language and culture. The downside to this, apart from intensifying problems in relations with Japan, is to accentuate a divide between 'us and them', as was evident for example in the course of the parading of the Olympic torch in various international cities prior to the Olympic Games in 2008 or in the reaction in China to press reports of disturbances in Tibet earlier that year.[109]

One of the determinants of the security of the Asia-Pacific in the years ahead will be the extent to which China's rulers will be willing and able to moderate the nationalism which fuels their demands to claim the islands and maritime resources in the name of China's sovereignty and territorial integrity if it is to reach settlement acceptable to neighbours with whom that sovereignty is in dispute, especially now that America has joined the diplomatic fray.

Notes

1 Susan L. Shirk, *China: Fragile Superpower: How China's Internal Politics Could Derail Its Peaceful Rise* (Oxford: Oxford University Press, 2007).

2 See the brief discussion of the different views within the Chinese domestic academic community in David Shambaugh, 'China: an Unpredictable Global Power', *China Review* (London: Great Britain–China Centre) 50 (Summer 2010), pp.2–5.

3 For the period up to 1994, see the East Asian Analytical Unit of the Australian Department of Foreign Affairs and Trade, *Overseas Chinese Business Networks in Asia*, 1995. For the period since then see, Hung-gay Fung, Changhong Pei, Kevin H. Zhang, *China and the Challenge of Economic Globalization: The Impact of WTO Membership* (Armonk, NY: ME Sharpe, 2006), pp.31–35.

4 Statistics taken from China's Ministry of Commerce (MOFCOM) website.

5 Leslie Hook, 'China denies IEA claim on energy consumption', *Financial Times*, 20 July 2010.

6 Peter Hays Gries, *China's New Nationalism: Pride, Politics and Diplomacy* (Berkeley: University of California Press, 2004).

7 Shirk (*op. cit.*), especially ch. 4, 'The Echo Chamber of Nationalism, Media and the Internet', pp.79–104.

8 Dai's talk at the China-US Strategic and Economic Dialogue, 28/29 July 2009. Cited by Orville Schell, 'China Defending its Core Interest in the World – Part I' in *Yale Global Online* p.2 at http://yaleglobal.yale.edu/content/china-defending-its-core-interest-world – Part-I (accessed 11 April 2010).

9 For Zhao Ziyang's perspective on the conflict between conservatives and reformers, which brought him down, see *Prisoner of the State: The Secret Journal of Premier Zhao Ziyang*, translated and edited by Bao Pu, Renee Chiang and Adi Ignatius (New York: Simon & Schuster, 2009).

10 Joseph Fewsmith, *China Since Tiananmen*, ch. 2, 'Deng Moves to Revive Reform' (Cambridge University Press, 2001), pp.44–71.

11 For a full discussion of inner Party debates and policies see David Shambaugh, *China's Communist Party: Atrophy and Adaptation* (Washington, DC: Woodrow Wilson Center Press & Berkeley: University of California Press, 2008).

12 Saw Swee-Hock, Sheng Lijun and Chin Kin Wah, 'An Overview of ASEAN-China Relations' in their joint (eds.), *ASEAN-China Relations: Realities and Prospects* (Singapore: Institute of Southeast Asian Studies, 2005), eds. p.1.

13 Percy Cradock, *Experiences of China*, 'Chapter Twenty-Three, The Airport Agreement' (London: John Murray, 1994) pp.237–46.

14 James Mann, *About Face: A History of America's Curious Relations with China, From Nixon to Clinton* (New York: Alfred A. Kopf, 1998), pp.249–50.

15 See, Scott Snyder, *China's Rise and the Two Koreas: Politics, Economics, Security*, ch. 2, 'China's Shift to a two Korea Policy' (Boulder, CO: Lynne Rienner, 2009) pp.23–46; see also, Don Oberdorfer, *The Two Koreas* (Boston: Addison Wesley, 1997), ch.10, pp.229–48.

16 See, Jusuf Wanandi, *Asia-Pacific After the Cold War* (Jakarta: Centre for Strategic and International Studies, 1996).

17 For an account of its origins and early development, see Michael Leifer, *The ASEAN Regional Forum* (London: Oxford University Press, for the International Institute of Strategic Studies, Adelphi Papers no.302, 1996).

18 See the discussion of China's threat perceptions in David Shambaugh, *Modernizing China's Military* (Berkeley: University of California Press, 2002), ch.7, pp.284–327.

19 Originally directed against challenging Gorbachev on ideological grounds in 1991, but since cited by Chinese scholars to refer to foreign affairs more generally and the handling of the US particularly. See my chapter in David Shambaugh (ed.), *Deng Xiaoping: Portrait of a Chinese Statesman* (Oxford: Clarendon Press, 1995), p.156.

20 Shambaugh, *Modernizing China's Military* (*op. cit.*), p.69ff.

21 Robert L. Suettinger, *Beyond Tiananmen: The Politics of U.S.-China Relations, 1989–2000* (Washington, DC: The Brookings Institution, 2003), p.143.

22 Address by W. Anthony Lake on 17 May 1994 at the School for Advanced International Studies, Johns Hopkins University, Washington DC, online at www.mtholyoke.edu/acad/intre/lakedoc.html.

23 For an informed account, see Mann, *About Face* (*op. cit.*), ch.16, pp.292–314.

24 According to American official figures. By 2003 it was to reach US$120 billion and by 2008 $268 billion, before declining somewhat because of the recession to $227 billion in 2009. Nevertheless the $34 billion deficit of 1995 was considered sufficiently large at that point to become a political issue in domestic American politics and, hence, in Sino-American relations.

25 For a succinct account of the two statements, see Alan D. Romberg, *Rein in at the Brink of the Precipice, American Policy Toward Taiwan and US–PRC Relations* (Washington, DC: Henry L. Stimson Center, 2003), pp.163–64.
26 This and the following paragraph rely heavily on Suettinger, *Beyond Tiananmen* (*op. cit.*), chs 6, 7; and on Romberg, *Rein in at the Brink of the Precipice* (*op. cit.*), pp.164–76. See also, Robert L. Suettinger, 'U.S. "Management" of Three Taiwan Crises' and Niu Jun, 'Chinese Decision-Making in Three Military Actions Across the Taiwan Strait' in Michael Swaine, Tuosheng Zhang and Danielle Cohen (eds), *Managing Sino-American Crises* (Washington, DC: Carnegie Endowment for International Peace, 2006) pp.251–92 and 293–326, respectively.
27 See the discussion by Michael Leifer, 'China in Southeast Asia: Interdependence and Accommodation' in David S.G. Goodman and Gerald Segal (eds), *China Rising: Nationalism and Interdependence* (London: Routledge, 1997), pp.156–71.
28 For a more detailed account, see Reinhard Drifte, *Japan's Security Relations with China Since 1989* (London: RoutledgeCurzon, 2003), pp.91–101.
29 Francois Godement, *The Downsizing of Asia* (London: Routledge, 1999), p.188.
30 For detailed analysis on which this and the subsequent two paragraphs are based, see Nancy Berkhopf Tucker, 'The Clinton Years: The Problem of Coherence' in Michel Oksenberg, Ramon H. Myers and David Shambaugh (eds.), *Making China Policy* (Lanham, MD: Rowman and Littlefield, 2001), pp.59–69. For the disparagement of Japan, see Michael Yahuda, 'China: Incomplete Reforms' in Gerald Segal and David S.G. Goodman (eds), *Towards Recovery in Pacific Asia* (London: Routledge, 2000), p.91.
31 See, Christopher R. Hughes, *Chinese Nationalism in the Global Era* (London: Routledge, 2006).
32 This and the next paragraph draw considerably on Fewsmith, *China Since Tiananmen* (*op. cit.*), ch.7, pp.190–220.
33 Cited in 'Sino-American tensions', *Strategic Comments* (London: IISS) 5, 5, June 1999.
34 Shirk, *China: Fragile Superpower* (*op. cit.*), pp.215–16.
35 For details, see Romberg, *Rein in at the Brink of the Precipice* (*op. cit.*), pp.180–89.
36 David Finkelstein, 'China Reconsiders its National Security: The Great Peace and Development Debate of 1999', Alexandria: The CNA Corporation, 2000. Available online: www.cna.org/centers/china/publications.
37 For analysis and representations of the Chinese intellectual debates at the turn of the twenty-first century about the country's paths of development, see Chahua Wang (ed.), *One China, Many Paths* (London: Verso Press, 2003); and Lin Chun, *The Transformation of Chinese Socialism* (Durham and London: Duke University Press, 2006).
38 For an assessment of the initial impact of WTO membership, see Margaret M. Pearson, 'Lessons from China's Early Years in the World Trade Organization', in Alastair Iain Johnston and Robert S. Ross (eds), *New Directions in the Study of China's Foreign Policy* (Stanford University Press, 2006), pp.242–75.
39 Danny Schechter, *Falun Gong's Challenge to China: Spiritual Practice or 'Evil Cult'* (New York: Akashik Books, 2000).
40 Mann, *About Face,* (*op. cit.*), 'Prologue', pp.3–12.
41 See Elizabeth Economy and Michel Oksenberg (eds), *China Joins the World: Progress and Prospects* (New York: Council on Foreign Affairs, 1999). See also William R. Feeney, 'China and the Multilateral Economic Institutions' in Samuel S. Kim (ed.), *China and the World* (Boulder: Westview Press, 4th edn, 1988), pp.239–63.
42 Alastair Iain Johnston, 'China's International Relations: The Political and Security Dimensions' in Samuel S. Kim (ed.), *The International Relations of Northeast Asia* (Lanham, MD: Rowman and Littlefield, 2003), p.70.
43 For an analysis of the significance of this, see Rosemary Foot, *Rights Beyond Borders* (Oxford: Oxford University Press, 2000).

44 International Crisis Group, Policy Report, 'China's Growing Role in UN Peace-keeping', Asia Report No. 166, 17 April 2009.
45 See the discussion by Guoguang Wu, 'Multiple levels of Multilateralism: The rising China in the turbulent world', Guoguang Wu and Helen Landsdowne, *China Turns to Multilateralism: Foreign policy and regional security* (London: Routledge, 2008), pp.267–89.
46 See the discussion in Johnston, 'China's International Relations' (*op. cit.*), pp.65–100. See also the analysis of the Chinese strategic debate, David Finkelstein, *China Reconsiders its National Security* (*op. cit.*).
47 For an account of the developments that led to this new approach, see David Shambaugh, 'China and the New Asian Landscape' in David Shambaugh (ed.), *Power Shift: China and Asia's New Dynamics* (Berkeley: University of California Press, 2005), pp.1–20.
48 See Carlyle Thayer, 'China's New Security Concept and Southeast Asia' in David W. Lovell (ed.), *Pacific Security Policy Changes* (Singapore: ISEAS, 2003), pp.89–107.
49 Ralf Emmers and See Seng Tan, 'The ASEAN Regional Forum and Preventive Diplomacy: A Failure in Practice.' *RSIS Working Paper #189* (Singapore, 7 December 2009).
50 Author's conversation with a senior Chinese diplomat in Seoul, 23 December 1996.
51 See David Shambaugh, 'China and the Korean Peninsula: Playing for the Long Term', *Washington Quarterly* (Spring 2003), pp.43–56.
52 Bates Gill, *Rising Star: China's New Security Diplomacy* (Washington, DC: Brookings, 2007), pp.21–74.
53 Anne Booth, 'China and Southeast Asia: Challenges and Opportunity' in David Shambaugh, *Charting China's Future, 2010–2015* (forthcoming 2010).
54 See Wang Gung Wu, 'China and Southeast Asia: The Context of a New Beginning' in Shambaugh (ed.), *Power Shift* (*op. cit.*), pp.187–204.
55 The texts of these and other statements may be found on the ASEAN website, online at www.asean.sec.org/home.htm.
56 For background see, Barry Wain, 'Manila's Bungle in the South China Sea', *Far Eastern Economic Review* 171, 1 (2008), pp.45–48.
57 Richard Weitz, 'Global insights; China's Military Buildup Stokes Regional Arms Race', *World Politics Review*, 4 July 2010.
58 Robert L. Suettinger, 'The Rise and Descent of "Peaceful Rise"', *China Leadership Monitor*, 12 (30 October 2004), pp.1–10. See also Speeches of Zheng Bijian 1997–2005, *China's Peaceful Rise* (Washington, DC: Brookings, 2005).
59 ASEAN Secretariat website.
60 Joel Rathus, 'The Chiang Mai Initiative's multilateralization: A good start', *East Asia Forum*, 23 March 2010.
61 Wang Gung Wu, *The Chinese Overseas: from Earthbound China to the Quest for Autonomy*, (Cambridge, MA: Harvard University Press, 2000). For the new difficulties as experienced by contemporary overseas Chinese see, Geremie Barme, 'Strangers at Home', *The Wall Street Journal* 19 July 2010.
62 For details see ASEAN Secretariat website.
63 Bates Gill and Matthew Oresman, *China's New Journey to the West* (Washington, DC: CSIS, 2003).
64 John W. Garver, 'China's Influence in Central and South Asia: Is it increasing?' in Shambaugh (ed.), *Power Shift* (*op. cit.*), pp.205–27.
65 Pepe Escobar, 'China Plays Pipelineistan' *Asia Times On Line*, 24 December 2009 and M.K. Bhadrakumar, 'China resets terms of engagement in Central Asia', parts 1, 2 and 3. *Ibid.*, 24 December 2009.
66 Mark Katz, 'Russia and the Shanghai Cooperation Organization: Russia's Lonely Road from Bishkek to Dushanbe', *Asian Perspective* 32, 3 (2008), pp.183–87.

67 M. Taylor Fravel, *Strong Borders Secure Nation: Cooperation and Conflict in China's Territorial Disputes* (Princeton: Princeton University Press, 2008).

68 AP, 'US Wades into South China Sea', 25 July 2010 and Greg Torode, 'How the US ambushed China in its backyard', *South China Morning Post*, 25 July 2010.

69 See Evan Medeiros and M. Taylor Travel, 'China's New Diplomacy', *Foreign Affairs* (November–December, 2003), pp.22–35.

70 Robert G. Sutter, *Chinese Foreign Relations: Power and Policy Since the Cold War* (Lanham, MD: Rowman & Littlefield, 2008), pp.173–75. See especially footnote 36.

71 Sutter, *China's Foreign Relations (op. cit.)*, pp.174–75.

72 Bates Gill and Matthew Orensen, *China's New Journey to the West (op. cit.)*.

73 See Andrew Small, 'China's Caution on Afghanistan and Pakistan', *Washington Quarterly*, 33, 3 (July 2010), pp.81–97. See also, Michael Swaine, 'China and the "AfPak Issue"', *China Leadership Monitor*, no. 31, 15 February 2010, pp.1–22.

74 Jonathan Hoslag, *China and India: Prospects for Peace* (New York: Columbia University Press, 2010), pp.76–81; and Satyajit Mohanty, 'Sino-Indian Trade Ties: an Uncertain Future', Institute of Peace and Conflict Studies #3053, 2 February 2010. www.ipcs.org/sino-indian-trade-ties-an-uncertain-future-3053-2010.

75 For a thoroughly researched analysis of the history of the relationship, see John W. Garver, *Protracted Contest: Sino-Indian Rivalry in the Twentieth Century* (Seattle: University of Washington Press, 2001).

76 See chs 5 and 6 of Hoslag, *(op. cit.)*. See also M.K. Bhadrakumer, 'The Dragon spews fire at the Elephant' *Asia Times Online*, 17 October 2009; and Vikas Bajaj, 'India worries as China builds ports in South Asia' *New York Times*, 16 February 2010.

77 For a non-realist view see, Amardeep Athwal, *China-India Relations: Contemporary Dynamics* (London: Routledge, 2009). For a Chinese view see, Wang Hui, 'Gnawing issues in China-India relations', *China Daily*, 9 April 2010. For an Indian view see, Rajesh Kumer Mishra, 'China-Indian Relations not independent of US-China relations' *South Asia Analysis Group*, paper number 172. Available online: www.southasiaanalysis.org/%5Cpaper.172.htm.

78 For a brief, but good, overview, see, Chietigi Bajpayee, 'China-India Relations: Regional Rivalry Takes the World Stage', *China Security*, 2010/ Issue 17, June 2010. Available online: www.chinasecurity.us/index.php?option=com_content&view=article&id=469&ltemid=8. Accessed 23 June 2010.

79 See Jonathan Spence, *In Search of Modern China* (London: Hutchinson, 1990), relevant chapters.

80 *Tokyo Shimbun*, 27 September 1972. Cited in Ross Terrill, *The New Chinese Empire* (New York: Basic Books 2003) p.284.

81 See, Michael Yahuda, 'Sino-Japanese Relations: Partners and Rivals?' *Korean Journal of Defense Analysis*, 21, 4 (2009), pp.365–79.

82 Gries, *China's New Nationalism (op. cit.)*.

83 See Yahuda *(op. cit.)*.

84 Much of the analysis is drawn from Scott Snyder, *China's Rise and the Two Koreas*, (Boulder, CO: Lynne Reinner, 2009).

85 IMF, *Direction of Trade Statistics* 2009.

86 On the first crisis, see Oberdorfer, *The Two Koreas (op. cit.)*, ch.13. On China's role in the Bush period, see 'The Koreas: Dangerous Defiance' in International Institute of Strategic Studies, *Strategic Survey 2002/2003* (Oxford: Oxford University Press, 2003), pp.194–209.

87 For an explanation by a senior Chinese academic of his country's commitment to the North, see Wang Chong, 'China must not abandon North Korea', *Global Times* (Beijing), 23 June 2009. For an account of China's economic efforts to shore up the North, see Gordon G. Chang, 'Beijing is Violating North Korean Sanctions', *Wall Street Journal*, 15 October 2009.

88 Bonnie Glaser and Brad Glosserman, 'China's Cheonan Problem', Hawaii: CSIS, *PacNet* #31, 18 June 2010.
89 Richard Bush III, *Untying the Knot: Making Peace in the Taiwan Strait* (Washington, DC: Brookings, 2005).
90 For an analysis of the Chinese claims, see Alan M. Wachman, *Why Taiwan?* (Stanford: Stanford University Press, 2007).
91 See Richard Bush III, *Untying The Knot* (*op. cit.*); and Alan D. Romberg, *Rein in at the Brink of the Precipice: American Policy Toward Taiwan and US PRC Relations* (Washington, DC: Henry L. Stimson Center, 2003).
92 See Zhidong Hao, *Whither Taiwan and Mainland China: National Identity, the State and Intellectuals* (Seattle: University of Washington Press, 2010).
93 Its leading bank official also suggested that IMF Special Drawing Rights could be an alternative. But not even Chinese officials presented this as a serious means of addressing the current financial crisis.
94 The official *China News Agency*, 28 July 2009, as cited in *China Digital Times*, 29 July 2009, http://chinadigitaltimes.net.
95 These themes are explored in depth in William A. Callahan, *China the Pessoptimist Nation* (Oxford: Oxford University Press, 2010).
96 For a discussion of various views about the international significance of the Chinese economy and the dependence of the Chinese economy on the international economy, see Sutter, *Chinese Foreign Relations* (*op. cit.*) ch. 4, pp.91–129.
97 See James Manicom and Andrew O'Neil, 'Accommodation, realignment, or business as usual? Australia's response to a rising China', *Pacific Review* 23, 1 (March 2010), pp.23–44.
98 Statistics drawn from China's Ministry of Commerce website, English.mofcom.gov.cn/statistic/statistic.html.
99 See R. Evan Ellis, *China in Latin America: the Whats and Wherefores* (Boulder, CO: Lynne Rienner, 2009).
100 Among the extensive literature on Sino-African relations the following are especially notable: Chris Alden, *China in Africa* (London: Zed Books, 2007); Sarah Raine, *China's African Challenges* (London: Routledge, for IISS, 2009); Deborah Brautigam, *The Dragon's Gift: The Real Story of China in Africa* (Oxford: Oxford University Press, 2009) – from which the statistics are drawn, p.184; and Julia Strauss and Martha Saaveda (eds), *China and Africa: Emerging Patterns in Globalization and Development* (Cambridge: Cambridge University Press, China Quarterly Special Issue, 2009).
101 See Fred Bergsten, 'A Partnership of Equals', *Foreign Affairs*, 87, 4 (July/August 2008), pp.57–69; and Zbignew Brzezinski, speech in Beijing on the thirtieth anniversary of the establishment of US-China diplomatic relations, 13 January 2009.
102 See, for example, Bates Gill, *Rising Star* (*op. cit.*), Alastair Iain Johnston, *Social Status: China in International Institutions, 1980–2000* (Princeton: Princeton University Press, 2008); David M. Lampton, *The Three Faces of Chinese Power: Might, Money and Minds* (Berkeley: University of California Press, 2008); and Evan S. Medeiros and M. Taylor Travel, 'China's New Diplomacy' *Foreign Affairs* 82 6, 2003.
103 See, for example, Avery Goldstein, *Rising to the Challenge: China's Grand Strategy and International Security* (Stanford: Stanford University Press, 2004) and; Shirk, *China: Fragile Superpower* (*op. cit.*).
104 See, in particular, William A. Callaghan, *China the Pessomist Nation* (Oxford: Oxford University Press, 2010).
105 The most recent of relevance to the analysis here are Christopher R. Hughes, *Chinese Nationalism in the Global era* (London: Routledge, 2006) and William A. Callaghan, *China the Pessopimist Nation* (*op. cit.*).
106 For analyses of the significance of the CCP and Leninism, see Richard McGregor, *The Party: The Secret World of China's Communist Rulers* (New York: Harper Collins, 2010); see also David Shambaugh, *China's Communist Party: Atrophy and Adaptation* (Berkeley: University of California Press, 2008).

107 Helen Milner, 'International Theories of Cooperation among Nations: Strengths and Weaknesses', *World Politics*, 44, 3 (April, 1992), p.467.

108 Robert O. Keohane, *After Hegemony: Cooperation and Discord in the World Economy* (Princeton: Princeton University Press, 1984), pp.51–52.

109 For accounts and analyses of these dimensions of Chinese nationalism, see Shirk and Gries (*op. cit.*), but see especially Callaghan, *China the Pessoptimist Nation* (*op. cit.*).

11 Japan

Coping with relative decline

In the two decades since the end of the Cold War Japan has been transformed from a country that was seemingly on the cusp of supplanting the United States as the world's leading economy to a country that is seemingly gripped in a downward cycle of relative decline. The decline is encapsulated in the fall of Tokyo's Nikkei Stock average from its all-time high of 38,915.87 on 29 December 1989 to its post-bubble low of 7,054.98 in 2009. In mitigation of this image of drastic decline, it should be noted that the immensity of the asset bubble that burst in 1991 (when the value of Tokyo's real estate was said to exceed that of the whole of the US) exaggerates the steepness of the decline. In fact real GDP rose by 25 per cent between 1990 and 2008. Nevertheless the Japanese economy did experience relative decline, as may be discerned from the comparison with the United States, whose GDP grew by 84 per cent in the same period.[1] Indeed, writing in July 2010 a former vice-minister of the once acclaimed MITI (Ministry of International Trade and Industry), pointed out that Japan's share of global GNP had fallen from 14.3 per cent in 1990 to 8.9 per cent in 2008 and that it was due to sink below that of China. He further lamented that Japan had lost its top positions in the production of traditional industrial goods to China, one after another, and that Japanese manufacturers lag behind South Korean and Taiwanese makers of LED, 3D and other high-tech products.[2]

The end of the Cold War did not in itself precipitate Japan's economic decline, but it changed fundamentally Japan's international and political environment in ways that required corresponding political and economic adjustments that its domestic system proved unable to bring about. The Japanese political and economic systems were both the product of the arrangements made at the end of the American occupation in 1952, which had resulted in one-party rule by the conservative Liberal Democratic Party since 1955. The result was a political system in which the triangular arrangement between the LDP, big business and the government bureaucracy became embedded and all three had vested interests in obstructing change. The economic system too was resistant to change as the interlocking mechanisms by which banks were invested in the major companies to whom they extend loans, which had worked so well when the economy was growing fast, turned into a kind of gridlock once the economy began to decline. The massive loans to companies that remained on the books of the banks could not be repaid and the banks could not bankrupt them without bankrupting themselves. At the same time the LDP, which was tied up with the major companies, had a vested interest in resisting major reform.[3]

The unexpected and rapid end of the Cold War left Japan unprepared to address the strategic challenge of developing a more independent role now that the bargain of the Yoshida Doctrine was no longer viable. The trade-off between allowing the United States to provide security for Japan, and to use the country as a base for its dominance of the Western Pacific, while Japan pursued economic development along neomercantilist lines, had suddenly broken down. The Japanese economic model was in disarray and the United States now wanted Japan to contribute militarily to the security dimensions of the American provision of global public goods.

Yet the international changes brought about by the end of the Cold War required significant adaptations by Japan. The rapid expansion of economic globalization caught the country rather flat footed and, unlike its taking of the lead in earlier technological innovations, it was not well placed to take a leading role in the new communications technological revolution associated with the internet. It was in the US that the World Wide Web began in 1992, Yahoo, Amazon and Netscape in 1994 and Google in 1997. As late as October 2009, a Japanese scientific adviser to the government complained that Japan was stuck in an outdated business model and confessed that he was pessimistic about the momentum for change towards a new business model of horizontal integration and open innovation.[4]

The end of the Cold War changed Japan's international environment and it also contributed to a partial transformation of Japanese politics. But it did not lead to a transformation of Japan's position in the world. Japan remained constrained from pursuing a truly independent role by the long-standing inhibitions arising from its past history and the pacifistic consensus at home centring on the 'peace constitution'. Thus the security alliance with the United States remained the cornerstone of Japan's foreign and security policies, even after the demise of the Soviet Union, which had long been considered to be the main threat around which the alliance was formed.

Nevertheless, within the framework of the alliance, Japan began to fashion new approaches and initiatives that suggested that the country was beginning to assert a new international role for itself, however slowly and hesitantly. Partly at American prodding, Japan broke several taboos by first agreeing to participate actively in regional security from the late 1990s and then into the twenty-first century by sending troops abroad. These developments remained controversial within Japan, but under enhanced military threats from North Korea and China they indicated a 'distinct shift' to a 'greater degree of focus on Japan's independent military capability and power'.[5]

From the outset Japan found that it had to deal with the new Russia separately from the US. The same became true of Japanese relations with Southeast Asia. More broadly, however, the Japanese increasingly sensed that their interests did not always coincide with the United States. There was a degree of resentment at being expected to contribute to what were seen as American wars in the Balkans, the Middle East and Central Asia, which were not always regarded as being in the interest of Japan and on which the Japanese were not effectively consulted. What made matters worse was that on issues closer to home, such as China and North Korea, the US could not always be relied upon to act in accordance with the Japanese interest. In other words, Japan was in danger of facing one of the classic problems of an alliance partner, of entrapment or abandonment. There has been concern at times in Japan that it might be 'bypassed' (or abandoned) by the US as it cultivated China. At other times Japan has been wary of being dragged into commitments in the Middle East that it would prefer to avoid (an example of entrapment).

Japanese thinking about the country's future role may be seen as divided between two major groups: first, conservatives who looked forward to Japan becoming a 'normal' country, with its own independent military force and strategy, and hence becoming a great power in its own right; and second, those of a more leftist or reformist persuasion who, drawing on the pacifistic outlook developed since the defeat in 1945, seek to focus more on political economic power and to develop Japan as a country that would abjure conflict and make its mark as a country uniquely devoted to the promotion of peace and the new global agenda of non-traditional security. Both in their different ways seek to establish a more distinctive Japanese international identity. Thus the claim that Japan should become a permanent member of the UN Security Council, first aired in 1993 when there was caution within Japan about its readiness to take part in UN PKO and then pursued in earnest in 2005, enjoyed universal support, even though the two groups had different ideas as to the role Japan would play.[6] There were differences within each of the two groups as to how to balance the alliance with America with the relationship with China. Both recognized that 'preventing the worst' requires a strong alliance with the US, but 'constructing the best' requires an East Asian community that includes China. In other words, what Richard Samuels has called Japan's 'strategic convergence' demands 'hedging'.[7]

The constraints on developing a new role

Sluggish Japan is part of a region with fast-changing balances of economic and political power and uncertain relations of cooperation and competition between several great regional powers. Three new nuclear powers emerged in the 1990s and all states in the region (with the partial exception of Japan) have been increasing their defence budgets and modernizing their military forces. The region has lacked multilateral security institutions capable of defending the national interests of members and is characterized by divergent political systems with unresolved territorial and maritime disputes. In addition the competition over energy and other necessary resources is growing. The pace of change, the fluidity and uncertainty of future developments in the region, all combined to present Japan with a much more confused, if perhaps less immediately threatening, regional security environment than was true of the four decades of the

Cold War. However, as Japanese began to rethink their place in the world they were subject to both domestic and external constraints, which both shaped and restricted their options.

First, the country was wedded to the famous peace Article Nine of the Constitution. At no point was there a realistic possibility of obtaining the two-thirds majority in the legislature, followed by a majority in a national referendum, that would have been needed to revise it. It was only through careful reinterpretations by successive LDP governments and through the passage of specific legislation that it became possible for Japan's Self Defence Forces, beginning in 1991, to participate in UN PKO missions and to be deployed abroad in support of American combat missions – but only under conditions that precluded the Japanese from taking part in actual combat. Although Japan developed powerful modern forces and an effective coastguard, these were firmly geared towards self-defence and not towards the projection of force.[8]

Second, Japan was constrained by inability or unwillingness to carry out bold new economic policies and substantive institutional reform, which kept the country in economic stagnation for much of the 1990s. Even when a modest economic recovery began after 1998 it arose from the greater volume of exports to the rapidly growing economy of its giant neighbour, China, rather than from major structural reforms at home.[9]

Third, the domestic economic difficulties led to a curtailment of Japanese external investment, especially in Southeast Asia, which contributed to the sense of Japanese decline relative to the rise of China. Much of this was due to the perception of a rising China and of a Japan in decline rather than to a consideration of the actual amounts of capital involved. For example, little was made of Japan's contribution of some $44 billion to the IMF and the ASEAN countries during the 1997 Asian financial crisis, even though it exceeded by far China's contribution of just over $2 billion. But China's contribution, and its refusal to devalue its currency, were praised within the region and by American leaders, with the Chinese held up as virtual saviours of the region.[10] Nevertheless the perception of decline had a basis in fact. Japanese ODA, which had been a key instrument in Japan's foreign policies towards East Asia, has been declining since the bursting of the Japanese bubble.[11]

Fourth, Japan faces a problem of a declining population. It peaked at just under 128 million in 2005 and it has been declining ever since. By 2050 government demographers calculate that the population will have dropped to 87 million. The number of children has declined for twenty-seven consecutive years and children constitute only 13.5 per cent of the population as a whole (the lowest among the thirty-one leading countries). About 22 per cent of the population is sixty-five or older. These trends will continue. According to government demographers, the elderly will outnumber children by about 3:1 in 2020 and by about 4:1 in 2040.[12] Although Japanese will remain wealthy, household wealth will stop growing and by 2024 household wealth will have returned to 1997 levels. Tax revenues and savings will diminish, which in time will confront Japan with increasingly difficult choices about priorities and the provision of services.

Defence spending will come under greater pressure and military recruitment will become even more difficult. Given Japanese aversion to immigration, these trends are unlikely to be reversed.[13]

Fifth, externally, Japan has been under constant pressure by its American ally to contribute more to American military and security commitments in the region and beyond. Japan can hardly disavow its key protector without facing huge new problems of how to arrange for its own national security and to assure itself of regional stability in Northeast Asia, which is characterized by strategic distrust between the resident states. The post-Cold War environment has raised anew the old problem of how to balance Japan's Asian and Western identities, or put differently, how to balance relations between China and America. At the same time, as indicated by the problem of relocating the Futenma American marine base, the extent to which Japanese people are prepared to pay the monetary and social costs of what Americans perceive as Japan's share of the burden of defence of Japan and the region has been thrown into doubt as never before.[14]

Sixth, Japan has been constrained in refashioning its identity, by demands from South Korea and China in particular, that it address more openly its fifty-year history of aggression until its defeat in 1945.

Finally, despite the recognition of a need for reform, most Japanese resisted reform in practice. With a per capita GDP of nearly $40,000 perhaps life was too comfortable to face the upheavals that systemic reform would entail. Indeed successive opinion polls suggested that most Japanese recognized the need for fundamental reforms, but felt threatened by the future.[15]

Relations with the United States

The partnership with the United States has continued to remain central to the economies and security arrangements of both states, but shorn of the glue provided by the common enmity towards the Soviet Union, the alliance has been subject to new strains and old problems have acquired greater salience. Nevertheless, one issue that went back to the American rapprochement with China in 1971–72 was Japanese concern at what was seen as an excessive American preoccupation with China, often to the neglect of Japan. The key issues in the post-Cold War period were primarily political and strategic rather than the economic ones that had caused so much discord and acrimony in the late 1980s and the first year of the Clinton administration. Much of that soon dissipated after the bursting of the Japanese bubble. In 1996 the two countries were able to reinvigorate their alliance, but the relationship was characterized by continued American pressure on its Japanese ally to contribute more militarily to its strategic needs, which even sympathetic Japanese prime ministers found difficult to satisfy. That demonstrated differences of interest and outlook between the two allies.

These differences were manifested early on in the Gulf War of 1991. Although Japan had broken a taboo that year by sending a team to contribute to the UN PKO in Cambodia, it was unwilling to contribute manpower to participate in the US-led war. Regarding the war as essentially an American affair, Japanese assistance was late, grudging and largely confined to money ($13 billion – considered a huge amount in Japan) although the Japanese did send some mine-sweepers to the Gulf after hostilities had come to an end. The Japanese response puzzled and angered American opinion and revived the old suspicions about the Japanese as freeloaders. The episode also served to fuel American disquiet about the terms of trade with Japan, especially as that was no longer tempered by Cold War considerations about Japan's strategic importance. Japanese differences with the United States over the Gulf War took place against a background in which only a year or so earlier at the height of the hubris over the Japanese bubble opinion polls on both sides of the Pacific showed that each regarded the other as its key economic adversary.[16]

Japanese quiescence, and what appeared to Americans as its excessive parochialism, became evident in the diplomacy over the North Korean problem in 1993 and 1994. Prior to that, in 1990, the then leading LDP politician had gone to Pyongyang, desperate about Gorbachev's impending recognition of the South, and all but agreed to a proposal by Kim Il Sung that relations be normalized with reparations being paid not only for the period of annexation (1910–45), but for the period after 1945 as well. Nothing came of the proposal, but the Japanese politician had failed to inform, let alone consult, the South Korean or American governments.[17] When the nuclear crisis broke out in 1993 the Japanese government was aware of the difficulties of overcoming a Chinese veto; it nevertheless insisted that it would not carry out sanctions against the North without a UNSC resolution authorizing them. At one point the threat of warfare on the peninsula was real; nevertheless the Japanese government refused to risk confronting a Korean organization operating within Japan that was responsible for transferring an estimated US$1–1.5 billion a year to the North – its main source of hard currency. Yet the Japanese government did not dispute that if the North were to acquire a nuclear capability the consequences for Japan would be very serious. The parochial Japanese approach seemed to typify what many in America saw as 'free-riding'. Once again Japan's main contribution was to be economic, in providing funds to help implement the Framework Agreement and to supply agricultural and other provisions to North Korea. It became clear that the situation could not endure in which Americans risked their lives in Korea on behalf of Japan *inter alia*, while Japanese bickered at home as to whether or not to provide food and supplies. American dissatisfaction with its ally as a 'free-rider' was only matched by Japanese concern about entrapment.[18]

It was the recognition of that, coupled with the sense that the alliance had been allowed to drift for some years, which led to its revamping. Two major defence reviews, one by the United States (known as the East Asian Security Review and also as the 'Nye initiative') and the other by Japan (known as the National Defense Program Outline – NDPO), that were released in 1995 set the terms for revitalizing the alliance. Interestingly, the NDPO was carried out by a coalition government, which had replaced the LDP for less than a year, whose head was the Socialist Party leader, Tomiichi Murayama, which ensured that it did not meet with the customary opposition in the Diet. Murayama is best remembered for his open apology for Japanese aggression in the Pacific War, but his leader-ship in promoting the revitalization of the alliance was important, even if it was at the instigation of the LDP majority in his cabinet. The Japanese review recognized the alliance as indispensable for the defence of their country and as the key for regional peace and security.[19] By the time an agreement was reached between the two sides in April 1996, the socialist prime minister, Murayama, had been replaced by the more hawkish LDP leader, Hashimoto, and opinion in Japan had been affected by China's attempt at coercive diplomacy by firing missiles in waters near Taiwan, which at their northerly point were less than 200 miles from Japan's most southerly small island. Although it was North Korea, rather than China, that had been uppermost in the determination of the new security guidelines, it was the March 1996 crisis over the Taiwan Strait that was the catalyst and that ensured that the China question would loom larger afterwards.[20]

The new guidelines went beyond those of 1978 so as to allow Japan to co-operate militarily with the United States, not only in the defence of Japan itself, but also in the defence of the 'areas surrounding Japan'. In other words, Japan accepted that stability in the region was linked to Japanese security and that in the new international circumstances Japan would go beyond allowing the Americans to use bases in Japan by providing active logistic support to American forces. The revised guidelines were made public the following year, and in May 1999 the relevant legislation was passed by the Japanese Diet without full debate. Meanwhile, in August 1998, the North Koreans increased the growing unease about security issues in Japan, by test-firing a suspect Taepodong-1 missile into the sea across the Japanese archipelago. That facilitated the signing in August 1999 of a memorandum of understanding with the US, committing the two to deepen their cooperation in researching the development of theatre missile defence (TMD).[21]

This seemingly smooth consolidation of Japan's relations with the United States had been interrupted first by differences over the handling of the Asian financial crisis in 1997–98 and second by the China factor. To take the financial crisis first, America seemed to behave less like a sensitive ally and more like a rival anxious to assert its supremacy. Despite their economic stagnation at home the Japanese did respond positively by proposing to establish what was called an 'Asian Monetary Fund'; in fact this had been suggested even before the July crisis and was continually proposed throughout 1997, only to be blocked by the United States on the grounds that only an international response in accordance with international rules would do. Others suspected that the US feared that it was in danger of being frozen out of Asia with its leading role being usurped by Japan.[22]

The key role in addressing the financial crisis was played by the IMF, in which the American voice was pre-eminent even though Japan contributed more to the financial bail-out of Thailand, Indonesia and South Korea (Japan committed US$21 billion to the US's US$14.2 billion and Japan advanced an additional $23 billion to the IMF).[23] Yet Japan was widely blamed, not least by the Clinton administration, because of its failure to reform its domestic economy. What made the situation more galling was the exaggerated praise for China (as noted earlier).

Perhaps at a deeper level the economic crisis shattered the myth of the alleged superiority of the Japanese economic model, paralleled by the so-called Asian developmental state. This now stood condemned for encouraging a lack of transparency in business and financial institutions and the development of crony capitalism. The image of Japanese leadership in the guise of flying geese was seemingly exposed as a mirage. Japan no longer provided the stimulus for regional economic growth as it no longer provided the market that once stimulated Asian growth, and as direct investments in its neighbours' economies continued to decline the regional institutions such as ASEAN and APEC, on which so much Japanese diplomatic capital was spent, proved unable to rise to the challenge of the crisis. Although it may be argued that they were not designed to serve such a purpose, they nevertheless lost much of the élan they once had. The Japanese aspiration of establishing a Pacific community, which had appeared to be approaching fulfilment in the early 1990s, now seemed forlorn. As a distinguished Japanese columnist put it at the time, 'Japanese hopes for peace through economic development and integration have been compromised'.[24]

The China factor also contributed uncertainties to the viability of the alliance as seen from Japan. It was not so much the effect of Chinese criticism of the enhanced security role that Japan had assumed with the concurrence of the US that was at the root of the problem; rather, it was the warming of America's relations with China. Japan has naturally always been sensitive to the conduct of relations between America and China. While in principle favouring American policies of engagement as opposed to confrontation with China, the Japanese have been concerned lest their main economic partner and provider of security should seek to cultivate relations with China at the expense of Japan.

Not surprisingly, there was considerable dismay in Japan at the conduct of Clinton's presidential visit to China in June 1998. Not only were Japan and every other Asian country left out of Clinton's itinerary, but he and his closest aides also went out of their way to praise China and to disparage Japan on Chinese soil. In the course of the visit, US Secretary of the Treasury Robert Rubin praised China as an 'island of stability' amid the Asian economic storm, and simultaneously sharply criticized Japan.[25] Japanese Foreign Ministry sources expressed concern that 'the United States may try to use both a China card and a Japanese card'. Other high-level diplomats were privately speculating that under such conditions Tokyo might be forced to review its strategy and become a political superpower that could contend with the United States and China.[26] After Clinton's return Washington sought to mollify Japan, and in any case Sino-American relations began to deteriorate, making the idea of their forming a 'constructive strategic partnership' recede in significance. Nevertheless, the episode increased Japanese uncertainties.

9/11, however, saw an immediate reconfirmation of the depth of the alliance. The Japanese government, led by Prime Minister Koizumi, reacted speedily by passing legislation that enabled Japan to dispatch a small number of ships, including three destroyers, to help refuel American and coalition ships on mission to the fighting in Afghanistan. A public opinion survey in October 2001 registered 71 per cent in support of the American war on terrorism, but the margin in favour of sending Japanese forces overseas was narrower, 49 per cent for and 40 per cent against.[27] This was the first time that Japanese naval forces had been sent to support combat since the Second World War and it had met with little domestic opposition. More controversially, Koizumi went even further at the end of 2003 by agreeing to dispatch up to 200 Japanese from the Self Defense Force to provide humanitarian help and to contribute to reconstruction work in Iraq, despite the opposition of Japanese public opinion and the growing risks to foreign workers there. In 2004 the air force (ASDF) controversially contributed to flying supplies to Iraq. Koizumi and President Bush established close personal relations, but his successors after 2006 were short-lived as prime ministers and did not develop such familiarity with Bush.

The contingent was duly withdrawn from Iraq once its mandate ran out in 2006 and the ASDF was pulled back in 2009. The incoming DPJ government withdrew the naval mission in the Indian Ocean once its mandate ran out in December 2009. Whatever the precise military value these missions may have had, they were seen as important politically by both the Bush and the incoming Obama administrations and they constituted precedents for the dispatch of SDF overseas should a future Japanese government wish to do so again.

The advent of the DPJ government in September 2009 changed the tone and perhaps the character of the alliance, as it came to power with the idea of establishing a more 'equal' relationship with the United States and with the aim of emphasizing the Asian dimension of Japan's foreign relations. Prime Minister Hatoyama also sought to establish an Asian Community based on what he called 'yu'ai' (commonly translated as 'fraternity'), from which the Americans would be excluded. However the immediate issue with the United States focused on a 2006 agreement to relocate an American base in Futenma, Okinawa, from a densely populated urban centre to a less populated site and to relocate several thousand of the US marines stationed there to the American island of Guam, some 1,400 miles away in the Pacific. The LDP government had made the agreement in 2006, but had not implemented it because it had become deeply controversial. Much to the initial indignation of the American side the DPJ government wanted to renegotiate the agreement. The American Secretary of Defense, Robert Gates, on a visit to Japan on 20 October 2009, went so far as to rule out any renegotiation. But Washington soon recognized that it was dealing with a democratic ally, with which it had to come to terms. Part of the problem was that Japanese ministers expressed different opinions and Hatoyama was inconsistent. Nevertheless he continually insisted that the relationship with the United States was the 'cornerstone' of Japan's foreign policy. Hatoyama proved to be disappointing as a leader and, having promised to reach a decision on Futenma by the end of May he endorsed it and promptly resigned. Meanwhile resistance to the relocation of the base had intensified in Okinawa and it was by no means clear how the new Prime Minister, Naoto Kan, would be able to implement the agreement, especially after he was held responsible for his party's poor performance in the elections to the Upper House in July, only weeks after becoming prime minister. His loss was necessarily bad news for Washington too.[28]

The alliance with the United States, however, still remains at the core of Japan's foreign relations, but since the end of the Cold War the strains of the alliance have increased as the differences between the identities and interests of the two states have become more evident. Under the LDP, Japanese assertions of their national identity began to shift from the liberal pacifistic side of the spectrum towards a point at which the use of force beyond Japan's territorial bounds might be acceptable. The threat from North Korea shifted the debate in Japan. Topics that were formerly taboo, such as collective defence, offensive missiles, launching pre-emptive attacks and even considering the feasibility of becoming a nuclear power, have entered the Japanese mainstream of acceptability for debate. But the DPJ government shifted the agenda in a more pacific direction. The DPJ has yet to articulate a view of its strategic and foreign-policy priorities. The alliance may serve the current status quo, but there is much to be rethought about its purpose and future development, including the number of American forces, the status of forces agreement and the location of American bases.

Of equal significance in the development of the alliance has been the weakening of the social and non-governmental ties between the two allies, whose governments have not followed up on the rhetoric of the overwhelming significance of their relationship. This was true of the last decade of the LDP administrations[29] and it was clearly a factor in the falling out between the Obama and Hatoyama administrations in the early period following the election of the DPJ, when they had even fewer personal contacts. The relationship had come to depend on the dedication of a few principal figures on both sides and on a small number of officials who enjoyed good working relationships. The advent of the Hatoyama administration, which combined inexperience with a determination to take policy making away from bureaucrats and unelected officials and ensure that policy would be made by ministers, meant that neither the new American nor the new Japanese administrations enjoyed familiarity with the other, or with their policy-making processes.

It is perhaps early days to judge the impact that the new DPJ government and its new approach will have on the relationship with the US. But it is clear that the Obama and Kan administrations will not only have to work out their differences, but they will have to ensure that the alliance is not allowed to fall into disrepair when it is left primarily to a relatively small number of officials to manage the relationship.

From a Japanese perspective the alliance is indeed the cornerstone of both its domestic and foreign politics. At a time in which the country is facing daunting indebtedness and huge and pressing economic and social problems, Japan could ill afford to raise its military expenditures to the levels necessary to stand alone as a fully fledged independent great power. However, the alternative of accepting some kind of Chinese leadership has little support within the country. The latest provocation from North Korea in the sinking of a ship, coupled with apparent tacit Chinese support, has pushed Japanese sentiment closer to South Korea and the United States. At issue is the extent to which the United States will be sensitive to Japanese fears of abandonment as it focuses on China, while coming to terms with Japan's decline, which seems set to continue.

Relations with China

The importance of Japan's relations with America is only matched by its relationship with China. The key question in Japan's foreign policy since the Meiji revolution of 1968 has been how to balance Japan's ties to Asia with its ties to the West. In the post-Cold War period this has morphed into balancing the relationships with China and the US. America is the indispensible ally, which provides for the defence of Japan and the security of the region. China has become Japan's major trading partner and the two economies are now inter-dependent. America and Japan are fellow democracies and share many liberal values, whereas China and Japan share something of an East Asian identity. The difficulty in balancing relations between China and the US is the divergence between the economic and security dimensions of the two relationships. As China's economic importance is growing at the relative expense of the US, the provision of security by the United States is rising to counter growing Chinese military assertiveness and the provocations of North Korea (enabled by China).

In the immediate post-Cold War period, as China pursued policies seeking integration in the international economy, it appeared as if Japan would be able to establish an enduring, more positive relationship with its giant neighbour. Because of its less pronounced interest in human rights and because of the greater priority given to regional stability as expressed in orderly economic relations, and because of the Japanese view that it has a primary interest in the continued sta-bility of China, Japan did not share the same enthusiasm for imposing sanctions on China after 4 June 1989 as did its American ally. Indeed, Japan was the first of the G-7 countries to resume ODA. In fact Sino-Japanese relations rapidly improved after 1990, and by 1994 had reached what both sides regard as the best period of their relations yet. After a certain delay Japanese FDI in China reached new heights and in 1993 Japan once again became China's most important trading partner. Relations seemed to have reached a new and exalted level that the Japanese hoped would enable the Chinese to give less prominence to their troubled history when the emperor himself visited China in 1992 and offered his own, albeit reserved, apologies for the war. The official website of the Chinese Ministry of Foreign Affairs noted that this was the first such visit and added cryptically, 'it [the visit] filled in the gaps in the history of Sino-Japanese relations'.[30] This paved the way for many-sided dialogues and exchanges that have taken place since then between the two sides. These also included high-level meetings between military representatives. This was also a period in which Japan was seeking to define a new post-Cold War international identity that would be centred on the UN, while China was seeking to overcome its isolation by cultivating relations with its neighbours. Japan was actively promoting what was to become the ARF, primarily with the intention of establishing a multilateral framework that would induct China into security discussions with countries of the region.[31]

But at deeper levels problems remained, and they soon surfaced as China's leaders began to regain self-confidence in their country's ability to survive and prosper and as their Japanese counterparts re-emphasized the significance of their alliance with the United States. The two are incipient rivals within the region and the Chinese were concerned, on the one hand, by the prospect of Japan becoming an active regional partner of the US in security matters, thereby becoming once again an effective regional military power in its own right, while also contributing to the possibility of a US containment of China. On the other hand, the Chinese also worried about the consequences if the American commitment to remain militarily engaged in the region were to be found to be less enduring than was presently asserted. In particular they feared that Japan might seek to become a military power once again if the Japanese were to be suddenly bereft of the American military presence. For their part, the Japanese were concerned as to what China's military modernization might portend and called in vain for greater transparency on the Chinese side.

In 1995, following a Chinese nuclear test, carried out only three days after it was announced that an international conference embracing nearly all states had agreed to renew the NPT indefinitely (and within a context in which the other declared nuclear powers had stopped conducting tests since 1992), the Japanese government took the unprecedented step of cancelling the aid of US$92 million that had been promised for the year. Japan was also prominent in its sharp criticism of China's creeping assertiveness in the South China Sea in the dispute with the Philippines over Mischief Reef in March 1995. Both developments were much resented in China. Japanese attitudes towards China were also beginning to harden.[32]

The Japanese government had already publicly expressed its concern about the possibility that China might use force to resolve the Taiwan question even before the Chinese responded in 1995–96 to what they regarded as unacceptable provocations with threatening military exercises and the launching of missiles near Taiwan's two main ports. The Japanese government expressed its concern in public at missiles being directed to the north of Taiwan near the territorial waters of one of its most southern islets. The episode also affected Japanese public opinion so that the announcement in April 1996 of the agreement about strategic guidelines with the US did not attract much domestic criticism. Yet not long before, popular opposition to the American military presence had been raised, significantly as a consequence of the rape of a Japanese teenager by three American marines in Okinawa.

The Japanese government did not modify the guidelines or back down in any way in the face of Chinese criticisms that they could involve combat in the Taiwan Strait. The official view was that this was a commitment in principle that did not have clearly defined geographical limits, but the chief secretary to the cabinet publicly asserted that they did cover the Taiwan Strait. Interestingly, the Japanese government ignored the Chinese protests and neither confirmed nor denied his statement. The Japanese meanwhile had become increasingly concerned about the annual double-digit percentage increases in China's military budget, the effort to acquire a power projection capability and the advanced weapons purchases from the Russians. They pressed the Chinese for greater transparency.[33]

Further indications of the deterioration of relations between the two greatest regional powers emerged from their dispute over Japan's confirmation of its participation in the American-led research to develop a theatre missile defence system. Claiming that this would provide cover for Taiwan too, the Chinese protested that this would alter the strategic balance to their disfavour. It would degrade their nuclear missile capabilities, which were the only counterweight they had to the superiority in conventional forces enjoyed by the US and its allies in the region. The Japanese paid little heed to the Chinese protests, in part because they had become alarmed by the growing threat of missiles from North Korea after one of these traversed the main island of Japan to splash down in the seas beyond. But also because the Chinese side appeared to be pressing for the long-term withdrawal of American forces from Japan without the Chinese acknowledging that the Japanese had any legitimate security needs of their own. On the contrary, any attempt by the Japanese to identify these, still less to prepare for them, evoked customary accusations about the alleged revival of Japanese militarism and demands that the Japanese atone for their past aggression. The Japanese too protested at naval intelligence-gathering by Chinese ships in Japan's exclusive economic zone. After reaching a good stage of relations in the mid-1990s the decade ended amid distrust and recriminations as President Jiang Zemin completed a visit to Japan in November 1998 that was marked by acrimony.[34]

Within Japan attitudes towards China had changed over the decade for a number of complex reasons. The younger generation that had replaced the post-war leaders of the LDP no longer had the latter's emotional attachment to China and were irritated by Beijing's tendency to play the history card whenever it sought something from Tokyo. By the same token they were disturbed by Beijing's failure to make clear to its own people the extent of Japanese aid and soft loans to China that accounted for over 50 per cent of all bilateral assistance received by China since 1978. It was only in the course of Jiang's visit that an official document was signed in which China formally thanked Japan for its assistance, which Premier Zhu Rongji in October 2000 acknowledged had been 'a major help in the development of the Chinese economy and the construction of the Chinese state'.[35] Yet none of this was apparent in the patriotism campaigns launched by the Chinese authorities in the early 1990s. Policy towards China was traditionally the provenance of the Ministry of Foreign Affairs, which had been driven continuously by the strategy of engaging China so as to encourage its development towards a more open and stable society at home, to push towards taking on greater responsibilities as a member of the international community.

In the latter half of the 1990s that approach began to be challenged by the defence establishment, and in 1997 the annual report of the Self Defense Agency for the first time mentioned China as a potential threat. Generally, as Japan itself has become more nationalistic, partly in response to the harsher regional environment, policy towards China has been subject to more debate.[36]

The mutually dependent economic relations they have been able to foster since the early 1990s, however, have mitigated Japan's difficulties with China. Japan became China's second most important trade partner and China ranked as Japan's first in 2007, but if the trade with Hong Kong were included the relative change took place in 2003. The value of trade trebled from US$18.2 billion in 1990 to US$62.2 billion in 1996, and then increased to over US$132 billion in 2003. By 2009 it reached $232 billion and China's share of Japanese trade exceeded 20 per cent. Although trade has not been without friction, trade disputes have been far more amenable to resolution than those of the political or territorial variety.[37]

These developments did not prevent a souring of relations. Chinese began to characterize the relations as 'cold politics, hot economics'. As noted in the previous chapter, nationalistic anti-Japanese passions were inflamed on the Chinese side, over the alleged failure of the Japanese to atone properly for their wartime brutal aggression. Prime Minister Koizumi's visits to the Yasukuni Shrine, where the souls of millions of Japanese dead soldiers and those of twelve A-Class war criminals were located, stoked the fire of Chinese anger. Koizumi regarded Chinese protests as undue interference in Japanese internal affairs. In 2005 the downturn in relations reached an all-time low as anti-Japanese violent demonstrations broke out in many of China's cities, culminating in destruction of Japanese property in Shanghai. China's leaders called a halt to the riots and Koizumi's replacement by Shizo Abe in October 2006, coupled with Hu Jintao's weakening of Jiang Zemin's Shanghai group in the Poliburo, paved the way for 'breaking the ice' in relations between the two countries. A joint statement was signed in which the Chinese not only expressed appreciation for Japanese aid and investment that helped kick-start China's economic growth, but they also acknowledged for the first time that Japan had pursued policies of peace since the end of the war in 1945. Additionally, the two sides agreed in effect to leave the history issue to be decided by historians by setting up a joint group of historians to carry out a study and report later. For his part Abe tacitly pledged to refrain from visiting the Yasukuni Shrine.

Ironically, the agreement was reached with one of the most right-wing politicians to become prime minister in the post-Cold War period. It was Abe who took the lead on the question of North Korea's abduction of Japanese citizens, which in effect blocked any possible separate deal with the North at the same time, and it was he who proposed a quasi-alliance of democracies that in effect would constitute a regional grouping that would exclude China. However, the October 2006 rapprochement signified a recognition by both sets of leaders that they had much to lose, and much to gain from establishing a good working relationship. The initial breakthrough was followed by a succession of top-leader visits to each country and the signing of many agreements to upgrade socio-political relations. Perhaps the most striking was the agreement to go in for joint development of oil and gas exploration and extraction in one of the disputed areas near the maritime border claimed by Japan for its Exclusive Economic Zone. It was agreed that Japan could invest in what the Chinese called the Chunxiao field, which the Japanese claimed extracted resources from the Japanese EEZ.

Both sides have placed greater emphasis upon increasing exchanges in different sectors, including students, tourists and even the military at all levels. As already mentioned, China's leaders began to acknowledge openly the significance of Japanese assistance. Japanese leaders visiting China have made a point of going to key sites commemorating the war. The two sides have sought to work together in promoting a fund to facilitate currency stability as part of the ASEAN Plus Three network. But difficulties remain. Chinese evince suspicions about Japan's policies towards Taiwan, which does not resonate with Japanese on the moderate left who feel sympathy for Taiwan as a democracy and a corresponding distaste for China on grounds of human rights and poor governance. At the same time the territorial dispute over the Senkaku (or Diaoyutai) Islands continues to inflame nationalist sentiment on both sides. Further afield, Japan and China are more rivals than partners elsewhere in Asia. The development of a new national consciousness in each state leads to greater mutual suspicion as evidenced by Chinese objections to Prime Minister Koizumi's visits to the Yakusuni shrine and by Japanese disquiet at growing Chinese assertiveness in the region, especially with the continued growth of Chinese military power. Japan's Defence White Papers of 2008 and 2009 noted the increasing presence of the Chinese navy in the waters around Japan, including in Japan's EEZ. The two sides also disagreed about nuclear matters as the Chinese side has angrily rebutted Japanese complaints about China's lack of transparency about its nuclear weapons and strategy. The paradox is that their growing economic interdependency has not led to a corresponding improvement of relations in other spheres.

Relations with Russia

With the end of the Cold War Japan's relations with Russia ceased to be directly linked with the American security guarantee and they began once again to centre on bilateral and regional questions. Two issues in particular came to dominate the diplomacy between them. The first was the territorial dispute over the group of four islands immediately to the north of Japan, which the Russians claimed were part of the Kurile chain and the Japanese claimed were extensions of Japan, calling them 'the Northern Territories'. The second was the economic question about forging links between the Russian Far East and Japan and in particular whether the Japanese would invest significantly in Russia and whether Russia would supply Japan with oil, gas and timber. Underlying these two issues were deeper ones about the balance of power in the region and about the political identities of these great powers who had lost ground in the 1990s. If the Russians tended to vacillate about how to balance their foreign policy between a Western and a Eurasian orientation and about the significance to attach to China, the Japanese also varied between a nationalistic emphasis on the recovery of territory and the geopolitical advantages of forging closer relations with Russia. But in the absence of pressing reasons for a compromise, nationalist forces in both countries were able to ensure that little progress was made. Indeed, it was not until after 9/11 when Russia drew closer to the United States that the prospects for an accommodation improved. These prospects became linked with complex geopolitics on the subject of whether a putative oil and gas pipeline from eastern Siberia would be directed to China or to the Russian port of Nakhodka and thence to Japan and South Korea. In other words, the question of the China factor surfaced as an important consideration.[38]

As Gilbert Roznan has argued, the potential for a Russo-Japanese deal emerged from their diplomacy in the Gorbachev period. It would have involved a revival of the 1956 agreement by which two of the islands would be transferred to Japan with an agreement to develop the other two jointly. That would enable a formal peace treaty to be signed that in turn would open the gates to deepening economic ties and Japanese economic assistance, leading eventually to a resolution of the two remaining islands.[39] However, during the course of the 1990s little of concrete significance was achieved, even though various attempts at making a breakthrough took place. Economic and trade relations also fell short of previous expectations as the value of trade in the 1990s rarely exceeded the Soviet–Japanese peak of US$6.1 billion reached in 1989 and Japanese FDI fell short of that of the UK, let alone those of the US and Germany. In addition to residual historical problems, Japanese caution in business also stemmed from the poor Russian record of settling its past commercial debts (US$1.1 billion was still owed in 1996) and from its uncertain domestic business climate.[40]

The political sphere was no more rewarding. In an attempt to settle the past legacy and to deepen Russia's engagement with the Asia-Pacific region, Yeltsin in 1992 sought to put relations with Japan on a new footing by proposing to sign a peace treaty and by saying that he saw Japan as 'a potential alliance partner'. In the end, however, Japan was accorded a lower priority as Yeltsin abruptly cancelled his visit to Japan that was due in September that year and travelled the following month to South Korea and then to China in December. He did not visit Tokyo until October 1993, and all that was agreed was that there was in fact a dispute over the four islands and that it would be settled in due course according to 'justice and international law'. The next major attempt followed Prime Minister Hashimoto's declaration of a new 'Eurasian diplomacy' in 1997. That led to the 'no necktie' summit in Krasnayorsk in November that year and an agreement to settle matters by the year 2000. But each side misunderstood the other. The Japanese thought that the territorial issue had finally been all but settled in their favour, whereas the Russians thought that economics had been decoupled from the territorial issue and that massive Japanese economic investment was coming their way. The Russians then offered to conclude a peace treaty in advance of a territorial settlement. Nationalist sentiments in both countries opposed concessions, and none of the leaders were persuaded that the possible geopolitical advantages of a settlement outweighed the political costs of confronting the domestic opposition.[41]

Russo-Japanese relations took a turn for the better after 9/11. Russia became in effect a partner of the United States in the war against terror and its strategic partnership with China lost some of its lustre. As Japan found its economic and diplomatic standing in much of Asia increasingly challenged by the rising significance of the Chinese economy, the advantages of a new deal with Russia became more evident. Prime Minister Koizumi forged a new relationship with President Putin. Much emphasis was placed on the building of a new pipeline to shift Russian oil from eastern Siberia to Nakhodka and thence to Japan. The Japanese offered to pay US$7 billion for the pipeline and a further US$2 billion to develop the area. Russia had already all but agreed with China on an alternative pipeline to Daqing in China's northeast. The latter was temporarily put on hold as different vested interests in Russia fought over the respective lines. Of course, at issue were decisions of important geopolitical consequences and it seemed that by the spring of 2004 the Japanese proposal had won favour, in part because of the political problems of Yukos Oil, which was associated with the Chinese project, and in part because of the commercial advantage of being able to access more countries. However, the preference shown to the Japanese project is of international geopolitical significance as it illustrated the complexity of the interactions between the major powers in the Asia-Pacific. Notwithstanding Russia's strategic partnership with China and the strategic significance of oil, Russia nevertheless at first appeared to chose Japan. To be sure there were economic reasons for doing so, but the choice may be seen as an example of the way the major powers both cooperate and compete for advantage.

However, the issue dragged on, and was without resolution by 2010. In the intervening period Japan began to play an important role in helping develop oil and gas exploration and extraction in the Sakhalin Island fields. Japanese investment in developing the Russian Far East was seen by some elements of the Russian government and energy conglomerates as vital for the development of the region and for enhancing Russian engagement in the Asia-Pacifc. Others preferred a partnership with China for both economic and political reasons. A Sino-Russian agreement was reached to build a pipeline to Northeast China that it was suggested would become in due course but a spur of a line linking the Russian oil and gas fields to maritime East Asia. Meanwhile Russia and China carried out extensive military exercises in Northeast Asia in 2005 that were continued in subsequent years. By 2008 Japan's annual Defence White Paper underscored the instability in northeast Asia by adding a resurgent Russia to the traditional threats to peace posed by China and North Korea. This suggested that whatever the attraction of Japanese investments and technology transfers, China was the preferred partner for Russia. In part this had to do with the intransigence of both the LDP and DPJ governments over what they called the 'Northern Territories' and the Russians called the 'Southern Kuriles'. The Japanese Diet passed a resolution in 2009 claiming that all four islands were an 'integral part of Japan', thereby ruling out the various compromises that had been considered by each side. As a result no formal peace agreement could be contemplated and the only practical issue around which cooperation could be reached was the economic one of Japanese investment and Russian supply of energy.[42]

Japanese policies in Asia

Japan has continued to be a major player in Asia. In the 1970s and 1980s it played a key role in promoting the 'East Asian economic miracle' and its trade and accumulated investments continued to be critical for the economic development of South Korea and most of the Southeast Asian countries. Rapid economic growth was seen by most of the Asian governments as a key factor in enabling them to stay in power and consolidate their often fragile political systems. At the same time Japan remained an important counterbalance to China's growing economic penetration.

Notwithstanding its relative economic stagnation and the difficulties in reforming its political system, Japan was quite proactive in the politics of the region for much of the 1990s. In part this was due to the end of the bipolar structure of international politics of the Cold War, which provided more freedom of manoeuvre for great and medium powers, especially within their own region – what was described in Japan as the 'loosening of the bonds of unipolarity'.[43] Japan also felt the need to meet the challenge of a rising China by enmeshing it within the regional groupings and to address problems created in the region by the Asian financial crisis.

By this time Japan had already been a key player, 'a leader from behind', in the formation of both the key regional economic and security groupings of APEC and the ARF.[44] In their first few years both institutions demonstrated a degree of activity as they worked out the scope of their activities. As we have seen, Japan was instrumental in 1994–95 in preventing APEC from going beyond its original conception as a consultative forum geared to facilitating economic cooperation to become a mechanism for enforcing free trade. After consolidating the alliance with the United States, Prime Minister Hashimoto made a point of making his first foreign visit to Southeast Asia rather than the US as was customary. In what was to be called the 'Hashimoto Doctrine' he argued that the alliance with the US was of benefit to the region as a whole and sought to tighten relations with ASEAN, arguing that the stability and development of the two sides were inseparable. Specifically, he sought institutionalized exchanges with ASEAN and each of its members, in terms of regular meetings of leaders, cultural exchanges and joint actions to meet the new security problems of terrorism, the environment, health, governance and so on.[45]

However, the outbreak of the Asian financial crisis half a year later not only exposed the weakness of the region's consultative institutions, but it also revealed problems in Japan's attempts to provide leadership as its proposal to establish an Asian monetary fund was effectively vetoed by the US. To add salt to the wounds, China received all the kudos for what were far more limited contributions than Japan's to addressing the region's financial meltdown.

The Japanese offer of a regional fund was later agreed in a modified form at an ASEAN meeting in Chiang Mai, Thailand, in May 1999 in the form of a currency swap mechanism. But this was more of symbolic significance, as it was not thought that it could be effective in the event of another major currency crisis.[46] After bickering between China and Japan over its leadership, the Chiang Mai Initiative was eventually agreed in May 2009 – and even then agreement was made possible by the onset of the international financial crisis. China and Japan each contributed 30 per cent of the initial fund of $120 billion (assuring them of equal voting rights) with ASEAN and South Korea contributing the rest.[47]

Ironically, Japan's relative decline removed some of the external constraints which had hitherto prevented Japan from playing a more prominent international role. By the opening of the twenty-first century, Southeast Asians were more concerned at a possible scale-back of Japan's economic weight, especially in view of the rapid rise of the Chinese economy that was challenging the neighbouring economies. As they were being drawn into closer interdependent ties with China, Southeast Asians saw the advantage of balancing or hedging against Chinese dominance. Thus a Japanese offer at the ASEAN meeting in May 1999 in Hanoi to provide up to US$30 billion was accepted as a major contribution to facilitate economic recovery. In the new multilateral setting of ASEAN Plus Three (APT) that included China, Japan and South Korea and was institutionalized in late 1999, Japan has found itself cast in the role of counteracting China. China's agreement in November 2000 to establish a free-trade agreement with ASEAN to be implemented in ten years evoked a rapid reaction from the new Japanese Prime Minister, Koizumi, who set off on a tour of Southeast Asian capitals during which he proposed a model of regional integration to be based on the Asia-Pacific region rather than East Asia. In January 2002 Koizumi launched an initiative to expand Japanese socio-economic relations in Southeast Asia. He also sought to dilute the APT, in which Japan was losing ground to China, by calling for the inclusion of Australia and New Zealand. Koizumi also began the trend for Japan of establishing separate free-trade agreements with individual ASEAN states, notably Singapore, while further FTAs were being considered with Thailand and South Korea.

However, by the time of the APEC meeting in October 2003 it seemed as if Japan had been greatly outshone by China. A leading Japanese commentator, Yoichi Funabashi, lamented Japan's diminishing presence and its 'inability' to adapt to the rapidly changing environment in Asia. While China was successfully advancing a China-centred pattern of regional integration, Japan was so bogged down by its own special domestic interests, notably in agriculture, that it was unable even to start negotiations with Thailand. The Thai premier complained of Japan as 'a strange country where the Ministry of Agriculture does not listen to decisions of the Prime Minister'. Singapore's Senior Minister, Lee Kuan Yew, observed that 'it has become the norm in Southeast Asia for China to take the lead and Japan to tag along'. Yet in 2001 Japan's trade with ASEAN was more than three times that of China, and its investment was many more times greater, both in terms of current flows and overall accumulated stock. The test for Japan was to 'convert its market strength to diplomatic strength'.[48]

Both the strengths and weaknesses of Japan's relations with ASEAN emerged at the ASEAN–Japan Commemorative Summit held in Tokyo in December 2003 to mark the thirtieth anniversary of Japan's relations with the association. It was a meeting heavy in symbolism and in tribute to the past rather than a forward-looking one with a dynamic agenda for the future. It was widely seen as an attempt by Japan 'to play catch-up' with China. It provided an opportunity for ASEAN to express its appreciation for Japan's positive role and it was therefore fitting that this was the first occasion on which an ASEAN summit meeting was convened outside Southeast Asia. A declaration was issued calling for deepening ties and enhancing cooperation in the fields of political and security affairs, as well as in financial policies and information technology. More aid was offered and economic partnerships were established or endorsed. Further talks were announced on establishing free-trade agreements with Malaysia, Thailand and the Philippines, but no indication was given that a way had been found to over-come the objections of Japan's powerful agricultural lobby. The latter had demonstrated its effectiveness in these matters only two months before in blocking an FTA with Mexico. But the summit raised the profile of Japan and it reaffirmed Japan's long-standing position as a major contributor to and upholder of ASEAN, with whom it shared a deep history and a commitment to common values. The summit also provided a reminder that, despite the attention currently being paid to China as the new economic hub of the sub-region, Japan's trade with ASEAN still exceeded by far that of China. According to ASEAN statistics, trade with Japan in 2001 was valued at US$122.3 billion, while that with China was US$55.4 billion.[49] Moreover, the prime minister of Singapore, Goh Chok Tong, expected Japan's position as the most important trading partner and investor in ASEAN to remain 'unchallenged' for the next twenty years, but in fifty years' time Japan would 'have to share that position' with China.[50] But by 2008 China was catching up fast, at least in trade. Its trade with ASEAN came to $192 billion, only $20 billion behind Japan.[51]

Rivalry with China is evident also in Japan's dealings with South Korea. There is much that divides the two democracies, especially over their respect-ive treatment of the history of Japan's colonization of Korea in the first half of the twentieth century. Relations were only normalized in 1965 and, despite their both being allies of the United States, there were few or no military relations between the two in the Cold War period. Since then, relations have improved substantively, especially as the effects of the democratization of the South brought the two sides closer. Notably, that extended to the historically sensitive domain of military relations. Military talks begun in 1991 led to the holding of joint military exercises in 1998. Meanwhile, Japan joined South Korea in managing the KEDO initiative that grew out of the framework agreement the Americans signed with the North in 1994. Following the Taepodong incident, Japan joined the South and the US in the Trilateral Coordination and Oversight Group that coordinated the approaches of the three to the North. Moreover, a breakthrough was reached when the great human-rights figure, Kim Dae Jong, was voted into office in the South. That made possible reconciliation in 1998, when Japan issued a significantly worded apology for its past history. Interestingly, that written apology was not issued to the Chinese president, Jiang Zemin, on his visit to Japan later that year. Nevertheless, that apology did not lead to a decent burial of the history issue, as a row about new Japanese history textbooks erupted again eighteen months later. Although Japan played a major role in the economic development of the South, little of that has brought them closer in other spheres. Amid a surge of new nationalism in both, negative feelings about the other continued to prevail. Although Japanese economic contributions were significant in enabling the South to recover from the disasters of the Asian financial crisis, opinion in governing and popular circles in the South entertained much more favourable views about China, with whom economic relations were booming.[52]

Japan had been excluded in the first multilateral talks on Korea involving China, the US and the two Koreas meeting in New York in so-called 'two plus two' talks arising out of the armistice at the end of the war in 1953. But these meetings came to an end with the advent of the Bush administration. Although both the South and Japan favoured a negotiated outcome to the problem of the North, they had different agendas. The South now looked to Russia and especially China for help in handling the North. Kim Dae Jong also fashioned a new policy of engagement with the North, the so-called 'sunshine policy'. Although controversial in the South, it was highly emotionally charged, as it was driven in part by the desire of some 15 million (a third of the population) who had relatives in the North and in part by a new nationalist assertiveness that desired reunification. It culminated in an unprecedented summit in June 2000 between Kim and the leader of the North, Kim Jong-Il. Perhaps less worried by the nuclear and WMD issues, the South was more concerned by the thousands of artillery pieces deployed by the North within reach of Seoul, the interests of the South clearly favoured reconciliation and engagement with the North. Japan, however, especially, after the Taepodong incident, was more concerned by the missile and WMD threat. Its initial response was to launch its own first spy satellite in order to be able to monitor developments in the North independently of its American ally. It also suspended support for KEDO (which was only resumed under American pressure). The navy and coastguard were instructed to pursue and if necessary to fire on intruders into Japanese waters, and in December 2001 a ship (thought to be North Korean) was indeed pursued and sunk. This first use of naval force since 1945 met with public approval (which would have been unthinkable only a few years earlier). Moreover, public support was forthcoming for the decision to support the deployment of TMD, notwithstanding the known opposition of China.[53]

With the advent of the Bush administration, the attempts at engagement of the North by the previous Clinton administration came to an end, much to the embarrassment of Kim Dae Jong. However, with Washington preoccupied with the coming war on Iraq, the Japanese prime minister took the initiative to hold his own summit with the leader of the North, Kim Jong-Il, in September 2002.

The summit had been reasonably well prepared and it took place with the blessing of America, China and the South. Washington had been unable to agree on a clear policy and, like the other countries of the region, Japan hoped for some kind of a negotiated settlement, as the alternatives of conflict or a collapse of the regime in the North would have been highly damaging to Northeast Asia as a whole. In addition to the prospect of masses of refugees destabilizing the South and the adjacent parts of China, the chaos and the cost of reunification would be too much for the South to bear. Japan would be expected to help with vast amounts of capital at a time of economic stagnation. Additionally, a region marked by rapid economic growth and development would suddenly be blighted. In principle the summit was a success, as the North hoped that reconciliation with Japan would open the door to huge reparation funds that would help revive its decrepit economy and that an understanding with Japan would lead to new relations with the US. Accordingly, the North readily agreed to suspend missile tests and acknowledged that it had indeed abducted Japanese citizens in the past. But the lack of humanity in the way the abductees had been treated by the North and the dearth of relevant information soured relations almost immediately. So that, rather than leading to reconciliation, the summit in the end left Japan and the North even further apart. Nevertheless Koizumi visited Pyongyang for a second time in May 2004 and although he made a little progress regarding the abductees, no breakthroughs were achieved.[54] Japan then rejoined the negotiation process with the North as part of the multilateral approach demanded by the Americans, which was made possible by the part China played as a facilitator and host for talks that began in Beijing in August 2003. Once again it was China that was gaining the plaudits for its deft diplomatic role, while Japan was left to a lesser role. Japan meanwhile had created difficulties in relations with South Korea by resurrecting its claim in the spring of 2005 to the islands of Takeshima/Dokdo, which stirred up all the historical animosity of the South towards Japan, which had seemingly been addressed by Obuchi's written apology to Kim Dae Jong back in 1998. It also led to a temporary break-up of the joint approach with the South and the US.[55]

In any case, as noted in chapter 9, each of the three states had different as well as common interests in addressing the North. Much to the irritation of the other members of the 6PT, the Japanese side, driven by domestic pressures, insisted on keeping the question of its abductees on the agenda of the talks. Indeed the Japanese required American support in order to ensure that it remained on the agenda. However, as the American lead negotiator pursued a more unilateral diplomatic approach from the summer of 2005, the Japanese side began to feel excluded. In particular it complained in vain about the announcement by the White House in June 2008 of the intention to remove North Korea from the State Department's list of states sponsoring terrorism, as that was seen as weakening its position regarding the abductees. However, by the time the North was removed from the list in October, Shinzo Abe, who had replaced Koizumi as prime minister and who had ridden to power as the principal political advocate of the cause of the abductees, had himself been replaced by the more moderate

Yasuo Fukuda in September 2008, and the question of the abductees was no longer given the same prominence.

The rapidity of the change of prime ministers in Japan (five since Koizumi stepped down in September 2006) has been seen as illustrative of the weakness of the Japanese political parties and the failure of leadership to carry out needed reforms and to chart a course for Japan's future. The fall of the first three was seen as a product of the decay of the Liberal Democratic Party, which had ruled the country almost without a break since 1955, but its successor, the Democratic Party of Japan, has so far been a disappointment too. Gerald Curtis, the leading expert on Japanese politics, lamented in June 2010 as the last prime minister, Naoto Kan, faced a setback in the elections to the Upper Houee: 'the public is ready to be led, but it has no leaders'. He noted that no one was 'addressing a number of pressing issues – from reforming the taxation system, to immigration and national security'.[56]

Nevertheless, the different prime ministers have offered different visions on which to base Japan's foreign policy. Shinzo Abe, a conservative nationalist, had sought a revision of the famous Article Nine of the constitution in order to promote a more independent and militarily powerful Japan able to accept the responsibilities of collective security. In office he and his foreign minister Taro Aso (the next prime minister but one) tried to encourage the formation of a coalition of democracies, including Australia, the United States, India and Japan, to be called 'the arc of freedom and democracy'. China was purposively excluded, despite the improvement in bilateral relations initiated by Abe himself.[57] Not surprisingly, little came of that. On the other hand, a major joint military exercise was held in February 2007 in the Indian Ocean drawing on the navies of the United States, India, Australia, Singapore and Japan, which was then followed up by a quadrilateral meeting at assistant ministerial level by the four countries, excluding Singapore, that drew a démarche from China in June. A trilateral arrangement then emerged between Australia, Japan and India, from which Australia withdrew in 2008 out of deference to Chinese concerns. But the highlight this aspect of Abe's foreign policy was the signing of a security pact with Australia in March 2007, in which *inter alia* they agreed to share intelligence and coordinate policies in East Asia – a pact that has endured beyond changes of governments in both countries.[58]

Yasuo Fukuda, who also lasted only a year as prime minister, changed the emphasis of foreign policy from cultivating partners to balance against China, to shifting the orientation to working with China and to deepening the Asian orientation of Japan's identity and foreign relations. Thus the signing of a Sino-Japanese joint statement and a press conference on 7 May 2008, between Fukuda and Hu Jintao, dwelt on the importance of 'promoting a mutually beneficial relationship based on common strategic interests'. The two pledged to work together on various issues, including competing claims in the East China Sea and more generally regional development.[59] As noted in the previous paragraph, Taro Aso, his replacement as prime minister, was inclined more to the Abe approach.

Yukio Hashimoto, the first prime minister of the DPJ, which had been elected with a huge majority in 2009, came to office determined to have a more 'equal' relationship with the United States, renegotiate the existing intergovernmental agreement on relocating the American Futenma base in Okinawa, while maintaining the alliance as the 'cornerstone' of Japan's foreign policy. At the same time he sought to establish an Asian community centring on China that would be based on what he called 'yu-ai', fraternity. The community proposal was vague and it was unclear whether or not it would allow participation by the United States. But he too resigned after less than a year in office, in part because of his vacillations over the Futenma base in the face of American insistence that the agreement be honoured. He conceded to the American demand and promptly resigned on 10 June 2010 after less than nine months in office. His successor, Naoto Kan, has agreed to accept the Futenma agreement and has reaffirmed the centrality of the alliance for Japan, but it is unclear how he will overcome domestic opposition in Okinawa to the relocation of Futenma. He has not yet indicated where his foreign policy preferences lie and given his weakened position after the poor showing of the DPJ in the July elections to the Upper House, Kan will only be in a position to develop credibility if he were to win the DPJ leadership election due in early September.[60]

By way of conclusion, it is clear that the alliance with the United States remains the cornerstone of Japan's foreign relations at least for the medium term. It may also be seen as the defining instrument for the American ability to continue to be responsible for overall strategic stability in the Asia-Pacific. At the same time it is also clear that differences between the two allies have increased in the period since the end of the Cold War. These have not challenged the alliance itself, but Japan has become more wary of being 'abandoned' by its pre-eminent ally, especially with regard to China. At the same time, Japan has been divided internally over the question of being entrapped by American demands that it participate actively in its wars, as in Afghanistan and Iraq. Meanwhile Japan has its own sense of vulnerability to North Korean WMD and ballistic missiles, as it also keeps a wary eye on China's rapid military modernization. More positively, Japan has also developed more independent foreign policies in the Asia-Pacific region as it has formed an alliance with Australia and engaged in complex patterns of competition and cooperation with the other major powers, principally China, but also Russia and India. Whether Japan will remain the 'lynchpin' of American strategy in the region will depend on whether it can address its structural problems arising from an economy in need of reform amid the challenges of adjusting to a declining population.

Notes

1 For the data on Japan, see Mure Dickie, 'The Spectre of Stasis', *The Financial Times*, 22 December 2009 and for that of the US see 'DATA 360', available online: www.data360.org/dataset.aspx?Data_Set_id=354. Accessed 7 February 2010.

2 Shiji Fukukawa, 'How Japan regains vitality', *The Japan Times*, 13 July 2010. Available online: http://search.japantimes.co.jp/print/eo20100713sf.html.

3 For an argument that this was true for Japan only up to 1998, after which there was a major shift in the strategy of Japanese corporations, see Ulrike Schaeke, *Choose and Focus; Japanese Strategies for the 21st Century* (Ithaca: Cornell University Press, 2008).
4 Kiyoshi Kurokawa in *The Japan Times*, 18 October 2009.
5 Narushige Michishito and Richard J. Samuels, 'Hugging and Hedging: Japanese Grand Strategy in the 21st Century', as summarized in Sigur Center for Asian Studies, *Policy Brief - July 2010*, 'Rising Powers and Domestic Attitudes on Hard Power', p.3.
6 For analysis of the issue in the 1990s see Reinhard Drifte, *Japan's Quest for a Permanent Security Council Seat* (New York: St. Martin's Press, 2000).
7 Richard J. Samuels, *Securing Japan: Tokyo's Grand Strategy and the Future of East Asia* (Ithaca: Cornell University Press, 2007) pp.198–205.
8 Thomas Berger, 'Japan's International Relations: the Security and Political Dimensions' in Samuel S. Kim (ed.), *The International Relations of Northeast Asia* (Lanham, MD: Rowman & Littlefield, 2004) pp.135–69.
9 On the difficulties in carrying out domestic political reform, see J.A.A. Stockwin, *Governing Japan* (Oxford: Blackwell Publishers, 4th edn, 2008).
10 See Michael Yahuda, 'China: Incomplete Reforms' in Gerald Segal and David S. Goodman (eds), *Towards Recovery in Pacific Asia* (London: Routledge, 2000), p.91.
11 See Dennis Trinidad, 'Japan's ODA at the Crossroads', *Asian Perspective*, 31, 2 (2007), pp.95–125. Available online: www.asianperspective.org/v31n2-e.pdf. Accessed 14 July 2010.
12 See *Kyodo News*, 'Population probably shrank even more in 2009, ministry estimates' *Japan Times*, 1 January 2010; and Blaine Harden, 'Japan Steadily Becoming a Land of Few Children', *Washington Post*, 6 May 2008). Meanwhile Japan has fallen from fifth to tenth place in the UN Human Development Index (Editorial, 'Tenth Place and Falling', *Japan Times*, 18 October 2009).
13 See, Brad Glosserman and Tomoko Tsunoda, 'The Guillotine: demographics and Japan's security options', *PacNet* Number 45, Pacific Forum CSIS, Honolulu, Hawaii, 17 June 2009.
14 Steve Clemons, 'Jeff Bader's Tough Love Talk on Japan, Futenma & Hatoyama', *The Washington Note*, 7 June 2010. Available online: www.thewashingtonnote.com/archives/2010/06/jeff_baders_ton.
15 For a convincing analysis of the changes in Japanese political life since the end of the Cold War, see Gerald L. Curtis (ed.), *The Logic of Japanese Politics* (New York: Columbia University Press, 1999). For a fascinating discussion of the limits to reform, see ch.1, 'The Politics of Complacency', pp.25–64.
16 See Robert Neff *et al.*, 'What Americans think of Japan Inc', *Business Week*, 8 (August 1989), p.51; and Robert Neff, 'Japan's Hardening View of America', *Business Week*, 18 (December 1989), p.62. For an account of Japan's response to the Gulf War, see Yusuhiro Ueki, 'Japan's UN Diplomacy: Sources of Passivism and Activism' in Curtis (ed.), *The Logic of Japanese Politics* (*op. cit.*), pp.356–60.
17 Don Oberdorfer, *The Two Koreas* (Indianapolis: Addison-Wesley, 1997) pp.220–22.
18 See the brief discussion by Michael J. Green, *Japan's Reluctant Realism* (New York: Palgrave, paperback, 2003) pp.120–21.
19 For the text, see Appendix 6A in Michael J. Green and Patrick M. Cronin (eds), *The US–Japan Alliance: Past, Present and Future* (New York: Council on Foreign Affairs, 1999), pp.359–67. For analysis of the complex Japanese politics that lay behind the endorsement by the coalition government, see Curtis, *The Logic of Japanese Politics* (*op. cit.*) chs 3, 4 and 5.
20 Yoichi Funabashi, *Alliance Adrift* (New York: Council on Foreign Affairs, 1999), pp.368–419.
21 Patrick M. Cronin *et al.*, 'The Alliance Implications of Theatre Missile Defense' in Michael J. Green and Patrick M. Cronin (eds), *The US–Japan Alliance* (New York: Council on Foreign Relations, 1999), pp.170–85.

22 Fred Bergsten, cited in Francois Godement, *The Downsizing of Asia* (London: Routledge, 1999), pp.46–47.

23 *Ibid.* Calculated from table 3.2, p.77.

24 Yoichi Funabashi, 'Tokyo's Depression Diplomacy', *Foreign Affairs* (November/December 1998), p.27.

25 See footnote 10.

26 See Ted Galen Carpenter, 'Roiling Asia: U.S. Coziness with China Upsets the Neighbors', *Foreign Affairs* (November/December 1998), pp.2–6.

27 Cited by Thomas Berger, 'Japan's International Relations: The Political and Security Dimensions' in Samuel S. Kim (ed.), *The International Relations of Northeast Asia* (Lanham, MD: Rowman and Littlefield, 2004), p.157.

28 See *The Nelson Report* (Washington, 12 July 2010).

29 That is the main theme of Kent Calder, *Pacific Alliance, Reviving U.S. – Japan Relations* (New Haven: Yale University Press, 2009).

30 See online: www.fmprc.gov.cn.eng/wjb/zzjg/yzs/gjlb/2721/default.htm.

31 For a similar account see, Glenn D. Hook *et al.*, 'Sino-Japanese political relations in the post-Cold War period' in their *Japan's International Relations: Politics, economics and security* ((London: Routledge, 2002), pp.170–73.

32 Green, *Japan's Reluctant Realism* (*op. cit.*) pp.80–82.

33 For a discussion of the controversies about the new guidelines and about the question of transparency, see Reinhard Drifte, *Japan's Security Relations with China since 1989* (London: RoutledgeCurzon, 2003), pp.94–101 and p.80, respectively.

34 *Ibid.*, pp.163–65. See also BBC News: Asia-Pacific (26 November 1998).

35 Cited in the statement by the Japanese Ministry of Foreign Affairs, 'Economic Cooperation with China', online at www.mofa.go.jp/policy/oda/region/e_asia/china-2.html.

36 Green, *Japan's Reluctant Realism* (*op. cit.*), pp.90–98.

37 Figures drawn from the websites of the two foreign ministries.

38 For accounts of Russia's continuing, if reduced, significance in the region, see Watanabe Koji (ed.), *Engaging Russia in Asia Pacific* (Tokyo: Japan Centre for International Exchange, 1999).

39 G. Rozman, 'A Chance for a Breakthrough in Russo-Japanese Relations: Will the Logic of Great Power Relations Prevail?', *The Pacific Review* 15, 3 (2002).

40 This account of Japanese–Russian relations in the 1990s also draws on Chikahito Harada, *Russia and North-east Asia* (London: Oxford University Press, for the International Institute for Strategic Studies, *Adelphi Papers* no. 310, July 1997).

41 Rozman, 'A Chance for a Breakthrough in Russo-Japanese Relations' (*op. cit.*), pp.331–33. See also his chapter, 'Russian Foreign Policy in Northeast Asia' in Kim (ed.), *The International Relations of Northeast Asia* (*op. cit.*), pp.207–11.

42 Re the Northern Islands see, for example, Kyodo, 'Okada wins no concession in talks with Russia on island dispute', *Japan Times*, 29 December 2009. Re the economic dimension see Kyodo, 'Japan not ready to settle isle issue: Putin', where he promises support for Japanese companies wishing to build car assembly plants in the Russian Far East and where he claims that the oil pipeline linking Eastern Siberia with the Russian Pacific coast is being built on schedule. *The Japan Times*, 10 May 2009.

43 For an argument along these lines, see Takashi Inoguchi, 'Japan Goes Regional' in Takashi Inoguchi (ed.), *Japan's Asia Policy: Revival and Response* (New York: Palgrave Macmillan, 2002), pp.8–15.

44 The apt term, 'leader from behind', was coined by Alan Rix. See his 'Japan and the Region: Leading from Behind' in R. Higgot *et al.* (eds), *Pacific Economic Relations in the 1990s* (St Leonards, NSW: Allen and Unwin, 1993). In his words, 'it is a style of leadership that aims at creating long-term Japanese influence in the region, and has been a successful form of long-standing "entrepreneurial" leadership that has carved out a regional role for Japan as investor, trader, aid donor and political actor' (p.65).

45 For a detailed account of Japan's new initiatives, see Suedo Sudo, *The International Relations of Japan and South East Asia* (London and New York: Routledge, 2002).
46 Peter Drysdale in Inoguchi (ed.), *Japan's Asia Policy* (*op. cit.*).
47 Joel Rathus, 'The Chiang Mai Initiative's Multilateralism: A good Start' *East Asia Forum*, 23 March 2010. Available online: www.eastasiaforum.org/2010/03/23/the-chiang- mai-initiatives-multilateralism-a-good-start/. Accessed 16 July 2010.
48 Yoichi Funabashi, 'All's Not Yet Lost in the Land of the Waning Sun', *The Straits Times* (3 November 2003).
49 31 See the ASEAN website, www.aseansec.org/home.htm.
50 *Straits Times* (3 December 2003).
51 www.aseansec.org/18137.htm. Accessed 16 July 2010.
52 For brief discussions of relations between Japan and South Korea, see Berger, 'Japan's International Relations' (*op. cit.*), pp.149–52; and Chung-in Moon and Taehwan Kim, 'South Korea's International Relations: Challenges to Developmental Realism', also in Kim (ed.), *The International Relations of Northeast Asia* (*op. cit.*), pp.259–61.
53 Berger, 'Japan's International Relations' (*op. cit.*), pp.150–51.
54 For a detailed account see Yoichi Funabashi, *The Peninsula Question: A Chronicle of the Second Nuclear Crisis* (Washington, DC: Brookings, 2007), chs 1 and 2, pp.1–92.
55 *Ibid.*, pp.425–31.
56 See Roy K. Akagawa, 'Curtis: Responsible leadership elusive', *Asahi Shimbun*, 30 June 2010.
57 See Abe's address to the Indian parliament on 23 June 2007, available online: www.asianews.asia.com/ … /four-power-'arc-of-freedom-alliance-with-Japan-but-not-china-10125.html. And Aso's talk of 12 March 2007, available online: www.mofa.go.jp/policy/pillar/address/0703.html.
58 Hisane Masaki, 'The emerging axis of democracy', *Asia Times Online*, 15 March 2007.
59 For the press conference and a lead to the joint statement see http://kantei.go.jp/foreign/hukudaspeech/2008/05/07/'kaiken_e.html.
60 See the account by Mike Green and Nicholas Szechenyi, 'US-Japan: New Realism' in *Comparative Connections*, 17 July 2010. This electronic quarterly journal published by the Hawaii branch of the Washington based CSIS provides the best up-to-date analysis of developments in Japan's foreign relations and, more broadly, for the region as a whole. See www.csis.org/program/pacific-forum-csis.

Conclusion

In looking ahead when writing in the second edition in 2004 I confidently suggested that 'American pre-eminence is likely to endure for the foreseeable future',
although I recognized that it would not be on a scale that will allow the United
States to dictate the character of politics in the region. Several reasons can be
advanced as to why that forecast seems to have gone awry. First, is the debilitat-
ing effects of the American-led long wars in Iraq and Afghanistan and the high
material and psychological costs they entailed as well as the damaging effect they
brought about to America's standing in the world. Second, is the damage
wrought to the US and indeed to Europe and Japan by the 2008 financial crisis
and the resulting economic recession, whose effects will be felt for some time yet.
Third is the extraordinarily rapid rise of China to become a global player of significance. Finally, there are the unpredictability, the fluidity and the rapidity of
change in the current era.

Nevertheless, not all the forecasts of six years ago seem to have been overtaken
by events. For example, the boundaries of the region have continued to 'become
less precise' as Central and South Asia increasingly impinge on Southeast and
Northeast Asia. The pattern of competition and cooperation still characterizes
relations among the great powers. In the absence of a clear structure for international politics, domestic politics continue to loom large in the foreign policies,
causing inconsistencies in the policies of the major powers in particular.
The diplomacy of the region continues to be shaped by 'a complex mosaic of
multilateral arrangements that are varied and multi-textured'.

The final point made then was that how the world, the region and the United
States come to terms with a rising China would be the most important factor to
shape the evolution of the region. That is indeed proving to be the case. China has
become the economic locomotive driving most of the economies of the region
through complex supply chains of production. China's trade with America's most
important allies and friends in the region exceeds in value their trade with the
United States. That has led to a growth of Chinese political influence, making the
resident states much more careful to avoid the appearance of disagreements,
especially on such sensitive issues as Taiwan. They are also cognizant of the fact
that although the rise of China is seen as a challenge to United States leadership it
is they, as China's neighbours, who will first have to face Chinese new assertiveness.

Coping with China

China's continuing rise as both an economic and a military power will continue to pose challenges as well as provide opportunities to the countries of the region and to the wider world. A disjunction has arisen between the region's economic dependence on China and its strategic dependence on the United States. Ideally the states of the region would like the United States to play the role of an off-shore balancer that would provide a kind of insurance against China's growing military power, without at the same time allowing its own relations with China to become too confrontational lest they be forced to choose between the two. At the same time the resident states would not like to see too close a relationship between China and the United States lest that lead to a condominium in which their interests might be neglected. Hence they were uneasy in the first year of the Obama presidency, when it appeared that far from balancing China, America would establish a comprehensive partnership with China – a so-called G-2 – that would jointly exercise leadership over the region and manage global problems such as climate change.

That American effort appears to have been rebuffed by a more nationally assertive China convinced of its own success amid American decline. China's new-found assertiveness has not been confined to words. In March 2009 an American surveillance ship was harassed within China's EEZ off Hainan Island. The US claimed that according to international law the ship was in international waters, but the Chinese claimed that they had certain entitlements within the EEZ waters. This recalled a similar claim over the airspace of the EEZ in the 2001 EP-3 incident. The Chinese navy has carried out vigorous patrolling in the Sea of Japan, where Japanese ships were 'buzzed', and in the South China Sea. At the time of writing (July 2010) the countries of Northeast and Southeast Asia, with American participation and leadership, are confronting a China which is more assertive in pushing its maritime claims in the Yellow, Japan and South China Seas.

In the first six months of 2010 a greater wariness is evident in American dealings with China. Moreover, the Chinese government has begun to show less regard than previously for the views and interests of its maritime neighbours. By appearing to condone the aggression of North Korea in sinking a South Korean ship and in seeking to prevent South Korea and the United States from conducting military exercises in the seas around the Korean peninsula (especially in the Yellow Sea) the Chinese deepened the concerns of Japan and South Korea, as well as the United States. This came on top of claiming for the first time in March 2010 that the South China Sea was a 'core interest' (putting it on a par with Taiwan and Tibet) and that China was pursuing a strategy of 'deep sea defence'.

In response to that and to concerns expressed by regional states in Washington, the US Secretary of State, Hilary Clinton, declared at a meeting of the ASEAN Regional Forum in July for the first time that the US has a 'national interest' in resolving the disputed claims to islands in the South China Sea and that it 'supports a collaborative diplomatic process' to this end and that 'we oppose the use or the threat of force by any claimant.' Other states at the Forum joined her in calling for a collective approach to the South China Sea. The Chinese Foreign Minister, caught off guard, simply repeated Beijing's long-standing opposition to 'internationalizing' the disputes.

The immediate future is likely to be characterized by sharper diplomatic exchanges and probes and counter-probes at sea. However, severe military clashes are unlikely, although the occasional skirmish is highly possible. The balance of naval power is strongly in America's favour and the Chinese goal is essentially one of seeking to deny the American navy unconditional access to certain waters, rather than to challenge the crucial American interest of keeping the sea lanes open. In the longer term, new issues will arise as China seeks to protect its own trade routes.

At issue, however, is not just the question of adapting to a rising power on which there is a rich, but not particularly helpful, International Relations literature,[1] but also how China will define itself as a nation and what entitlements it will claim. If the current trend were to continue, of a nationalism which emphasizes China's grievances against the West and Japan and which accentuates its claims as the successor to the alleged domains of the Qing Dynasty, it will presage a period of contention.[2] Such a China would see the world in terms of 'us against them' and it would be troubled by senses of insecurity at home as well as abroad. A China of this kind, especially as ruled by a Leninist party, would still be secretive and would be limited in its capacity to integrate with a world whose main powers and key institutions would still be guided by liberal principles. A further problem arising from Chinese nationalism is that it militates against a Chinese capacity to develop a sense of regional order that will appeal to the other regional states. If all Chinese maritime claims are 'indisputable', no space is left for the claims of others, or for a means of resolving the conflicting claims. The Chinese suggestion that resolution can be postponed in favour of joint development of resources in the disputed areas lacks appeal, because other claimants sense that China's relative strength will grow with the passage of time and hence postponement will favour China.

As against such pessimism, note should also be taken of China's economic interdependencies, the adaptability and sophistication of its diplomacy and its participation in the international system as a 'responsible great power'. If the resilience of China's ruling communist party is partly due to its embrace of nationalism and its presentation of itself as the inheritor of China's past greatness, it also rests on the performance of the Chinese economy. The maintenance of high economic growth rates is seen as essential for social stability and hence for continued party rule. International trade and access to advanced technology are crucial to China's economic growth. That in turn relies greatly on the public goods provided by the United States. Arguably China and the United States have become economically interdependent, especially as China holds a high proportion of American indebtedness, with currency reserves of over US$2.4 billion. These considerations go a long way in mitigating the potential for conflict.

American decline?

Much has been made over the years of the prospect of the decline of the West and in particular the decline of the United States since the German Spengler first published a book on the topic at the end of the First World War. As noted in earlier chapters, the topic was in vogue just before the end of the Cold War, when Japan was supposed to be the next hegemon. The first decade of the twenty-first century has spawned a new series of books on American decline in the face of the rise of China, by itself, or combined with others. As noted in previous chapters, the United States has paid and is continuing to pay a heavy price in many respects for its bleeding in the wars in Iraq and Afghanistan. The great financial crisis has left its economy in recession and the nation in long-term indebtedness.

But as many have pointed out, America has many strengths that should help it to recover from its present problems. It has a culture of innovation and creativity, and a can-do spirit; it is blessed with excellent universities and top research institutes that attract and retain talent from all parts of the world. It is the world's leader in the development of and research into high technology. Its political institutions are stable and enduring. Whatever its current economic travails, its GNP still accounts for about a quarter of the world's GNP and it is still some three times as much as the next country. Its military is still by far the world's most powerful. Finally, there are signs that America's two wars in Iraq and Afghanistan will be drawn down in the near future. Meanwhile America remains the most important country in the world in terms of the economy, the military, intellectual innovation and mass culture, with values that still attract admiration and which underpin most of the international organizations.

The United States, however, is no longer the hegemon and its unipolar moment has passed. The US cannot exercise dominion over world affairs and certainly not in the Asia-Pacific. But the United States remains the only country capable of offering world leadership, whether it is in promoting international economic rules, action on climate change, non-proliferation or contributing to the settlement in regional disputes and conflicts from the Balkans, through the Middle East and even into the Asia-Pacific. The United States is still the main upholder of security in the Asia-Pacific through its key alliances and partnerships. The US may require partnerships, but the partners would not be able to act on their own behalf without the United States. Moreover the United States has no territorial claims on any regional state. The United States still holds the key to the management of the two 'hot spots' of Taiwan and North Korea

Great power relations

Great powers in the region continue to find ways to cooperate and to compete. They have not been able to cooperate sufficiently to balance against the United States, or for that matter against China. Attempts by Japanese Prime Ministers Abe and Aso to establish some kind of league of democracies to the exclusion of

China did not materialize and both Japan and Australia have made clear that their newly formed alliance is not directed at China.

India is too independent a great power to be willing to balance against China despite the problems posed by China's support for Pakistan, the disputed borders, China's cultivation of India's close neighbours and a growing rivalry in the Indian Ocean. The two great powers of Asia have developed a complex relationship as their economic relationship has thickened and as they share interests on some issues such as climate change and Iran and diverge on others. India too is becoming a more important player in East Asia. The distrust between Delhi and Beijing is deep, but the likelihood of major conflict remains small.

Japan, which we have seen has declined since the end of the Cold War, is nevertheless a wealthy country, with highly advanced technologies and innovative capacities. Its military may be constrained, but its naval forces are still formidable and China still fears its potential. The two cooperate and compete, especially in Southeast Asia. Japan and China may be seen as both partners and rivals.

It will be seen therefore that the prospects for any kind of regional concert of powers is limited if non-existent.

Regionalism and non-traditional security

As noted in earlier chapters, the end of the Cold War has provided geopolitical space for regional institutions to form and to flourish in the Asia-Pacific. As also noted, building on the experience of ASEAN, these have been primarily of a consultative nature, whose resolutions are non-binding on member states and whose main organizational ethos has been consensus-orientated and based on non-interference in the domestic affairs of member states. Nevertheless, that ethos was challenged in the case of ASEAN by its adoption of a charter which includes an affirmation of the importance of democracy and human rights. The main effect is manifested in the case of Burma, whose military dictatorship continues to embarrass ASEAN internationally. ASEAN, however, has not become much more cohesive, despite many declarations and attempts to bring about deeper integration. In terms of economics, intra-ASEAN trade may have grown greatly, but it still accounts for only about 25 per cent of total trade. And that militates against fuller integration, even though tariff barriers have dropped and the long promised ASEAN Free Trade Area seems at last within reach by 2015. The main obstacle, however, remains cross-border disputes, political antagonisms and divergent threat perceptions. ASEAN remains what it became in the course of the Third Indo-China War – a diplomatic community.

It is as a diplomatic community that its international role has been enhanced in recent years. Because of their mutual distrust and their strategic rivalries the great powers involved in the region have looked to ASEAN to provide leadership for many of the regional bodies in which they are engaged. These include the ARF, ASEAN Plus Three, the Easy Asian Summit and so on.

The growing saliency of non-traditional security issues, such as terrorism, piracy, natural disasters, international crime, including the trafficking of people, narcotics and money laundering, and the need for better coordination between countries in conducting sea rescues, have prompted new forms of functional cooperation between states in the region. In particular they have provided a focus for the institutionalized meetings between ASEAN Ministers of Defence, begun in 2005. In addition, sub-regional groupings have emerged to deal with geographically specific problems such as the Indonesian, Malaysian and Singaporean cooperation to cope with piracy and navigational problems in the Straits of Malacca or the Mekong grouping to facilitate cooperation between the riverine states.

Looking ahead

One aspect of the politics of the region that has not been considered is the coming demographic crisis in the region. I have not done so as it is not yet a pressing regional problem. However, within the next ten years and increasingly thereafter most of the East Asian states will face demographic problems similar to those currently experienced by Japan, namely ageing populations and declining birth rates. In terms of the distribution of power and influence within the region, the most important country to be affected will be China. Unlike wealthy Japan, China is still in many respects a developing country, especially in the regions beyond the east coast. There are already signs of this being reflected in declining numbers of new recruits for the sweated labour production centres in Guangdong Province. But these will intensify and China will also experience many more additional social problems, not only because of the inadequacies of its fledging social security systems, including the provision of health care, but also due to the ill-effects of its thirty-year-old 'one child family' policy, which is responsible for an unhealthy disparity between the numbers of males and females.

There can be little doubt, however, that in the immediate future the principal strategic problem will remain coping with the rise of China, whose determination to assert control over wide reaches of adjacent seas and sovereignty over the islands within them challenges not only other resident states, but also the United States and its insistence on universal rights to international waters in accordance with generally accepted international law.

Notes

1 Aaron L. Freidberg, 'The future of U.S.–China Relations: Is conflict Inevitable?' in *International Security* 30, 2 (Fall 2005), pp.7–45.
2 For a full account of the problems arising from this Chinese nationalist form of identity see, William A. Callaghan, *China, The Pessoptimist Nation* (Oxford: Oxford University Press, 2010).

Index